The
Three
Boxes
of Life

Books by Richard Nelson Bolles

The Three Boxes of Life
and How To Get Out of Them

Where Do I Go From Here
With My Life?

What Color Is Your Parachute?
A Practical Manual for Job-Hunters
& Career-Changers

The Three Boxes of Life

And How To Get Out of Them

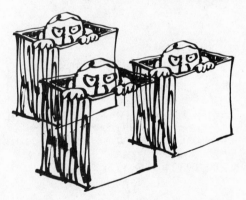

An introduction to life/work planning

RICHARD NELSON BOLLES

TEN SPEED PRESS

Bolles, Richard Nelson.
    The three boxes of life.

    Bibliography: p.
    Includes index.
    1. Vocational guidance. 2. Education.
3. Retirement. 4. Success. I. Title.
HF5381.B635 12   650′.14   78–17000
ISBN 0-913668-52-4
ISBN 0-913668-58-3 pbk.

Designed by Richard N. Bolles and Beverly Anderson
Cartoons on cover and title pages by Ed Renfro
Type set by Mary Fran McCluskey

This book is dedicated to
DON BOLLES
1928-1976
reporter, hero,
and
my beloved brother

Contents

Financial survival. Emotional survival. The husband and wife in retirement: idyl or nightmare. Three rules for dealing with stress. Principles of spiritual survival. The secret of healing.

Meaning and Mission during retirement / page 354: The life-cycle of housewives. Geriacracy: its meaning and power.

Effectiveness in retirement / page 358: Your life review, and how to do it; how to draw your Life Line. Tools for making joint decisions. Alone and what to do about it. Singledom. What to do so that people won't run when they see us coming.

Lifelong Leisure or Playing / page 374: How much leisure you should have. When you're too busy to find time for leisure. How to deal with the Puritan within you. The importance of an Alternating Rhythm in your life. The error of labeling 'leisure activities.' How to be more satisfied. How to find variety in your leisure. Constructing a map of your leisure activities. Games, crafts, and guidebooks. A word about playfulness.

The Preface

Hello, dear reader. You're browsing here in order to try to find out what kind of a book this is, right? You've flipped through the pages, back to front, the way we all do, and you've seen that it has lots of interesting cartoons, charts, and flair. You've perused the table of contents. And now you're checking out the preface.

Welcome. You want to know what this book is about? Well, it's essentially a book of ideas. Ideas about School, Work, and Retirement—what's wrong with them, what could be right with them, and how you might do something about that in your own life...now. There are separate books on the market already that deal just with School, or just with Work, or just with Retirement, but this book is unusual because it deals with all three at once. The reason for that is that this book is an introduction to LIFE/work Planning. And L/w P, by definition, means looking at all the parts of your life, together.

I volunteered, very reluctantly I might add, to write this book. I am the head of a project of United Ministries in Higher Education, which is called the National Career Development Project. We put out a Newsletter, run workshops, and create needed materials (more about this, at the very end of this book). People also ask us a lot of questions. And one of the most persistent has been, Where can I lay my hands on a good book that explains what LIFE/work Planning is all about? Well, there really isn't any (that we *know* about, anyway). So we decided that with all the experience the Project has had, in this field, we probably ought to fill the void.

I cannot *possibly* tell you the sacrifices that have had to be made, the mountains that have had to be climbed, the deserts that have had to be crossed, the rivers that have had to be swum, in order for this book to be completed. God knows. (Also my dear office-person at that time, Erica Chambré, who regularly beat off callers from the entrance to my cave, while I typed away inside.)

Anyway, here it is. A book of ideas, some of them really dazzling. I know; because they aren't mine. If you are enamored of a particular idea, you will of course want to know where it

came from. Wherever possible, I tell you. I feel exceedingly pro-
tective toward idea people. They are creatures who are often
given little recognition or reward—in this life at least. I mean,
if you invent a product, *everybody remembers*. Every time there
is a car accident, people automatically think of Old Whatsisname.
But an idea? Ah that is a different kettle of fish. *Nobody*
remembers who first thought of collecting garbage. Idea-people
are like that. Unsung heroes and heroines, rarely getting rich
off their ideas, going to their anonymous grave, The Tomb of
the Unknown Idea-Person. While we all are enriched by the
opulence of their minds.

And what shall we do with these ideas, thus gathered in this
book? Read them, to be sure. Savor them, turn them over and
over in the mind, apply them to our lives wherever we can. And
preserve them just as they are? Well, not exactly. It would help
us all, I think, to picture the whole world of ideas as a series of
relay races. You know the sort of thing I mean: where runners
are in teams, and each team sends one runner out to run a lap
or two with a stick or baton in his or her hands. At the end of
which, another member of their team is waiting, and the stick is
passed on to him or her. So it is with ideas. Someone gets a
brainstorm, and runs with it as far as he or she can. Then someone else takes that idea from there, and runs it still further.
Following which still another person picks it up, to carry it
further still.

By the time the third runner has finished with the idea it is
sometimes difficult to recognize it as the idea with which the
race was begun. And so it is with this book. Wherever I know
the original source of an idea, I will tell you. But it is important
that you not imagine you have, thereby, had a good exposure to
the ideas of that person, as he or she originally expressed them.
This *is* a relay race, I am the second or third runner, and I *have*
run with the ideas—sometimes Quite Quite Far. While I am
anxious to give them all due credit, I am equally anxious to
deliver them from unjust blame, for that which is my interpre-
tation, not theirs. Incidentally, many of the overall conceptions
and ideas in this book are actually mine. They are identifiable
as the ones that either sound strange, or make you want to write
your Congress-person.

Now, of course, it is your turn. To run with these ideas, I mean. Do not think that it is your job to preserve them just as they are. Au contraire. Run them through your own brain, distill them through your own experience, express them through your own personality. These ideas are not meant to be guarded in some Platonian cave. They are meant to be impressed upon your own life, first of all, and then shared with others—in your own distinctive style and voice.

And so, dear reader, here is my book. Here is your baton. May you run with it just as far as you can, with the wind at your back, the sun on your face, and your hand stretched out to those who wait for your life to touch them.

Peace, and shalom.

R.N.B.

P.S. I would like to express my profound gratitude to all those people who helped make this book what it is, and to six in particular:

— to John C. Crystal and John L. Holland, geniuses in the world of ideas, for being the source of so many of the tools which I have here used and applied;

— to Beverly Anderson, a genius in the world of design, for designing this book as she has all my earlier publications and books, with flair and imagination;

— to Phil Wood, my publisher, for his infinite patience and understanding through all the factors that made this book a year late—the very model of what one would hope a publisher would be;

— to Neil Severance, who—while on leave of absence as a Danforth Fellow from his home base in Slippery Rock, Pennsylvania—gave me invaluable assistance with my research, as he brought order out of chaos;

—and last, but hardly least, to Erica Chambré and friends, who not only helped get this manuscript ready for the printer, but took much of my normal work-load off my back, so that I might have the time to complete the writing, in quietness and peace.

3

So, what's wrong with
boxes? I love boxes.
Pandora

t times in my life I have felt really boxed in. Apparently you have too. No way to turn. Nowhere to escape to. Really in a box. As we grow older, however, we learn how to cope with that feeling. That's one of the benefits of growing up. We become not so afraid of the little boxes anymore. All that remains then is to learn how to deal with the Big Boxes of life— I mean, the *really* big ones. The ones called: EDUCATION. WORK. And RETIREMENT.

To be sure, these are not normally called "boxes." Lying out on some hillside, on a warm summer day, with our arms behind our head as we contemplate the sky and the mysteries of life, we are more likely to think of them as "periods" of life. Our whole life, we tell ourselves, is divided into three periods. The first period is that of "Getting an Education." The second period is that of "Going to Work, and earning a living." While the third and last period is that of "Living in Retirement." Thus, our total lifespan on Earth looks—in theory—something like this:

The World of Education	The World of Work	The World of Retirement

In point of fact, of course, it ends up looking quite differently from this. First of all, the segments or periods on either end— namely, Education and Retirement—have been getting longer and longer. That is to say, a lot of people are delaying their entrance into the World of Work until a later and later age, as

5

they pursue more and more Education; and, a lot of people are retiring much earlier than they used to, sometimes at age 50. [1] So, the periods begin to look more like this, overall:

The World of Education	The World of Work	The World of Retirement

Secondly, these periods have become more and more isolated from each other. Life in each period seems to be conducted by those in charge without much consciousness of—never mind, preparation for—life in the next period. Despite all the talk about 'career education,' for example, a survey of graduating high school seniors in one U.S. school district revealed that 63% felt they had received little or no training in school which would help them find a job.[2] Likewise, those coming to the end of their time in the World of Work feel they have been given little or no help by that world, in preparing for Retirement. The most that the average organization does is to offer a pension plan, as a sort of bribe to keep an employee working for that particular organization. And often, despite recent legislation, the employee finds that this bribe fails to materialize, when the chips are down and Retirement is almost within grasp. So, these three periods—in their isolation from one another—end up looking (or feeling) like three boxes:

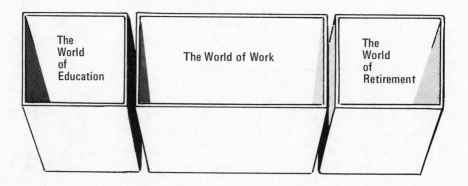

The box-like nature of these three phases of our lives is further accentuated by what it is that happens to us, timewise, in each one. If we look, for example, at the time devoted to 'getting an Education,' the cultural expectation is that while we are in the first box (from age five through 18, 22 or whatever) the major portion of our time will be devoted to that task.

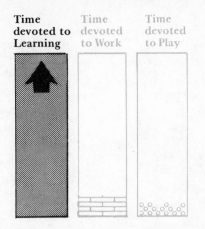

in The First Box of Life

While we are in the second box, however, the cultural expectation is that only a relatively small proportion of our time will be devoted to formal education—and that, mostly to upgrade our work skills or to prepare us for a change in career.

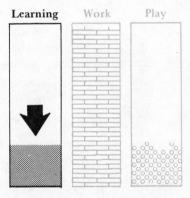

in The Second Box of Life

And when we enter the third box (usually between ages 50 and 68) it is assumed that we will devote little time to formal schooling thereafter, since clearly our brain has atrophied by then!

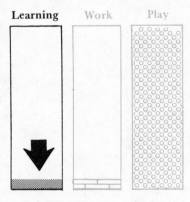

in The Third Box of Life

7

The First Box of Life

Turning now to look at the question of how much time we devote in each box to 'Working,' 'holding down a job,' or to 'formal achievement for pay,' we see a very similar imbalance. The cultural expectation is that while we are in the first box, a comparatively small proportion of our time will be devoted to Working—just enough, in fact, to help underwrite our expenses in connection with 'getting an Education.'

And if we complain that the time devoted to Working, while we are in this first box, seems disproportionately small to say the least, the response we customarily receive is that of The Postponement Principle. Namely, "You may not be able to work as much as you like, right now. But just be patient, and after you get out of school you'll be able to work yourself to death."

The Second Box of Life

Sure enough, it turns out to be as was predicted. In the second box the largest proportion of our time is indeed devoted to working—more than making up for the deprivation we felt earlier.

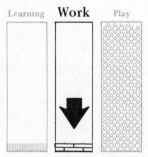

The Third Box of Life

When we get to the third box, however, the cultural expectation is that we will get out of the job market—since clearly our needs, in retirement, are expected to turn modest; and younger bodies now need the jobs that we hold.

Well, what is left? Clearly, the time devoted to Leisure or Re-creation. In the first box, we are told that we should not expect to have a lot of time for Leisure. Just enough to recharge our batteries, as it were, in order that we may be ready to go back to our studies.

The First Box of Life

In the second box, we are again told that we should not expect to have a lot of time for Leisure. Just enough to recharge our batteries in order that we may be ready to go back to work. And if we feel, by this time, like complaining about the disproportionately small amount of our time which Leisure commands, The Postponement Principle is once more invoked — "You may not be able to play as much as you would like, right now; but just be patient. Once you retire, you will be able to play yourself to death." Which turns out to be true, sometimes in an ironic sense. For we read of the couple who waited for forty years to take that trip to Bermuda, or whatever, and then one of them has a fatal heart attack on the eve of their departure.

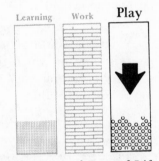

The Second Box of Life

But—leaving such rare occurrences aside—most of us can count on an inordinate amount of time being devoted to Leisure, Play, or Re-creation during the time that we are in the third box of life.

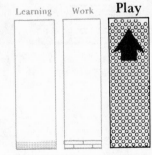

The Third Box of Life

What all of this adds up to, is an imbalance between the time spent on Learning, the time spent on Working, and the time spent on Play, in all three boxes of life. And it is precisely this which helps make them into boxes.

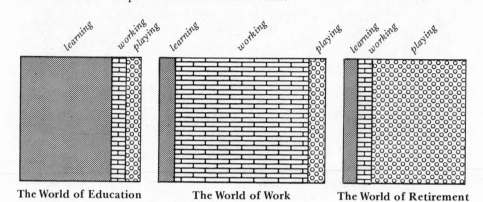

The World of Education   The World of Work   The World of Retirement

What we could all envision is a quite different way of doing this: one in which there was more of an equitable balance between Learning, Working and Playing in *each* of the three boxes. Thus, they would end up looking more like this:

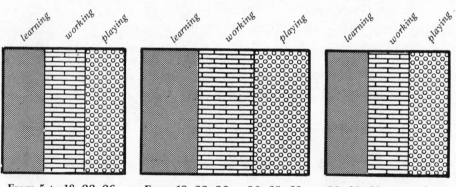

From 5 to 18, 22, 26   From 18, 22, 26 to 50, 65, 68   50, 65, 68 years of age
years of age   years of age   to death

How you can go about building this better balance in your own life is precisely what life/work planning (and this book) is all about, as we shall see.[3]

What's Happening?

First, however, we need to notice another characteristic of these three periods in our life, which turns them into boxes. This is the fact that there are different issues, perplexities or problems in life that we all have to wrestle with. And that these issues have a kind of logical order in which we tackle them. I believe this can best be illustrated with the aid of a fantasy. Imagine that tonight you go to sleep in your own familiar bed, in your own familiar room. Tomorrow morning, you awaken. You are still in your own bed, but to your absolute astonishment you and your bed have been transported into the middle of some mysterious jungle. All around you, ferns and tall trees, exotic-looking flowers, mysterious sounds, and sunlight filtering down through the trees. Now, what kinds of issues, perplexities, or problems do you have to work through? Well, the first issue— or family of issues—that you would have to work your way through, it seems to me, is one which we might entitle: WHAT'S HAPPENING? You know the kind of questions that would naturally occur to you, right off the bat: Where am I? How did I get here? What on earth is happening? Is this truly a jungle? What kind of a jungle is it? Are there dangerous beasts or people here? What kind of food and drink is available? And so forth. Your absolute first need would be to settle this question of WHAT'S HAPPENING—or, at least, to get a kind of temporary 'fix' on it. Until that happens, the question would preoccupy your attention, and you would be pretty well immobilized, and thus prevented from doing anything else.

Survival

When you had, at least for the time being, gotten enough of an answer to satisfy you, you would then be able to take your attention off this issue, and go on to the next one. That would be, in the very nature of the case, one which we might entitle: SURVIVAL. Granted I have some elementary idea about what's happening, what's going to happen to me? Am I going to make it, or not? These are the kinds of questions that would just naturally occur to you. SURVIVAL, like its predecessor WHAT'S HAPPENING, would turn out to be not simply one issue, but a whole family of issues. There would be the issue of

11

physical survival: is there food and water? Can I survive the weather, and any hostile environments? And so forth. Then there would be the issue of *emotional* survival: there's a whole different role for me here, than the one I am accustomed to. Have I got what it takes to survive all this emotionally? Or will I become a basket-case? Along with this, there would be *spiritual* survival: I've always believed myself to be a certain kind of person, with certain kinds of values and things I believe in; will this experience so change me, that I won't even recognize myself any longer? Or not? If you were not in the jungle, but in the midst of some sort of civilization, you would also have the issue of *financial* survival. Thus SURVIVAL ends up being this whole family of issues, and while such members of the family as spiritual survival may not be terribly urgent, other members of that family—such as physical survival—would immediately rivet your attention. Until you had some kind of resolution of your worry about it, in at least a temporary sort of way, it would be about all that you could think about.

Meaning or Mission

When you had solved the issue of SURVIVAL to your immediate satisfaction at least, you would then be ready to deal with the next family of issues. And that, it seems to me, is one which we might call: MEANING OR MISSION. Once you were assured that you had some idea of what is happening, and that you were going to survive, then of course you would have to decide what you were going to do with your time. It appears that there are four answers which people come up with, in everyday life—and, I suppose, in the jungle:

1. "All that is important, about the use of my time, is that I manage to keep busy." If this is your answer to the issue of MEANING OR MISSION, in the jungle, then you will probably say, "I'll wake up each morning and figure out what I'm going to do that day. That's as far ahead as I intend to plan." Of course, you may—in time—turn to another answer:

2. "It isn't enough just to keep busy. I want to enjoy what I'm keeping busy with; so I'm going to determine what kinds of things I enjoy." If this is your preferred answer to the issue of MEANING OR MISSION, in our jungle fantasy, then neces-

sarily you will search for those things which give you the most pleasure there: lying in the sun, doing woodcarving, bathing in a stream under a waterfall, weaving a grass skirt, or whatever. Your goal would be to give maximum time to those activities—frivolous or essential—which you particularly enjoy, and minimum time to those activities you did not enjoy. This answer to the issue of MEANING OR MISSION might satisfy you for some time. Then again, it might not. In which case, you would search for another answer.

> Synonyms and
> Related Words for
> *Mission*
> *or Meaning*
>
> My Goal
> My Target
> My Purpose
> My Objective
> My Plan
> My Aim
> My Intention
> My Design
> My Ambition

3. "It isn't enough to just enjoy myself; I want to have some meaning to my life, and I want my activities to furnish that meaning." Tracing out what this means there in the jungle, you might decide to give time and thought to those questions about existence which have puzzled all thinking men and women for centuries, to see if you could ferret out some new answers. And—thus playing philosopher—write down those answers, in the hope that posterity would find them, and share them with the civilized world. Were you not in the jungle, you might decide to find meaning by helping other people, someway, somehow. In any event, you would have moved beyond "busy" and "enjoy" to the deeper issue of "meaning." And whatever, for you, made your life meaningful, would determine how you used your time.

4. There yet remains however, one still deeper answer to the issue of MEANING OR MISSION. That is to find, beyond meaning, some ultimate goal or mission for your life, that drives you on with a kind of sacrificial, burning passion. It is the kind of mission that drove Pasteur, Schweitzer, Einstein, and many lesser names. It is the kind of drive that—in any or every profession—distinguishes some men and women from the rest of 'the common herd.' So, in the jungle of our fantasy, you might decide to search for some ultimate goal, some heroic mission there, that would be a burning driving force in your life. If you had to build a tree-hut, you might decide to become the most innovative architect and builder of tree-huts in the history of the world, finding some whole new principle of design and of materials. Or whatever.

14

Effectiveness

Well, whatever principle you use to determine the use of your time—busyness, enjoyment, meaning, or mission—you are still wrestling with this family of issues regarding what you choose to do, once "what's happening" and "survival" are no longer preoccupying you. Only when you have solved this question of MEANING OR MISSION, is your attention sufficiently freed up to notice and deal with the next family of issues—namely, that of EFFECTIVENESS. This is the whole question of "Am I preoccupying myself with the sorts of activities that I really want to be doing, or ought to be doing? And, if so, am I doing those activities in the most effective, efficient, and competent manner possible? Am I building this tree-hut in the best manner possible, for me? Should I be building this tree-hut at all; or is there some better use I could find for my time? That sort of question. We might call this the issue of Evaluation and Re-evaluation, except that Evaluation is so often interpreted these days as something that *others* do for you (or to you). Effectiveness, however, is essentially a self-actuated, self-directed form of questioning. It springs out of a desire to improve your performance, of a particular task; and to improve the way in which you are working toward your goals.

The Pyramid of Issues

What's Happening; Survival; Meaning or Mission; and Effectiveness—these seem to me to be the four major *families* of issues that you would have to wrestle with, in a jungle. They also seem to me to be the four major families of issues that people are wrestling with, everywhere. And at any stage of their lives.

There are a number of ways these could be depicted. We could represent them in a circle:

What's Happening

Survival

Effectiveness

Mission or Meaning

We could represent them in
a straight line, horizontally:

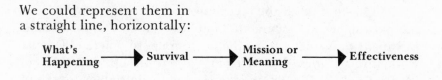

What's
Happening → Survival → Mission or
Meaning → Effectiveness

Or on a downward vertical line:

What's Happening
↓
Survival
↓
Meaning or Mission
↓
Effectiveness

Or an upward vertical line:

Effectiveness
↑
Meaning or Mission
↑
Survival
↑
What's Happening

We could even place this vertical line on a pyramid, if that fig-
ure had not become so identified, in many people's minds, with
Abraham Maslow (and his *hierarchy of values*)[4] or with the
Egyptians:

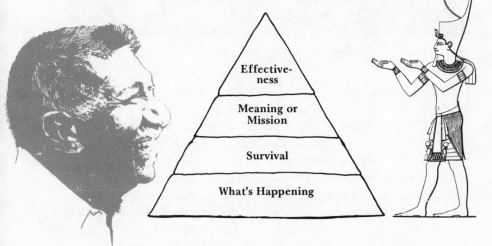

Effective-
ness

Meaning or
Mission

Survival

What's Happening

I think that of all the preceding possibilities, the pyramid is the most appealing. "Pyramid" implies that, even as the ancient Egyptians built theirs from the bottom up, so you (and I) must work through these issues, from the bottom up, step by step, level by level. "The Pyramid of Issues" even *sounds* nice; and infinitely preferable, it seems to me, to the designation other figures would require. (For example, "The Straight Line of Issues" just doesn't make it.)

So, the pyramid it will be—for the rest of this book, albeit dressed up a little bit three-dimensionally, as follows:

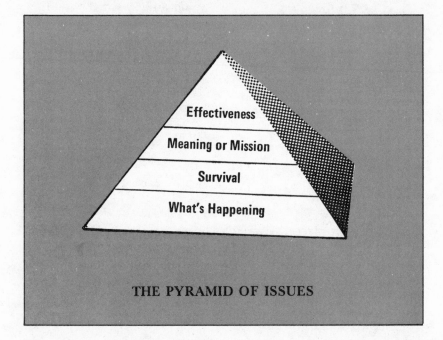

THE PYRAMID OF ISSUES

Incidentally, it has been suggested that there ought to be a fourth level added at the bottom of this pyramid—an even more basic one, entitled something like "Drifting." This, in order to take into account those people who will not even wrestle with the issue of "What's Happening"; they just don't seem to care. Upon reflection, however, it seems that "drifting" is not in itself an issue, let alone a family of issues, but rather *a way of* dealing with the issues already on the pyramid. Or a way of non-dealing. Two other ways of dealing with these issues might be defined: namely, *superficially* or *in depth*. Thus, a complete picture of the pyramid would come out looking something like this:

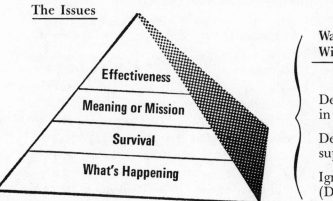

The Issues

Ways of Dealing With Those Issues

Effectiveness

Meaning or Mission

Survival

What's Happening

Dealing with them in depth.

Dealing with them superficially.

Ignoring them. (Drifting).

Boxes and Pyramids

Now, as I said earlier, this pyramid seems to me to represent the four major families of issues we have to wrestle with, at *any* stage in our lives. The answers we discover, say during the time that we are in the first box of life (the World of Education), will generally serve us during the rest of the time that we are in that box. But when we go out into the World of Work, it soon becomes clear that the answers which served us so well while we were in the first box, no longer apply. We have to, as it were, work our way up the pyramid all over again. What's Happening in the World of Work is entirely different from What's Happening in the World of Education. How you survive in the World of Work is also quite different.

When the time comes for us to move into the World of Retirement, once more we have to work our way up the pyramid all over again. For the World of Retirement *is* a whole new world. Thus, in essence, we have to work our way up the pyramid of issues three different times—three *major* times, anyway. This fact, alone, does not help to turn these three periods of our life into boxes. For if everyone who taught in the World of Education or administered that world were conscious of the fact that the place where their students are going, after they leave that world, is precisely to the World of Work where the Pyramid of Issues will require quite new answers; and if every educator consequently concluded that *part* of the task of Education is to acquaint students with those answers, then the pyramid would not (in and of itself) turn these periods of life into boxes.

Or again, if every employer in the World of Work were extremely sensitive to the fact that people in that world—employee and employer alike—are going to go, next, into the World of Retirement, where the Pyramid of Issues will need to be wrestled with, all over again; and if every employer consequently concluded that it was part of his or her task to help prepare people for that experience, ahead of time, then once more the pyramid would not—in and of itself—isolate one box from another.

It is precisely because each period or world (Education, Work, and Retirement) is a whole new ball-game, *and* very little help is given to prepare us for the next ball-game coming up, that these worlds become isolated from each other and thus become even worse boxes, than before. All that we are given (at best) to aid us in the transition from one box to the next is *a single* advisor, office or department. It is supposed to do it all. We may therefore think of that advisor, office or department as a "Token Bridge-keeper." "Bridge-keeper," because they stand (alone) at the entrance to the bridge which leads from one box or world (Education, or Work) to the next. And "Token," because they are asked to do a monumental task *which ought to be the concern of everyone who 'runs' that world, rather than being shifted off onto the shoulders of one small office.* When that task proves to be too monumental, when for example the Career Planning & Placement office at a college just can't 'place' a sufficient percentage of its graduating students, you would suppose that the whole philosophy of "Token Bridge-keeper" would be subjected at last to long-overdue examination. Not so. Rather, it is customarily assumed by the college that something is wrong with that particular placement or career planning director. So he or she is fired (thus becoming "Scapegoat Bridge-keeper"), and a new Token is elected to this Mission Impossible.

The same situation obtains, of course, in the World of Work, except that there the Token Bridge-keeper is the Personnel Director, or the Personnel Department. Now, of course, some of you will object that you know some sterling exception to all of the foregoing: some college or some organization within industry, that takes very seriously the next world into which its students or employees will be going, and does everything possible to help them before the time. I know such exceptions, too. The problem is, they *are* exceptions. In general, the boxes remain. Looking, overall, somewhat as follows:

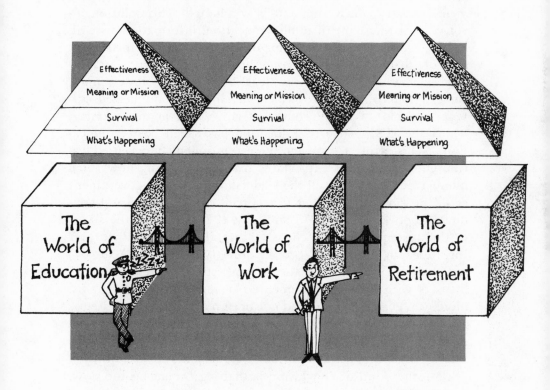

Not forgetting the imbalance within each box, noted earlier, between time devoted to Learning, and time devoted to Working, and time devoted to Playing.

They *are* boxes. We *are* in them. And the problem that faces us all is: *how* to get out of them.

Systemic Answers

How do you stop Education, Work, and Retirement from becoming three boxes? Generally speaking, the proposed solutions have tended to divide into two separate families, as it were. The first is one we might call The Systemic Family. This stresses the fact that the three boxes of life are essentially too formidable and too overwhelming for any one individual to deal with; therefore, it is the whole system which must be changed. The conclusion normally drawn from this is that therefore we must press for mammoth legislative change, or mammoth institutional change, in the whole way that Education, or Government/Industry, or Retirement is conducted. This solution involves a vast amount of public education, information-dissemination, lobbying or other forms of pressure, and so forth. This sort of change, if it does come about, is slow, but certainly legal. Or perhaps I should say, legal but certainly slow. I think, for example, of the most widely-heralded and publicized systemic attempt to unify education and work, in this country, which the U.S. Office of Education has called "career education". This effort to impact the estrangement between education and work in all fifty states has been ongoing now for a number of years, with all the leadership the federal government could possibly give it. Yet in a survey commissioned and conducted between June 1975 and May 1976, assessing the status of this systemic effort to change things, the American Institutes for Research of Palo Alto, California (which did the survey) revealed that only 3% of the nation's students were in school districts with broadly-implemented career education programs. Moreover, even educators had not been reached by this systemic attempt (so far), as revealed by the fact that the nation's school districts rated Placement (i.e., the former students' ability to find a job) as *the least important outcome* of career education.

Another kind of conclusion is that legal change is too slow, and therefore what is needed is a change that is revolutionary—a rapid and radical change, even at the expense of overthrowing much of what is commonly regarded as the essential social structure of our society.

Both of these solutions, the legislative and the revolutionary, are at their roots the same: Systemic. They want to

Handy Guide to Public Policy Proposers
and Their Proposals

Ideological Positions	View of Present and Future	Proposals for Future
Horrified Humanist	A slim chance of surviving our chaos and obsolescence.	Sweeping reforms, world government, national planning.
Languishing Liberal	Troubled times.	More money and programs; racial integration.
Middling Moderate	No thoughts: cross-pressured.	Various platitudes to avoid offending other policy proposers.
Counteracting Conservative	Crime, centralization, and crumbling civilization.	Law, order, soap, haircuts, Truth and Morality.
Rabid Rightist	It's getting *Red*der all the time.	Wave flags and stockpile arms (public and private).
Primitive Populist	Domination by pointy-headed pseudo-intellectuals.	Throw briefcases in Potomac, restore common sense.
Passionate Pacifist	A garrison state	A peaceable kingdom
Radical Romantic	A cancered civilization.	Small experimental communities.
Rumbling Revolutionary	A repressive, racist, imperialist, capitalist, establishment.	Confront and destroy The System (other details worked out later).
Apocalyptic Apostle	Armageddon coming to a sinful world.	Be saved.

Role-Related Positions

Urgent Urbanist	Decline and fall of cities.	More funds and programs sidestepping states.
Emphatic Ecologist	Decline and fall of everything else.	Control contaminators and restore nature.
Boiling Black Man	Here a pig, there a pig, everywhere a pig pig.	Black everything.
Status-Seeking Sibling Sender	Crisis in our schools and colleges.	More funds and programs, tax deductions.
Multi-Megamuscled Militarist	Growing Chinese and/or Russian capabilities.	More National Security regardless of national security.
Technocrat-on-the-Take	No thoughts; not within scope of specialty.	Well-funded studies and use of arcane models.
Sincerely Sorry Scientist	Profligate technology.	Think of alternative futures and their consequences.

(Over)

Role-Related Positions

continued	View of Present and Future	Proposals for Future
Bullied Budget-Binder	Up-tight.	Making this year's budget and getting more for next year.
Tortured Taxpayer	Growing gaps between income, aspirations, and expenditures.	Cut Cut Cut Cut Cut Cut Cut Cut Cut
Stultified Student	Entrapment in *their* world.	Inner and interpersonal exploration, and other relevant learning.
Contracting Conglomerator	Cybernation, diversification, and internationalization.	Withering of the state.
Hi-throttle Highwayman	Paving the nation.	Re-paving the nation.
Frustrated Feminist	Futility, frivolity, and frigidaires.	Fun-filled fulfillment.
Star-Struck Spaceman	Up, up, and away.	Science must not be impeded.
Bonded Bureaucrat	Six years to go until retirement.	Longer coffee breaks.

by Michael Marien, Educational Policy Research Center, Syracuse University Research Corporation. Reprinted with permission from Public Administration Review, Volume XXX, No. 2, March/April 1970. Bi-monthly publication of the American Society for Public Administration, 1225 Connecticut Avenue, N.W., Washington, D.C. 20036.

change the whole thing at once. They despair of the power of the individual to do it alone. It is The System that must change, before there can be any hope. That is the *credo* of most of the reformers in modern history; and it is the solution (to most problems) that the majority of people in our country tend to subscribe to.

Sometimes systemic change is admittedly absolutely essential. But with our preoccupation with this kind of change, we must not forget that there is another possibility—complementary to the first, if less popular, This is the possibility of giving the individual person some tools by which he or she can begin now to change the system *at least as it affects his or her life.*

Individual Change

If, for example, Education, Work and Retirement have become three boxes of life, we can work on legislative and institutional ways of changing the whole system. *And, at the same time*, we can try giving individuals some tools, to see if he or she can at least change the box-like nature of Education, Work, and Retirement, *for his or her own life.*

In its most primitive motivation, this Individual Change solution is a kind of "every person for themselves" theory. It is as though an ocean liner had become impaled upon some reefs, and everyone were running for the lifeboats, heedless of what happened to the rest of the passengers. However, in its most mature motivation, this Individual Change approach is itself a theory and form of Systemic Change. If enough individuals were to change, it argues, then the system would have to change. Or, if enough individuals were to change, then willy nilly the system itself would already be changed.

In comparatively recent history, the best example—perhaps—is that of the so-called Vietnam peace movement. It began with a few individual voices being raised on some of our nation's college campuses. In time, as these individuals persuaded others, the movement became a kind of juggernaut. Eventually it was so powerful that a President of the United States—associated in people's minds with that unpopular war—found he could not be re-elected, in all probability. Thus, what began as individual change became, in the end, systemic.

But we do not have to appeal to history, in order to establish how systemic change may thus begin by changing a few individuals. A theoretical foundation may equally be found in biology, by appealing to the human body. There we see first one individual cell change, and then another. And then another. Eventually, however, as a consequence of these individual cell changes, the whole body is constitutionally different from what it was when it began.

The Point of This Book

In dealing with the problem of the three boxes of life, and how to get out of them, it is not my intention to dismiss the importance of systemic change. I believe that that is absolutely essential. But this is intended to be a book dealing with individual approaches: a kind of *What To Do Until Systemic Change Arrives.* Or a kind of *How to Bring In Systemic Change By Each of Us Taking Responsibility for What Happens In Our Own Life, Now.* This is to be a book of Tools for the Individual, designed to help you arrive at some kind of balance in your own life—and throughout your whole life—between Learning, Working, and Playing. This book is designed to help you alter the three boxes of life, at least for yourself, so that they are no longer boxes.

This whole approach, when it deals with Tools for the Individual, is traditionally called "Life/Work Planning." There are probably a million better names than that; but "Life/Work Planning" is the name that has become most popular and probably best known. So, this is a book about *that*. The three boxes of life, and how you as an individual can get out of them.

If enough individuals try out these tools, successfully and therefore effectively, then we may—in the end—see genuine systemic change for everyone. No more boxes. For anyone. Instead a society which sees Learning, Working, and Playing as essential parts of a whole life—in our youth, in our middle years, and in our old age. Someday, perhaps.

But for now, let's begin by concentrating just on YOU.

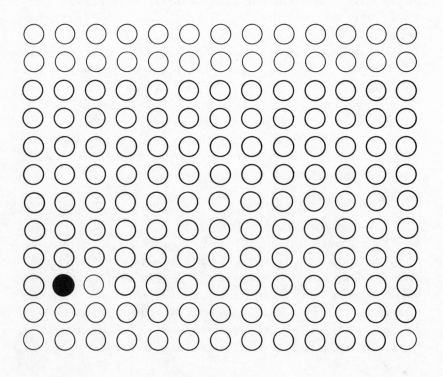

Chapter One Footnotes

1.   Peter Drucker points out that when Social Security began there were seven people who received benefits for every one hundred in the labor force. Now it is down to (or up to) twenty five or thirty persons for every one hundred in the labor force. (*Quoted in* The Claremont Collegian, *January 16, 1975*.) Robert J. Samuelson predicts that by 2030 there may be 45 beneficiaries for every one hundred workers. (*Quoted in* The Los Angeles Times, *June 4, 1975*.)

2.   In Orange County, California.

3.   I want to acknowledge my great indebtedness to the ideas of the late Philip Arnow for much of the preceding. I also want to acknowledge my indebtedness to Bill Batt, of the National Center for Productivity and The Quality of Working Life, for introducing me to Phil's thoughts. Over the years, a number of articles have appeared in newspapers and magazines on this subject of the separation between Learning and Work, or between Work and Retirement. Among the more influential of these, was the series on "Education for the World of Work," which appeared in the October 1975, December 1975, and January 1976 issues of *Fortune* Magazine. (See your local library's magazine reference section, for a look at these well-researched articles.)

4.   Maslow, Abraham H. *Motivation and Personality*, 2nd. ed. New York: Harper and Row, 1970.

When a man knows
he is to be hanged in a fortnight,
it concentrates his mind wonderfully.
Samuel Johnson, 1777

Chapter Two
How to Get Out of Them:
LIFE/work Planning

ou want some tools, then, to help you build a better balance (throughout your whole life) between Learning, Working and Playing? That activity, by definition, is called Life/Work Planning. There are, of course, an infinite number of variations on that title (Make Life Work; Life Works; Life Planning; Life Designing, etc.); but "Life/Work Planning" is the one that has stuck, and become best-known.

This activity has become increasingly popular across the country and throughout all age groups: among college students, housewives returning to work, people facing retirement, and so forth. Yet despite its popularity, Life/Work Planning has not (yet) become a science, with any well-defined rules or methods. There is still a lot of exploration going on, in many quarters, about how to do it better. And a lot of disagreement, as to how to do it best. Thus there is no one accepted way to go about it, period. And that is perhaps as it should be. For 'one person's meat is another person's poison,' and tools which are very helpful to some people, are very unhelpful to others. So it is understandable that it remains a kind of 'smorgasbord,' from which you pick and choose what helps you best.

Notwithstanding, this activity, field, art or whatever you want to call it, has been around long enough now for some of its broadest outlines anyway, to become rather clear. Some of us by now have had enough experience with teaching it and living it, to be able to make some definite statements about what Life/Work Planning is, or is not. I would like to share these with you, for I believe them to be very important.

Definitions of Life/Work Planning

The first word in its title is *Life*, for three reasons. In the first place, the scope of Life/Work Planning's attention is indeed all of life. Youth, middle-age, and old-age. Learning, Working, and Playing. Any program which calls itself Life/Work Planning, but only deals with *Working* man and woman is deceiving people. It ought to call itself, in such a case, by a more limited name, such as "Work Planning."

In the second place, *Life* is the goal of Life/Work Planning. Full, abundant, whole life. The kind of life, as someone has said, where we climb more mountains, and swim more rivers and watch more sunsets, and yield to all those impulses to help those around us, gently and lovingly.

In the third place, *Life* means that this sort of thinking and planning is to be lifelong. Life/Work Planning is emphatically not the mastering of some tools which are used once, and then discarded. Life/Work Planning is, rather, a continuous process; and the tools to be used are useful tools for the rest of your life.

The second word in the title is (as you will have noticed) *Work*. That word is there for two reasons. First of all, Work is the most difficult box for people to get out of; or—which is more to the point—the most difficult box to get into. In dealing with the three boxes, Life/Work Planning consequently has to spend an *inordinate* amount of time on the subject of Work. In this respect, it is as though the three boxes—Learning, Working, and Retirement—were three rooms with locks on their doors. The locks on two of the doors—Learning and Retirement—are relatively easy to open; but the lock on the third door—Working—is inordinately difficult to unlock. As a result, it is at this door that we linger the longest, and it is for this door that we need the most powerful tools.

The second reason that *Work* is in the title Life/Work Planning is that it describes the arena where most people discover the *motivation* for doing Life/Work Planning. If you are troubled about not having sufficient Education, or sufficient Play in your life, this may be bothersome to you—but you would rarely describe it as a crisis. If, however, you are out of work or trying for the first time to get into the World of Work, and you cannot find any Work, *that* is a crisis. And at that point you may, for the first time, discover the motivation to get involved with Life/ Work Planning. As Samuel Johnson said . . . well, I'm sure you read his sentence at the beginning of this chapter.

The Chinese character for "crisis" is, incidentally, one which means "dangerous opportunity." I think we all perceive the "danger" in a crisis-time, but I am not always sure we perceive the "opportunity." So, let me belabor this for a moment. Imagine that a friend of yours is in a crisis situation and you want to be helpful to him or her. We are all so hypnotized by the virtue of 'being helpful,' that we rarely stop to think about the fact that there are two principal ways of being helpful. One is *to render services.* The virtue of this is that if you are successful, you will pull your friend out of the crisis (like, being without a job), and he or she will be very, very grateful to you. However, the difficulty with (if I may say) *merely* rendering services is that your friend who received your help usually hasn't even a clue, when it is all over, as to how you did it. And, therefore, no idea as to how to pull it off the next time that that same crisis, or one like it, occurs in his or her life. This kind of help therefore, might as well be an act of magic, for all the comprehension your friend has afterwards as to how to solve the problem the next time.

Fortunately, there is a second way of being helpful. And that is to take tremendous care as you go through the process of helping your friend with his or her crisis, so that your friend clearly understands you are *using this particular crisis to teach him or her how to solve that kind of crisis for himself or herself, ever thereafter.* In order to do this, of course, you will need to use no exercises or test-instruments which your friend does not fully understand; to undertake no step in the process without explaining to your friend what is being done, and why; and to offer him or her no additional 'helpers' without explaining why you are offering them, what their virtues and limitations are, and how you found them. I call this latter form of helpfulness *Empowerment,* not because that word was made popular in the late sixties, but because I don't know a better way to describe a process in which both the goal and the acknowledged outcome is that your friend becomes stronger and more in control of his or her life, rather than merely grateful or dependent. And this, because of the way in which you set about to help him or her deal with their 'dangerous opportunity.'

All of this is equally important, if not more so, when it is *your* life which has a crisis in it. You can find help—from books or people—which merely renders you services; or you can find help which is truly Empowering to you. You must set the goal. An Empowering sort of help will be one which helps you learn a method and/or pick up tools which you can relatively easily master, remember, and use all the rest of your life.

It will not come as any great surprise to you that the intention of this book is completely that of Empowering you, rather than merely rendering you a service. This is why, for example, we are employing from the beginning such devices as the Pyramid of Issues. It is a way of helping you to master and remember an empowering sort of framework or structure, that will stay with you once you have used it. Hopefully for the rest of your life. It is this which will turn any crisis you face, from hereon out, into a dangerous opportunity—though more of an opportunity than a danger.

Well, as I said earlier, running into trouble at Work is the crisis that brings more people to Life/Work Planning than any other. Nonetheless 'Work' is still subordinate to 'Life', which is why there is a 'slash' (/) between the two words. It ought to read, actually, like this:

$$\frac{\text{LIFE}}{\text{work}} \text{ Planning}$$

But it is too awkward to take two lines every time one wants to say the phrase; so the straight-line (—) is turned on its side (/) in order that it may all (LIFE/work Planning) fit on one line.

So much for the second word in our title: *Work*.

The third—and last—word in the title is that of *Planning*. This is, admittedly, a rather misleading word. *Planning* means many different things to many different people. Most people, when they first hear of it in this connection, think that what is being talked about is the laying out of a detailed plan about what they are going to be doing a year from now, two years from now, five or even ten years from now. Unfortunately, there are some people in this world who are super-planners, and when they talk about LIFE/work Planning, they mean precisely this very thing. I know of one man who changes jobs every three years, on the precise day, going step-by-step up the career ladder that he has plotted for himself. But if you take such super-planners as your model, you will inevitably be driven to drink—or into a stupefying depression. Most of us just can't pull it off like that. We need a lot more spontaneity and impulsiveness in our lives. Room for the unexpected and the surprise.

Moreover, we know the difficulty of predicting the future.[1] Even those men and women who are supposed to be experts at it—the so-called 'futurists' of our era—who make it their business to forecast the future shape of our environment, our institutions, and so forth — have compiled really rotten score cards, in most cases. There is always the random unpredictable event that comes crashing in, to upset the 'best-laid plans of mice and men.' What is true of society, is true also of our own individual lives. Consequently, most of us simply cannot plan in any detailed or far-reaching sense, down the corridor of our years. The best that we can hope to do is to organize our luck. Or (to put it more accurately) the best we can do is to organize ourselves and our knowledge or picture of what we are looking for, in such a way that we will be prepared to take advantage of whatever may come along—by accident, luck, circumstance, serendipity, fate, Providence, or an act of God.

> LUCK is a crossroad where preparation and opportunity meet.
> —*Anon.*

33

Planning, as that word is used in LIFE/work Planning, seems to involve three distinct processes:

(1) *Pre-developing pictures in one's mind.* Stop for a moment, and think of the most enjoyable moment or evening that you have had during the past two weeks. I am willing to bet that you probably had a picture leap into your mind, rather than merely a string of words. That is to say, we tend to store our memories in terms of pictures. Now think if you will of the event you are most looking forward to during the next two weeks. It is extremely likely, again, that a picture leaped into your mind. Thus we see how much we live by *pictures* in our head. The difficulty is, we often concentrate too much on our pictures of the past (e.g., our memories) and not enough upon our pictures of the future (e.g., what kinds of things we would most enjoy doing, the kinds of places we would most enjoy being, etc.). As a consequence, many people look right at a job they would like, or a thing they would like to do, and pass on by it without even a sign of recognition. Life/Work Planning therefore uses tools to aid you in pre-developing such pictures ahead of time, within your heart and mind, so that if you should find yourself staring right at it, there will be instant recognition, and you will be able to take advantage of the opportunity which matches your predeveloped pictures.

> If you have built castles in the air, your work need not be lost; that is where they should be. Now put the foundations under them.
> —Thoreau

(2) *Pre-testing decisions in one's mind.* If each of us was going to live for 500 years on this Earth, there would perhaps be no need to pre-test decisions. Given that much time to live, we would all have ample opportunity to play smorgasbord with life, and dabble at a hundred different possibilities. We could learn what we like, or don't like, about each experience. We would gradually learn what we are good at, and what we are not good at. We would gradually learn what turns us on so much in our activities, that the line between play and work begins to blur, until working, playing and learning all seem different aspects of one experience. *If* each of us was going to live for 500 years, on this Earth. It is precisely the fact that we are not, which creates the need to *compress* a longer life (as it were) into the rather limited time span that we do have. Life/Work Plan-

ning does this by speeding up the learning process regarding the various possibilities and the alternatives that stretch out in front of us. It accomplishes this by using tools which enable us—within the laboratory of our own head and heart—to pre-test the possibilities, rather than having to laboriously live them out. This pre-testing may best be compared to the housewife (or woman with homemaking skills) who is planning to bleach a dress, and first dips a small sample of the fabric in the bleach—before immersing the whole fabric. What Life/Work

Planning does is to pre-test experiences and possibilities *ahead of time*, by allowing us *to dip ourselves* (as it were) into a small sampling of them, before we decide to go all the way and immerse ourselves in them. By doing this pre-testing, we are able to discard (with relatively little "time-cost" to ourselves) those possibilities which we find to be unattractive or unfitting for us. Thus, we are able to use most of our time to explore and experience those things which this pre-testing has indicated to be worth further exploration and experiencing.

It works out, at best, something like this:

WITHOUT LIFE/WORK PLANNING:

1)
Two possibilities ahead: **A** is chosen without pre-testing.

START HERE:

2)
A is discovered to be bad news; time to get out of **A**, and try **B**.

3)
And **B** is worse.
Decision time: another two possibilities to choose from.
    C is chosen, without pre-testing—just on impulse.

5)
D is found to be very satisfying.

4)
C is discovered to be bad news *for you*; time to get out of **C**, and try **D**.

35

WITH
LIFE/WORK PLANNING:

START HERE: ● ● ● ➤

A ??? ➔

B

D

1)
Decision time, between
two possibilities that lie ahead,
A and **B**; Pre-testing is done in your
own heart and head: **B** is revealed to be
the better choice.

C ??? ➔

2)
Decision time again: two
possibilities lie ahead. **C**
and **D**; Pre-testing is done
in your own heart and head:
D is revealed to be the
better choice.

> To err is human,
> but when the eraser
> wears out
> ahead of the
> pencil, you're
> overdoing it.
> —J. Jenkins

You should not presume from what I
have just said that Life/Work Planning is
intended to eliminate all mistakes. *Oy
gevalt!* Clearly it does not. Some of the
best Life/Work Planners I know, still do
make an occasionally terrible decision.
What conscientious or systematic Life/
Work Planning *is* intended to do is to cut
these down to a minimum, if possible.

Now, to the third process involved in the word *Planning*:

(3) *Pre-determining what one's alternatives are.* You can call
this preparing a lifeboat before going on board a ship. Or you
can call it strapping on a parachute, before flying an airplane.
Or you can call it developing a *plan B*, in case your *plan A*
(whatever that may be) doesn't work. It doesn't much matter
what you call it; it's the not having all your eggs in one basket,
that is the point. I know so many job-hunters, for example,
who—when asked how things are going—reply, "Oh, just great. I
know this magnificent place down the road that I've been told
needs someone just like me. So I'm going down there next week
to ask for an interview, and I'm just sure I'll land a job there."
To which I respond (after expressing appropriate optimism, that
it will indeed be that simple): "But if it doesn't work out,

36

what's your plan B?" There is *almost always* a surprised look, and a hesitant, "Gee, I haven't thought that far ahead." Which bears out what a friend of mine once observed: It is important to help people look down the road a ways; most people are focussing just at headlight range.

Pre-determining what your alternatives are means not waiting until a crisis is upon you, and the thing you counted on has fallen through. It means knowing ahead of time what alternatives are open to you. And of all those alternatives, which one is the one about which you have the most enthusiasm. Done well, this process is not invoked merely for crises, but represents a

---

No "Plan B"

GRANNIS, Ark. (AP) — Twenty-four people waiting for the second coming of Christ aren't worried about a threat to repossess the home they are living in. They believe they will be gone — along with the rest of the world — before marshals come to evict them.

"We don't think God will let us be broken up, so we don't believe we'll be here when they come to take the house," said Elizabeth Nance Bard.

The deadline for them to appeal the repossession of their home is Wednesday, but it's not certain yet when eviction will be attempted.

The U.S. attorney's office in Fort Smith has filed suit against Mrs. Bard's brother, Gene Nance. They say he defaulted on a $15,000 loan to buy the house where the vigil began last Sept. 29.

In April, the Farmers Housing Administration took legal possession of Nance's home. But the vigil members—who have been waiting for redemption for nine months — refused to leave, and legal proceedings were started.

Court officials say that if Nance fails to respond by Wednesday, a default judgment probably will be handed down. U.S. Atty. Robert Johnson says that would probably result in marshals traveling to this southwest Arkansas community and evicting the vigil members.

Mrs. Bard said the group won't fight eviction.

"The sooner the better," she said. "Maybe something will happen. Our great hope is that the end will occur before they come.

"We don't think God will let them split us up," she added.

Mrs. Bard said the vigil members have no idea what they will do if the second coming hasn't occurred by the time the marshals arrive.

"We have no plans at all," she said. "It would be foolish to resist physically. We wouldn't scatter very far ... We don't know, we just haven't made any plans, to move anywhere else. It isn't possible."

[P.S. They were evicted.]

"Switch to Plan B"

way of continually dealing with your whole life. Let us say, for example, that you are going to see a member of your family who lives fifty miles away. You know, of course, the road you are going to take. So, you plan to go down that road or highway. But, it may turn out to be blocked, due to a bad accident or whatever. If you are pre-determining your alternatives, you will look at the map *before you leave home* to see what is the best other way to get to your destination, should you need it. You will have a plan B, in case your plan A doesn't work.

This is basically a *way of thinking* which can become a habit, if you just exercise and develop it continually, as you would exercise a muscle in your body. Every time you think of what it is you are going to do, or how you are going to accomplish a certain task, you *also* stop and think: what is another thing I could do, or another way I could accomplish this task, if my first plan falls through? If this whole way of thinking sounds very strange and perplexing to you, there is an exercise you may want to try:

A Week's Journal of Plan Bs

Instructions: At the end of each day, for a week, write down five different decisions you made that day. List these in column A. (See example given below.)

After you have listed your five for that day, go to column B and try to list what you might have done, if your decision in column A *hadn't* worked out.

EXAMPLE: Column A The thing I decided to do:	Column B The alternative plan (plan B) I could have developed ahead of time:
Go into city today and buy shoes at my favorite shoe store.	*Look up name, ahead of time, of other shoe stores, in case the first one doesn't have what I want.*

Column A The thing I decided to do:	Column B The alternative plan (plan B) I could have developed ahead of time:

FIRST DAY

1 _____ _____
2 _____ _____
3 _____ _____
4 _____ _____
5 _____ _____

SECOND DAY

1 _____ _____
2 _____ _____
3 _____ _____
4 _____ _____
5 _____ _____

THIRD DAY

1 _____ _____
2 _____ _____
3 _____ _____
4 _____ _____
5 _____ _____

FOURTH DAY

1 _____ _____
2 _____ _____
3 _____ _____
4 _____ _____
5 _____ _____

FIFTH DAY

1 _____ _____
2 _____ _____
3 _____ _____
4 _____ _____
5 _____ _____

SIXTH DAY

1 _____ _____
2 _____ _____
3 _____ _____
4 _____ _____
5 _____ _____

SEVENTH DAY

1 _____ _____
2 _____ _____
3 _____ _____
4 _____ _____
5 _____ _____

The point is that having a 'Plan B' is a habit; a habitual way of thinking about making decisions. And, like all habits, it is best developed simply by doing it. That is the purpose of this exercise.

LIFE/Work Designing

F THIS FIELD were starting from scratch, and we could name it anything we wanted to, I think I would prefer to call it LIFE/Work Designing.

"Designing" has the image of doodles, pretty colors, and beautiful patterns, drawn freehand on the pages of life; and that is closer to what this field is all about, than the word "Planning" suggests.

The Familiarity of Life/Work Planning

Now, most people—when they first hear about Life/Work Planning—feel a genuine interest in it, but hesitate to get involved with it because it seems like a strange and unfamiliar activity. Fortunately, however, it is familiar to us all. Almost everyone does Life/Work Planning in some area of his or her life—though without using that title for it.

If you get up on a Sunday morning and you think of eight different things you might do that day, before discarding five of them in your head and deciding to do the remaining three—that is Life/Work Planning, in at least a primitive form. Again, if you think about your vacation time coming up next summer, and start out by imagining three different ways you could spend it, before you finally decide which of those three possibilities is most interesting or even fascinating to you—that also is Life/Work Planning—in a primitive form.

In other words, the title may be new to you, but the activity itself is something that almost all of us—including the most dedicated drifter or dreamer among us—has already experienced. If you decide to do Life/Work Planning, therefore, in the systematic way that is laid out in the rest of this book, you are only resolving to do more thoughtfully and thoroughly that which you already do occasionally and without much thought.

In this sense, it is rather like your determining to take up walking as a regular daily exercise. Clearly, you are not beginning a totally new activity. You already walk. But it may be that, previously, you just ambled around the house, or took at best a ten minute walk to the nearby store. To choose walking as an exercise is to determine to walk at a brisker clip, and for (let us say) an hour each day. But, at the heart of it, you are only expanding something you already do. Life/Work Planning represents the same kind of decision and expansion. If you do the exercises in this book, you are simply taking a mental activity that you already do in an ambling sort of way, and for some parts of the year; and resolving to do it in some kind of disciplined way, more regularly and for a larger bloc of time.

Of course, just exactly what "some kind of disciplined way" means, will vary from one person to the next. Life/Work Planning is a broad field, and if you undertake to walk across that field there are a number of different routes that you can take.

To make these clear, let's take a little quiz:

How do you want to do

a) ☐ In smorgasbord fashion, picking out an exercise here
and an exercise there, as it pleases you?
OR
☐ Systematically, designing a way to blend Learning,
Working and Playing for each part of your Life?

b) ☐ One time in your life, kind-of once and for all?
OR
☐ As a lifelong process, so that your goal the first time
out is not only to do it, but also to master the tools
and framework so that you can repeat it as needed?

c) ☐ In an "action" way, keeping busy doing exercises
without taking the time to reflect upon the learnings
which come out of those exercises?
OR
☐ In an "action + reflection" way, making sure that after
each exercise is completed you make time for sitting
and just thinking?

d) ☐ Using only those exercises which depend heavily on
your being good with words, and which use the
analytical side of your mind?
OR
☐ Using only those exercises which depend heavily on
your being good with pictures, images or music,
and which use the intuitional, holistic side of your
mind?
OR
☐ Using both of the above kinds of exercises?

e) ☐ Enjoying the exercises, as an end in themselves?
OR
☐ Keeping in mind how the exercises fit within an overall
empowering framework, and enjoying them as they
help toward empowerment?

43

Now, obviously the above questions are 'loaded' in the sense that you can see, within each pair or trio, which alternative seems to be more desirable, or comprehensive, or 'mature' than the others. But, few of us will unfailingly choose that alternative from each of the above pairs or trios. So, in the end, every statement above comes out as an accurate description of how *some* people do Life/Work Planning. And only when all the statements are taken together, do you have a complete description of how Life/Work Planning gets done, in this country.

Can You Find The Time?

Well, of course, you want to get out of the three boxes of Life, and build a balanced life for yourself. And of course the idea of some self-empowering exercises, toward that end, while you are waiting for our country to come up with a more global, systemic kind of change in the three boxes, sounds rather attractive. But there is always the $64,000 question: how do you find the time?

To be sure, if you are undertaking Life/Work Planning in a classroom or other group setting, or if you are unemployed or on vacation, time may not be a problem at all. But if you are in school, or working, or running a home, with a very busy schedule to say the least, it probably is a problem. So, what to do?

Most of us—truth to tell—do find time for whatever is for us most important.[2] Therefore, the most important question for you to wrestle with, I suppose, is: how high is Life/Work Planning among your priorities? You may further be helped by reflecting upon the fact that Life/Work Planning doesn't really require extra time *when looked at in the perspective of your total life.* You and I both know what our lives are like without any systematic Life/Work Planning in it: kind of trial and error, trying this, rejecting that, meandering, ambling—and, in general, wasting a great deal of time. By contrast, the time involved in Systematic Life/Work Planning is relatively small. It's just that you have to invest that time *consciously, regularly,* and *now.*

This comes out feeling like hard work. Not merely because of the self-discipline and determination that is needed, but because of the nature of the exercises involved. Their essence, as I mentioned earlier, in most cases has to do with developing pictures in your mind. Such pictures only develop after you have

put together a sufficient number of pieces—rather like assembling a jig-saw puzzle. Each exercise is, consequently, complete and satisfying in itself to a certain degree. But, in another sense, each exercise is also to a certain degree incomplete, and frustrating, because it only contributes one piece toward the total picture. What that total picture is, does not become clear until you have all the pieces. Or almost all. (Jig-saw Puzzle addicts will immediately understand.)

This feels like hard work because of the biding patience that is required of you. And because you have to keep plodding—as it were—until you have manufactured all the pieces. And—most importantly of all—because you have to do a lot of hard thinking along the way. Hard thinking is always work. Most of us would rather flip the television set on, and wave Hard Thinking goodbye.

In the end, so far as Systematic Life/Work Planning is concerned anyway, this comes out to be something of a trade-off. It works like this: are you willing to put in some hard-thinking time on this now, in order to save a lot of trial and error time further down the road? Or do you prefer to do a lot of your life by just trial and error, investing that kind of time in order to save yourself from having to do a lot of hard thinking? Only You can decide.

What we have tried to do, in this book, is describe the exercises necessary to put together the whole picture of your life. *And* we have tried to make these exercises somewhat playful, somewhat enjoyable, without denying the complimentary *hard thinking* that you will necessarily have to do, as the exercises progress. Put another way, we have tried to blend Learning, Work, and Play in the very structure of the exercises themselves—so that (to use an overworked phrase) the medium contains the message that we want to convey.

The Three Boxes in Your Life

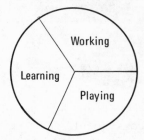

*Here is a circle. Consider this circle
to represent either a year, or a month,
or a week in your present life. If your
life were **ideally** balanced between
Learning, Working and Playing,
the circle would look like this.*

*You may, or may not, want your life as perfectly divided as that.
How would you like your life divided, right now, between Learning, Working and Playing? Divide up this circle so that it shows
this:*

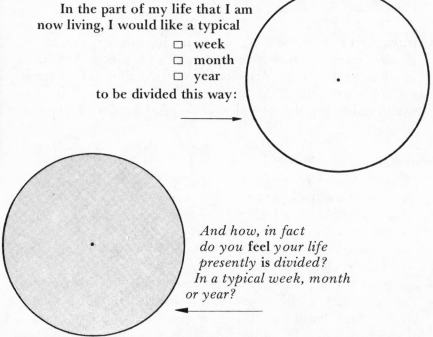

**In the part of my life that I am
now living, I would like a typical**

☐ week
☐ month
☐ year

to be divided this way:

*And how, in fact
do you **feel** your life
presently **is** divided?
In a typical week, month
or year?*

This exercise may have proved very useful to you, in visualizing
how much of your present life is in one of the three boxes. Or,
you may have found the exercise very difficult, because you are
just not sure how your time is spent, presently. In that case, the
next exercise is for you:

Keep this time-log for a week (or for a whole month if you prefer; in which case, take extra sheets of paper and simply reproduce this log three more times). Enter the hours or minutes you spend on each Category, in the log.

THE THREE BOXES TIME LOG	Mon.	Tues.	Wed.	Thurs.	Fri.	Sat.	Sun.	Weekly Total
LEARNING/EDUCATION								
Reading books, magazines, newspapers, journals— in order to learn								
Educational TV								
Day school								
Night school								
Weekend seminars								
Studying, homework								
Other learning activities								
Total Learning Time:								
ACHIEVEMENT/WORK								
Full-time job								
Part-time job								
Volunteer work								
Working at home (typing, crafts, etc.)								
Commuting or waiting to commute								
Other work activities:								
Total Working Time:								
LEISURE/PLAY								
Television								
Socializing with family, friends								
Love—giving and receiving								
Games, sports								
Reading for fun and for pleasure								
Other leisure/play activities								
Total Leisure Time:								
SUBSISTENCE								
Eating, preparing meals								
Sleeping								
Personal care, dressing, undressing								
Exercise								
House-chores, errands, shopping, etc.								
Other:								

PRACTICAL EXERCISE NO. 2

When the log is completed, at the end of the week, total up the number of hours and minutes that you have spent on Learning, Achievement, and Play, and put them on the graph below:

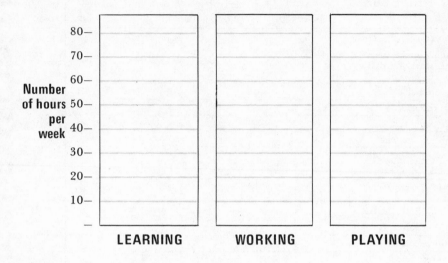

When you have completed this graph, it will look something like this:

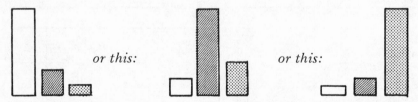

in all likelihood.

And now you know the dimensions of the problem. It is no longer: the three boxes of life. But: the three boxes in YOUR life.

How much you will be able to get out of them, depends on a number of factors. How burdensome your present schedule is, with things you just *have* to do. How ingrained your habits are. How much you are willing to take risks, and try new things. How strapped you are, financially (there is no denying that the more money you have, the easier it is to build a balanced life; however, you'd be surprised what you can do even if your income is in the poverty range, as we shall show).

But, most of all, how much you can get out of the three boxes in Your life, depends upon the degree to which you have licked, or can lick:

The Victim Mentality

For, if you happen to have the Victim Mentality in any great degree, it will inevitably undo the usefulness and effectiveness of any tools that we could ever hand you—including the exercises in this book. Victim Mentality, simply defined, is that outlook or attitude which says:

66 My life is essentially at the mercy of
vast powerful forces (or a vast powerful force)
out there and beyond my control.
Therefore I am the victim of,
and at the mercy of:

√ [Usually at least four are selected]

☐ My history, my upbringing, my genes, or my heritage.
☐ My social class, my education (or lack of it), or my
I.Q. (or lack of it).
☐ My parents, my teachers, or an invalid relative.
☐ My mate, my partner, my husband, or my wife.
☐ My boss, my supervisor, my manager, or my co-workers.
☐ The economy, the times we live in, the social structure,
or our form of government.
☐ The politicians, the large corporations, or the rich.
☐ Some particular enemy, who is out to get me, and who
has great power: an irate creditor, an ex-boyfriend or
ex-girlfriend, a combine, or the Devil.

...As a consequence, it makes little difference
what I want out of life; I have had to
learn to settle for whatever I
can get, since I am relatively
powerless. **99**

49

The Victim Mentality ultimately discharges you from any responsibility for your life, since clearly what is happening to you is not your fault. You don't have to lift a finger. The exercises in this book, which suggest you can take initiative, and actually change your life?—they are clearly for *other* people, who aren't up against what you're up against. So runs the thinking of the Victim Mentality.

Now, to be sure, there is a sense in which we *are* victims, in our culture. We often are at the mercy of forces that we have no control over. A good hurricane or earthquake will remind you forcibly of that fact. So will even a moment's contemplation of what it means to live in The Nuclear Age, where sometime, somewhere, the rulers of some country that we have absolutely no control over, could decide to plunge this whole world into a nuclear holocaust—that would end life, as we know it, for us all.

Beyond these general truths, we are starkly reminded that some people in our society—most especially those who are members of minorities, the poor, and the downtrodden—have a vast amount of compelling evidence that they are more particularly at the mercy of peculiar powerful forces: discrimination, racism, sexism, uncaring officials and bureaucrats, idiotic laws, blind justice, and the like. Their claim that they are peculiar victims of our society hardly needs substantiation.

Nonetheless, there is a vast difference between being a victim (which we all are, in some areas of our life) and having the Victim Mentality. Being a victim, means there are some areas of my life where I am battling powerful forces, *but I will still do battle with them.* Whereas, having the Victim Mentality means giving up: *what's the use? why even try? I have no power at all; the things you suggest may help other people, but they can't offer any hope to me.*

I want to state a simple truth, and that is, I believe every individual has more control over his or her life than he or she thinks is the case. I have seen some dramatic examples of this, in my own experience. Some years ago, a lovely woman named Maryann was pointed out to me, by a mutual friend. The friend pleaded with me to try to help her. Maryann was allegedly the victim, though in her twenties, of multiple sclerosis; she was quite paralyzed, and could walk only with the greatest of difficulty. A neurologist, I was told, had examined her, and said there was nothing he could do. A psychiatrist had examined her, and added there was nothing he could do, either. Maryann was brought in to see me. She entered the office very slowly, walking with an extreme amount of stiffness. I asked her how she felt. She said, Hopeless. When I asked her why, she replied that everyone who had examined her professionally had concluded there was nothing they could do, and had counseled her that she would just have to learn to live with this. I then asked her, "Maryann, do you know what multiple sclerosis is?" "No, I don't," she replied. "Neither do I," I said, "but let us suppose that it is almost purely physical, caused by a virus or something like that, that you have no control over, and the doctors have no antidote for. Let us suppose that 98% of it is physical, then. There is still that other 2% that is under the control of hidden forces within you—your emotions, or your mind, or something that is consciously or unconsciously under the control of your will. Now, we can't work on the 98%, or whatever, that is out of your control; but we certainly can work on that 2%, or whatever the percentage is." The upshot of our conversation was that she agreed to meet with me regularly, so that we could work on that part of her disease which was within her control and power. In time, she lost so much of the paralysis, that she was able to resume a normal life. In fact, she became a clothes model, on fashionable 57th Street in New York. P.S. The doctors, of course, attributed this change to "spontaneous remission, which is typical of this disease." All I know is that Maryann worked very hard on that 'spontaneous remission.'

I tell this story because it is an illustration of something that I believe wholeheartedly: no matter how much of our life we perceive to be unchangeable, because it is in the control of someone or something else, there is always That Part that is under our control, and that we can work on to change. Be it 2%, 5%, 30% or whatever, it is almost always *more* than we think.

I once knew a man who made a dramatic discovery of this. He was, at that time, married, but he was going through a very difficult time with his wife, and was thinking very seriously about divorce. Consequently, he went to see a marriage counselor. "Tell me," said the counselor to the husband, "what kind of problems are bothering you." "Well," replied the husband, "to put it quite simply, my wife is a nag. The other night, for example, she wanted to go out to a meeting, so I offered to stay home and put the kids to bed. I did that, and in addition, I did all the dishes left over from earlier in the day. When she got home, do you think she thanked me? No, she looked in the kitchen and saw that there was one pan I had forgotten to wash. And all she said was, 'Why didn't you do that pan?' " "Very interesting," said the counselor. "Incidentally, why didn't you do that pan?" In the days following, the husband thought about that question; and a revelation came to him. He realized that every time his wife asked him to do something, he would always leave one little tiny part of it undone. He hadn't created her explosive temper; she had it, before they had ever met. But he did 'play into it,' and in that sense, he had some control over the situation. He knew how to trigger her anger, by leaving one part of any task undone. In other words, he had more power over the situation with his wife, than he had at first supposed. He was not so much a victim as he had thought.

This truth applies, even when we are not dealing with another human being, but with (what we suppose to be) some force of nature. I have worn contact lenses for some years, and some time ago I found myself baffled by some very strange occurrences with those lenses. When I needed to remove them from my eyes, I would let the lens drop into my outstretched hand—held at about the level of my chin. But when I then looked into my hand, to retrieve the lens, it was no longer there. The lens had mysteriously disappeared, through no apparent action on my part. Clearly, some mysterious force was at work, for the lens would disappear even in a room where there was no breeze or any air current to explain it. I was sure I was dealing with Something beyond my control or power. One day, however, I decided to study just exactly what occurred when I dropped the lens out of my eye and into my hand. I discovered that as I was 'popping' the lens out of my eye, I was instinctively holding my breath for a moment, until the lens was safely out. Then I would start breathing again, but—of course—a sudden snort of air would rush out through my nostrils; and as my hand was only an inch away from my nose, the air would hit the palm of my hand and blow the lens right out of my hand. I learned, consequently, to hold my breath just a little bit longer, until I had in fact plucked the lens out of my palm. And thereafter, no lens ever "mysteriously" disappeared. So it is that I believe there are many such situations in our lives, where we think some force outside our control is making us the victim. When, in fact, we are doing it to ourselves.

Boxes, Victims and Hope

The assumption that your life has three stages to it is very pervasive and powerful. Our society simply takes it for granted that when you are young, you will study; and when you become an adult, you will work; and when you are old, you will do nothing. Indeed, this assumption has powerful institutional forces and structures (such as required schooling in the early years, or mandatory retirement at a Certain Age) that are very difficult to combat.

But if you have resisted the Victim Mentality (and are resisting it), you will know that you must have more power to begin changing this situation in your own life at least, than you had at first supposed. This power begins by holding firmly in your mind a vision of what our society *could* be and *can* be. That Vision is one of *Flexible Lifetime Patterns,* where—whether you are young, middle-aged, or old—you have the following options or choices:

a) a better balance between education, work and leisure—or learning, working and playing—within Each Day. For example, the morning for study, the afternoon for work, the evening for leisure;

OR: **b)** a better balance between education, work and leisure—or learning, working and playing within <u>Each Week</u>. For example, three days a week devoted to work, two days a week devoted to leisure or playing, and two days a week devoted to education or study;

Sunday	Monday	Tuesday	Wednesday	Thursday	Friday	Saturday

OR: **c)** a better balance between education, work and leisure—or learning, working and playing—within <u>Each Month.</u> For example, ten days a month devoted to education or study, ten days a month devoted to working, and ten days a month devoted to leisure or playing;

	1	2	3	4	5	6
7	8	9	10	11	12	13
14	15	16	17	18	19	20
21	22	23	24	25	26	27
28	29	30	31			

OR: **d)** a better balance between education, work and leisure—or learning, working and playing—within <u>Each Year</u>. For example, four months a year devoted to working, four months a year devoted to leisure or playing, and four months a year devoted to education or study;

Jan.	Feb.	Mar.	April	May	June	July	Aug.	Sept.	Oct.	Nov.	Dec.

OR: **e)** a better balance between education, work and leisure—or learning, working and playing—within <u>Each Decade</u>. For example, four years devoted to working, three years leisure or playing, and three years to education or study.

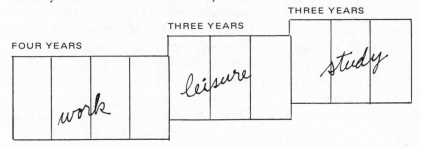

FOUR YEARS — *work*

THREE YEARS — *leisure*

THREE YEARS — *study*

Our power to make one of these visions come true in our own life, i.e., to obtain the Flexible Lifetime Pattern that appeals to us the most, is up against three major obstacles:

(1) *Lack of a strong will or desire on our part to see this happen.* Many of us don't know what we would do with more leisure or more time for study. We need clearer goals and objectives as to how we would use this time. Much of the following chapters, consequently, are devoted to helping you set clearer goals and objectives. When you want something to happen so strongly that you can taste it, you will move heaven and earth to make it happen for you. That depends upon surfacing a vision of what your leisure and your education or study time could be, and could mean, to you.

(2) *Lack of money to pay for the leisure time or the study time.* The further down you get on the Flexible Lifetime Pattern Scales above (i.e., the further away from "a" and the more toward "e") the more you need savings from your period of working to pay for your periods of study and leisure. Yet the typical American wage-earner "has no more than $50 laying around the house, a checking account that falls near zero at the end of every month and very little saved " (San Francisco Examiner, April 19, 1976). This difficulty need not, however, prevent you from *moving toward* one of the Flexible Lifetime Patterns above. For example, "a" above can be adapted at least to mean Working five days a week, having Education or Study three nights a week at a nearby community college (because of its inexpensiveness), and planned Leisure on the weekend, regardless of how little money you may have.

(3) *The difficulty of getting back into the World of Work, once you have left it.* This difficulty increases, of course, the older that you become. But it is a great problem at any age. It really holds us back. We could go off and get some further education, or take some time off for leisure, playing, and recreation, *if* we knew with some confidence that we could get back into the World of Work when our time for education or leisure was up.

The fact that usually we do not have this confidence about ease of Readmission explains why so many of us allow our Life to stay indeed Three Boxes: Education only when we are very young, Work only in our middle years, and Leisure only when we are old. What we need, plainly, is a process for Job-hunting that works so well, regardless of age, we can be confident about leaving the World of Work when we wish, and re-entering it when we wish. That is, if there is such a process. At the National Career Development Project, we have accumulated a vast amount of impressive evidence that there is. It is described in our later chapter on Work. It seems to work equally well for the young and the old, for men and for women, for drop-outs and the well-educated, for Wasps and minorities, for inner-city dwellers and surburbanites, for high-verbal skilled and low-verbal, for the ex-perienced and the inexperienced, for ex-offenders and psychiatric out-patients, for the assertive and for the shy, for the artist and the executive. In a word: for all sorts and conditions of men and women.

With these three obstacles clearly in mind, we will turn now to consider—in subsequent chapters—Lifelong Learning, Lifelong Working, and Lifelong Leisure. And the tools you need in order to build a balance between these elements in your own life—be you sixteen or sixty, nineteen or ninety. The chapters are not of equal length. The first one (Lifelong Learning) is by far the longest, for a number of reasons. One of these is that the principles of Life/Work Planning have been throughly applied to Lifelong Working, in my previous books: *What Color Is Your Parachute?* and (in coauthorship with John C. Crystal) *Where Do I Go From Here With My Life?* But how these principles apply to Lifelong Learning is not so clearly understood, by any means. Therefore, the explanation is more detailed and more lengthy. Another reason for the length of the chapter on Lifelong Learning is that this is our first "climb" up the Pyramid of Issues. The tools required for that "climb", whether the Pyramid be encountered in the World of Education, or the World of Work, or the World of Leisure and Play, are virtually the same. But it is in the chapter on Lifelong Learning that we first encounter those tools, and it is there that they consequently receive detailed explanation.

Before going on, we take one last look back. Here is the sum of all that has been said so far:

You are in charge of your life.

No matter how many forces there may be which seem to influence or even dictate part of your life, there is always That Part over which you have control. You can increase that control. If you decide what it is that you want out of your Learning, and out of your Working, and out of your Playing, you will be infinitely less *powerless* and *"victimizable."* Because you are clear about what it is you want, you will not accept cheap substitutes willingly. You will not be easily seduced into thoughtlessly exchanging your birthright for a mess of pottage. (If this allusion is lost upon the reader, consult Genesis, chapter 25.) You will no longer be vulnerable to being sold a bill of goods by any passing stranger. It is your life. Not hers. Or his. Or theirs. Yours.

Chapter Two Footnotes

1. But for those who would like to try, there is:

    Sheldon, Eleanor Bernert and Moore, Wilbert E. ed. *Indicators of Social Change: Concepts and Measurements.* New York: Russell Sage Foundation (230 Park Avenue, New York, NY 10017), 1968. $15, or at your local library.

    Bell, Daniel. *Toward the Year 2000: Work in Progress.* Boston: Beacon Press, 1968. $2.95.

    Hansot, Elisabeth. *Perfection and Progress.* Cambridge, Massachusetts: M.I.T. Press, 1976. $17.50 or your local library.

    Roemer, Kenneth M. *The Obsolete Necessity.* Kent, Ohio: Kent State University Press, 1976. $10 or your local library.

2. For help with time management, see:

    Lakein, Alan. *How To Get Control of Your Time and Your Life.* New York: Peter H. Wyden, Inc. (750 Third Avenue, New York, NY 10017), 1973. $6.95. Also out in paperback.

    Cooper, Joseph D. *How to Get More Done In Less Time.* Garden City, New York: Doubleday & Company, Inc., 1971. $7.95.

Two men were walking along a crowded sidewalk in a downtown business area. Suddenly one exclaimed: "Listen to the lovely sound of that cricket." But the other could not hear. He asked his companion how he could detect the sound of a cricket amid the din of people and traffic. The first man, who was a zoologist, had trained himself to listen to the voices of nature. But he didn't explain. He simply took a coin out of his pocket and dropped it to the sidewalk, whereupon a dozen people began to look about them. "We hear," he said, "what we listen for."

— Kermit L. Long

Chapter Three
Toward a Balanced Life:
Life-Long Learning

t will come as no surprise to most of you that the whole educational system of America is under tremendous attack these days—and has been for some time. A new book criticizing our elementary system, our high schools and/or our colleges, appears almost every month. So continuous has this assault been, that you could be pardoned for assuming that a chapter on "Our Educational System and You" is a waste of time, since—in the face of so much dissatisfaction—nobody could possibly be enrolled in our schools these days.

Well of course, if you are in school at the moment you know that is just not true. And if you are not in school, you may be interested to know that in point of fact some sixty million people are enrolled in some kind of school today. Close to nine million of these are in college (two million of them in community or two-year colleges), some fifteen million (plus) in high schools (grades 9-12), and a little less than 34½ million in elementary schools (grades kindergarten through eighth). When you add to these our nation's teachers (some three million), school administrators (about 300,000) and maintenance staff, it turns out that nearly one out of every three people in the U.S. are involved in the World of Education. Moreover, our educational system has become the Nation's largest enterprise, spending over $110 billion per year. [1]

That system is no longer simply for the five to twenty-two year old — if indeed it ever was. Today 48.3% of all students who attend college are over twenty-two years of age, and 10.4% are over thirty-five years. [2] This means that on our nation's college campuses, one out of every ten students is what we would today call 'middle-aged' or older.

The latter age group is also well-represented at those numer-

30-YEAR-OLDS GIVE LOW GRADES TO HIGH SCHOOL EDUCATION

Most 30-year-olds are disappointed in the quality of education they received, a NIE-supported survey has discovered. A 15-year-follow-up of Project Talent participants, the survey was designed to determine how well schools are meeting the needs of their students.

Interviews with a national sample of 1000 Project Talent men and women first quizzed in 1960 while still in high school revealed that, although they rate the quality of their lives as "quite good," most believe that their high school education did little to help them along.

Over 90 percent of those interviewed felt that their health, love life, and job were most important to them, and about three-fourths were pleased with those aspects of their lives. However, although 84 percent believed intellectual development to be important, only 54 percent were satisfied with their lives on that count.

High on the list of criticisms was the failure of secondary schools to help students develop long range educational goals or plan for a career.

For over three-fourths of the 30-year-olds, the schools' lack of adequate vocational and education guidance was "an important factor in interfering with the present quality of life." For most participants—especially those who did not attend college—schools seem to have done a poor job of helping them discover their interests and talents or plan for the future.

According to the study report, written by John C. Flanagan and Darlene Russ-Eft of the American Institutes of Research, this lack of guidance was the schools' biggest failure. "It is very clear," they say, "that these students were unrealistic in their career expectations because they lacked an understanding of both the education needed for particular jobs and their own level of abilities and interest."

REAL LIFE SKILLS

Although 47 percent of the 30-year-olds said they use skills learned in high school on the job, many felt that what they learned in school just wasn't relevant to the skills they really needed. "I learned everything I know from skipping school and working in the garage," said one. In addition, 65 percent said they could have benefited from more individual help, and about a third felt they had been hurt by a failure to get understanding, counsel, or support in their schools.

How did they perceive the quality of teaching in the schools? Reactions were equally divided. About half said a teacher had been a positive influence, while an equal number said a teacher had influenced them negatively. Either way, the report states, "(The) effects of both good and bad teachers on the quality of life of these students are clearly evident many years after these students have left these teachers' classrooms." Students most admired those teachers who had a sincere interest in both their subject and their students and who were hard taskmasters.

Copies of the survey report, *An Empirical Study to Aid in Formulating Educational Goals*, are available from: John Flanagan, American Institutes for Research, P.O. Box 113, Palo Alto, Calif. 94302. The NIE project monitor is Richard Harbeck, Basic Skills Group.

From INFORMATION, Vol. 2, No. 1, May, 1976. The Quarterly Newsletter of the National Institute of Education.

ous other places besides colleges where an adult can go for further education. In a recent year, for example, more than seven million people age thirty-five or older were enrolled in some form of adult education outside of colleges. And 1,363,000 of them were fifty-five years or older.

What this means, of course, is that people are beginning to perceive that Education *ought not to be* a box which they are in from age five to twenty-two, and then *that's it*. A lot of us are beginning to realize that Education is a life-long activity. And therefore must be built in as part of our life while we are in the World of Work and as part of our life—if possible—while we are in the World of Retirement.

SO, THIS CHAPTER IS FOR ALL AGES. WE ARE TALK-ING ABOUT LIFE–LONG LEARNING.

And it will hopefully be helpful to all ages. But, however enlightened *we* may be about all this, let us not forget:

It's Still A Box For Most of the Population

You have only to look at the following table or chart to see this clearly.[3] From 1957 to 1975, the percentage of the population participating in some kind of adult education activity almost doubled. But even so, those participating as late as 1975 only represented 13.3% *of all those who could have partici-pated.*[4]

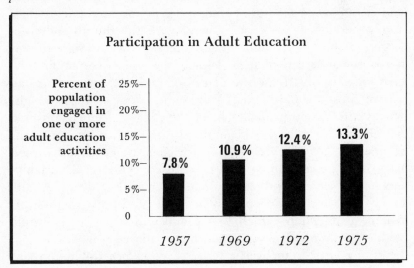

Participation in Adult Education

Percent of population engaged in one or more adult education activities

1957   1969   1972   1975

7.8%   10.9%   12.4%   13.3%

To put it another way, out of the 135 million adults who could have participated in some kind of formal-educational activity, 117 million (or 86.7%) did not.[5] Partly, of course, this is because they perceive the validity of the criticism which is being leveled against the World of Education by its critics. But partly, also, it is because they have bought in on the idea that Education is something you do primarily between the ages of 5 and 22. They have made a box out of the World of Education—in their heads.

How You Get Out of That Box

Let us notice that there is something heartening about all the criticism being leveled at the educational establishment in our country. Such criticism could not take place were it not for the fact that an increasing number of people—parents and students—are asking, what am I supposed to be getting out of all this schooling? Or: what is my child supposed to be getting out of all this schooling? It used to be left up to the schools themselves to define this for us, and now increasingly we are taking this responsibility upon ourselves. That is most heartening.

Yet we have a great deal to overcome. A plane trip I took several years ago, drove this home to me. I was seated by a window. Next to me was an empty seat, while on the aisle sat a very sweet looking middle-aged woman. She was reading a manuscript, which she had placed on the tray-table in front of her, and all the while she was reading she kept absent-mindedly massaging her left-hand wrist, slowly, with the thumb and forefingers of her right hand. I was sure she was unaware of this nervous mannerism of hers. I knew she was a veteran air traveler, since the briefcase she placed on the seat between us had one of those "100,000 miles" tags on it. "Poor dear," I thought to myself, "she's probably been traveling too much, pushing herself too hard, and is beginning to develop this unconscious mannerism." Well, this went on for some time, while I turned back to my own reading, and tried to concentrate. Eventually, lunch was served, and we both put our reading down. As the lunch trays were being placed in front of us, my manuscript-reading companion turned to me and with the sweetest smile said, "You know, I never would have believed it would take so long for a wrist to recover, after it's been in a cast. Why, do you know, I have to massage my wrist this way for at least a half hour every day in order to get my blood really circulating again!"

I, of course, wanted to crawl under my seat, for what I had been thinking. I was very relieved that she had set me straight. At the same time, it occurred to me that there was a profound parallel between her experience, and that of our young adults who are in school. Many—if not most—of the students in high school feel as though they too have been in a cast: a decision-making cast for their whole psyche, which kept them rather immobilized during most of the years till they were sixteen or more. They were told where they had to live, where they had to go to school, what kinds of courses they ought to take, what time they were to be home, how long they were supposed to spend on their homework, when they could start dating, what time curfew was, and so on. Suddenly they graduate from high school, and are ready to go on to college or out into the World of Work. *Then* we suddenly tell them, "Okay, you're a decision maker now. Start making some decisions. Do you want to go to college? If so, where, and what do you want to study? It's your decision. Or you prefer to go out and get a job? If so, what do you want to do, and where do you want to work? It's your decision. You're graduating from high school, and that means you've become *A Decision-Maker.*"

It's not exactly surprising that the students just sort of sit there, staring at us. Perhaps if they started symbolically massaging their left-hand wrist with their right hand, then at least we would understand that after being in *A Non-Decision-Making Cast* for so long, it's likely to take them some time before they get their decision-making-powers really circulating. We would not wonder if they go into a kind of paralysis for a while, either not making any real decisions or else making a few very tentative gestures toward the life-bending issues we suddenly put in front of them.

Back Up The Pyramid Again

Suppose you are that student in high school. And suppose you've decided to go on to college, as almost one out of every two high school graduates does, these days. You may have had some genuine sense of being at home in the high school world. You knew what was happening, you knew how to survive there, you knew what was most meaningful to you, and you knew how to be effective in doing that thing, or those things. Now you are going on to college. What is so difficult about that? You will be facing the same issues. Yes, *but now those issues have new answers, and so—in effect—you have to start at the bottom of the pyramid, all over again.*

The Educational Pyramid

What's happening in college? does not have the same answer as What's happening in high school? So, you have to wrestle with that issue all over again.

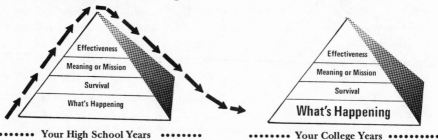

It is amazing how many students spend half their time in college just trying to figure out what's happening. Trying to discover what's going on there, what options are open to you, and so forth, can be a full-time occupation. Sometimes the question is only fully-solved, the options are only finally uncovered, as you are about to depart from that scene. *Then* you realize what you might have been able to choose between, what paths you might have explored. And the familiar regrets flood in upon you: "Gee, I sure didn't take the best courses I might have." "Wow, I wish I had known that I could have..." And so forth.

Some students in college never get much higher than the level of "What's Happening" and "Survival," during all the time they are there (particularly those between ages eighteen and twenty-two or so). By contrast, when we attend college at an older age, either for the first time or as a returnee seeking to 'upgrade our skills,' we are generally able to move on to the next levels, and perceive our Education in terms of the Meaning we are seeking for our lives, or in terms of up-grading our Effectiveness.

Eventually, then, if Education is truly a lifelong process *in our own lives at least*, we will need to know the best tools and resources for getting at the four levels of the Educational Pyramid. For we will have the need to work through those four levels again and again, in high school, in college, in our middle years, and in retirement. The earlier we learn how to do that, the more occasions we will have for using that knowledge.

The First Issue on our Educational Pyramid: ● WHAT'S HAPPENING

To begin with, the World of (Formal) Education is a very large world. That means we have a lot of choices available to us, at any age. Most of us never know that. Lacking an overview of that World, we tend to choose our educational opportunities in a relatively haphazard way. In our teens and twenties. In our thirties, forties and fifties. And in our sixties, seventies and eighties. We act as though there were only a couple of possibilities to choose from. We choose our card, as it were, from something less than a full deck.

In high school, if we decide to go on to college, we choose the college where our parents or older friends went. Or those colleges with which our high school guidance counselor happens to be familiar. Which is to say, only a small number of the actual possibilities ever get really examined, or even looked at.

In later years, our information-gathering-system about the educational opportunities, possibilities, and options that are open to us, doesn't usually get much more sophisticated or extensive. If we're financially strapped, we decide that our only option is the local community college. Indeed, the local community college may be our *best* option—but it is hardly our *only* option. To think that it is, is to give up some of our freedom. For, no one is truly free until he or she has at least two things to choose between.

Clearly we need a better information-gathering-system, about What's Happening in the World of Education. And that better system begins with an overview of All The Possibilities. It comes out looking something like this: [6]

A Picture of the World of

Elementary Education	Secondary Education	Postsecondary (Higher) Education

Elementary or Primary Schools

General Senior High Schools

— or —

Specialized High Schools

Vocational-Technical Institutes

— or —

Public or Private Career Schools

— or —

Community Colleges

— or —

Doctor's degree study

Post-doctoral study and research

Kinder-gartens

or

Nursery Schools

Middle Schools

— or —

Vocational-Technical High Schools

— or —

Trade School

— or —

General Educational Development Test (GED)

Master's Degree Study

Undergraduate Colleges Liberal Arts or General (in residence or attendance).

— or —

Junior High School

— or —

Combined Junior-Senior High Schools

External Degree Programs (Certified for Work Done Outside the College)

—or— —or— —or—

Professional Schools (Teaching, Medicine, Theology, Law, Etc.)

— or —

Special Schools

— or —

Special Schools

— or — — or —

Corre-spondence Schools

Corre-spondence Schools

TYPICAL AGE:

3	4	5	6	7	8	9	10	11	12	13	14	15	16	17	18	18	19	20	21	22	23	24	25	26	27	28	29

School year	N	K	1	2	3	4	5	6	7	8	9	10	11	12	13	14	15	16	17	18	19	20	21	22

Education (AN OVERVIEW

Continuing Life-long Educational Opportunities

Technical Institutes

or

Private Career Schools

or

Community Colleges: 6 month–1 year programs
Community College 2 year programs (AA)
Community College 3 year programs

or

Non-profit agencies giving training to special clients
with particular backgrounds or traits: women; minorities;
people with physical, emotional, or mental handicaps;
ex-offenders; drop-outs, etc.

or

Government Manpower Training or Educational Programs—
(MDTA, CETA, etc.)

or

Armed Forces Schools and Training Programs
(for those who enlist)

or

Training or Educational Projects in Industry
- apprenticeships (for 350 trades)
- entry training-programs
- education and development programs done by industry or industry/college

or

Programs or Schools in Your Community
- adult or continuing education programs run by school district or community college

  or
- university/college extension programs

  or
- Y/church/synagogue schools or programs

  or
- "open" schools/universities without walls

or

Workshops offered by organizations, schools, or individuals

or

Training/indoctrination programs of various organizations

or

Miscellaneous: Therapies/groups/gurus/tutors/private instructors

or

Home Study
- TV/local college
- Correspondence courses
- Cassettes

AT ANY AGE WHATSOEVER, AFTER 16–18

69

No particular school year

Now, of course I could go on to a whole series of descriptions and Fascinating Statistics concerning each part of this World of Education. For example, under correspondence schools, I could enter the fact that there are more than 300 such schools in this country, including 115 that have national accreditation, which enroll some two million pupils, less than a third of whom complete their courses (from *Fortune,* December 1975).

There are three reasons, however, why you will not find such a detailed recital here:

(1) I would like this to be a practical manual, of manageable length, dealing with *your* education, *your* work and *your* leisure. How many other people are involved in educational enterprises is, in the last analysis, irrelevant to you—except as such statistics may indicate how wide and varied your options are. Believe me, they are *very* wide and varied.

(2) Until you know what you want to learn, or how you want to learn, you cannot really deal with all this information. You need some principles of exclusion, by which you can 'cut the territory down to manageable size'. Let me give an example. In a recent year, a survey was conducted to determine why adults were pursuing further education. These were the findings:

Participants' Reasons
for Taking Adult Education

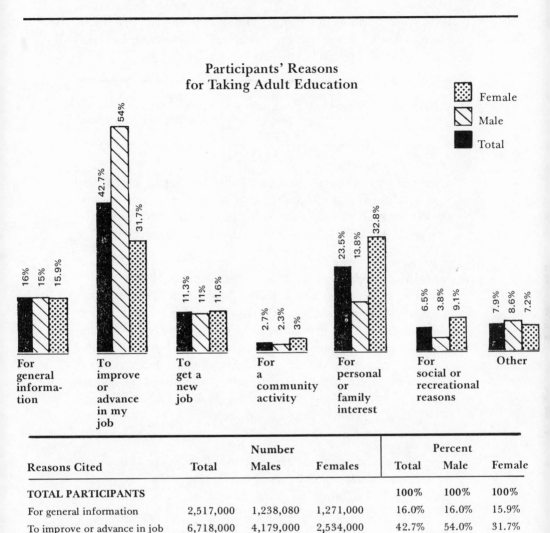

Reasons Cited	Number			Percent		
	Total	Males	Females	Total	Male	Female
TOTAL PARTICIPANTS				100%	100%	100%
For general information	2,517,000	1,238,080	1,271,000	16.0%	16.0%	15.9%
To improve or advance in job	6,718,000	4,179,000	2,534,000	42.7%	54.0%	31.7%
To get a new job	1,778,000	851,000	927,000	11.3%	11.0%	11.6%
For community activity	425,000	178,000	240,000	2.7%	2.3%	3.0%
For personal or family interests	3,697,000	1,068,000	2,622,000	23.5%	13.8%	32.8%
Social or recreational reasons	1,023,000	294,000	728,000	6.5%	3.8%	9.1%
Other	1,243,000	665,000	576,000	7.9%	8.6%	7.2%
Not reported	94,000	54,000	40,000	0.6%	0.7%	0.5%

Totals add to more than participants, as more than one course was taken by some.

Source: U.S. Department of Health, Education, and Welfare, National Center for Education Statistics, *Participation in Adult Education, 1972.*

With these findings in hand, it is relatively easy then to divide the whole World of Education (an overview of your options) into manageable segments. Thus:

Your Reasons for Further Education —
and, Places to Look for What You Need:

For general information
Community colleges; undergraduate colleges; correspondence schools; adult or continuing education programs; university or college extension programs; open schools; university without walls; TV/college courses; cassettes; tutors

To improve or advance in job
Vocational/technical institutes; community colleges; undergraduate colleges; external degree programs; correspondence schools; Master's or Doctor's degree study; Armed Forces Schools & Training Programs; professional conventions; education and development programs done within your industry or company; adult or continuing education programs in your community; university/college extension programs; workshops offered by organizations, schools or individuals; TV/college courses; cassettes; tutors

To get a new job
Vocational/technical institutes; public or private trade schools; community colleges; undergraduate colleges; external degree programs; correspondence schools; Master's or Doctor's degree study; non-profit agencies giving training to special clients with particular backgrounds; government manpower training or educational programs; Armed Forces; apprenticeships; entry-training programs in industry; adult or continuing education programs; university/college extension programs; open schools; universities without walls; workshops offered by organizations, schools or individuals; TV/college courses; tutors

For a community activity
Community college; undergraduate college in your community; adult or continuing education programs; Y/church/

synagogue schools or programs in your community; open schools or university-without-walls in your community; workshops offered by organizations, schools or individuals in your community; training/indoctrination programs of various organizations (TA, P.E.T., est, Lifo, etc.); gurus; miscellaneous community education events

For personal or family interest

Community colleges; undergraduate colleges; correspondence schools; non-profit agencies giving training to special clients with particular backgrounds; some educational programs within industry for employees; adult or continuing education programs; Y/church/synagogue schools and programs; university/college extension programs; open schools; universities without walls, workshops offered by organizations, schools, and individuals; training/indoctrination programs of various organizations (TA, P.E.T., est, Lifo, Synanon, A.A., Delancey Street, etc.); therapies (Esalen, etc.)/ groups/gurus; TV/college courses; cassettes; tutors

For social or recreational reasons

Community colleges; undergraduate colleges; adult or continuing education programs; university/college extension programs; Y/church/synagogue schools or programs; open schools; workshops offered by organizations, schools, or individuals; universities without walls; groups

---

The minute you have decided on the primary reason why you want further education, you have—in a sense—adopted a principle of exclusion. There are, as a result of your decision, a whole bunch of places you *don't* need to look at. They are excluded.

(3) Our concern, as was stated earlier, is to give you a process by which you can find out What's Happening in the World of Education *anytime that you want to, for the rest of your life.* I am, therefore, more concerned with detailing *how* you find out What's Happening, than I am with detailing *what* you will find out. The 'what' keeps changing, as our educational system evolves and new institutions are developed or new technologies unfold (such as 'programmed instruction,' 'computer-assisted learning,' and so forth). The 'how' does not essentially change.

How You Find Out What's Happening

We have already seen the beginning of some basic principles. Now it is time to arrange the whole subject systematically. It goes like this:

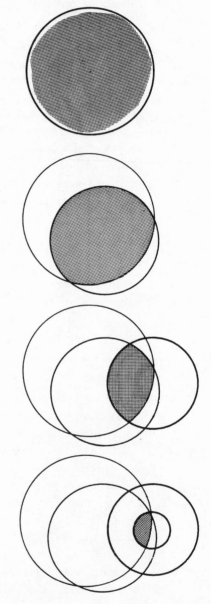

1 Overview. You begin with some idea of 'the broad picture' of the whole area you are interested in, so you know how large your options are. *For example, the whole World of Education, or all colleges, etc.*

2 Cutting it down. You make some decisions. These act as principles of exclusion, eliminating a large number of things you now do not need to look at. *For example, "I don't want to go to a college with over 10,000 students" is a decision which eliminates the need to look at colleges over 10,000.*

3 Use of printed resources. Each time you turn to a book, directory or catalog, you make some more decisions, further cutting down the territory you need to look at. *For example, "I like colleges in the Western part of our country" and "I don't want a campus that's right in the heart of a city" may become clear to you, as you read some books or see pictures.*

4 You talk to people. What you can't find out from printed stuff, you find by talking to appropriate people. They can give you current information that enables you finally to zero in on the one (or two or three) places or things you most want to learn about. *For example your high school guidance counselor; or alumni of particular colleges; or family friends, etc. Who you talk to depends on what you want to know.*

There's the whole process, in a nutshell. Once you've mastered it, you can use it—for the rest of your life—to find out almost anything you could possibly want to know. *What*'s happening may keep changing; but you will always know *how* to find out what. **Now, to flesh out the outline:**

Step **1** OVERVIEW. We have already seen what an overview looks like, with our earlier *A Picture of the World of Education*. There are overviews available on almost every subject you can think of. I have listed a number of examples below, under "Step Three." Your local librarian will be able to tell you where additional overviews are to be found. In some instances, incidentally, you may only uncover the overview as you go along —in which case you will do the narrowing down, after that.

Instead of going like this:

– it may go like this:

1.
Overview

2.
Narrowing down

3.
Use of printed resources

4.
Talk to people

5.
Find what you want

1.
Start with one idea

2.
Use printed resources

3.
Talk to people

4.
Get overview at last

5.
Narrow it down with aid of steps 2 and 3

6.
Find what you want

Step **2** CUTTING IT DOWN IN SIZE. The overview, regardless of when you finally grasp it, always includes too much information. You have only to look back at our *Picture of the World of Education* to see this clearly. If you tried to find out even a limited amount of information concerning each segment depicted in that diagram, you would have a full-time task on your hands for the next half-year. But the moment you make *any* decision, or state any preference, you have reduced the size of the world that you need to find out about. Suppose, for example, that you are just finishing high school, and you decide to go on to college. That decision, in and of itself, eliminates a lot of segments in that world *Picture*. Or suppose you are in middle or later life, and you decide you want further education "for personal and family interest." Our chart, back on page 68 would immediately enable you to eliminate a lot of educational opportunities that you *would not* need to look at. Every decision you can make will cut down, in size, the territory you need to explore. Thus, if you leap to *The Third Issue on Our Educational Pyramid: MEANING AND MISSION* (page 114) and do the exercises there, since they are *decision* exercises, they will reduce the amount of time you need to expend on "What's Happening" here. Or, to put it another way: he or she who *will not* take the time to make some *decisions* about where he or she is going, will then *have to* spend a lot more time just figuring out "What's Happening."

Step **3** USE OF PRINTED RESOURCES. Once you've got a clue as to what you're looking for (like: *I want to go on to college*. Or: *I want some further education to help me with my personal or family interests*) you turn to library resources, to find out what there is in print or in audio-visuals that can help you. Your best friend here is your friendly neighborhood librarian (particularly *research librarian*, if your library is large enough to have one). Don't overlook your school library, either. You have only to tell your librarian what it is you are trying to find out—or find out more about—and she or he can direct you to the proper directory, book, catalog, or whatever.

You will need, of course, to take with several grains of salt *anything* that a book tells you (including, of course, *this* one). Some of us get positively hypnotized when we see something in print. Well, typesetters only set in type the things which authors tell them to. And authors are as fragile, vulnerable, and ofttimes mistaken, as the rest of the human race. To give an example, there are guides purporting to evaluate various colleges around the country—but it is rarely if ever made clear how extensive the interviewing was (on a particular campus) or what percentage of the total student body shared the opinions of the interviewees. Such books, if you take their findings as Clues, can be very useful. But if you treat them as Absolutely True, because they are in print, you are in big trouble, friend.

Another thing to remember when examining any book, is: look at the most recent copyright date, on the back of the title page. The oldest copyright date is when the book first was printed. The most recent copyright date is when the book was most recently printed *in a revised form*. Needless to say, if there's only one copyright date, that date is both the first and the last time it was revised. *Printing* dates don't mean anything for our present purposes. Thus, a book which reads: *Copyright 1960, First Paperback Edition 1974, Fifth Printing 1976*, still has information in it no more recent than 1960. The Copyright date is the giveaway. You can figure the information in the book is even older—at least a year or so older than the Copyright date, in most cases—given the time it takes a publisher to get a book into print and out into the bookstores *after* the manuscript is completed.

When trying to evaluate the information in a particular book, therefore, it will help you to remember that information has *got* to be: *(Check one)*

☐ virtually current   ☐ terribly dated
☐ slightly dated   ☐ absolutely outdated

This is why printed stuff, like books and directories, must always be checked out, by Interviewing People, afterwards.

Now, here is the *kind* of book which *may* be useful to you, if your friendly neighborhood librarian is out to lunch, or you don't live within 50 miles of a library, or you're trying to figure this all out by yourself—for whatever reason. This is, in other words:

If You're Looking For—
You Might Find This Helpful:

1. An overview of how you find out information

    Finding Facts Fast: How to Find Out What You Want to Know Immediately. A handbook for high school, college and graduate students, political activists, civic leaders and professionals . . . based on methods used by reference librarians, scholars, investigative reporters and detectives, by Alden Todd. 1972. Can be ordered directly from: Ten Speed Press, P.O. Box 7123, Berkeley, CA 94707, $3.95, paper. This book could turn out to be your very best friend in school and out. Highest recommendation.

2. An overview of Education in the U.S.

    The Condition of Education: 1976 Edition. A Statistical Report on the Condition of Education in the United States. The National Center for Education Statistics. (If your library doesn't have it, you can order it from: Superintendent of Documents, U.S. Government Printing Office, Washington, D.C. 20402. Stock No. 017-080-01521-8. $4.40, paper.)

    and/or

    Digest of Education Statistics: 1976 Edition, by W. Vance Grant and C. George Lind, National Center for Education Statistics. 1977. Superintendent of Documents (address above). $3.30, paper.

3. An overview of the future trends in Education in the U.S.

    Projections of Educational Statistics to 1984-85, by Kenneth A. Simon and Martin M. Frankel, National Center for Education Statistics. Obtainable, if your library doesn't have it, from Superintendent of Documents (address at No. 2, above), $3.00, paper.

4. An overview of other government publications on Education

   EDUCATION, Price List 31. Free from Superintendent of Documents (address at No. 2, above).

5. An overview of publications about Career Education

   Write to: ERIC Clearinghouse in Career Education, Center for Vocational Education, Ohio State University, 1960 Kenny Road, Columbus, Ohio 43210.

6. An overview of publications about adult or lifelong education, and a directory of resources available

   Write to: NIU Information Program, Clearinghouse on Adult Education and Lifelong Learning, 204 Gabel Hall, Northern Illinois University, DeKalb, Illinois 60115.

7. An overview of all the colleges in the U.S., arranged according to States

   The Education Directory, Part 3 (Higher Education). Available, if your library doesn't have it, from Superintendent of Documents (address at No. 2, above).

8. An overview of some colleges in U.S., in greater detail

   The Underground Guide to the College of Your Choice, by Susan Berman, 1971. At your local library, bookstore, or from: Signet Books, The New American Library, Inc., P.O. Box 999, Bergenfield, New Jersey 07621. $1.50, paper.

   and/or

   The Insiders Guide to the Colleges, compiled by the Staff of the Yale Daily News. At your college bookstore, or from: Berkley Publishing Corp., 200 Madison Avenue, New York, N.Y., 10016. $2.50, paper.

   The Handbook of Private Schools, 1976. Porter Sargent Publisher, 11 Beacon St., Boston, MA 02108. 1,536 pages. $21.00 Or, see your library. Description of over 2,000 independent schools in the U.S.

9. An overview of all vocational/technical/career/trade/training educational opportunities

> *The Guide to Career Education*, by Muriel Lederer. 1974. In your bookstore, or order directly from: Quadrangle/The New York Times Book Co., 10 East 53rd Street, New York, New York 10022. $6.95, paper.
>
> and/or
>
> *Lovejoy's Career and Vocational School Guide: A Source Book, Clue Book and Directory of Institutions Training for Job Opportunities*, by Clarence E. Lovejoy. Available from: Simon and Schuster, Rockefeller Center, 630 Fifth Avenue, New York, New York 10020, or your bookstore. $3.95 paper.

10. An overview of private trade and technical schools

> *Getting Skilled: A Guide to Private Trade and Technical Schools*, by Tom Hebert and John Coyne. 1976. Available in your bookstore, or from: Sunrise Books, E. P. Dutton & Co., Inc., 201 Park Avenue South, New York, N.Y. 10003. $4.95, paper.

11. An overview of work/study programs (cooperative education)

> *Directory of Cooperative Education: Its Philosophy and Operation in Participating Colleges in the United States and Canada.* 1973. Available from: Cooperative Education Association, Drexel University, Philadelphia, Pennsylvania 19104. $6.00
>
> *"Undergraduate Programs of Cooperative Education in the U.S. and Canada."* From: National Commission for Cooperative Education, 360 Huntington Avenue, Boston, Mass. 02115. Free.

12. An overview of career education, with activities and programs of each State

Career Education: The State of The Scene. 1974. Available from: Office of Career Education, U.S. Office of Education, 7th & D Sts., S.W., Washington, D.C. 20202, or from Superintendent of Documents (address at No. 2, above).

Bridging the Gap: A Selection of Education-to-Work Linkages. Final and Supplemental Reports. 1975. From: College Entrance Examination Board, Box 2815, Princeton, N.J. 08540. $4.00.

13. An overview of apprenticeships and internships

"The National Apprenticeship Program" 1972. Manpower Administration, U.S. Department of Labor. From: Superintendent of Documents, U.S. Government Printing Office, Washington D.C. 20402.

and

A Directory of Undergraduate Internship Programs in the Public Sector. 1976. From: The National Center for Public Service Internship Programs, Suite 601, 1735 Eye Street, N.W., Washington, D.C. 20006. $6 (for non-members) pre-paid.

and

Directory of Public Service Internships: Opportunities for the Graduate, Post-Graduate, and Mid-Career Professional. From same publisher immediately above. $6 (for non-members) pre-paid.

14. An overview of short week-end residential educational programs for adults, and directory of centers offering these

The Weekend Education Source Book, by Wilbur Cross. 1976. Available in your library, bookstore, or from: Harper's Magazine Press, Harper & Row, Publishers, Inc., 10 East 53rd Street, New York, N.Y. 10022. $6.95, paper.

15. An overview of degree programs for part-time students
    *On-Campus/Off-Campus Degree Programs for Part-time
    Students,* edited by Linda W. Gordon and Judy H.
    Schub. 1976. From: National University Extension
    Association, One Dupont Circle, Suite 360, Washington,
    D.C. 20036. $4.

16. An overview of educational opportunities in industry
    Education in Industry by Seymour Lusterman. 1977.
    The Conference Board, Inc., 845 Third Ave., New York,
    NY 10022. $5, Educational; $15, Non-Associate. See
    also: *The National Guide to Credit Recommendations
    for Noncollegiate Courses,* 1978 Edition. Office on
    Educational Credit, American Council on Education,
    One Dupont Circle, Washington, D.C. 20036. $7.50 +
    50¢ postage.

17. An overview of home/study courses and directory of schools
    or colleges offering them
    Directory of Accredited Private Home Study Schools.
    Free from: Accrediting Commission, National Home
    Study School Council, 1601 Eighteenth St., NW.,
    Washington, D.C. 20009. And *1977-1979 Guide to
    Independent Study through Correspondence Instruction.*
    1977. National University Extension Association, Book
    Order Department, P. O. Box 2123, Princeton, New
    Jersey 08540. $2.

18. An overview of the different kinds of therapies that are
    available for personal development
    You Are Not Alone, by Clara Claiborne Park with Leon N.
    Shapiro, Atlantic Monthly Press Book, Little Brown and
    Company. It's $15, so try your local library.
                        and/or
    *A Complete Guide to Therapy: From Psychoanalysis to
    Behavior Modification,* by Joel Kovel. Pantheon Books.
    $10, so again try your local library, first.

19. An overview of the places in your geographical area which are 'brokers' of continuing education for adults, and can tell you what programs are available that you haven't even thought of

Write: National Center for Educational Brokering, 405 Oak Street, Syracuse, N.Y. 13203 for your nearest 'brokering' agency or center.

Well, that's your printed *sampler*. Now, on to:

4

Step **YOU TALK TO PEOPLE.** There will be at least two reasons why you will need to talk to people, before, after, or during the time you are referring to your printed resources. First of all, you will encounter some useful information amongst the printed stuff, that you want to *check out* for its accuracy, currentness, and that sort of thing. Secondly, you will sometimes search printed resources in vain for the information you want, and it will finally become clear that it hasn't been written down yet. If you are ever to find out what you want to know, you're going to have to go talk to those people who have the information, thus far only in their head or on their desk.

It will immediately occur to some of you that if this is the only way to find out What's Happening, you are in big trouble. Because you are *too shy* to go talk to people. You have, of course, lots of company. Including the people that you may need to go talk to. A Survey on Shyness, done a couple of years ago at Stanford University, revealed that one out of every two people considers himself or herself shy.[7] (I'll buy that. In spite of speaking to groups all-year-long, and having done this for years and years, I am still innately shy.)

If you are shy, and you go out to talk with other people, the odds are very great that what you will be encountering is One Shy Person Talking With Another Shy Person—although one or both of you may be doing your best to try to cover up the shyness.

What will help you further, I hope, is the realization that when you go out *interviewing for information*, both of you will be talking to each other about a mutual Enthusiasm—not just passing the time of day, or talking about the weather. For example, if you are trying to find out what workshops there are that deal with Overcoming Shyness (commonly called 'assertiveness training,' as you would quickly discover), you may start with a woman whom you've heard is 'into' assertiveness training, or who has been to such a workshop. When you go to see her, then, it will be two (perhaps Shy) people talking with each other concerning something you are both enthusiastic about.

Stanford Shyness Survey

**PERCENTAGE OF SHY STUDENTS
WHO SAID THEY FELT SHY IN VARIOUS SITUATIONS**

SITUATIONS	*PERCENTAGE OF SHY STUDENTS*
where I am focus of attention—large group—(as when giving a speech)	72.6%
large groups	67.6%
of lower status	56.2%
social situations in general	55.3%
new situations in general	55.0%
requiring assertiveness	54.1%
where I am being evaluated	53.2%
where I am focus of attention—small group	52.1%
small social groups	48.5%
one-to-one different sex interactions	48.5%
of vulnerability (need help)	48.2%
small task-oriented groups	28.2%
one-to-one same sex interactions	13.8%

OTHER PEOPLE	
strangers	69.7%
opposite sex group	62.9%
authorities by virtue of their knowledge	55.3%
authorities by virtue of their role	39.7%
same sex groups	33.5%
relatives	19.7%
elderly people	12.4%
friends	10.9%
children	10.0%
parents	8.5%

And the easiest conversations in the world are those where two people are talking about their common Enthusiasm.

Since this is merely a search for Information, there is—moreover—no need for you to go alone. If you feel painfully (or even moderately) shy, you can take someone—friend, brother, sister, or acquaintance—with you, and let that person take the lead in the talking or interview until you get the hang of it.

The two major problems you will probably encounter during this Person-Search-for-Information are *a)* whom do you talk to?

and *b)* how do you know whether what they are telling you is accurate, or not?

As for the first, there are basically two types of people to talk to: those who know the information you want, and those who know who might know. The latter are 'Switchboards' or 'Resource Brokers,' connecting you with the people you ultimately need to talk to.

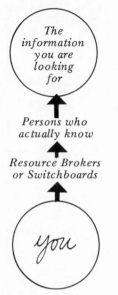

The information you are looking for

Persons who actually know

Resource Brokers or Switchboards

you

If you can immediately figure out who knows the information you are looking for, you can of course dispense with the intermediary: the Switchboard or the Resource Broker. Otherwise, the latter is your key to finding The Person Who Knows. Who the Switchboard person might be, for you, depends of course upon what it is that you are trying to find out. For example, if you wanted to find out what was happening in the music world of a particular town, your Switchboard people would likely be the music teacher at a local college, or the organist at a local church.

The way you define your particular Switchboard Person is to ask yourself, "What is it that I want to know? And who has an investment in knowing who knows that information?" To return to our earlier example of 'assertiveness training,' suppose you wanted to find out where there are such workshops, how long they are, how much they cost, and so forth. If you asked your friends a few questions about it, you would quickly learn—if you did not already know—that such training has become extremely popular particularly among women. So, your question to yourself—"who else has an investment in knowing about assertiveness training?"—would inevitably yield the answer: women's groups, or women's resource centers. Your local newspaper, local weekly, Yellow Pages, bulletin-boards at laundromats, etc. would be likely places to discover the address of such women's resource centers.

The *kinds* of Switchboards to keep in mind as good places to start, for almost any information search, are:

> *Resource librarians*
> *Underground newspapers (or mildly above ground)*
> *Post offices or mailmen or mailwomen*
> *Yellow Pages*
> *TV or radio stations*
> *United Way headquarters*
> *Churches, synagogues and Y's*
> *Fire departments*
> *Colleges (the appropriate department or teacher)*
> *Chambers of Commerce*
> *Collectives or resource centers*

These, or others like them, should lead you to the people who *can* tell you exactly what you want to know.

You then have only the one problem remaining: how do you know whether what they are telling you is accurate, or not? Well, let us take a particular example. Suppose you wanted to know where it was that you could find some training in cosmetology (or whatever particular skill you wanted to master). Your local cosmetic salon would be the obvious place to start your information search. So, you go there, and ask them: what places around here give training in cosmetology? They *might* conceivably respond: well, we got our training in another part of the country, and that was fifteen years ago; we don't think there is any place around here, where you could get such training. Do you conclude from this answer that there is no place nearby? No way! Instead, you ask them your next question—which is designed to ferret out where a resource broker might be: who around here might know more about this sort of thing than anybody else? Or is there, somewhere in the country, a national headquarters for cosmetologists, or an association that I could write to, for such information?

You are, in other words, declining to take one person's word *about anything*. Always talk to two, three or more persons. In a sense, your task is not unlike the 'triangulation' practiced during the Second World War, when a hidden radio transmitter was being searched for. Directional receivers would be set up at three different points; and where their directional beams intersected, the transmitter was assumed to be to be located.

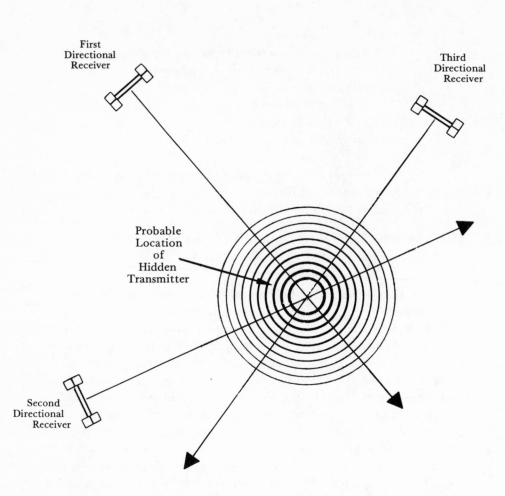

First
Directional
Receiver

Third
Directional
Receiver

Probable
Location
of
Hidden
Transmitter

Second
Directional
Receiver

Instead of a hidden transmitter, you are looking for the truth about What's Happening, in a particular area of interest to you. It too is likely to be where three different people's statements overlap and confirm each other.

The one major exception to this rule is where:

(1) *The answer is negative (i.e., your hopes are dashed upon the ground) AND*

(2) *The person you are interviewing has an emotional investment in that negative answer—in all likelihood.*

Suppose you want to know, for example: could I ever get to be a professor in a college, without having a Ph.D. degree? You may talk to one professor, whom you happen to know or whom you arrange to meet, and he may tell you, "Absolutely not." So you try two others, and they tell you the very same thing. You have 'triangulated' the question, and their answers all coincide. Do you assume that the answer indeed is No? Not exactly. Not even if eighteen professors, deans, or college presidents told you NO. It is a negative (i.e., hope-dashing) answer. And the people-you-are-talking-to all have an emotional investment in that answer, since they had to go get *their* Ph.D. way back when.

You may, then, need to rephrase your question. As it stands, your question could be interpreted as asking about "the usual route" to a Professorship. That isn't really what you want to know. Rather, you really want to know: "Have you *ever* heard of anyone who became a Professor, without having a Ph.D.?" And: "If you haven't, who might know about such things?"

You are most likely to turn up something, with this re-phrased question, if you go and talk to people who do not have as much of an emotional investment in the answer. This might be a college president: "Have you ever hired, or heard of any-one ever hiring, a Professor who did not have a Ph.D. degree?" And he might respond, "Well, yes, Professor so-and-so over in the Business School had an exceptional history in the business world, so on the basis of his experience we hired him, even though he only had a Master's Degree in Business Administra-tion." You would, of course, then ask where you could find him, and having found him, say, "Tell me just how you did it." He, or she, indeed, may know of other people who have done the same thing. Birds of a feather may not necessarily flock to-gether, but they do tend to have heard of each other at least. So, when you have one specimen of a particular species, he or she will usually lead you to others. *Now* you are triangulating on the proper people for information; and you will at last learn what you want to know.

I have explained in some detail and at great length just exactly how you find out What's Happening in the world of ed-ucation. Because this *process*—Getting an Overview, Cutting It Down in Size, Using Printed Resources, and Talking to Peo-ple—is the very same one, with some minor adaptations, that you use to find out What's Happening in the world of work, or in the world of leisure, as we shall see.

The Second Issue on our Educational Pyramid:
⬤ *SURVIVAL*

Effectiveness

Meaning or Mission

Survival

What's Happening

Let us begin with a parable. Imagine a mildly arthritic seventy-five-year-old man beholding a football game for the very first time, in his whole life (he's probably been living on Mars). Nonetheless, so committed to sports in general is he, so anxious to be an active participant rather than merely a spectator is he, that he rushes down onto the football field and enlists in the game—before he has the foggiest notion of what the rules are, or how the game is played. What do you anticipate would be his chances of survival?

Beyond the first ten minutes of the game, not very great— one would imagine. All the Guidelines for Survival that we might hatch for him on the spur of the moment would be of little avail—*because the basic problem is that he is playing in the wrong game, to begin with.* And, clearly, he is going to get creamed. Better he should have been playing croquet.

Survival in the World of Education must begin with the very same consideration. In a sense, the different parts of the World of Education (page 68)— that is, the different kinds of educational opportunities that are available to you all your life long— are not unlike different games or sports. Some of those games— like croquet—you can survive in quite well, given a few cautionary Guidelines about Survival. But others may 'cream' you, no matter how many Guidelines we might hatch. Because you are playing in what is—for *You*—the wrong game, to begin with.

Therefore, the first consideration for Survival in the World of Education—at any age—is: BE SURE YOU ARE PLAYING IN WHAT IS, FOR YOU, THE RIGHT GAME.

If you enjoy books, you can do some cautionary reading about the World of Education in general, and various parts of it in particular. For example, one or two of the following might prove very helpful to you, in deciding which game you want to play in:

90

The Case Against College, by Caroline Bird. 1975. David McKay Company, Inc., New York. $9.95, hardcover. Also out in paperback. *Probably the best summary of what's right and wrong about the game called college.*

Teaching as a Subversive Activity, by Neil Postman and Charles Weingartner. 1969. Delta Books, Dell Publishing Co., Inc., 1 Dag Hammarskjold Plaza, New York, N.Y. 10017. $3.25, paper. *This is absolutely my favorite book about what's right (or could be) and what's wrong with the whole game called school.* These authors also wrote *The Soft Revolution* and:

The School Book, by Neil Postman and Charles Weingartner. 1973. Delacorte Press, New York. *A tremendously helpful summary of all the books which have been written criticizing the game called school, together with a lengthy lexicon of terms employed in that criticism, and thumb-nail sketches of significant critics and thinkers.* $7.95, hardcover.

Other historically-important books which can provoke some cautionary thoughts in any reader are:

death at an early age, by Jonathan Kozol. 1967. Bantam Books, 666 Fifth Avenue, New York, N.Y. 10019. $1.25, paper. Its subtitle—The Destruction of the Hearts and Minds of Negro Children in the Boston Public Schools—tells it all.

The Underachieving School, by John Holt. 1969. Dell Publishing Company, Inc., 1 Dag Hammarskjold Plaza, New York, N.Y. 10017. 95¢, paper. By the same author: *How Children Learn*, and *How Children Fail.*

Why Johnny Can't Read, and What You Can Do About It, by Rudolf Flesch. 1955. Perennial Library, Harper & Row, 10 East 53rd Street, New York, N.Y. 10022. $1.50, paper.

Education and Ecstasy, by George B. Leonard. 1968. Dell Publishing Company, 1 Dag Hammarskjold Plaza, New York, N.Y. 10017. $2.25, paper.

Schools Without Failure, by William Glasser. 1969. Harper and Row, 10 East 53rd Street, New York, N.Y. 10022. $1.95, paper.

For additional reading see the section called "People," in Postman's and Weingartner's *The School Book* (above).

Okay, but suppose you don't particularly like to do a lot of reading (on the one hand) but you still want to know just how to choose the right game for you (on the other). Well, there are several questions you can ask yourself, that might help point you in the right direction . . . at any age. The questions can be put in terms of opposites, although sometimes it's possible that you may prefer both parts of a particular pair—depending on the season, where you are with your self-identity, the full moon, and several other factors:

1. Which do you prefer as you plan on additional educational opportunities for yourself? (*Check one*)
☐ Working on your education by yourself
☐ Working on your education with other learners

2. Which do you prefer as you plan on additional educational opportunities for yourself? (*Check one*)
☐ Working on your education at your own pace
☐ Working on your education at the pace of a group (of fellow-learners)

Comment: if your experience in school was that you always seemed to take longer to understand a concept or to master a process than the rest of the class, you will probably want to check the first alternative above.

3. Which do you prefer as you plan on additional educational opportunities for yourself? (*Check one*)
☐ Learning by lecture, etc. (pedagogically)
☐ Learning by experiencing (andragogically)

Comment: "Pedagogy" is derived from two Greek words meaning "the leading of a child"; so it is, by definition, the art or science of teaching children. "Andragogy" is derived from two Greek words meaning "the leading of a grown man, or adult"; hence it is the art or science of teaching adults. Professor Malcolm S. Knowles, President of Knowles Enterprises in Raleigh, North Carolina, introduced this concept to the United States. The contrasts between the two methods of teaching are hinted at below.[8] The question is, leaving labels like "pedagogy" and "andragogy" aside, which of the two methods do YOU most prefer for the subject matter you want to learn about?

Relation Between Teacher and Learner

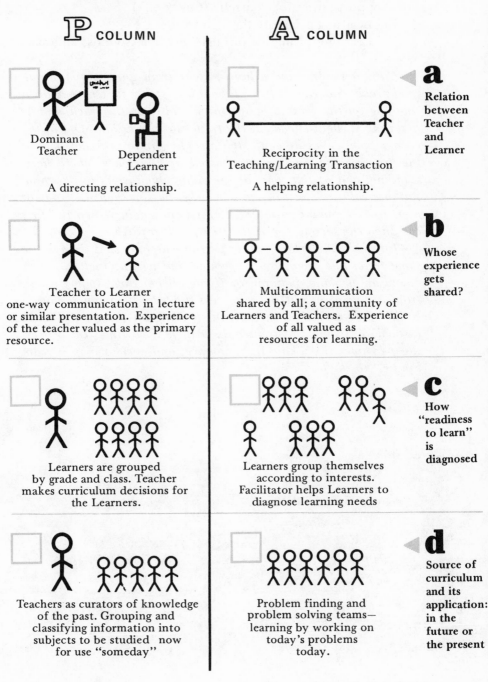

P COLUMN   **A** COLUMN

Dominant Teacher — Dependent Learner

A directing relationship.

Reciprocity in the Teaching/Learning Transaction

A helping relationship.

a Relation between Teacher and Learner

Teacher to Learner one-way communication in lecture or similar presentation. Experience of the teacher valued as the primary resource.

Multicommunication shared by all; a community of Learners and Teachers. Experience of all valued as resources for learning.

b Whose experience gets shared?

Learners are grouped by grade and class. Teacher makes curriculum decisions for the Learners.

Learners group themselves according to interests. Facilitator helps Learners to diagnose learning needs

c How "readiness to learn" is diagnosed

Teachers as curators of knowledge of the past. Grouping and classifying information into subjects to be studied now for use "someday"

Problem finding and problem solving teams— learning by working on today's problems today.

d Source of curriculum and its application: in the future or the present

4. Which do you prefer as you plan on additional educational opportunities for yourself? (*Check one*)

☐ Learning primarily through words

☐ Learning primarily through pictures, sounds, and such

Comment: Imagine a long freight train going down a railroad track and two different people viewing it. One person is standing on the ground about three feet from the track, and he is staring straight ahead—at the train as it passes him. Out of the corner of his eyes he can catch a slight glimpse of that part of the train which has already passed by the place where he is standing, and of that part of the train which is yet to pass him. But basically all he can see is what is passing right in front of him, from moment to moment. First the engine, then the first car, then the second car of the train, and so forth.

Imagine, however, another person watching that train at the same time. She is not on the ground, but way up high in the air . . . in an airplane, balloon, or flying on her own. In any event, from her great height she perceives the train below in an entirely different way than the person standing on the ground does. Instead of seeing the train only a little at a time, car by car, she perceives the whole train at once, and every car in it from the first to the last.

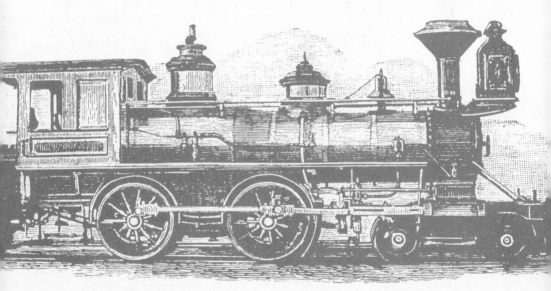

Now, I have asked you to picture this scene in order to describe to you the nature of the human brain. For that one brain which each of us has in our heads is divided into two sides. And these two sides of our brain process information in quite different ways. The left side of the brain (except in some left-handed people) processes information in much the same way that the person standing on the ground, above, processed information about the train: sequentially, one by one, bit by bit. On the other hand, the right side of the brain (except, again, in some left-handed people, where the situation is reversed) processes information in much the same way that the person way up in the air, above, processed information about the train: holistically, all at once, intuitionally. Robert Ornstein, who has been the popularizer of much of the research on the two sides of the brain, makes the following sorts of distinctions:[9]

The Two Sides of Our Brain

(TWO MODES OF CONSCIOUSNESS AND PERCEPTION)

The Left Side	The Right Side
Connected to the right side of the body, and the right side of each eye's vision.	Connected to the left side of the body, and the left side of each eye's vision.
Deals with inputs one at a time.	Demands ready integration of many inputs at once.
Processes information in a linear manner.	Processes information more diffusely.
Has a lineal and sequential mode of operation.	Has a nonlineal and simultaneous mode of operation.
Deals with time.	Deals with space.
Responsible for the faculty of verbal expression, or language.	Responsible for gestures, facial and body movements (or "body language"), tone of voice, etc.
Responsible for verbal and mathematical functions.	Responsible for spatial and relational functions; awareness of one's own body, for sports and dancing; our orientation in space; recognition of faces; crafts, artistic endeavor; musical ability and recognition of pitch.
Specializes in memory and recognition of words or numbers.	Specializes in memory and recognition of objects, persons and places, music, etc.
Normally tends to specialize in logic and analytical reasoning or thinking.	Normally tends to specialize in intuition and holistic perception or thinking.
The seat of reason.	The seat of passion and of dreams.
The crucial side of the brain for wordsmiths, mathematicians and scientists.	The crucial side of the brain for artists, craftspeople and musicians.

Your one brain functions because both sides work comple-
mentarily and simultaneously. Or, to return to our earlier
picture, because both the person standing beside the train and
the person hovering way up over the train are in constant com-
munication with each other, sharing what they perceive. None-
theless, some of us do tend to prefer one side of the brain (i.e.,
one mode of consciousness or perception) over the other. In our
society, we call people who prefer the left side of the brain
'verbal people'; while we call people who prefer the right side of
the brain 'non-verbal people.' The latter label is obviously out-
dated, because instead of labeling such people in terms of what
they do not have ('non-verbal'), we ought to label them in terms
of what they do have. If, for example, the strength of those
who prefer the right side of the brain is that they deal well with
space and are good at picturing things, then we might call them
'picturing people.'

The issue for you is: do you favor one side of your brain
over the other, i.e., do you prefer learning through words rather
than learning through pictures? Or vice versa? If so, then this
says a lot about the kind of learning place you ought to seek
out. Not to pay attention to this factor is to guarantee your
Non-Survival in education—particularly if you are a 'picturing
person' and you get locked into an educational system which
teaches almost exclusively by means of words.

Well, there you have it: four different (sometimes lengthy)
questions to ask yourself, in order to ensure that you do indeed
survive by getting into the educational *game* (so to speak) that
is right for you.

How do you put it all together? Well, by using the Spinning
Wheel on the next page, first putting a check mark by the answers you have just given—as they appear on the inner circle.
And then following the arrows by those checked answers, on
out to the outer circle.

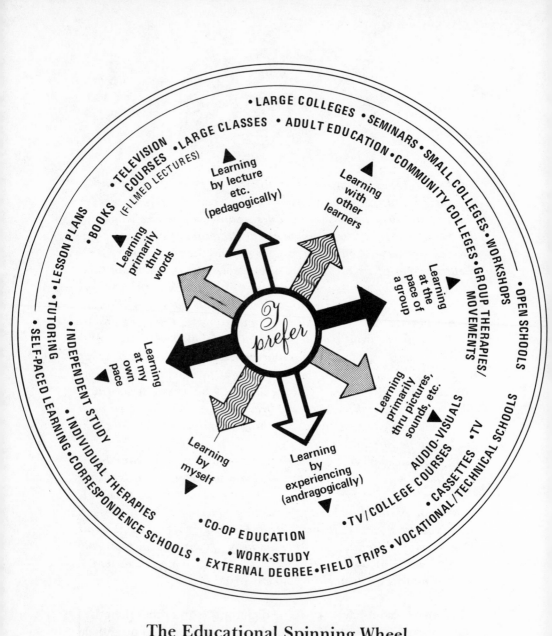

The Educational Spinning Wheel

TO BE SURE YOU ARE IN THE RIGHT GAME (FOR YOU)

You now should have identified from four to twelve games—i.e., educational options—that are right for you; and it might help if you listed them here:

1._____ 7._____

2._____ 8._____

3._____ 9._____

4._____ 10._____

5._____ 11._____

6._____ 12._____

If you need to know, out of all these options, which is absolutely *best* for you, there is a simple three-step process by which you can decide:

(1) Take the four factors that you checked on the inner circle (e.g., "learning with other learners," or whatever) and Prioritize these, using the exercise in Appendix A.

(2) Rearrange those factors, now, in the order of priority, starting with the factor that is most important to you, then the factor that is next most important, etc.

(3) Starting with the most important factor, look on the Educational Spinning Wheel to see which educational opportunities on the outer circle correspond to (are out at the end of the arrow leading from) your most important factor. On the list above, put a star beside those opportunities. Now you know which of the twelve (or however many you have listed) are the best for you. They are the ones which give you Your Most Important Factor.

The Most Overlooked Key
to Educational Survival

Out of all the factors above, if we had to list the one which has caused the most difficulty for students trying to survive in our educational system today, we would have to choose the two-sidedness of our brain. While this picture is changing, due to a concentrated effort on the part of educators who are sensitive to the issue, it still remains true that *in the main* our whole educational system *heavily favors* the left side of the brain (even this book is words, words, words—although we have tried to put in lots of pictures and diagrams, for the sake of 'picturing people'). Students who are at home in 'the world of words,' that is to say students who prefer the left-brained 'mode of perception' —verbal, logical, analytical—find our educational system relatively easy to survive. But those of us who—for whatever reason—favor the right-brained 'mode of perception' (and therefore: pictures, music, spatial design, etc.), often find the educational system quite difficult to survive. Instead of pictures, dance, music, crafts and such, which would be the proper and congenial learning environment for 'right-brained people,' there are words, words, words: a foreign-tongue for many of us. Survival, consequently, is tenuous, at best. And, to compound the felony, the survivors ('verbal people') put a label on *the non-survivors* ("Well, they are 'non-verbal' people") instead of upon the *educational methodology*, where the real problem lies ("Well, it *is* a system that favors the 'verbal people'").

If the right side of the brain gets rather ignored (in us all) in any particular classroom, it is liable to go seeking pictures, on its own. In the classroom, it may be simply the pictures that come in through the eye: what the classroom looks like in all of its parts, what scenes are going on outside the window, etc. 'Verbal people,' teachers especially, of course have a name for this right-brained activity: it is called 'daydreaming' or 'not paying attention' (i.e. to the teacher's *words*). 'Picture-starvation' would be a more apt title for the malady.

Outside the classroom, the right side of the brain will often 'glom' on to any media which 'feed' it, regardless of the quality of that feeding —as a person who is starved

---

**ENGLISH 198.
Self-Reliance
in a Technological
Society.**
Theory and practice of self-reliance in today's world. In addition to reading and discussing concepts of self-reliance as reflected in literature, students will become members of a legally registered corporation set up just for this class. As members of the corporation they will get a bank loan, purchase a rundown wreck of a house near the university, work on redesigning and remodeling the house, then sell the house and divide the profits. Not for cowards or cleanliness freaks. Both men and women welcome. Enrollment limited to 15 students. Four credit hours.

*Lehigh University
List of Courses
1976*

for food will settle for nutritionally lousy food, if nothing else is available. Thus, young and old alike will stay 'glued' in front of the television set, not simply because they are 'lazy' (as has been alleged), but also because TV feeds the brain with pictures, pictures, pictures. The quality of that feeding is admittedly, for the most part, educationally lousy — but 'picture-starved' brains aren't always as discriminating as one might wish. Any more than food-starved stomachs are.

All that we have said about television is also true, of course, about motion pictures. As individuals, we have tended to take whatever resources there are in our culture, and give a larger percentage of our time to those resources which will help us to *perceive* in the mode our brain most prefers — leaving aside such loftier considerations as "But are we *learning* anything?" As we are all well aware, now, the medium is the message.

If you are choosing an educational experience, opportunity, or whatever you want to call it, it will help your survival chances immensely if:

A. You notice whether or not you tend to favor the right side of your brain. One clue: do words 'turn you on,' or are they your Waterloo? Do you prefer to learn from words, or from pictures? (If both, you probably do not *favor* one side of the brain over the other.)

B. If you do favor the right side of your brain (artists, musicians, actors/actresses and craftspeople Particularly Take Note) you are probably going to have to ask a lot of questions at whatever institutution/school/training program/workshop/ correspondence course, etc., you are thinking of attending.

C. Your survival will depend upon your knowing The Kind of Teacher, The Kind of Textbook, The Kind of Teaching Methodology that *you* will be actually taking. Talking to students who have been in those classes before, or are just now finishing up, should give you a lot of the information you want. Obviously, you cannot totally escape Words—in your learning process—but you can at least ask for a heavy input of 'right-brained' activities, so that you are in a learning situation which *operates in a language that you are at home with:* pictures, body movement or expression, images, music, and so forth.

If all of the above is just too much work to do ahead of time then obviously you're going to just plunge in—and see what happens. You may 'luck out' or you may not, but at least now you will know Why.

Once You're in the Right 'Game' (For You), How Do You Survive?

Once you've chosen the right educational opportunity (for you), be it a small college, a workshop, a correspondence school, or whatever, there are three sides to the Survival issue:

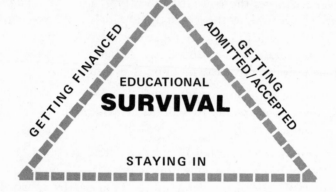

Let's look at each of these, in turn.

GETTING FINANCED

That reader who has been flipping through the book, here and there, like a seagull dipping into the sea of truth, and who has at last alighted upon this section without reading anything that has gone before, is not likely to understand much of what I am about to say. On the other hand, those of you who have plodded faithfully through, from the first page until now, probably will understand.

So, I shall state the principles very briefly:

(1) No matter how young or old you are, there is a lot of money 'out there' to help you with furthering your education—regardless of what method of education you may choose.

(2) It takes work or hard effort on your part, if you are to find out where that money is, and then gain access to it. Most people are simply not willing to take the time and make the effort. Consequently, they will tell you: "There is no money to

help you with your education." That is more convenient for them to claim. Take what anyone tells you (about "no money") with large grains of salt.

(3) When people do go looking for financing for their education, their so-called 'luck' turns out to be (usually) directly proportional to two factors:

- How badly they want to find it.
- How clear they are about why they want this further education.

I remember once receiving a phone call from a man who *desperately* wanted to attend one of the two-week Life/Work Shops run by the National Career Development Project. He was *positive* that the University he attended would not put up any funds for this special education. I proposed an experiment to him. "Sit down," I said, "and think out just exactly what benefit it would be to your University, if you got this training. Then, take one week, and go ask every Dean, professor, or administration official that you know, if he or she knows *who* might have access to Special Funds that could be used for underwriting your attendance at that Workshop. You should not ever ask *them* for money; this is an information search. You are asking them to point you to a third person. But, as you conduct your information search, take care to acquaint each person you talk to, with what kind of education you hope to get out of the Workshop, and what benefit it will be to the University after you get back."

A week later, I received a jubilant phone call. "I got the money," he said. "Was it a lot of work?" I asked. "Easiest thing I've ever done," he replied. "Not only did I get the money but I educated a whole lot of people along the way, about why the University needed Life/Work Planning, and what kinds of events I could run for the University once I got back. I was going from Dean to Dean with my question, when suddenly one of them said to me, '*I'm* the one who has the kind of Special Undesignated Funds you're looking for. And, in view of what you've just told me, I'd be happy to pay all your costs.' "

If you know *why* you want the educational experience, you will be able to think of some source that *you can arrange a 'payoff' for*, if they put up the money. That source may be a community organization, a service organization like Rotary, a school, a church, or whatever. The place where you work (if you work) is an obvious place also to try. The 'payoff' will usually be that you will run a workshop for their members or employees free, or produce a product or render a service or offer a long range program that will benefit them, etc. Sometimes you can get all the money you need for your educational program, school, event or whatever from one source; other times you will need to apply to several sources. One man we know wrote to a number of clergy friends, asking them to contribute something out of their "Discretionary Fund" toward his Master's Program; he received enough money as a result to underwrite his whole two years at a university.

So, at any age, and regardless of the type of educational experience you choose, there *is* money out there. Here are some resources to give you further ideas about where, and how, to find it:

1. *Making It: A Guide to Student Finances* written by Harvard Student Agencies, Inc. 1973. If your local bookstore doesn't have it—and don't forget your local college bookstore—you can order it yourself directly from the publisher: E. P. Dutton & Co., Inc., 201 Park Avenue South, New York, N.Y. 10003. $4.95, paper.

2. *Cash for College*, by S. Robert Freede. 1975. In your local library, bookstore, or from: Prentice-Hall, Englewood Cliffs, N.J. 07632. $3.95, paper.

3. *Stopping Out: A Guide to Leaving College and Getting Back In*, by Judi R. Kesselman. 1976. Distributed by: M. Evans and Company, c/o J. B. Lippincott Company, East Washington Square, Philadelphia, PA 19105. $3.95, paper.

4. *Sylvia Porter's Money Book: How To Earn It, Spend It, Save It, Invest It, Borrow It—And Use It To Better Your Life*, 1975. In your library, bookstore, or from Doubleday & Company, Inc., 277 Park Avenue, New York, N.Y. 10017. $14.95, hardcover (yeah, I know; but it's a BIG book). Also out in paperback. Has a chapter entitled, "A College Education and How to Finance It," which includes a budget outline for computing college costs.

5. *General Information for the Returning Student.* Catalyst Education Opportunities Series.   From: Catalyst, 14 East 60th Street, New York, N.Y. 10022.   30 pp.   Aimed particularly at women returning to school after a period of child-raising and home-making. Deals with finances as well as other problem-areas.

6. *Don't Miss Out.* Octameron Associates, Box 3437, Alexandria, VA 22302. Lists scholarship and tuition assistance sources by field of interest.

7. For additional suggestions — if none of the above apply to you—see bibliography "Sources of Financial Aid: A Listing of Information Sources", the April 1976 (Volume 4, No. 9) issue of the *Career Resource Bibliography.* Available for 75¢ from The National Career Information Center, 1607 New Hampshire Ave. N.W., Washington D.C. 20009.

The above resources are, admittedly, primarily (but not exclusively) for students going to college. The costs of such education may be found in a booklet entitled *Student Expenses at Postsecondary Institutions,* available for $2.50 a copy from the College Entrance Examination Board, Publication Orders, Box 2815, Princeton, N.J. 08540. Our earlier comments on finding money from non-traditional sources applies to all other educational options outside of college.

GETTING ACCEPTED

Getting in is admittedly a problem. An almost insurmountable problem to some people, particularly if their marks in school were not so hot and they are thinking of Further Education only in terms of some college with stringent entrance requirements. But – as we have graphically seen by now – Further Education should not be thought of only in terms of colleges.   There are a whole variety of places to get Further Education, at any age, and some of them are ridiculously easy to get into. Indeed we could make a list of Further Education Opportunities in terms of the difficulty of Getting In —putting the most difficult at the top, the next most difficult beneath that, and so on. Such generalizations—to which there are undeniably exceptions— would come out looking something like this:

The most difficult to get into

The most easy to get into

Post-doctoral study and research
Professional schools (teaching, medicine, theology, law)
Doctor's degree study
Master's degree programs
Universities
Prestigious colleges (4 year)
Other colleges (4 year)
Community colleges (2 year)
Public or private career schools
Vocational-technical institutes
External degree programs
University extension programs
Open schools / universities without walls
Adult or continuing education programs
Y/Church/Synagogue schools or programs
Workshops offered by organizations, schools, or individuals
Home study (television/local college/ correspondence courses/cassettes)

Thus, the first way of dealing with the difficulty of getting into certain kinds of Further Education is to keep some such chart as this nearby, and if it proves ABSOLUTELY impossible to get into a particular school of your choice, look at the chart and see what is the next kind of education below that (and hence, easier to get into). For example, if you just could not get into any college, you would look at this chart, and see that the next line down, below "Other colleges (4 year)" is: "Community colleges

(2 year)." So, you would seriously investigate what the possibilities are for beginning there at a nearby community college—and maybe *later* transferring to a four year college that is more in line with what you ultimately want. Paradoxically, once you had completed those two years in a community college where it was easy for you to get in, you would have a much better chance at getting into the college whose doors were formerly closed to you.

What it all comes down to is this. There is nothing on earth that can keep you from Getting In to *some kind* of further education. That is true even if, or especially if, you have reading difficulties, learning disabilities, etc. You (or your family) have only to research, through talking to school counselors and to others, what kinds of Further Education try especially to deal with that sort of difficulty, in the geographical area you are interested in. You can always get into Something.

But suppose you have your heart set on a very particular kind of Further Education, and a very particular school. Is all hope lost? Not necessarily. Getting into a school involves the very same process as Getting Hired.

Therefore, if you are not familiar with the process of getting hired, you will have to read the next chapter in this book, as well as chapters 5, 6, and 7 in *What Color Is Your Parachute?* (Ten Speed Press, Box 7123, Berkeley, CA 94707, $6.95 paper; or at your local bookstore). You will discover that when you translate "Getting Hired" into "Getting into School", the following steps will appear:

1. Research the schools to death (as they say), by
   a) reading everything your local library can tell you;
   b) reading everything your local reference librarian
      can guide you to;
   c) talking to every school counselor in your area;
   d) talking to alumni in your area, from the school(s)
      that interest(s) you.

2. Research all procedures for admission. Find out from the alumni what they think influences admissions officers. Read helpful books on this subject.

3. Use your contacts (alumni, etc.) to find out as much as you can about the admissions officers, their personal

Peterson's Guide to College Admissions, Monarch Press, a division of Simon & Schuster, 1 West 39th St., Dept. J, New York, N.Y. 10018. $4.95

How to Prepare for College Entrance Examinations (SAT) by Samuel C. Brownstein and Mitchel Weiner. Barron's. 1975. 672 pages. $4.50

ACT for College Entrance by Gary R. Gruber. Simon & Schuster, 1974. 522 pages, $4.95

How to Prepare for the ACT edited by Murray Shapiro, Barron's, 1973. 478 pages. $4.50

SAT for College Entrance by Edward C. Gruber and Morris Bramson. Simon & Schuster, 1975. 481 pages. $4.95

Preparation for College Board Examinations by Henry Regnery, 1972. 547 pages. $3.95

College Entrance Examinations by Louis K. Wechsler, Martin Blum and Sidney Friedman. Barnes & Noble, 1970. 391 pages. $3.50

preferences, things they look for, etc. Get them to put in a word on your behalf, if possible.

4. Be very clear in your own head why you want to go to that particular school, what its advantages are over other schools—so far as you are concerned—and make notes, if necessary.

5. Always go face to face with the admissions people if humanly possible. Use your vacation or whatever to get to that school and see the people in person. Don't count on a piece of paper (tests, letter, or whatever) to speak for you. When you go face to face, be clear about why you want to get into that school, and say so.

To illustrate these points, let us take the typical case history of a mother in her late thirties, who decided she wanted to get into a management program, at a prestigious school. This is her story:

"I'd been accepted by Harvard's Ed School at the beginning of April, but for better or for worse, I wanted the Management Program at MIT's Sloane School: twice as hard, twice as long and twice as valuable to me, as the M.Ed. I began by preparing for the entrance exams and to my amazement got a 97 percentile score. Then I worked on a personal statement of why I wanted to be in that Management Program, and what my background was, and what use I would make of the degree. It took hours and hours of writing, and many discarded pages. I talked to lots of people. When the Assistant Dean finally sent a letter asking if I wanted to be put on the waiting list, I requested an appointment and replied in person. And I'd thought through what I'd be asked and what I wanted to be sure to get across. I made notes on 3 by 5 cards. When at one point I started to get flustered, I reminded myself that I had that reply in my hand, looked at it, and went on to give a good answer. By the middle of May, I was notified that I'd been removed from the limbo of the waiting list, to the ranks of The Elect — those admitted to Sloane School."

If you are willing to work hard at it, regardless of your age, you may be able to achieve that Impossible Dream and get into the school of your choice. But if not, remember there are other possibilities. Consult the chart (page 106) and GET IN, somewhere. No-one, ultimately, can frustrate your desire for Lifelong Learning.

STAYING IN

The first condition of survival in most educational institutions is some kind of minimum grade. The second condition is something called your 'attitude.' Most people know how to deal with the first. If there is a course that is worrying you, you go ask the students who took that course last semester, "What was the course like? What did old (or young) Dr. So-and-So expect? What was the exam like? What kind of things did he or she look for? How did you prepare for it, and how did you pass it?" For most of us, that is sufficient research.

Going to talk to Dr. So-and-So directly is, of course, a more adventuresome method. Especially if you are determined to ask the same sorts of questions. But it also has a much better pay-off. You are getting some information directly from the source, rather than by second-hand guessing.

As for the second condition of survival—your attitude— a lot depends upon the kind of institution you are in. If it's a huge university, and most of your classes are large, your attitude isn't going to matter all that much. In a smaller, more intimate atmosphere, it may matter a great deal. A friend of mine has a few simple rules about Attitude, which may be worth sharing.

1. "Nobody," he says, "loves a smartass. Even if you do know the answers all the time, don't feel it is necessary to raise your hand every time the teacher asks a question. Let other people take their turn."

2. "Remember," he says, "good listeners are harder to find these days than good talkers. Be sure, outside the classroom particularly, that when you are talking with people you spend only half the time on You, and the other half on Them (Him or Her)."

VANDALISM in the nation's schools was appalling enough. Each year, the damage it caused was estimated to cost more than $600 million—more money than had been spent nationwide for textbooks in 1972, or enough to hire 50,000 more teachers.

But that wasn't the worst of it, according to Senator Birch Bayh (Dem.-Ind.), whose sub-committee on juvenile delinquency had just completed three years of Senate hearings on school violence and vandalism. Last weekend it released results of a nationwide survey of 757 school systems enrolling about half of the nation's public elementary and secondary students.

"Even more shocking" than the vandalism, said Bayh, were the "70,000 serious physical assaults on teachers and the literally hundreds of thousands of assaults on students perpetrated in our schools annually."

The subcommittee had found that problems of violence were not limited to large cities but existed as well in small towns and affluent suburbs.

"While certainly not every school in the country is faced with serious crime problems," said the Bayh report, "it is clear that for a growing number of students and teachers the primary task is no longer education, but self-preservation."

San Francisco Sunday Examiner & Chronicle, March 6, 1977

3. "Everybody in life," he concludes, "fumbles the ball *sometimes*. What separates the men from the boys and the women from the girls is whether or not they are willing to admit it. So when you fumble, admit it briefly, candidly and without long apologies. People will *identify* with you immediately, and that—when all is said and done—is the secret of whether people like your attitude or not."

These points aside, 'staying in' may be something you rarely have to think about; or it may be something you spend half of every twenty-four hours worrying about. If the latter, just remember that there are some people who are "born survivors." Nobody has to educate them in how to survive. They just do it, and they have always done it. If you happen to know one of these people, go talk to them and ask: What has been the greatest challenge you have had to face, so far, and how did you go about dealing with it? And: when have you been the most worried about surviving in school, and what did you do about that worry? It *is* possible, in this fashion, to learn how to survive—for those of us who weren't born Knowing.

Never be afraid to interview fellow students. Ask your friends who they think is the best student that they know of, and then go interview him or her to find out what kind of study habits he or she has, and so forth. Occasionally you may run into someone who resents this sort of questioning. But most will be happy (even flattered) beyond words to share with you their 'secrets.' Your only cost for this extra-curricular education will be speaking those eight words so many people find impossible to say: "I don't know; will you please help me?" You will, inevitably, learn a lot. And, in the end, you may reflect how ironic it is that students sit in the company of other students—a rich resource—and so often take no advantage of that resource, but allow each other to pass like ships in the night.

There may be times in your life, of course, when you elect to do your learning alone, at home, by yourself. Obviously, this casts a different light upon the problem of survival. It is no longer a matter that somebody else makes a decision about. It is delivered, now, entirely into your own hands. It is a question of self-discipline and self-motivation. Books by the reams have been written on this subject, and yet I think we are as far away from knowing how to *induce* self-motivation as we ever were. If you are one of those individuals who has a lot of both qualities—self-discipline, and self-motivation—survival during your independent study will be a relatively easy matter. But what do you do if you don't have much motivation? You've set yourself the task of this particular learning experience, you've enrolled or received the books, or whatever; and suddenly, you find that you're running out of gas. Your original enthusiasm just doesn't seem to be there. What to do? Just let it drop, and have the books sit there reproachfully glaring at you? Or try to find some new source of motivation, some rekindling of the original burning desire?

There are two ways of going about that rekindling. One is to sit down and list the ten things in life that are most important to you right now:

**Ten Most Important Things
In Life, To Me:**

1.	
2.	
3.	
4.	
5.	
6.	
7.	
8.	
9.	
10.	

Then, in a second column, put down *how* your independent study relates to, or will help in some way, one or more of those ten enthusiasms of yours. The goal of this exercise, of course, is to Hook Up the enthusiasm you are trying to have, to an enthusiasm you already have.

A second method of helping rekindle your self-motivation is to build a kind of 'support community' for yourself. For example, if you are taking a home study course from some school, institute, or organization, you can write to the place that is sending you the lessons, and request the names of other individuals in your geographical area who have enrolled in the same course recently, because you would like to arrange a group meeting with them. You may thus be able to find another individual, or two, with whom you can meet regularly—thus enabling you to help, challenge, and motivate one another.

In the absence of any such fellow students, you can always ask your mate, or some friend, to be a 'weekly supervisor' for you—to whom you will report, on a regular day each week, how you are doing, and what your progress has been. Once you are talking to a Person, rather than just to your Books, it becomes *very* embarrassing to report week after week that you just didn't work on the course at all. Consequently, you may find this helps you to keep your self-discipline going—now that another person is cheering you on, week after week.

Summary

If you choose the kind of education that is most appropriate to your needs, and you want that education badly enough, then no matter who you are, how young or old you are, you *can* find the money for it, you *can* get in and stay in. You can begin the learning *and* stick with it. You can put the issue of Educational Survival safely to rest, once and for all.

The Third Issue on our Educational Pyramid:
● *MEANING OR MISSION*

Pyramid diagram labels (top to bottom): Effectiveness / Meaning or Mission / Survival / What's Happening

You are eighteen,
> or twenty-two,
> or thirty-five,
> or fifty or sixty,
> or whatever.

You have decided to get some further education.
You have decided that this can be best obtained, so far as you are concerned (and your finances)
> at your local community college,
> or a weekend seminar,
> or an evening extension course from a nearby university,
> or a distant college,
> or by correspondence (home-study).

The only problem is: you are not totally sure just what it is you want to study, or what courses you want to take. You only know you want some more education.
Because: it's there. Like Mount Everest.
And because it's good for you. Like vitamins.
So, you're ready to go.
Off to the great adventure called Aimlessly Dipping Into the Sea of Truth.

I was there once. After being out of college for some twenty years, I decided that I would go back. In a different section of the country, and assuredly to a different school. But back, nonetheless. I didn't have the foggiest notion why, of course. I just had the idea that "some more education" would be, in and of itself, A Good Thing. So, I picked a couple of courses out of the college catalog of my choice. I picked them haphazardly. My only criterion was that these two courses looked mildly interesting. In this, I proved to be a prophet. They were *only* mildly interesting. From that day (1970) until this, the knowledge I picked up in those courses has proved almost totally irrelevant to my day-to-day life. Talk about a waste of time! Yi!

Education chosen without knowing why, can be a disaster. It must have some meaning, for you. You must have some sense of mission. And it is up to you to define this meaning and choose this mission, in your own life. No one else will do it for you. Not your friendly local college registrar. Nor the dean. Nor the faculty advisor. Nor your counselor. They will all respond, like the building-manager of the late Freddy Prinze: "Eets not my job."

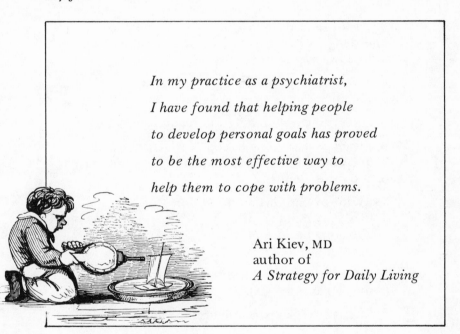

In my practice as a psychiatrist,

I have found that helping people

to develop personal goals has proved

to be the most effective way to

help them to cope with problems.

Ari Kiev, MD
author of
A Strategy for Daily Living

It is *your* job. Yours, and yours alone.

But there are helps.

Specifically, a check-list — which you can use every time in your life that you want to get some more formal education. You can make up your own check-list. Add any items that you learn about from your own experience. Or that you hear on television. Or that you learn from others. But here is the base with which you may want to begin:

The Ten Purposes of Education

A Check List for Myself

**I want to take a course or
go to school because:**

($\checkmark$ *as many items as apply to you at the present moment*)

☐ 1. I want to enlarge my mental, emotional and/or
spiritual horizons.

☐ 2. I want to learn how to learn and how to
think clearly.

☐ 3. I want to learn the virtues and the limits of
knowledge; what we can know, and what we can
not know.

☐ 4. I want to learn reading, or writing, or
arithmetic.

☐ 5. I want to develop myself in relationship to others.

☐ 6. I want to learn how to cope with change and
with constancy—especially when there is too much
or too little of either.

☐ 7. I want to find further 'food' for
    ☐ a. my mind, and/or
    ☐ b. my heart, and/or
    ☐ c. my will

☐ 8. I want to have a chance to meet other people
(with similar interests).

☐ 9. I want to pick up/polish up the required skills
that I need for
    ☐ a. a particular field or line of work in which
        I need accreditation,
    ☐ b. a particular job (present, or contemplated),
    ☐ c. a particular role that I have, or want to
        have, in life

☐ 10. I want to develop my philosophy of life.

This list needs, of course, some elaboration and illustration. So, let us look at each of the ten purposes of education — as outlined above — *before* you give your final answers to the check list.

"I want to enlarge my mental, emotional and/or spiritual horizons."

There are many intriguing questions we might raise about each new person that we meet (and some of our old friends as well), but the most intriguing of all is to wonder how large his or her world is. The obvious answer: "As large as the world that God has made" or "As large as Reality", is rarely the true one. God, Providence or Life has given to everyone of us the power to narrow our attention, restrict our consciousness, and limit our mental horizons, so that each of us can create for ourselves—in effect—a world that is much smaller than the World That Is.

Indeed, we begin with such a world—in the natural order of things. We all came into life as infants, conscious only of a very small world, bounded by our mother's arms, or—at best—not wider than our crib. But all the processes of growth that were implanted in our nature, clearly were not willing to leave the matter there. Life, Providence or God—depending on your point of view—seemed bent upon moving us, willy-nilly, into an ever larger world. Each new week, each new experience, each new learning, accomplished this in us. With the coming of our sight, our infant world grew larger than our mother's arms; as large, in fact, as our room. With the coming of crawling, our world grew as large as our home. With the advent of walking, as large as our yard or our street. In time, as large as our neighborhood, or the town. The older we grew, the larger the world *that we were conscious of* was destined to become—the further out our mental, emotional and spiritual horizons were pushed.

Once grown, if our horizons were to shrink, it would only be because we fell ill or fall ill. Whether that illness be physical, emotional, mental or spiritual. We all know, for example, when a man falls physically ill, how his conscious world becomes

The first 'possible reason' for taking further education

much much smaller. Indeed the sicker he is, the smaller it becomes. His attention becomes restricted, his interests become elemental, the horizons of his consciousness often no larger than his room or (if he is seriously ill) no larger than his body. He loses interest in the world, in the daily papers, in the running of the hospital, and can think or talk only about what is going on in his body and being. He is like a general whose central headquarters are under attack, and who consequently withdraws all his troops from the field in order to defend those central headquarters. Only when this defense has been successful are the troops then sent out into the field again. And so with sickness: one of the signs that our man is beginning to get well is that his energies begin to go 'out into the field' again. He notices now what is going on in the rest of the hospital ward. He begins to complain about his food. He asks to see a daily paper. He is getting well. His world is expanding. And just as this is true of physical illness, and its healing, so it is true of illness that is emotional, mental or spiritual.

If illness is the principal enemy of Growing, and Our Expanding Horizons, Education is its principal ally. For example, through geography, we become conscious of a world as large as the world. Through history, we become conscious of a world as far back as recorded time. Through prophecy, as far ahead as we can imagine. Through philosophy, we become conscious of the unseen world of Ideas. Through atomic physics and science, our world expands to include the sub-particles of our very being. Through astronomy, our world expands to include the universe and the stars. So, one of the reasons you may want to take some further education is—quite simply—because you want to expand your mental, emotional, and/or spiritual horizons.

The
second
'possible
reason'
for
taking
further
education

There is a marked difference between Learning, on the one hand, and Learning How To Learn, on the other—just as there is a marked difference between helping people by rendering services to them, and helping people by empowering them. When you render services to someone, you rescue them from the situation they are floundering in; but they are left without the foggiest clue as to how to deal with that same situation the next time it happens. Whereas, when you empower them, you teach them how to rescue themselves from the situation they are floundering in; and the next time that same situation occurs, they will now know exactly how to get out of it on their own. Or at least they will know clearly what resources they need to call upon.

A lot of people go to college and come out of college—or out of any other educational experience—with some Learning firmly in their grasp. And we account these to be educated people. But they have never learned How To Learn. In this sense they are like people who were rendered services, rather than empowered. To illustrate this distinction, let us consider the statistics with which we are all bombarded, day after day, on TV, in newspapers, in magazines and in books. Suppose, in one of these media, tomorrow the following headline should appear: People Who Eat Food X are Twice As Likely To Get Heart Attacks As People Who Don't Eat Food X. The person who has had some further education, but has come out only with "learning" will read this article and say, "Aha, I've just found some new learning. Don't eat Food X." On the other hand, the person who has had some further education, but has come out with having learned How To Learn, will read this article and say, "I want to know what the actual statistics are, on which this article is based." So he or she will search the article for those statistics. If the statistics are in the article (and if this is a typical article in our time) they may well turn out to be something like this: "Heart attacks occur in 7 out of every 1000 people who don't eat Food X, but in 14 out of every 1000 people who do eat Food X." The person who has learned

How To Learn will then reprocess the information in a different way, in order to see what it truly means. "Let's see, that means that of the people who don't eat Food X, 993 out of every 1000 don't get heart-attacks. While of people who do eat Food X, 986 out of every 1000 don't get heart-attacks." The earlier impression conveyed by just the headline — that people who eat Food X were 'dropping like flies'—has now been put in perspective. Actually 986 out of each 1000 of them are avoiding heart-attacks even so.

> Some Yale scholars once determined the twelve most persuasive words in English: you, money, save, new, results, health, easy, safety, love, discovery, proven, guarantee...

If the statistics are not in the article, the person who has learned How To Learn will suspend final judgment about the headline's accuracy, until he or she has found the statistics—by calling the newspaper to find the source of the article, and how to get in touch with that source, or whatever. In a similar fashion, the man or woman who has learned How To Learn and How To Think Clearly will treat all information that is dispensed day by day in our land. Thus we see that his or her education truly empowered him or her, rather than merely rendered them a service.

If this is your goal then —or one of your goals— in getting further education, then obviously you will need to look at courses which deal especially with researching, analyzing, logic, intuition, creativity and such. But this goal also implies a certain alertness in *any* course that is taken, to watch how one learns about that particular subject, and what characterizes clear thinking vs. fuzzy thinking in that field. Thus will each course truly empower you, rather than merely rendering you a service, as it were.

> "The principal goal of education is to create men and women who are capable of doing new things, not simply of repeating what other generations have done—men and women who are creative, inventive and discoverers" who "have minds which can be critical, can verify, and not accept everything they are offered."
> —Jean Piaget

"I want to learn the virtues and the limits of knowledge: what we can know, and what we cannot know."

☐ ③

The third 'possible reason' for taking further education

In view of the tremendous knowledge explosion that has taken place in this country (and the world) during the twentieth century, we sometimes like to imagine that we can know anything that Is. We forget that the lens through which we look at everything is Ourselves; and that there are limits to what that lens is able to perceive, aided or unaided. For example, the room or place where you are sitting reading this chapter is filled with sounds at the moment. Yet your ears cannot hear them. If, however, you have a radio there, and you turn it on, the sounds will become evident to you. The radio does not create those sounds. It pulls them (or impulses of energy which carry them, anyway) out of the air, and translates them into sounds that your ear can hear. Thus are we reminded how limited (without the radio) our ears are. Again, the room or place in which you are sitting is filled with pictures. But your eyes cannot see them. If you have a television set there, however, and you turn it on, the pictures will become quite evident to your eyes. The television of course does not create those pictures. It only converts the electronic signals in the air into a form that our eyes can perceive. Thus are we reminded how limited (without the television) our eyes are.

These limits to our senses, and therefore to our Being, and therefore to our ability to know, are found everywhere. We know that dogs, for example, can hear sounds which no human ear can detect. And of late we are learning that dogs and other animals can detect such phenomena as earthquakes, days before they actually occur. One of the functions of further education, and one of the reasons you *may* want that education, is to learn not only what we can know, but also what we can't know. To learn the limits to the senses. And to learn about other means of apprehending phenomena, such as intuition, parapsychology, extra-sensory perception (esp), psychic reading, special experiences (such as those undergone by people who medically died, and then were revived) and the like. You must decide if this is, or is not, one of the reasons why you want further education.

121

"I want to learn reading, or
writing, or arithmetic."

**The
fourth
'possible
reason'
for
taking
further
education**

    This needs no comment, except to say that if you don't
know how to read, or to write, or to do arithmetic, and if you
decide you want to know how, this is a good reason for seeking
further education toward that end—no matter how old you are.

(Wide World Photos, Used with Permission)

Winter Park, Fla., February 24, 1977—LATE STARTER.
Ben Raymond is interested in making a careful study of the Bible
to help him become a better preacher, so at the age of 110 he's
enrolled in school to learn how to read. Born in Statesboro,
Georgia, Sept. 1866, Mr. Raymond is shown in Winter Park,
Florida, with his wife Leola Raymond who is 79.

"I want to develop myself in relationship to others."

The fifth 'possible reason' for taking further education

Self-development is one of the principal reasons people seek further education—particularly in the middle of life, as it is euphemistically called. (If you are destined to live to be 94 years old, the middle of your life is 47 years of age; but if perchance you are only destined to live to be 62 years of age, the middle of your life, technically, is 31.) People who have never been able to make decisions properly, decide at last that they want further education in how to make decisions. People who have never been able to assert themselves, decide they want further education in assertiveness techniques. And so on, with people who do not know how to handle conflict, or how to take risks with other people, or how to raise their children, or how to improve their sex life, or how to manage their money, or whatever. A weekend seminar, a course at the local Y, or church, or synagogue, or a course at the nearest university extension branch, may be the preferred form of this further education for self-development. But if this is why you want further education, and you are clear about what particular area you want help in, your education choices will be that much more focused, that much more relevant, and that much more useful to you—when the course is done. With one provision: that you check out, as best you can, the expertise of the particular instructor.

In no other area of education is it so easy for a novice to begin teaching without any credentials whatsoever, and with only the barest personal experience of the subject matter—often restricted to having read the most popular book in that field, and then deciding to teach it to others. Period. Through direct communication with the instructor, or through judicious use of your contacts (you know, all those persons who know you well enough to at least misspell your name) try to interview three (count them, three) people who have taken that particular course, or seminar, or workshop—to get their impressions of the usefulness of that experience. If your contacts don't know of anyone who has taken the subject with this particular instructor, and you are forced to ask the instructor for names, you will of course be aware that if the instructor has had 150 students so

123

far, 145 of whom were dissatisfied, and five of whom were favorable, in their view of the course, you will inevitably be given the three names you ask for from among the five, not from among the 145. One way to get around this (or at least to try), is to ask for the names of three people who were happy about the experience, *and* the names of three people who were at least mildly critical. If the instructor refuses to give you those last three names, well, even *that* fact should tell you part of what you want to know. Beware.

> Who can say more than
> this rich praise, that
> you alone are you?
> William Shakespeare

The sixth 'possible reason' for taking further education

"I want to learn how to cope with change and with constancy, especially when there is too much or too little of either."

There is a book which has become a modern classic, called *Future Shock,* by a man named Alvin Toffler. It details the way in which Change is occurring in our world at a faster and faster rate. The world in which we will all live ten to fifteen years from now, will be markedly different from the world in which we live today—in many respects.

The other side to this coin, so to speak, is that some things in this world which we wish with all our heart would change, seem to remain obstinately constant. Many of these things are rooted in human nature, which seems to possess a stubborn constancy down through the centuries.

For some people, the motivation for further education is that they may better understand what it is that is changing, and what it is that is remaining constant. For others, it is this *plus.* They want not only to understand the changes and the constancies, but to gain some tools for better dealing with Change and with Constancy. So that they do not, as Toffler says, go into shock. But that, rather, they are empowered to cope with both Change and Constancy. This may be one of the reasons why you want further education. If so, it will certainly give you some guidance and direction as to what kind of courses you ought to take.

"I want to find further 'food' for
(a) my mind, and/or (b) my heart, and/or
(c) my will."

The
seventh
'possible
reason'
for
taking
further
education

According to a very ancient psychology, each of us has not only a body but also a mind, and heart and will. These were not necessarily lodged in any particular physical organ or part of the body, but were three different ways of looking at man and woman, or three different ways of describing them. 'The mind' was—and is—a symbol for Man & Woman as a Thinking Being. 'The heart' was—and is—a symbol for Man & Woman as a Feeling Being. While 'the will' was—and is—a symbol for Man & Woman as a Choosing Being.

The goal of the mind was held to be Truth. The goal of the heart was held to be Beauty. The goal of the will, Perfection.

The proper 'food' for the mind, it was said, included ideas, concepts, theorems, theories. The proper 'food' for the heart included emotions, feelings, intuitions, the things which attract us, the things which repel us, our loves and our hates. While the proper 'food' for the will included values, ethics, morality, conscience-examination, decisions, judgments, and the like.

Our formal education was very likely to furnish 'food' for our mind—in abundance—but we may well feel that it did not furnish us with enough 'food' for the heart, or for the will. In which case, you may want to back for further education in order to 'feed' your heart or your will, as it were. To state it another way, you may want to seek further education in order to learn more about your emotions and feelings. Or in order to learn more about your values, ethics, and morality.

8

"I want to have a chance to meet other people (with similar interests)."

The
eighth
'possible
reason'
for
taking
further
education

In many circles this is either leaped over or dismissed as a reason for seeking further education. It is considered unworthy. But the truth is, I know many women who have been mothers, wives and homemakers for years, who then decide to go to college simply in order "to meet people." For some this may mean they want the opportunity simply to sit and listen to what other people are thinking and talking about. For others, this may mean they want the opportunity to meet with, and befriend, other people who share their interests ("I like psychology, and I'd like to meet with other people who are also interested in psychology"). Still others go to college because they hope to meet some member of the opposite sex—a meeting implicit with possibilities ranging from dating to marriage.

This perception of college or any other form of further education (except correspondence courses) primarily in terms of People, rather than in terms of Courses, is not—of course—restricted to the female. Many men also go to college or seek further education for the same reasons, if the truth were told. And why not? Colleges, seminars, workshops, and weekend courses certainly furnish a viable and improved alternative to the local pub—as a meeting-place. (Owners or frequenters of pubs, who wish to lodge a protest over the above comparison: my address is Box 379, Walnut Creek, CA 94596.) But this contrast between People on the one hand, and Courses on the other hand, is of course an artificial one. You meet People in Courses, and what kinds of people you meet depends markedly on what kinds of courses you choose. Maybe you know exactly what kinds (people and courses) you want to choose. But, suppose you don't. Here is an exercise that is kind of fun, and it also may help you decide. It begins with a Party.

THE PARTY EXERCISE:

At right is an aerial view (from the floor above) of a room in which a party is taking place. Here people with the same or similar interests have (for some reason) all gathered in the same corner of the room, as described:

The Party

R realistic

People who have athletic or mechanical ability, prefer to work with objects, machines, tools, plants, or animals, or to be outdoors.

I investigative

People who like to observe, learn, investigate, analyze, evaluate, or solve problems.

C conventional

People who like to work with data, have clerical or numerical ability, carrying things out in detail or following through on other's instructions.

People who have artistic, innovating or intuitional abilities, and like to work in unstructured situations, using their imagination or creativity.

A artistic

People who like to work with people— influencing, persuading or performing or leading or managing for organizational goals or for economic gain.

People who like to work with people —to inform, enlighten, help, train, develop, or cure them, or are skilled with words.

enterprising **E**

social **S**

1

Which corner of the room would you instinctively be drawn to, as the group of people you would most *enjoy* being with for the longest time? (Leave aside any question of shyness, or whether you would have to talk with them.) Write the *letter* for that corner here:

2

After fifteen minutes, everyone in the corner you have chosen, leaves for another party cross-town, except you. Of the groups *that still remain* now, which corner or group would you be drawn to the most, as the people you would most enjoy being with for the longest time? Write the letter for that corner here:

3

After fifteen minutes, this group too leaves for another party, except you. Of the corners, and groups, which remain now, which one would you most enjoy being with for the longest time? Write the letter for that corner here:

When you have completed this Party exercise, you are urged to consult John L. Holland's excellent little book, *Making Vocational Choices: a theory of careers* (see your local library, or if you want your own copy, order it directly from the publisher: Prentice-Hall, Englewood Cliffs, New Jersey 07632—that's the full address—$4.95 paperback, plus postage and handling). On pages 111-117 there, you will find a list of occupations, which you can easily use to identify the corresponding courses, in most cases.

NEXT, THE HEXAGON:

Youngstown State University in Ohio worked it out this way. The Career Planning Office there placed the courses (or majors) on a hexagon, corresponding to the Party exercise—so that you can see immediately some of the courses (or majors) that would provide the People Environment you feel most at home with:

Realistic

Pre-Forestry; Civil Engineering; Industrial Engineering; Mechanical Engineering; Civil Engineering Technology; Urban Planning Technology; Architectural Construction Technology; Dietary Technology; Architectural/Mechanical Drafting Technology; Police Science Technology; Private Security and Public Safety; Medical Technology; Mechanical Engineering

Investigative

Biology; Chemistry; Earth Sciences; Economics; Geography; Geology; Mathematics; Physics; Psychology; Chemical Engineer; Electrical Engineer; Biological Science; Electrical Engineering Technology; Electronics; Materials Science; Electrical Power

Conventional

Accounting: Accounting Technology; Transportation Management Technology; Computer Technology; Secretarial Studies: Executive Technology; Legal/Medical Office Management; Secretarial Studies: Word Processing; Clerk Typist; Stenographer; Court Reporting; Computer Science

Artistic

English; Art History; Art; Educational Media; Advertising Art; Commercial Art Technology; Public Administration Technology; Graphic Technology; Design Technology; Drafting, Studio Art—Commercial Art, Crafts, General, Painting, Printmaking, Sculpture; Theatre; Applied Music—Theory & Composition, Vocal, Instrumental, and History/Literature

Enterprising

Finance: General Administration; Industrial & Transportation Management; Industrial, Management & Retail Marketing; Public Administration; Management Engineering; Business Education; Real Estate; Marketing Technology; Law Enforcement Admin.; Advertising Technology; General Administration Technology; Business Management Technology

Social

American Studies; History; Anthropology; Five Foreign Languages; English; Health; Physical Education; Political Science; Sociology; Religious Studies; Speech; Special Education; Pre-Law; Communications; Child Care; Corrections; Dental Hygiene; Dietary Technician; Home Economics; Food & Nutrition; Medical Assistant; Russian Social Studies; Classical Studies; Elementary and Secondary Education; Nursing

▶ If you prefer a longer list, not on a hexagon figure, you may find the following list of the correspondence between People Environments and Courses (or Majors) suggestive:

Majors Offered at the University of Wisconsin Madison Campus Arranged According to the Holland Categories

(Compiled by James O. Bauer, for the Office of Continuing Education Services)

The R Corner

R   Agricultural—Middle Course (2 year certification program, no degree: Ag)
RI   Agricultural Engineering (B, M, P:Ag)
RI   Agronomy
RI   Biological Aspects of Conservation (B: L&S)
RI   Botany (B, M, P: L&S)
RI   Civil & Environmental Engineering (B, M, P: Engr.)
RI   Civil & Environmental Engineering & City Planning (B: 5 year double degree)
RI   Civil & Environmental Engineering & Construction Administration
     (B: 5 year double degree Engr:)
RI   Construction Technology—Agricultural (B: Ag)
RI   Conservation (B: Ag)
RI   Dairy Science (B, M, P: Ag)
RI   Electrical Engineering (B, M, P: Engr)
RI   Forestry (M, P: Ag)
RI   Forest Science (B: Ag)
RI   Horticulture (B, M, P: Ag)
RI   Mechanical Engineering (B, M, P: Engr)
RI   Metallurgical Engineering (B, M, P: Engr)
RI   Mining Engineering (B, M, P: Engr)
RI   Naval Science (B: Engr, Ag)
RI   Nursing (B, M: Nursing)
RI   Pre-Veterinary (2 or 3 year program, no degree: Ag)
RI   Recreation Resources Management (B, M: Ag)
RI   Soils Science (B, M, P: Ag)
RI   Wildlife Ecology (B, M, P: Ag)
RIA   Landscape Architecture (B, M : Ag)
RIA   Occupational Therapy (B: Allied Health)
RC   Agricultural Mechanization and Management (B: Ag)
RC   Business and Engineering (B: Engr; M: Bus—5 year double degree program)
RC   Related Art (B, M: FRCS)
RCE   Agricultural Education (B: Ag—certification Ed)
REC   Dietetics (B: Ag or FRCS)
RS   Physical Education (B, M, P: Ed)

The I Corner

I   Analytical Clinical Chemistry (M: L&S)
I   Anatomy (M, P: L&S)
I   Anthropology (B, M, P: L&S)
I   Astronomy (M, P: L&S)
I   Astronomy—Physics (B: L&S)
I   Bacteriology (B: Ag or L&S; M, P: Ag)
I   Behavioral Science and Law (B: L&S)
I   Biochemistry (B: Ag or L&S; M, P: Ag)
I   Biology (B: Ed)
I   Biomedical Engineering (M: Engr)
I   Biophysics (M, P: L&S)
I   Endocrinology—Reproductive Physiology (M, P: Ag or L&S)
I   Entomology (B, M, P: Ag)
I   Food Science (B, M, P: Ag includes specialization in food chemistry)
I   Genetics (B, M, P: Ag)
I   Genetics—Medical (L&S : M, P)
I   Geography (B: L&S or Ed; M, P: L&S)

I	Hospital Pharmacy (M: Pharm)
I	Mathematics (B: L&S or Ed; M, P: L&S)
I	Medical Microbiology (B, M, P: L&S)
I	Medical Science (B: L&S)
I	Medicine
I	Meteorology (B, M, P: L&S)
I	Molecular Biology (: L&S; M, P: L&S or Ag)
I	Neurophysiology (P: L&S)
I	Neurosciences (M, P: L&S)
I	Oceanography & Limnology (M, P: IES)
I	Oncology (M, P: L&S)
I	Pathology (M, P: L&S)
I	Pharmaceutical Chemistry (M, P: Pharm)
I	Pharmaceutical Biochemistry (M, P: Pharm)
I	Pharmaceutics (M, P: Pharm)
I	Pharmacology—Med (P: L&S)
I	Pharmacology—Pharm. (M, P: Pharm)
I	Physics (B: L&S or Ed; M, P: L&S)
I	Physiological Chemistry (M, P: L&S)
I	Physiology (M, P: L&S)
I	Plant Breeding and Plant Genetics (M, P: Ag)
I	Plant Pathology (B, M, P: Ag)
I	Poultry Science (B, M, P: Ag)
I	Quantitative Analysis (B, M, P: Bus)
I	Radiological Sciences (M, P: L&S)
I	Water Chemistry (M, P: Engr)
I	Water Resources Management (M: IES)
I	Zoology (B: L&S or Ed; M, P: L&S)
I	Chemistry (B: L&S or Ed; M, P: L&S)
IR	Applied Mathematics, Engineering & Physics (B: L&S)
IR	Botany (B: L&S or Ed; M, P: L&S)
IR	Chemical Engineering (B, M, P: Engr)
IR	Civil and Environmental Engineering (B, M, P: Engr)
IR	Computer Sciences (B, M, P: L&S)
IR	Earth Science (B; Ed)
IR	Electrical Engineering (B, M, P: Engr)
IR	Forestry (M, P: Ag)
IR	Forest Science (B: Ag)
IR	Geology (M, P: L&S)
IR	Geology and Geophysics (B: L&S)
IR	Horticulture (B, M, P: Ag)
IR	Industrial Engineering (B, M, P: Engr)
IR	Materials Science (M, P: Engr)
IR	Meat and Animal Science (B, M, P: Ag)
IR	Mechanical Engineering (B, M, P: Engr)
IR	Metallurgical Engineering (B, M, P: Engr)
IR	Mining Engineering (B, M, P: Engr)
IR	Nuclear Engineering (B, M, P: Engr)
IR	Nutritional Sciences (B, M, P: Ag)
IR	Ocean Engineering (M: Engr)
IR	Pre-Veterinary (2 or 3 year program, no degree)
IRC	Medical Technology (B: Allied Health)
IRC	Computer Science (B, M, P: L&S)
IRA	Occupational Therapy (B: Allied Health)
IRS	Physical Therapy (B, M: Allied Health)
IS	Behavioral Disabilities (B, M, P: Ed)
IS	Behavioral Science and Law (B: L&S)
IS	Rural Sociology (B, M: Ag)
IS	Dietetics (B: Ag or FRCS)
IS	Nutrition (B: FRCS)

IC   Information Systems Analysis and Design (B, M, P: Bus)
IC   Pharmacy (B: Pharm)
IC   Statistics (B, M, P: L&S)
IC   Quantitative Analysis (B,M,P: Bus)
IAS   Psychology (B, M, P: L&S)
IA   Classics (B, M, P: L&S)
IA   Linguistics (B, M, P: L&S)

Advanced degrees in most fields can be considered to have a high degree
of I-Theme, therefore it is difficult to categorize advanced degrees.
In addition, Area Studies, such as East Asian Studies, may be classed as
either *IA* or *AI*. Here they will be found under *AI*. Language studies
present the same problem and once again I have chosen to class them
with *AI*.

Education majors are another problem, A degree in, for example, Zoology
secondary education will possess high *I* scores and high *S* scores. It is
difficult to say which comes first. Therefore, a listing of degrees offered
by the Education Department arranged within themselves will come at
the end of this list.

The A Corner

A   Art (B, M: Ed)
A   Art Education (B, M: Ed)
A   Classics (B, M, P: L&S)
A   Communication Arts (B: L&S or Ed; M, P: L&S)
A   Comparative Literature (B: L&S or Ed; M, P: L&S)
A   Dance (B, M: Ed)
A   Library Science (M, P: L&S)
A   Music—Applied (BM, MM, A Mus D: L&S)
A   Music—BA (B: L&S)
A   Music—Composition (MM, P: L&S)
A   Music—Conducting (MM; L&S)
A   Music—Ethnomusicology (MM, P: L&S)
A   Music—History and Theory (BM: L&S)
A   Musicology (MM: L&S)
A   Music—MA (M: L&S)
A   Theatre and Drama (B, M, P: L&S)
AE   Art History (B, M, P: L&S)
AE   Arts Administration (M: Bus)
AE   Apparel Design (B: FRCS)
AE   Communication Arts (B: L&S or Ed; M, P: L&S)   ♦
AE   Interior Design (B: FRCS)
AR   Agricultural Journalism (B, M: Ag) (P=Mass Communications)
AS   English (B: L&S or Ed; M, P: L&S)
AS   Home Economics Journalism (B: FRCS; M: Ag)
AS   Journalism (B, M: L&S) (P = Mass Communications)
AS   Library Science (M, P: L&S)
AS   Philosophy (B, M, P: L&S)
AI   This theme to include all language studies and area study programs.
AI   African Languages and Literature (B, M, P: L&S)
AI   Afro-American Studies (B: L&S)
AI   Asian Studies (B: L&S)
AI   Buddhist Studies (P: L&S)
AI   Chinese (B, M, P: L&S)
AI   Classics (B, M, P: L&S)
AI   Communication Arts (B: L&S or Ed; M, P: L&S)
AI   English (B: L&S or Ed; M, P: L&S)

AI   French (B: L&S or Ed; M, P: L&S)
AI   French Area Studies (B: L&S)
AI   German (B: L&S or Ed; M, P: L&S)
AI   Greek (B, M, P: L&S)
AI   Hebrew (B: L&S or Ed)
AI   Hebrew & Semitic Studies (M: L&S)
AI   Humanities, Classical (B: L&S) [possible certification: Ed]
AI   Humanities, Modern (B: L&S) [possible certification: Ed]
AI   Ibero—American Studies (B: L&S or Ed; M: L&S)
AI   Italian (B: L&S or Ed; M, P: L&S)
AI   Japanese (B, M: L&S)
AI   Latin (B: L&S or Ed; M, P: L&S)
AI   Linguistics (B, M, P: L&S)
AI   Music History (P: L&S)
AI   Music Theory (MM, P: L&S)
AI   Music—History and Theory (BM: L&S)
AI   Polish (B: L&S or Ed)
AI   Portuguese (B: L&S or Ed; M, P: L&S)
AI   Russian (B: L&S or Ed; M: L&S) (P=Slavic Languages)
AI   Scandinavian Studies (B, M, P: L&S)
AI   Slavic Languages (P: L&S)
AI   South Asian Languages and Literature (P: L&S)
AI   South Asian Studies (B, M: L&S)
AI   Spanish (B: L&S or Ed; M, P: L&S)

The S Corner

For Education majors please see the category at the end of this index.

S   American Institutions (B: L&S or Ed)
S   Behavioral Disabilities (B, M, P: Ed)
S   Communicative Disorders (B: L&S or Ed; M, P: L&S)
S   Social Welfare (P: L&S)
S   Social Work (B, M: L&S)
SR   Agricultural Extension Education (B: Ag) (M, P= Continuing
        and Vocational Education)
SR   Agricultural Education (B: Ag) (Certification: Ed)
SI   Educational Psychology (M, P: Ed)
SI   History of Science (B, M, P: L&S)
SI   Science Education (M: Ed)
SI   Sociology (B: L&S or Ed; M: L&S; P: L&S or Ag)
SI   Sociology—Correctional Administration (B: L&S)
SI   Behavioral Science and Law (B: L&S)
SIR   Nursing (B, M: Nursing)
SIR   Physical Therapy (B, M: Allied Health)
SIA   Occupational Therapy (B: Allied Health)
SC   Child Development/Family Relations (M: FRCS)
SC   Child Development and Pre-School Teaching
SC   Elementary Education (B: Ed)
SC   Family and Consumer Economics (B, M: FRCS)
SC   General Home Economics (B, M: FRCS)
SC   Pre-school Kindergarten Education (B: FRCS—Certification: Ed—M:Ed)
SCE   Educational Administration (M, P: Ed)
SCE   Educational Policy Studies (M, P: Ed)
SE   Mass Communications (P: L&S or Ag) P for Journalism or Ag Journalism
SE   Rehabilitation & Counseling (B, M, P: Ed) Degree is Behavioral Disabilities
SE   Social Studies (B: Ed)
SE   Sociology—Correctional Administration (B: L&S)
SEA   History of Culture (B: L&S)

SEC Continuing & Vocational Education (M, P: Ed or Ag or FRCS)
SEC Counseling & Guidance (M, P: Ed)
SEC Educational Administration (M, P: Ed)
SEC Educational Policy Studies (M, P: Ed)
SA   Journalism Education (B:L&S) Certification: Ed.

The E Corner

Area Study programs, eg. South Asian Studies, may possess the E theme.
These programs are found under *AI*.

E   History (B: L&S or Ed; M, P: L&S)
E   History and History of Science (B: L&S)
E   Communication Arts (B: L&S or Ed; M, P: L&S)
E   Industrial Relations (M, P: L&S)
E   International Relations (B: L&S)
E   Law
EI   History (B: L&S or Ed; M, P: L&S)
ERC Agricultural Business Management (B: Ag or Bus)
ES   Apparel Design (B: FRCS)
ES   Political Science (B, M, P: L&S)
ES   Retailing (B: FRCS)
ESC Health Services Administration (M: Bus)
ESC Home Economics Education (B: FRCS Certification: Ed. M, P=
     Continuing and Vocational Education)
EC   Public Policy and Administration (M: L&S)
EC   Retailing (B: FRCS)
ECS Legal Institutions (M: Law)
ECS Program Administration (M: Bus)
ECS Urban and Regional Planning (M, P: L&S)

The C Corner

C   Accounting (B, M, P: Bus)
C   Actuarial Science (B, M: Bus)
C   Appraisal (M: Bus)
C   Business Construction Administration (B: Bus)
C   Business Diversified (B, M: Bus)
C   Business Statistics (B, M, P: Bus)
C   Finance, Investment and Banking (B, M, P: Bus)
C   Risk Management & Insurance
CI   Actuarial Science (B, M: Bus)
CI   Agricultural Economics (B, M, P: Ag)
CI   Appraisal (M:Bus)
CI   Operations Research (B, M, P: Bus)
CI   Pharmacy (B: Pharm)
CR   Business & Engineering (B: Engr; M: Bus 5 year double degree program)
CR   Family and Consumer Economics (B, M: FRCS)
CR   Related Art (B, M: FRCS)
CR   Textiles and Clothing (B, M: FRCS)
CRS Consumer Services in Foods (B: Ag or FRCS)
CE   Marketing (B, M, P: Bus)
CE   Management (B, M, P: Bus)
CES Business Teacher Education (B: Bus; Certification: Ed;
     M, P=Continuing & Vocational Education)
CES International Business (M, P: Bus)
CES Real Estate and Urban Land Economics (B, M, P: Bus)
CSE Distributive Education (B: Bus; Certification: Ed;
     M, P=Continuing & Vocational Education)
CSE Food Administration (B: Ag or FRCS)

Education Majors Arranged Within Themselves
(SED = Secondary Education Classification)

R Agricultural Education (B: Ag; Certification: Ed; M, P = Continuing & Vocational Education)
R Agricultural Extension Education (B: Ag; M, P=Continuing & Vocational Education)
I Biological Aspects of Conservation (B: L&S or Ed. SED)
I Biology (B: Ed. SED)
I Botany (B: L&S or Ed; M, P: L&S. SED)
I Chemistry (B: L&S or Ed; M, P: L&S. SED)
I Chemistry Course and Education (B: L&S; Certification: Ed)
I Earth Science (B: Ed. SED)
I Education and Botany (M: Ed)
I Education and Chemistry (M: Ed)
I Education and Geography (M: Ed)
I Education and Mathematics (M: Ed)
I Education and Physics (M: Ed)
I Education and Zoology (M: Ed)
I Geography (B: L&S or Ed; M, P: L&S. SED)
I Mathematics (B: L&S or Ed; M, P: L&S. SED)
I Natural Science (B: Ed. SED)
I Physics (B: L&S or Ed; M, P: L&S. SED)
I Science Education (M: Ed)
I Zoology (B: L&S or Ed; M, P: L&S. SED)

A Art Education (B, M: Ed)
A Comparative Literature (B: L&S or Ed; M, P: L&S. SED)
A Education and Communication Arts (M: Ed)
A Education and English (M: Ed)
A Education and Journalism (M: Ed)
A Education and Music (M: Ed)
A English (B: L&S or Ed; M, P: L&S. SED)
A Humanities, Classical (B: L&S. Possible Certification: Ed)
A Humanities, Modern (B: L&S. Possible Certification: Ed)
A Music Education (BM: L&S. Certification: Ed; MM: L&S; P: L&S and Ed. Jt. degree program)
A Theatre and Drama (B, M, P: L&S. SED)
AI Education and French (M: Ed)
AI Education and German (M: Ed)
AI Education and Latin (M: Ed)
AI Education and Spanish (M: Ed)
AI French (B: L&S or Ed; M, P: L&S. SED)
AI German (B: L&S or Ed; M, P: L&S. SED)
AI Hebrew (B: L&S or Ed. SED)
AI History (B: L&S or Ed; M, P: L&S. SED)
AI Ibero-American Studies (B: L&S or Ed; M: L&S. SED)
AI Italian (B: L&S or Ed; M, P: L&S. SED)
AI Latin (B: L&S or Ed; M, P: L&S)
AI Polish (B: L&S or Ed; SED)
AI Portuguese (B: L&S or Ed; M, P: L&S)
AI Russian (B: L&S or Ed; M: L&S. Ph.D.= Slavic Languages. SED)
AI Spanish (B: L&S or Ed; M, P: L&S. SED)
AS Communication Arts (B: L&S or Ed; M, P: L&S)
AS Education and Communication Arts (M: Ed)
AS Education and Journalism (M: Ed)
AS Journalism Education (B: L&S. Certification: Ed)

S	Communicative Disorders (B: L&S or Ed; M, P: L&S)
S	Education and Physical Therapy (M: Ed)
S	Education and Sociology (M: Ed)
SE	American Institutions (B: L&S or Ed. SED)
SE	Education and History (M: Ed)
SE	History (B: L&S or Ed; M, P: L&S. SED)
SE	Social Studies (B: Ed. SED)
SE	Sociology (B: L&S or Ed; M: L&S; P: L&S or Ag. PhD. is Sociology or Rural Sociology)
SC	Home Economics Education (B: FRCS. Certification: Ed. M, P = Continuing & Vocational Education)
E	American Institutions (B: L&S or Ed. SED)
E	Business Teacher Education (B: Bus. Certification: Ed. M, P = Continuing & Vocational Education)
E	History (B: L&S or Ed; M, P: L&S. SED)
E	Social Studies (B: Ed. SED)
C	Business Teacher Education (B: Bus. Certification: Ed)
CE	Economics (B: L&S or Ed; M, P: L&S. SED)

Needless to say, these lists may contain inadvertent errors of classification. Moreover, there is room for genuine disagreement as to *which* People Environments correspond to which courses, or majors. As John Holland's data on pages 132-135 of his book (op. cit.) reveals, within the similar classification codes for a particular occupation (and, therefore, for the corresponding courses or majors) there are variations. An accountant, for example, may be: CES, CRI, or ICS. A secretary may be SCA, CRE, or CIE. and so forth.

The correspondence between People and Courses is hardly an exact science. But it is several 'light years' more precise than the usual hazy way in which people gravitate toward a particular course on the ground that "I think I might meet some nice people there." *Education as Meeting Place* does not have to be a lousy motive for learning. It can be a rather more noble yearning than is commonly acknowledged. If it is yours, fly with it.

"I want to pick up/polish up the required skills that
I need for (a) a particular field in which I need
accreditation, (b) a particular job (present or
contemplated) (c) a particular role that I have
or want to have in life"

The
ninth
'possible
reason'
for
taking
further
education

This is 'the biggie,' among all the reasons why people seek
further education. As we saw earlier (page 71), over half the
people who go back for further education do so because of the
desire either to get a new job or to improve and advance in their
present job. Fundamental to this desire, is the perception of
education as a way to pick up or sharpen job-related skills. This
is a perception that is even shared by academics, who acknowledge however grudgingly that 'skill training' is *one* of the proper
functions of education. (Academics only bristle when you try
to maintain that the acquiring of skills is *the only* function of
education.)

This being the case, you would suppose that educators have
a well-thought out, carefully-reasoned understanding of Skills,
and their relationship to education. Unhappily, this is simply
not true. Generally speaking, I do not believe there is any concept more misunderstood by teachers, faculty, workshop leaders, seminar conductors, and the like, than the concept of Skills.
You cannot therefore rely upon someone else—with any confidence— to do this work for you. If you are going to seek further
education in order to acquire or polish up your job-related
skills, it is *You* who is going to have to puzzle out what this
means, and what sort of courses you ought to take.

A little humility is becoming to us all, as we take our first
hard thoughtful look at the true meaning of Skills. It is not
merely academics who imagine they thoroughly understand the
concept, when in fact they rarely do. The public at large has the
same illusion. Walk through a typical week in your life, and
listen intently to see how the subject of Skills insinuates itself
into everyday conversation. It would seem, at first sight, that
most people are very familiar with the general concept. A father
may be heard to say, for example, "My boy went through four
years of college without picking up one single skill, except surfing and sex. And tell me how he's going to make a living off
those, for God's sake." A frustrated worker may be heard to

say, "I'm really tired of doing this sort of work, after all these years, so I guess I'm going to have to go back to school to pick up some new skills." A mother who has stayed at home for a number of years raising her children may be heard to say, "I'm afraid that, much as I'd like to go out and get a job, I just don't have any marketable skills."

Very heart-warming. Except that the very sentences, just quoted, contain a number of erroneous ideas about Skills. Let us see what they are:

● First Erroneous Idea: *People are not born with skills; all skills must be acquired.* This is simply not true. There are—as we shall see—three different kinds of skills, and some of them (the

'IN THIS PROFESSION IT TAKES MORE EDUCATION. I GRADUATED LAST WEEK!'

most important and basic) seem to be inborn, or developed very early in infancy. There is a great deal of truth to the phrase: "She (or he) just seems to have a natural talent for that."

● Second Erroneous Idea: *Those skills which must be acquired, are acquired primarily in school environments.* Actually, some of our most basic skills seem to be acquired in the home, or 'in the street', or otherwise outside the classroom.

● Third Erroneous Idea: *If you have certain skills, you will be very aware that you have them.* Not true. There is a lot of evidence to show that people use and practice certain skills, often without the slightest awareness that they possess those particular ones. A process of 'skill awareness' or 'skill identification' is usually necessary for most people, before this part of their Total Reality penetrates their consciousness.

● Fourth Erroneous Idea: *Skills which are picked up in one field are only usable in that field; they are rarely transferable.* This is perhaps the biggest misconception about skills. To be sure, there are—as we shall see—some kinds of skills that are rooted in a particular field. But, again, the most important and basic skills are abundantly transferable from one field to another, *as long as they are taken out of the jargon-language that is peculiar to that first field.*

● Fifth Erroneous Idea: *There are only a relatively few skills that individuals possess, none of which may turn out to be 'marketable.'* How sad to find people thinking this about themselves, yet this is an almost universally 'popular' idea. At the National Career Development Project we find that when we get an individual to sit down and do skill identification in the most thoroughgoing manner that we know—based upon a written autobiography of himself or herself—that he or she will turn up from five hundred to seven hundred skills, which he or she possesses.[10] The number of marketable skills within such a list boggles the mind. And this—whether the individual is sixteen years old or sixty.

So much for the misconceptions, which are *everywhere* in our culture. It is obvious that if you are going to seek further education in order to pick up some skills, you are first going to need a clearer understanding of what it is you are trying to 'pick up.' Equally obviously — from the above — you are not going to pick up this understanding just by walking around listening or talking to people. So, let us take a short course — right here — in:

The Relationship Between Education and Skills

We can approach the subject of skills, first of all, by putting them in some kind of perspective. Technically speaking, skills are a sub-group of something called an activity, task, or role. And these, in turn, are sub-groups of something called a job. A job, in turn, is a sub-group of a field, and a field is a sub-group of a career.

Look at the diagram on the facing page. If you are visually minded (i.e., right-brained), it all comes out looking something like this. Except that for simplicity's sake and for lack of space only *one* Job, and *one* Activity is diagrammed. Actually the picture spreads over a very wide area when filled in.

So much for the context, in which skills must be understood. Now, how do we break skills down? Into what categories? The dictionary is practically useless here. *Webster's*, for example, casts a net so broad that it catches practically everything; viz.,
  "a. the ability to use one's knowledge effectively
  and readily in execution or performance
  b. dexterity or coordination esp. in the execution
  of learned physical tasks
  c. a learned power of doing something
  competently; a developed aptitude or ability"
No, we must turn to the experts in the field. A great many minds in our country have wrestled, over the years, with the question of skills.[11] But one man —named Sidney Fine— has laid out a particularly thoughtful and careful set of distinctions, and it is to him that we are all especially indebted in this field. Sidney's field is functional job analysis. He was for many years, prior to opening his present office in Washington D.C., a senior staff member of the W.E. Upjohn Institute for Employment Research. Before that, he worked for the Department of Labor, directing the research which culminated in the publishing of the monumental *Dictionary of Occupational Titles, 1965 edition* —of which he has consequently been called 'the father', as it has become the 'bible' of the vocational world in the U.S. for over a

THE CONTEXT OF SKILLS

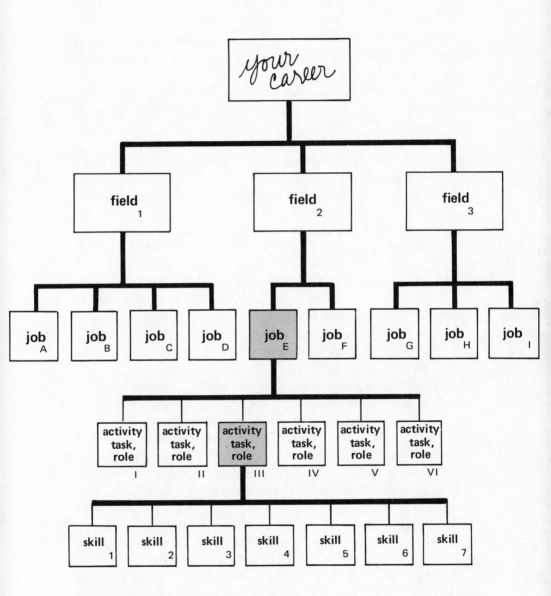

For simplicity's sake only the sub-components of one *job*, and of one *activity* are diagrammed here. The picture actually spreads over a wide area when filled in.

decade. Sidney is responsible for the basic distinctions I am about to explain, though not—I hasten to add—for my own peculiar formulations of them, nor for the use to which I put them.[12]

Skills, then divide into three basic families, which we may call (1) Self-Management Skills. (2) Functional or Transferable Skills. (3) Work-Content Skills.

Now, it may be that simply from these titles, you grasp enough of the distinctions to be able to answer the following questions:

If you are very punctual, and able to pace yourself well, in terms of the time needed to get a job done—which of the three kinds of skills is that?

If you are able to solve difficult problems in human relationships—which of the three kinds of skills is that?

And: if you know the names of all the parts of a car, or you have mastered a foreign language—which of the three kinds of skills is that?

If your answer to the first question was "Self-Management", your answer to the second, "Functional", and your answer to the third, "Work-Content"—then you have understood the titles very well, indeed (or you are a darn good guesser). If you didn't answer correctly, then a word of further explanation may be helpful to you.

■ (1) Self-Management Skills are the kind we are all aware of when we say about someone: "He really knows his stuff, and he's very competent, but in terms of being able to get along with anyone else, he's a mess." In *skill-language* (a species, I think, of Esperanto) what we have just said is: "His work-content skills and his functional skills are excellent, but his self-management skills are rather minimal." By definition, self-management skills include not only how you get along with others, but also how you relate to authority, how you relate to time, to space, to the control of your impulses, to the material world, to clothes and dress, etc., etc. Most of us are familiar with these things. We have just not thought of our relationship to them as constituting skills. We have described them instead as "Personality Traits" or "Character Traits." Yet a moment's reflection may convince us that they are indeed, skills. You have a friend, let us say, who does not get along with anyone in

authority. You, on the other hand, have learned how to relate to authority figures without being overawed by them (on the one hand) or hostile to them (on the other hand). Is that not a skill? Again, you have a friend who never seems to be aware of time, cannot keep time, is never on time, and so on. You, on the other hand, have learned how to manage yourself in relationship to time so that time and you have become sort-of 'friends.' Is that not a skill? Clearly it is. People who make up tests, for a living, tend to put Self-Management Skills (except they call them "Traits") on a kind of spectrum. A typical one would look something like this:

ATTITUDE TOWARD AUTHORITY:

| Hates people in authority, Thinks anything they say is wrong, and therefore rejects it immediately. | Has a balanced view of authority. Gives anything they say careful consideration, but weighs it carefully before deciding. | Loves people in authority. Thinks anything they say is right, without critical examination. |

The assumption is that someone who 'scores' in the center has 'good' skills at dealing with authority, while someone who scores at either end has 'bad' skills. In point of fact, however, there is a bias in the way that *this scale* is stated. It can be redrawn so that each 'score' is 'good'—in the sense that: there is a potential job where that 'skill' would be desirable and valuable; viz.,

Able to question the most basic assumptions; takes nothing for granted.	Strikes a balance between acceptance, and critical evaluation of facts or pronouncements.	Able to accept orders and follow instructions unhesitatingly.

▲

Thus restated, no matter where you score within that total spectrum, you would be perceived to have a 'good' skill—*provided that* you were able to be in an environment or job that was *appropriate* to that skill—i.e., an environment where that skill would be a 'plus' and not a 'minus.' For example, someone in charge of a research project needs the Self-Management Skill (in relation to authority) that lets him or her "question even the most basic assumptions, and take nothing for granted." While someone who is to be a private in the Army needs the opposite Self-Management Skill (in relation to authority) of being "able to accept orders and follow instructions unhesitatingly." Each skill, when it is used in the appropriate environment, helps that individual to *adapt* well to that environment. This 'family' of skills, then, may be legitimately called by other names than *Self-Management*. We might call them *Specific Environment Skills* or —as Sidney Fine calls them—*Adaptive Skills*. The name is not particularly crucial; but the distinction is.

There is no *authorized list* of Self-Management Skills, because there are so many ways in which each skill belonging to this "family" can be named. However, it includes the following kinds of skills:

SELF-MANAGEMENT SKILLS

Ability to choose, or
   make a decision
Alertness
Assertiveness
Astuteness
Attention to details,
   awareness,
   thoroughness,
   conscientiousness
Authenticity
Calmness
Candidness
Commitment to grow
Concentration
Cooperation
Courage, risk-taking,
   adventuresomeness
Curiosity
Diplomacy
Easy-goingness
Emotional stability
Empathy
Enthusiasm
Expressiveness
Firmness
Flexibility
Generosity
Good judgment

High energy level,
   dynamicness
Honesty, integrity
Initiative, drive
Loyalty
Open-mindedness
Optimism
Orderliness
Patience, persistence
Performing well
   under stress
Playfulness
Poise, self-confidence
Politeness
Punctualness
Reliability,
   dependability
Resourcefulness
Self-control
Self-reliance
Self-respect
Sense of humor
Sincerity
Spontaneity
Tactfulness
Tidiness
Tolerance
Versatility

Generally speaking, a Self-Management Skill will not take an object. A Functional Skill (as we shall see) not only takes one, but virtually requires one; the minute you see (for example) "analyzing", you feel like asking: "analyzing what?" A Self-Management Skill poses no such question. Courage is courage. Poise is poise. The only curiosity we might feel is: "Is there any kind of situation where you don't manage yourself in this fashion? But generally speaking a Self-Management Skill stands as it is.

Now we turn to the second kind of skills: Functional.

■ (2) Functional Skills are the kind required to deal—not with intangibles like the Self, Time, Space, Authority, Impulse, Style, Constancy and Change, as above—but with the basic tangibles of the everyday world, namely: Data (or Information), People and Things. Functional skills involve action verbs, describing how people *act upon* Information, People, and/or Things. The word "functional", as used here, has the implication of "basic" to it. These are actions which contribute to a larger action. And these actions are "basic" in a second sense. The research on functional skills began by analyzing—from the second edition of the D.O.T.—some four thousand job definitions and a couple of thousand action verbs. These were distilled down to thirty-one verbs, twenty-eight functions, in the most famous diagram of functional skills, namely this one:

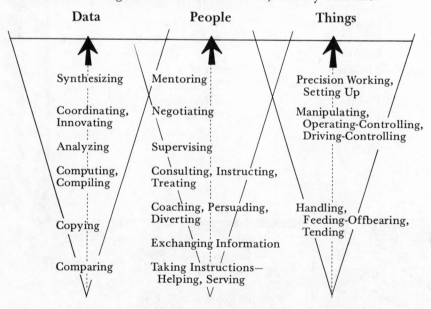

Data	People	Things
Synthesizing	Mentoring	Precision Working, Setting Up
Coordinating, Innovating	Negotiating	Manipulating, Operating-Controlling, Driving-Controlling
Analyzing	Supervising	
Computing, Compiling	Consulting, Instructing, Treating	
Copying	Coaching, Persuading, Diverting	Handling, Feeding-Offbearing, Tending
	Exchanging Information	
Comparing	Taking Instructions— Helping, Serving	

Note: Each successive function reading down usually or typically involves all those that follow it. The functions separated by a comma are separate functions on the same level separately defined. They are on the same level because empirical evidence does not make a hierarchical distinction clear.

The hyphenated functions: *Taking Instructions-Helping, Operating-Controlling, Driving-Controlling,* and *Feeding-Offbearing* are single functions.

Setting Up, Operating-Controlling, Driving-Controlling, Feeding-Offbearing and *Tending* are special cases involving machines and equipment of *Precision Working, Manipulating,* and *Handling,* respectively, and hence are indented under them. [13]

Longer lists of functional skills can be prepared, grouped around other principles than Data, People, Things. But the "basic" nature of functional skills remains.

So does their transferability; the *sine qua non* of functional skills is that transferability. This operates across time-frames. For example, if you were very good at problem-solving when you were five years old—say, in avoiding the bed-time that your parents had set—then you are probably still good at problem-solving today. True, your ability in this area may have gotten a lot more sophisticated, and may have become even sharper, but it is the same ability or skill they you had when you were five. The transferability of functional skills operates also across 'jobs' or 'fields.' If you are good at problem-solving in chemistry, you would probably be good at problem-solving in languages—just so long as (to be technical, for a moment) both kinds of problem-solving used the same hemisphere of the brain.

Now on to the third—and final—kind of skills: Work-Content.

■ (3) Work-Content Skills are those which deal with mastering a particular vocabulary, or procedure, or subject-matter. Thus, knowing a particular foreign language is a Work-Content Skill. So is knowing the parts of a car. Or the names of various psychological disturbances. Or the procedure for accomplishing a particular task. Because these masteries are not *necessarily* related to work—they may be called by a broader term, namely, Specific Content Skills. This is Sidney Fine's name for them. In any event, the distinguishing mark of this family of skills is that these skills are picked up or acquired as one goes on in life; and they involve, as the common mark of them all, the use of the

FAKING IT
WITH WORK-CONTENT LANGUAGE

A long-time bureaucrat has invented a way to let you sound as if you know what you're talking about.

Philip Broughton, for many years with the U.S. Public Health Service, hit upon what he calls the Systematic Buzz Phrase Projector. The system employs these thirty buzz words:

0. integrated	0. management	0. options
1. total	1. organizational	1. flexibility
2. systematized	2. monitored	2. capability
3. parallel	3. reciprocal	3. mobility
4. functional	4. digital	4. programming
5. responsive	5. logistical	5. concept
6. optional	6. transitional	6. time-phase
7. synchronized	7. incremental	7. projection
8. compatible	8. third-generation	8. hardware
9. balanced	9. policy	9. contingency

Broughton's procedure is simple. Think of any three-digit number, then select the corresponding buzz words from each column.

For instance, number 736 produces "synchronized reciprocal time-phase," a phrase you can drop into any report with a ring of authority.

"Nobody will have the remotest idea what you're talking about," he says. "But the important thing is that no one is about to admit it."

individual's memory. You may be instinctively good in the use of your hands—that is a Functional Skill. You do not have to 'remember' how to use them in any conscious sense. But using those hands to pick up various parts of a car in a certain prescribed order on an assembly line—that requires memory— and that is therefore a Work-Content Skill.

Let us look at some other examples that will contrast these last two types of skills. A baseball player may be very good in the muscular coordination between his eyes, his hands, and his feet. That is a Functional Skill. But he must also know the rules of the game, and how it is played—including all its intricacies. If he has mastered the game, that is a Work-Content Skill.

A seamstress may be very good in designing dresses. Her ability to visualize what the dress will look like before she draws the design is a Functional Skill. But her knowledge of various materials, ways of sewing, etc. is a Work-Content Skill.

A comedian may be very good in his instinctive sense of timing, and his stage presence in front of an audience. That is a Functional Skill. But if he has studied comedy, and knows the rules that apply to it, and if, further, he has memorized a great number of routines, one-liners and jokes, that is a Work-Content Skill.

A nurse may be wonderful in the way she relates to people —patients, fellow nurses, doctors and administrators alike. That is a Functional Skill. To the degree that she knows all the procedures to take with different kinds of patients, and what is called for in dealing with various emergencies, she also possesses a Work-Content Skill.

A teacher may have a tremendous ability to communicate his subject matter to his students with flair, enthusiasm, and clarity. That is a Functional Skill. His subject matter itself, to the degree that he has mastered it, involves—however—a Work-Content Skill.

For our present purposes, this should be sufficient definition and illustration of the three different kinds of skills. We may lay out the contrast between the three, now, in a sort of table. It will look like this:

SELF-MANAGEMENT SKILLS *Adaptive to Specific Environments*	FUNCTIONAL SKILLS *Instrumental or Transferable Skills*	WORK-CONTENT OR SPECIFIC-CONTENT SKILLS *Particular Job Conditions, Vocabulary and Artifacts*
Rooted in temperament	Rooted in aptitudes	Rooted in personal experience and preference
Acquired in early years, among family, peers, school; or, later in life, by intensive education.	Acquired either as natural-born talent, refined by experience and education; or by specific educational, vocational or avocational special training.	Acquired by private reading, apprenticeship, technical training institute, school, or (often) on the job.
Related to environments, and particularly to the requirements or demands for conformity and continuity *VS.* risk and discretion and change.	Related to People, Data and Things, in generalizable or transferable fashion (from one field, profession, occupation or job, to another).	Related to performing a job in a particular field, profession, or occupation, and according to the specifications and conditions of a particular employer.
EXAMPLES: Management of oneself in relation to: authority, space & time direction, moving towards or away from or against others, self-pacing, self-routing, punctuality, dress, care of property, impulse-control. *In Everyday Speech:* Regularity, dependability, initiative, resourcefulness, etc.	**EXAMPLES:** Tending and operating machines, comparing, compiling or analyzing data, exchanging information with or consulting, supervising people. *In Everyday Speech:* Artistic talent, a born problem solver, a natural salesman or saleswoman, a gifted writer, effective in dealing with many kinds of people, bringing new life to traditional art forms, etc.	**EXAMPLES:** Detailed knowledge of the various parts of a car. Knowing the names of all the muscles in the human body. Understanding the psychology of human motivation. *In Everyday Speech:* Financial planning and management; a skilled engineer; theatrical production planning and management; market research and analysis; making radio and TV presentations; personnel administration, etc.

Distinctions originated by Sidney A. Fine, as adapted by the National Career Development Project, particularly in the definition of Work-Content skills.

In thinking about the relationship of all this to your Education, there are four points to be kept in mind:

(1) You do *not* need to sit down and categorize all your skills, down to the last jot and tittle, in terms of these three different types. It is sufficient that you understand you *have* all three types—and that you know the major examples of same, in your own life.

(2) In every course, field, or major that you study, there are two basic components: that part of it which is *rooted* in that field or major, and not likely to be useful in any other field (or, at best, in only one or two others). *And* the other part which is so overlooked, namely, that part which is *absolutely transferable* to any other field or major. The first component, the rooted part, is—for the most part—what we mean by Work-Content Skills. And the second component, the transferable part, is—for the most part—what we mean by Functional Skills.

GRADS RATE COLLEGE AS TIME WASTE

BETHLEHEM, PA.—A study released here shows that fewer than half of college graduates believe their education is "very useful" in giving them the knowledge and skills they use in their jobs approximately 10 years after graduation.

The study, commissioned by the College Placement Council Foundation and the National Institute of Education, examined 4,138 graduates, all of whom began college since 1961.

To the question whether their education had given them the skills needed for their current jobs, only 38 per cent replied that it had been "very useful," with 50 per cent reporting "somewhat useful" and 12 per cent answering "not at all."

Responses varied with the degree to which the graduates were employed in fields that require highly specialized vocational training. More than half of accountants, health workers, engineers and educators rated their education "very useful." But only 25 per cent of administrators, including business executives, said their education had been "very useful" in their work.

The study offered several possible reasons for the reported inapplicability of college-learned skills. First, half the women and nearly two-thirds of the men studied chose their present careers only after leaving college. Moreover, education appropriate for entry-level jobs often becomes outdated when the jobholder is promoted—when an engineer becomes an administrator, for example.

The study also asked the graduates what courses they would recommend for job preparation, regardless of major. The leading areas of study recommended were business administration, English, psychology, economics and accounting.

The implication is that graduates felt they had neglected useful studies—communication, the handling of figures and business practices—and that such skills would be useful in any job.

(NYTNS)

By way of illustration as to how both of these elements are found in *virtually every* course you may take, let us suppose you took a course in physics, somewhere along the way. What did you pick up there? Well, first of all, obviously, a Work-Content Skill. You mastered the history, principles and applications of physics. Were you writing out a summary of your own skills, and were you being complete, you would put that down: "has a good grasp of the history, principles and applications of physics." This skill is clearly *rooted* in one particular field. Should you decide to be a family marriage counselor, it's not likely to be a terribly useful skill. But what else were you picking up in that course? Well, you were also learning how various great minds throughout history have tackled various puzzling problems and learned to solve them. As you studied how they did it, you probably became clearer about how you could go about tackling problems in your own experience. To the degree, then, that you had any aptitude or talent for problem-solving before you took the physics course, that aptitude was getting "polished up," as you went through the course. Thus you were picking up, or polishing up, a Functional Skill. "Adept at analyzing problems and identifying possible solutions" is a skill that will be useful in *any* field you may enter, during the rest of your life.

This skill, therefore, is patently *transferable* — i.e., not restricted in its usefulness merely to that one field, by any means. The moral, then, of this tale is quickly told: no matter how much you think that your education is only preparing you for one field, it is actually giving you — at the same time — some basic equipment that will prepare you for *any* field.

(3) Among the three types of skills, Functional Skills are the type it is most important for you to keep your eye on — and, at the same time, are the type it is the most difficult for you to keep your eye on. The first part of this paradox is quickly explained. Since the average person changes careers two or three times during his or her lifetime, knowledge of your Functional Skills will help you to change careers *without* going back to school *in order to restudy that which you already know, and to pick up skills which you already possess.* (A good inventory of the skills they already have would save a lot of people from taking Unnecessary Education. Especially an inventory of their

Functional Skills.)   But that leads us to the second part of our paradox. These are the skills it is the most difficult for you to keep your eye on because *in our culture we tend to describe our functional skills (to ourselves as well as to others) in* **work-content** *language, rather than in functional-skill language,* and so they end up sounding non-transferable—rooted in this one field.

Let us look at an example, to see how this works. Many of us, when we first get a job—say, in our teens—work as a waitress or waiter somewhere. Now, after working there for a while we may dream of getting into quite a different line of work, but— we say to ourselves—"all I know how to do is to be a waitress or waiter." If somebody presses us about this, we say, "Well, look, here is all I know how to do:

√ put on my uniform or costume,

√ set tables, with silverware, glasses, etc.

√ seat people,

√ hand out menus,

√ take orders,

√ deliver orders to the kitchen,

√ serve the people what they ordered,

√ suggest desserts,

√ check on them to be sure everything is okay,

√ give them the check or bill,

√ deliver them their change,

√ thank them, and

√ clear their table."

Because the *language* we use to describe what we can do is so splendidly *rooted* in this one field, it sounds as though there isn't a transferable skill in the whole bunch. Everything is *restaurant-y*: uniforms, set tables, menus, kitchen, serve, desserts, checks. But suppose we take **What We Do** out of this Work Content language, and put it in the functional language of **Information, People,** and **Things,** as follows:

Work-Content Language Job Description	What Am I Doing With Information?	What Am I Doing With People?	What Am I Doing With Things?
Put on my uniform			Handling
Set tables with silverware, glasses, napkins, etc.			Manipulating tools rapidly
Seat people		Helping	
Hand out menus	Distributing possibilities		Handling
Take orders	Interpreting difficult passages	Taking instructions	Writing clearly so as to be understood by others
Deliver orders to the kitchen	Communicating information to others		
Serve the people people what they ordered	Ability to prioritize information in a new sequence	Serving	Balancing a number of objects at the same time
Suggest desserts	Ability to memorize long and detailed lists	Coaching persuasively	
Check on them to be sure everything is okay	Checking back on information; seeking feedback	Helping, diverting, (when necessary)	
Give them the check	Copying, evaluating information received	Serving	Writing clearly so as to be understood by others
Deliver them their change			Transporting
Thank them		Dealing with people super-courteously	
Clear their table			Rapid manipulation of a multitude of objects

So, clearly, we are learning a number of things which are absolutely transferable from one situation to another, from one job or career to another. Or to put it another way if we are not learning these things (because we already knew them, and already possessed these functional skills) we are at the very least *demonstrating* them on this job.

From the foregoing example, you will note a couple of things. One is that in identifying Functional Skills (those used with information, people and things) you do *not* need to restrict yourself just to the thirty-one verbs in the table on page 146. You can use whatever verbs are most meaningful to *You*. The other is that you do not need to restrict yourself to using just a verb, by itself. You can use an object with that verb (provided the object is not rooted in that one field—e.g., "tools" is a better object than "silverware", even though they are referring to the same thing), and you can also use an adverb or adjective. Of your own devising, e.g.,

VERB   *OBJECT*   *ADVERB*
"Dealing with people supercourteously"

And the object could have been further expanded, if you wished, in order to say more definitively just what the skill is, that you possess:

"Dealing with people of all ages and temperaments supercourteously." Well, so much for your beginning lesson in *Skill-Identification*. Now at least, *you* know why Functional Skills are the most difficult of your skills to keep your eye on. And you also know the kind of exercises that are necessary in order to bring Functional Skills into your consciousness. This leads us to our fourth point, about the relationship of Skills to Education:

(4) In truth, almost *any* further education that you take will help you with all three types of skills: Self-Management, Functional or Transferable, and Work-Content. *However,* it is also true that education—looked at from the point of view of skills—divides into three basic families:

● Certain kinds of workshops, seminars or courses have as their *dominant*—though not exclusive—thrust, the aim of helping you with your Self-Management Skills. For example:

155

workshops, seminars or courses dealing with self-development, time-management, assertiveness training, meditation, and the like. Not to mention sensitivity groups, encounter groups, and the various kinds of therapies, group or individual. If you *major* (as it were) in this kind of education, you will probably need to spend some time identifying your skills in other areas, viz., your Functional Skills and your Work-Content Skills.

● Other kinds of workshops, seminars and courses have as their *dominant* — though not exclusive — thrust, the aim of helping you with acquiring Work-Content Skills. For example: almost all courses dealing with some body of subject-matter that you are required to memorize or otherwise master. And, all courses teaching procedures or processes—such as how to use a drill-press, how to sew, and the like. Language courses, technical or scientific courses, vocational courses, and so-called "skills" courses. From all of these you acquire, as *the major benefit,* new Work-Content Skills. If you major (as it were) in this kind of education, you will probably pick up—or polish up—many Functional Skills as well, but you may well need help in *deciphering* these out of their Work-Content language and form. The skills you will probably need the most help in identifying, however, are your Self-Management Skills.

● Finally—and certainly not surprisingly—still other kinds of workshops, seminars and courses have as their *dominant*—though not exclusive thrust—the aim of helping you acquire or polish up your Functional Skills. For example: liberal arts courses, and any courses whose major intention is to help you with the basic *functional verbs,* viz.,

— in relation to information: courses, seminars or workshops which deal with *comparing, copying, compiling, computing, analyzing, innovating, coordinating, or synthesizing.*

— in relation to people: courses, seminars or workshops which deal with *taking instructions — helping, serving, exchanging information, coaching, persuading, diverting, consulting, instructing, treating, supervising, negotiating, or mentoring (the latter, incidentally, comes from Mentor, the friend of Odysseus who was entrusted with the education of Odysseus' son, Telemachus; it consequently means tutoring or dealing with a person's total life adjustment).*

—in relation to things: courses, seminars or workshops which have as their aim the teaching of *handling, feeding-offbearing, tending, manipulating, operating-controlling, driving-controlling, precision working, or setting up.*

This last group of Functional Skills—those related to *things*—does tend to deal so much with procedures and processes, that the line between them and Work-Content gets very thin indeed. Faced with this, analysts who desire logic and neatness in all categories tend to go mad; the left-brain cannot cope. But intuitives, who live off what they sense and intuit, are content; the right-brain somehow *knows*. Beneath all the procedures and processes, there is something native and instinctual. Precision-working may be taught; but the best precision-workers are those who seem to have been born knowing how to do it. So, beneath the Work-Content, the Functional is still to be found.

If you major (as it were) in this kind of education, you will probably need help in identifying just exactly what your Functional Skills are, and *where* you want to use them. But you should not allow yourself to think (as liberal arts majors, in particular, so often do) that you have *no* skills usable in the marketplace. You are lacking only in certain Work-Content Skills—but these are the easiest to pick up, along the way, either by special study, or actually on the job.

How To Decide What Skills You Want To Pick Up Or Polish Up By Further Education

The simplest way to do this is simply to look at a list of Transferable Skills and check off the ones that you are interested in picking up from scratch, or polishing up, by further education. You can think of this as "What Skills Do I Need for Life?" or more particularly "What Additional Skills Do I Need In My Present Job, or in a Future Job or Career?" Anyway, here is a list for you to use:

Your "Shopping List" of Transferable Skills

(List A)

A. Using My Hands

☐	☐	1. assembling	as with kits, etc.
☐	☐	2. constructing	as with carpentry, etc.
☐	☐	3. or building	
☐	☐	4. operating tools	as with drills, mixers, etc.
☐	☐	5. or machinery	as with sewing machines, etc.
☐	☐	6. or equipment	as with trucks, stationwagons, etc.
☐	☐	7. showing manual or finger dexterity	as with throwing, sewing, etc.
☐	☐	8. handling with precision and/or speed	as with an assembly line, etc.
☐	☐	9. fixing or repairing	as with autos or mending, etc.
☐	☐	10. other:	

B. Using My Body

☐	☐	11. muscular coordination	as in skiing, gymnastics, etc.
☐	☐	12. being physically active	as in exercising, hiking, etc.
☐	☐	13. doing outdoor activities	as in camping, etc.
☐	☐	14. other:	

C. Using Words

☐	☐	15. reading	as with books; with understanding
☐	☐	16. copying	as with manuscripts; skillfully
☐	☐	17. writing or communicating	as with letters; interestingly
☐	☐	18. talking or speaking	as on the telephone; interestingly
☐	☐	19. teaching, training	as in front of groups; with animation
☐	☐	20. editing	as in improving a child's sentences in an essay, etc.
☐	☐	21. memory for words	as in remembering people's names, book titles, etc.
☐	☐	22. other:	

D. Using My Senses
(Eyes, Ears, Nose, Taste or Touch)

☐	☐	23. observing, surveying	as in watching something with the eyes, etc.
☐	☐	24. examining or inspecting	as in looking at a child's bumps, etc.
☐	☐	25. diagnosing, determining	as in deciding if food is cooked yet
☐	☐	26. showing attention to detail	as in shop, in sewing, etc.
☐	☐	27. other:	

**Want to
pick up
this skill**

**Want to
polish up
this skill**

E.   Using Numbers

☐	☐	28. taking inventory	as in the pantry, shop, etc.
☐	☐	29. counting	as in a classroom, bureau drawers
☐	☐	30. calculating, computing	as in a checkbook, arithmetic
☐	☐	31. keeping financial records, bookkeeping	as with a budget, etc.
☐	☐	32. managing money	as in a checking account, bank, store, etc.
☐	☐	33. developing a budget	as for a family, etc.
☐	☐	34. number memory	as with telephone numbers, etc.
☐	☐	35. rapid manipulation of numbers	as with doing arithmetic in the head
☐	☐	36. other:	

F.   Using Intuition

☐	☐	37. showing foresight	as in planning ahead, predicting consequences, etc.
☐	☐	38. quickly sizing up a person or situation accurately	as in everything, rather than just one or two details about them, etc.
☐	☐	39. having insight	as to why people act the way they do, etc.
☐	☐	40. acting on gut reactions	as in making decisions, deciding to trust someone, etc.
☐	☐	41. ability to visualize third-dimension	as in drawings, models, blueprints, memory for faces, etc.
☐	☐	42. other:	

G.   Using Analytical Thinking or Logic

☐	☐	43. researching, information gathering	as in finding out where a particular street is in a strange city
☐	☐	44. analyzing, dissecting	as with the ingredients in a recipe, material, etc.
☐	☐	45. organizing, classifying	as with laundry, etc.
☐	☐	46. problem-solving	as with figuring out how to get to a place, etc.
☐	☐	47. separating important from unimportant	as with complaints, or cleaning the attic, etc.
☐	☐	48. diagnosing	as in cause and effect relations, tracing problems to their sources
☐	☐	49. systematizing, putting things in order	as in laying out tools or utensils in the order you will be using them
☐	☐	50. comparing, perceiving similarities	as with different brands in the supermarket, etc.
☐	☐	51. testing, screening	as with cooking, deciding what to wear, etc.
☐	☐	52. reviewing, evaluating	as in looking at something you made, to see how you could have made it better, faster
☐	☐	53. other:	

Want to
pick up
this skill

Want to
polish up
this skill

H. Using Originality or Creativity

☐	☐	54. imaginative, imagining	as in figuring out new ways to do things, or making up stories, etc.
☐	☐	55. inventing, creating	as with processes, products, figures, words, etc.
☐	☐	56. designing, developing	as with new recipes, new gadgets
☐	☐	57. improvising, experiments	as in camping, when you've left some of the equipment home, etc.
☐	☐	58. adapting, improving	as with something that doesn't work quite right, etc.
☐	☐	59. other:	

I. Using Helpfulness

☐	☐	60. helping, being of service	as when someone is in need, etc.
☐	☐	61. showing sensitivity to others' feelings	as in a heated discussion, argument
☐	☐	62. listening	
☐	☐	63. developing rapport	as with someone who is initially a stranger, etc.
☐	☐	64. conveying warmth, caring	as with someone who is upset, ill
☐	☐	65. understanding	as when someone tells how they feel, etc.
☐	☐	66. drawing out people	as when someone is reluctant to talk, share
☐	☐	67. offering support	as when someone is facing a difficulty alone, etc.
☐	☐	68. demonstrating empathy	as in weeping with those who weep
☐	☐	69. representing others' wishes accurately	as when one parent tells the other what a child of theirs wants, etc.
☐	☐	70. motivating	as in getting people past hangups, and into action, etc.
☐	☐	71. sharing credit, appreciation	as when working in teams, etc.
☐	☐	72. raising others' self-esteem	as when you make someone feel better, less guilty, etc.
☐	☐	73. healing, curing	as with physical, emotional and spiritual ailments, etc.
☐	☐	74. counseling, guiding	as when someone doesn't know what to do, etc.
☐	☐	75. other:	

J. Using Artistic Abilities

☐	☐	76. composing music	
☐	☐	77. playing (a) musical instrument(s), singing	
☐	☐	78. fashioning or shaping things, materials	as in handicrafts, sculpturing, etc.
☐	☐	79. dealing creatively with symbols or images	as in stained glass, jewelry, etc.
☐	☐	80. dealing creatively with spaces, shapes or faces	as in photography, art, architectural design, etc.

160

Want to
pick up
this skill

Want to
polish up
this skill

☐	☐	81. dealing creatively with colors	as in painting, decorating, making clothes, etc.
☐	☐	82. conveying feelings and thoughts through body, face and/or voice tone	as in acting, public speaking, teaching, dancing, etc,
☐	☐	83. conveying feelings and thoughts through drawing, paintings	as in art, etc.
☐	☐	84. using words on a very high level	as in poetry, playwriting, novels
☐	☐	85. other	

K. Using Leadership, Being Up Front

☐	☐	86. beginning new tasks, ideas, projects	as in starting a group, initiating a clothing drive, etc.
☐	☐	87. taking first move in relationships	as with stranger on bus, plane, train, etc.
☐	☐	88. organizing	as with a Scout troop, a team, a game at a picnic, etc.
☐	☐	89. leading, directing others	as with a field trip, cheerleading
☐	☐	90. promoting change	as in a family, community, organization, etc.
☐	☐	91. making decisions	as in places where decisions affect others, etc.
☐	☐	92. taking risks	as in sticking up for someone in a fight, etc.
☐	☐	93. getting up before a group, performing	as in demonstrating a product, lecturing, making people laugh, entertaining, public speaking
☐	☐	94. selling, promoting, negotiating, persuading	as with a product, idea, materials, in a garage sale, argument, recruiting, changing someone's mind
☐	☐	95. other:	

L. Using Follow-Through

☐	☐	96. using what others have developed	as in working with a kit, etc.
☐	☐	97. following through on plans, instructions	as in picking up children on schedule
☐	☐	98. attending to details	as with embroidering a design on a shirt, etc.
☐	☐	99. classifying, recording, filing, retrieving	as with data, materials, letters, ideas, information, etc.
☐	☐	100. other:	

Now you have a rather complete list of the skills you would either like to pick up, or polish up, by taking some further education. If that's all the time you want to give to the task, then fly with this. Choose seminars, workshops or courses which will help you get or polish precisely those skills. If you are puzzled as to which courses will Accomplish That, talk to the counselor, academic advisor, or admissions officer at your local college or community college.

There is, however, another important step in all of this that you *ought* to take, first. I can explain it this way. Suppose as a teenager you've been away from home for awhile, and then at last you return. Your first night back, your Mom or Dad asks you to make a list of all the food you'd like to have in the house during the first two weeks you are there with them. So you make out the list. (Let's call that 'List A'.) The next day, it's time to go shopping for the food you want. Do you go right downtown to the supermarket, with List A? Not likely. *First, you would go into the kitchen, and inventory what foods are already there.* (Let's call that 'List B'.) *For, if you already have the foods, there's no need to go out and buy them.* Once this inventory was completed. you would subtract B from A, in effect, crossing off your list the foods you've already got. Now you need only go shopping for what is left on your list (A minus B).

It is the same way with skills. On the previous pages, you made out your 'shopping list' of skills. Your List A. But before you go down to 'buy' courses which will give you those skills, it is very important to go do an inventory *of the skills you already have.* Your List B. And to then subtract B from A, in effect crossing off the skills you've already got. Then you need only go 'shopping' for education which will give you what is left on your list (A minus B).

Make sense? Okay, here's how you get at your List B:

> Although men are accused of not knowing their own weakness, yet perhaps few know their own strength. It is in men as in soils, where sometimes there is a vein of gold which the owner knows not of.
> Jonathan Swift

Inventory of The Skills You Already Have
(List B)

Whether you are sixteen years old, or sixty-six, you already possess a number of skills—far more than you dream. You didn't just pick these up in the classroom. You picked some of them up in the home. And some 'in the street.' Some you were born with. In any event, here's how you get at Finding Out What They Are:

I "THE MAGNIFICENT SEVEN"
Your Seven Most Enjoyed or Satisfying
Accomplishments:

THE PARTY exercise on page 127, which you completed, is based on a simple truth discovered by Dr. John L. Holland: that we all tend to be attracted to the people who have the same (interests and) SKILLS as we do. Or at least the same Skills that we MOST ENJOY (or would most enjoy) using. So, what you have done in the party exercise actually, is to define (at least in a general fashion) the Skills you most enjoy using: just read back, in the diagram, the description of the people in each of the three corners you preferred: that is actually a description of YOU, and your Skills.

But now you *must have* more detailed information about your most enjoyable natural talents and developed skills. The first step toward this is for you to take

SEVEN SHEETS OF PAPER—

(lined paper if you are not going to type it). What you want to put on these seven separate pieces of paper is a description of some *experiences* in your life which you can then examine, to see what skills you were using when you were most enjoying yourself.

You have a choice as to what you write on the seven sheets of paper. Here are

TWO POSSIBILITIES:

(A) You can describe the seven *most satisfying accomplishments or achievements* in your life. At home, in a part-time job, in your hobbies, in extra-curricular or volunteer activities. An

"achievement" does not mean something you do better than anyone else; it only means something you learned to do, which once you could not do, e.g. "I learned how to sew my own dress" or "I succeeded in fixing my own car".

There are two ways of getting at this:

(1) Make the longest list you can, at first, of accomplishments from all different portions of your life—e.g., two or three achievements for each five year period of your life, thus far. Then from that longer list, choose the seven which TO YOU are the most meaningful. Make your own chart, after this model:

My Age	My Most Enjoyable Achievements	From the previous column: The Seven I Have Enjoyed The Most
1—5 years of age		
6—10 years old		
11—15 years old		
16—20 years old		
Etc.—		

OR:

(2) Make a list of *all* the things you have ever enjoyed doing, at play, at work, or while learning. Then, jot down the *most significant or best-remembered* occasion when you were doing each of these things—e.g. "Love listening to classical music." and: "Attended a symphony concert with my parents, when I was twelve." After all these significant occasions have been listed, choose the seven which seem TO YOU to represent the most achievement on your part. Make your own chart, after this model:

Things I Most Enjoy	Most Significant (to me) or best remembered occasions when I was doing the things in column 1	From the total previous column: The seven occasions I have enjoyed the most
AT PLAY LOVE LISTENING TO CLASSICAL MUSIC	Attended symphony concert with my parents when I was twelve	
AT WORK		
AT 'SCHOOL' **(LEARNING)**		

If you find it impossible to make a list of your achievements, then consider this alternative way of getting at your skills:

(B) Describe seven *roles* that you play (or have played) in life so far: e.g., wife, mother, cook, housekeeper, volunteer worker, student, and friend. Or whatever other ones you think of. If you can think of more than seven roles you have played (e.g., in addition to those above: being an individual, learner, teacher of others, sister, consumer, producer, citizen, etc.) then from this longer list choose the seven which you have ENJOYED the most.

II. THE FLESHING OUT

Whichever you choose, "A" or "B", put a separate item on each of the seven sheets, then go back and DESCRIBE IN DETAIL what you did under each of these items—in as much detail as if you were describing it to a five year old child (whom you could count on to know Nothing about the activity you are describing, say).

You may fill each sheet, and write on the back of it if necessary. You must *not* cut corners here, or you will simply not be able to do the next part of this Map. Here is an example of how detailed you will need to be. .

SAMPLE: "My Halloween experience when I was seven years old." Details: "When I was seven, I decided I wanted to go out on Halloween dressed as a horse. I wanted to be the front end of the horse, and I talked a friend of mine into being the back end of the horse. But, at the last moment he backed out, and I was faced with the prospect of not being able to go out on Halloween. At this point, I decided to figure out some way of getting dressed up as the whole horse, myself. I took a fruit basket, and tied some string to both sides of the basket's rim, so that I could tie the basket around my rear end. This filled me out enough so that the costume fit me, by myself. I then fixed some strong thread to the tail so that I could make it wag by moving my hands. When Halloween came I not only went out and had a ball, but I won a prize as well."

Color me "intuitive"

III. THE EXAMINING FOR SKILLS

When you have fleshed the seven out, *thoroughly*, look at the chart on the next page. In the seven columns at the top, put a brief title which will recall each sheet to your mind. e.g., we have called the story above, "The Halloween Experience".

Now, take column #1 (whatever title you have written in that space, and whatever achievement or role that title refers to).

Go down the list of one hundred skills, and with each new skill that you come to, ask yourself: in doing this experience, did I use this skill? (it's like saying: did I use this muscle?)

If the answer is "Yes", color in the box that is in column #1, and horizontally even with the name of the skill.

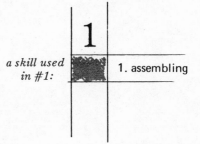

a skill used in #1:

1. assembling

If the answer is "No", that is to say, you did not use this particular skill in order to do this experience or achievement, then leave this space blank.

Go on to the next skill, and continue down the list of one hundred skills, until you have analyzed Experience #1, in terms of the complete list.

Then repeat the same procedure for Experience #2. Then for #3. And so forth. Until you have done all seven.

As you go, feel free to change the wording, fill in the blanks, or do whatever you wish in order to make this truly *your* list— not ours.

You may wish to study the "sample" first. It is the Halloween story, from page 166. Since you are familiar by now with that story (you didn't skip around, did you?) you may find it helpful to see which skills got colored in, in the sample column in the chart. If any colorings puzzle you, re-read the story.

Okay, now it's all yours:

sample: *The Halloween Experience*

Your Functional / Transferable Skills

func·tion (fungk'shən) *n.* one of a group of related actions, contributing to a larger action. (*Webster's*)

1	2	3	4	5	6	7	Name of Skill	Example of a situation where that skill is used
							A. Using My Hands	
							1. assembling	as with kits, etc.
							2. constructing	as with carpentry, etc.
							3. or building	
							4. operating tools	as with drills, mixers, etc.
							5. or machinery	as with sewing machines, etc.
							6. or equipment	as with trucks, stationwagons, etc.
							7. showing manual or finger dexterity	as with throwing, sewing, etc.
							8. handling with precision and/or speed	as with an assembly line, etc.
							9. fixing or repairing	as with autos or mending, etc.
							10. other	
							B. Using My Body	
							11. muscular coordination	as in skiing, gymnastics, etc.
							12. being physically active	as in exercising, hiking, etc.
							13. doing outdoor activities	as in camping, etc.
							14. other	
							C. Using Words	
							15. reading	as with books; with understanding
							16. copying	as with manuscripts; skillfully
							17. writing or communicating	as with letters; interestingly
							18. talking or speaking	as on the telephone; interestingly
							19. teaching, training	as in front of groups; with animation
							20. editing	as in improving a child's sentences in an essay, etc.
							21. memory for words	as in remembering people's names, book titles, etc.
							22. other	

169

When you have completed the grid,
you may cut out these four pages
and place them side by side
to see the total pattern.

1	2	3	4	5	6	7	Name of Skill	Example of a situation where that skill is used
							D. Using My Senses (Eyes, Ears, Nose, Taste or Touch)	
							23. observing, surveying	as in watching something with the eyes, etc.
							24. examining or inspecting	as in looking at a child's bumps, etc.
							25. diagnosing, determining	as in deciding if food is cooked yet
							26. showing attention to detail	as in shop, in sewing, etc.
							27. other	
							E. Using Numbers	
							28. taking inventory	as in the pantry, shop, etc.
							29. counting	as in a classroom, bureau drawers
							30. calculating, computing	as in a checkbook, arithmetic
							31. keeping financial records, bookkeeping	as with a budget, etc.
							32. managing money	as in a checking account, bank, store, etc.
							33. developing a budget	as for a family, etc.
							34. number memory	as with telephone numbers, etc.
							35. rapid manipulation of numbers	as with doing arithmetic in the head
							36. other	
							F. Using Intuition	
							37. showing foresight	as in planning ahead, predicting consequences, etc.
							38. quickly sizing up a person or situation accurately	as in everything, rather than just one or two details about them, etc.
							39. having insight	as to why people act the way they do, etc.
							40. acting on gut reactions	as in making decisions, deciding to trust someone, etc.
							41. ability to visualize third-dimension	as in drawings, models, blueprints, memory for faces, etc.
							42. other	
							G. Using Analytical Thinking or Logic	
							43. researching, information gathering	as in finding out where a particular street is in a strange city
							44. analyzing, dissecting	as with the ingredients in a recipe, material, etc.
							45. organizing, classifying	as with laundry, etc.
							46. problem-solving	as with figuring out how to get to a place, etc.
							47. separating important from unimportant	as with complaints, or cleaning the attic, etc.
							48. diagnosing	as in cause and effect relations, tracing problems to their sources
							49. systematizing, putting things in order	as in laying out tools or utensils in the order you will be using them
							continued next page	

171

When you have completed the grid,
you may cut out these four pages
and place them side by side
to see the total pattern.

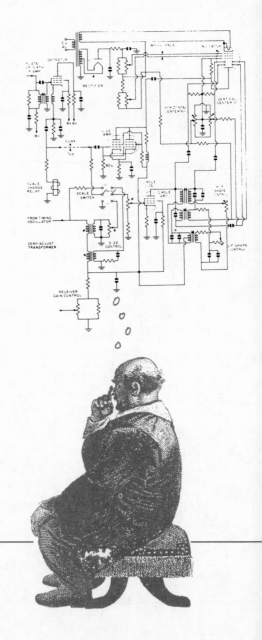

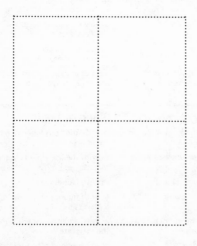

1	2	3	4	5	6	7	Name of Skill	Example of a situation where that skill is used
							50. comparing, perceiving similarities	as with different brands in the supermarket, etc.
							51. testing, screening	as with cooking, deciding what to wear, etc.
							52. reviewing, evaluating	as in looking at something you made, to see how you could have made it better, faster, etc.
							53. other	

H. Using Originality or Creativity

1	2	3	4	5	6	7	Name of Skill	Example of a situation where that skill is used
							54. imaginative, imagining	as in figuring out new ways to do things, or making up stories, etc.
							55. inventing, creating	as with processes, products, figures, words, etc.
							56. designing, developing	as with new recipes, new gadgets
							57. improvising, experiments	as in camping, when you've left some of the equipment home, etc.
							58. adapting, improving	as with something that doesn't work quite right, etc.
							59. other	

I. Using Helpfulness

1	2	3	4	5	6	7	Name of Skill	Example of a situation where that skill is used
							60. helping, being of service	as when someone is in need, etc.
							61. showing sensitivity to others' feelings	as in a heated discussion, argument
							62. listening	
							63. developing rapport	as with someone who is initially a stranger, etc.
							64. conveying warmth, caring	as with someone who is upset, ill
							65. understanding	as when someone tells how they feel, etc.
							66. drawing out people	as when someone is reluctant to talk, share
							67. offering support	as when someone is facing a difficulty alone, etc.
							68. demonstrating empathy	as in weeping with those who weep
							69. representing others' wishes accurately	as when one parent tells the other what a child of theirs wants, etc.
							70. motivating	as in getting people past hangups, and into action, etc.
							71. sharing credit, appreciation	as when working in teams, etc.
							72. raising others' self-esteem	as when you make someone feel better, less guilty, etc.
							73. healing, curing	as with physical, emotional and spiritual ailments, etc.
							74. counseling, guiding	as when someone doesn't know what to do, etc.
							75. other	

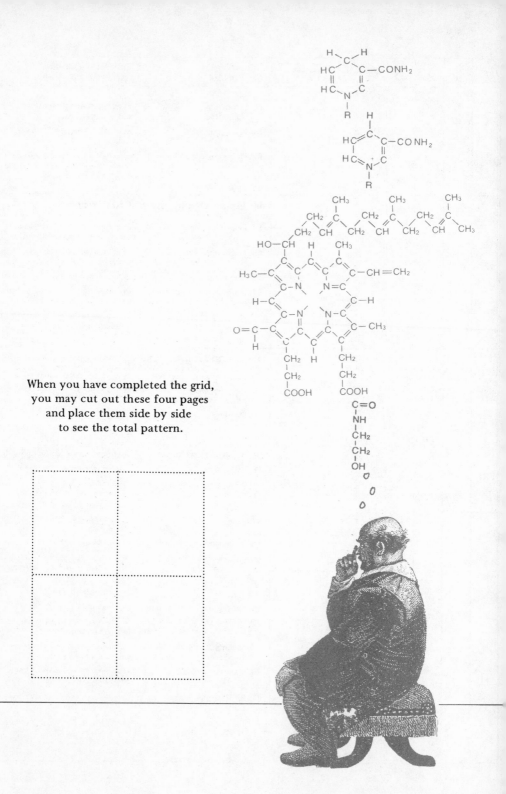

When you have completed the grid,
you may cut out these four pages
and place them side by side
to see the total pattern.

1	2	3	4	5	6	7	Name of Skill	Example of a situation where that skill is used
							J. Using Artistic Abilities	
							76. composing music	
							77. playing (a) musical instrument(s), singing	
							78. fashioning or shaping things, materials	as in handicrafts, sculpturing, etc.
							79. dealing creatively with symbols or images	as in stained glass, jewelry, etc.
							80. dealing creatively with spaces, shapes or faces	as in photography, art, architectural design, etc.
							81. dealing creatively with colors	as in painting, decorating, making clothes, etc.
							82. conveying feelings and thoughts through body, face and/or voice tone	as in acting, public speaking, teaching, dancing, etc.
							83. conveying feelings and thoughts through drawing, paintings, etc.	as in art, etc.
							84. using words on a very high level	as in poetry, playwriting, novels
							85. other	
							K. Using Leadership, Being Up Front	
							86. beginning new tasks, ideas, projects	as in starting a group, initiating a clothing drive, etc.
							87. taking first move in relationships	as with stranger on bus, plane, train, etc.
							88. organizing	as with a Scout troop, a team, a game at a picnic, etc.
							89. leading, directing others	as with a field trip, cheerleading
							90. promoting change	as in a family, community, organization, etc.
							91. making decisions	as in places where decisions affect others, etc.
							92. taking risks	as in sticking up for someone in a fight, etc.
							93. getting up before a group, performing	as in demonstrating a product, lecturing, making people laugh, entertaining, public speaking
							94. selling, promoting, negotiating, persuading	as with a product, idea, materials, in a garage sale, argument, recruiting, changing someone's mind
							95. other	
							L. Using Follow-Through	
							96. using what others have developed	as in working with a kit, etc.
							97. following through on plans, instructions	as in picking up children on schedule
							98. attending to details	as with embroidering a design on a shirt, etc.
							99. classifying, recording, filing, retrieving	as with data, materials, letters, ideas, information, etc.
							100. other	

When you have completed the grid,
you may cut out these four pages
and place them side by side
to see the total pattern.

When you're done with this INVENTORY OF THE SKILLS YOU ALREADY HAVE, you've got your 'List B'. The next step, obviously, is to subtract it from your SHOPPING LIST OF SKILLS on pages 158—161. Here's how you can go about doing that:

1. Tear out pages 169 to 176 (the ones with the actual inventory on them). Lay them out on a table, side by side. This is your *List B.*

2. *Now, turn back in this book to YOUR SHOPPING LIST OF SKILLS. This is your List A. Go down A, and each time you come to a skill that you checked off as desirable, look at your List B to see what your inventory turned up about it. On List B, you'll find one of these three situations:*

● *First Possibility: you have 'colored in' absolutely No squares opposite the skill in question. In this case, of course, your list A checkmark gets left as it is.*

● *Second Possibility: you have colored in absolutely most of the squares (from 5 to 7 in number) on your List B, opposite the skill in question. In other words, this is a skill that you have, and that you have used in almost every situation represented by the seven achievements or roles that you chose. On List A, cross off the checkmark opposite the skill in question—unless your intuition tells you you'd still like more training in that skill, and the checkmark is under the "Polish Up" column. You obviously have this skill, and—intuition aside—there's no need to take useless further education courses, seminars or workshops simply to acquire this skill that you already have.*

● *Third Possibility: you have colored in a few of the squares (from 1 to 4 in number) on your List B, opposite the skill in question, and it's a real question in your mind as to whether this means you actually have the skill or not. Well, look at your List A. Is the checkmark in the first column, under "Pick Up This Skill From Scratch"? If so, maybe—just maybe— you want to move the checkmark over to the second column. Or maybe all you wanted to do with this skill was just pick up a smattering of it, in which case your inventory may tell you that's exactly what you've already done; in that case, cross off the checkmark. Mission Accomplished. On the other hand, is the checkmark on List A standing there in the second column, under "Polish Up?" In that case, leave it alone—unless, again, your intuition tells you that you possess the skill alot more than even your List B would indicate.*

3. Continue down List A. Each time you come to a skill you've checked off on List A, go look to see what List B has to say about that. Be prepared, incidentally, for the situation where you have skills checked off (or 'colored on') List B, but there's no checkmark on A. Unless this uncovers an error you made on A (Oops, I meant to check that one), ignore this. You're bound to have more skills already in your possession than you want or plan to use in some future or present job. This is particularly true, the older you are. Your List B is liable to get overwhelmingly impressive—even to You.

Well, now, when this whole exercise is done, you have List A minus List B, and NOW you know what kind of skills you want to get some help with in your further education—be it courses, seminars, or weekend workshops. Be you sixty or sixteen.

Before we close this subject of the relationship between Skills and Education, let us note that there is another way you could prepare List A,— you know, Your Shopping List. You could make a list of the *roles* that you have, or want to have, in life. Since some of you may prefer this path toward the subject of Skills and Education, we will take a brief look at it.

Your Roles—Skills and Education

> role *n.* a socially expected behavior pattern usually determined
>   by an individual's status in a particular society; a part played
>   by someone, such as a singer or actor. (*WEBSTER'S*)

There are many ways of analyzing your total life. One of them is to think of the different "parts" or "roles" that you play, during a typical week, month, or year—or at different times in your life. Here are some possibilities; if you are interested in your roles, check off the ones that you think presently apply to you, or that—at the very least—you want to be prepared for, when they come:

ROLES

- ☐ 1. unique individual
- ☐ 2. member of a family
- ☐ 3. son/daughter
- ☐ 4. mother/father
- ☐ 5. husband/wife
- ☐ 6. homemaker
- ☐ 7. cook
- ☐ 8. consumer—purchaser
- ☐ 9. diner
- ☐ 10. sleeper
- ☐ 11. dresser
- ☐ 12. learner—student
- ☐ 13. teacher—advice-giver
- ☐ 14. job-hunter
- ☐ 15. job-holder—worker
- ☐ 16. volunteer (worker)
- ☐ 17. automobile driver
- ☐ 18. member of a community
- ☐ 19. friend
- ☐ 20. conversationalist
- ☐ 21. listener
- ☐ 22. writer, letter-writer
- ☐ 23. reader
- ☐ 24. customer—patron—client
- ☐ 25. gardener
- ☐ 26. raconteur
- ☐ 27. repairer, builder
- ☐ 28. decision-maker
- ☐ 29. believer—worshiper
- ☐ 30. sage—philosopher
- ☐ 31. ethical person
- ☐ 32. citizen
- ☐ 33. voter
- ☐ 34. others:

Once you are done with this list, you want to take each of your roles (present, or anticipated) and ask yourself: what skills are needed, in order to do this role well? Here beware, however: you do not want to lump all skills together, as some books or tests or educators do. Separate them, into the three types in a general sort of way, at least—without being rigid about it. Here are some examples of how you might go about it:

Your Role as a—	FUNCTIONAL SKILLS NEEDED	WORK-CONTENT SKILLS NEEDED	SELF-MANAGEMENT SKILLS NEEDED
● *Unique individual with self-identity*	Self-analyzing Having insight Conveying warmth and caring Expressiveness Goal-setting Evaluating	Knowledge of various therapies and procedures for preserving self-identity amidst external and internal pressures	Self-management Self-pacing Self-routing Impulse control
● *Consumer purchaser*	Budgeting, money management Planning Executing Computing Evaluating	Knowledge of how to maintain a checking account Ability to transact business and deal responsibly with our credit system Knowledge of how to budget time and money Ability to evaluate claims of advertisers	Impulse control—responding appropriately to emergencies Care of property Dress Assertiveness appropriate to the situation
● *Learner —student*	Reading Writing Computing Ability to articulate the questions that are on your mind Observing, surveying Diagnosing Determining Researching Information-gathering Analyzing Organizing Evaluating Generalizing, extrapolating; Applying.	Knowledge of resources Familiarity with libraries, card catalogs, etc. Knowledge of how to interview for information. Familiarity with concept of contacts and contact networks Knowledge of the steps in systematic research	Being in touch with your own curiosities, and the things that puzzle you Desire to seek answers Self-discipline, determination, stick-to-it-iveness

Your Role as a—	FUNCTIONAL SKILLS NEEDED	WORK-CONTENT SKILLS NEEDED	SELF-MANAGEMENT SKILLS NEEDED
● *Automobile driver*	Visual acuity Manual dexterity Eye-hand-foot coordination Motor coordination	Knowledge of how to drive a car safely. Defensive driving techniques. How to deal with emergencies. How to winterize, maintain & repair a car, or the resources which can help with these tasks. How to buy a new or used car. How to analyze auto expense and depreciation.	Alertness Sensitivity Consideration
● *Friend*	Careful listening Appreciating Empathizing Showing consideration. Collaborating, sharing Helping Supporting Giving feedback	Knowledge of the proper use of language in communicating courtesy, empathy, and/or appreciation. Knowledge of body language, knowledge of common elements and feelings in all human experience. Knowledge of right and wrong, fair and unfair.	Being in touch with your own feelings. Instinctively moving toward, rather than away from, others. Having firm and generous values. Having a sense of perspective and a sense of humor. Consideration of others (impulse control and impulse expression)
● *Citizen*	Caring, participating Making thoughtful decisions Acting upon your convictions Evaluating Risk-taking Having high sense of accountability	Knowledge of: community issues and needs; the basic structure and function of local, county, state and federal government; people's legal rights; how to make appropriate use of public agencies; how to evaluate rival claims and how to vote	Having a balanced attitude toward those in authority Desire to be involved

YOUR OWN CHART:

With these examples in mind, you can see how to make up, and fill out, your own chart. List the roles you checked off on page 179, in the left hand column. Then, put down any thoughts

My Role-Skill Chart

My Roles ↓	Functional Skills Needed	Work Content Skills Needed	Self Management Skills Needed
Unique Individual			
Daughter			
1, 1: 1 o			

you have about the three types of skills that are needed for each of those roles, in the other three columns. One very helpful way to get at this is to enlist others—fellow-students, friends, family—and brainstorm all of this with them.

If you want to give even more time to it, turn this into a project. Go interview people who are either Splendid Examples of those roles, or who teach people those roles; e.g., for "learner" interview someone who is a very good student or else interview a teacher and ask his or her opinion as to the skills a good student needs. For "Automobile driver", interview a driving-instructor. For "unique individual", interview someone who teaches seminars in self-development. And so on. You'll be surprised at what you learn. Just remember that you may have to "sift" and "classify" the information after they give it to you. Don't expect them to know the distinction between the three kinds of skills, but do listen to everything they say and ask intelligent questions like:

(For getting at Self-Management Skills) "What kinds of personal characteristics do you notice in people who are very good at this (role)?"

(For getting at Work-Content Skills) "What sorts of special knowledges does a person need to have in order to do this (role) well?"

(For getting at Functional Skills) "What kinds of actions does a person need to be good at, in order to do this (role) well?"

When you're all done (by whatever method: self-examination, brainstorming, or interviewing) filling in your Role-Skill Chart, you will have the equivalent of a 'List A', such as we saw on pages 158-161. You will still need to subtract from this your List B, i.e., the Inventory of Your Present Skills, as we saw on pages 163-165, before you will be able to decide what skills you want to seek further education regarding. If there are just too many skills, and you don't know which skills (or which Role) to tackle first, use the Prioritizing Exercise in Appendix A of this book.

What you have done, in sum, is so eminently sensible. You have listed the skills you want to have in order to help you do your present job, or your future career, or your various roles in life, better. You have subtracted from that list those skills which you already perceive yourself to have. And you are left with a list of those skills that you want to pick up, or polish up, in your futher education. That is the point at which to turn to a high school counselor, or a college counselor, or a community college advisor, to ask them what courses they think will help you sharpen up, or pick up, the skills that are on your final list. Just remember, there is a whole world out there that doesn't know much about skill-identification. Just by reading this chapter, you know more about this than probably 95% of the people you're going to meet. So, don't be surprised if the people you turn to for advice look at you rather blankly at first. *You* may have a chance to educate *them*, before they will be ready to go on and give some helpful counsel to you.

Anyway, you remember where we began with all this: "The Ninth 'Possible Reason' for Taking Further Education: 'I want to pick up/polish up the required skills that I need for a) a particular field or line of work, b) a particular job (present, or contemplated) c) a particular role that I have, or want to have, in life.' " If this is your reason (or one of your reasons) for wanting further education, you now possess a carefully laid out method for getting at this, which will save you a lot of time over the 'hit and miss' method that most of us otherwise might use.[14]

Incidentally, before leaving this ninth purpose, inasmuch as this is our 'work-related' one, let me mention that there are a number of people who choose Further Education not only to pick up (or polish up) their skills, but also in order that they may acquire Proof That They Have Those Skills. This is called "credentialing", and normally takes the form of a Bachelor's Degree, or a Master's, or a Doctorate. Since I have two or three of these myself, I'm not about to knock the idea. But I would like to utter a few words of caution:

(1) Don't assume you MUST have certification, or a degree in order to get a particular kind of job unless and until your own extensive research has convinced you that this is true. Go talk to people who are already in that line of work, and ask them if it is

      a) always absolutely always necessary to have a degree or a credential in order to do this sort of work; OR

      b) necessary most of the time; OR

      c) helpful but not necessary.

(2) Don't assume that IF you get the degree or the credentialing, you will automatically find that a job goes with it. Colleges turn out degreed people without ANY correlation between the number of diplomas on the one hand, and the number of vacancies 'Out There', on the other. A recent cartoon showed a restaurant in which the waiter was saying to the people he was waiting on, "Of course I added the bill up quickly—I'm a mathematics professor."

(3) Don't assume that you have to go the whole route on a college campus in order to get the degree you want. You may be able to gain credit for 'life experiences' or for the work experiences that you have already had, and thus acquire substantial credit toward your degree—shortening the time you need to 'finish off' the degree or the credential. MUST READING for you is the book entitled, *National Directory of External Degree Programs,* by Alfred Munzert, Ph.D. (1976). If your library or bookstore doesn't have it locally, write directly to the publisher: Hawthorn Books, Inc., 260 Madison Avenue, New York, N.Y. 10016 and order it. (It's $4.95 paper in the U.S.A.; $5.75 in Canada.) It will give you all the details on who, what, where and how.

(4) If you do decide to go for a degree, don't have your eyes so fixed upon that goal, that you pay no attention to what you're doing along the way. Even if you are choosing the

courses you choose because the degree requires them, you can still set your own goals within each course, as we have been suggesting throughout this section. That way, you'll be managing your courses, instead of your courses managing you.

(5) If you decide not to seek a degree, remember that this does not make you inferior to those who have a degree. You possess other qualities that make you infinitely valuable, and (sometimes) more helpful in whatever place you decide to

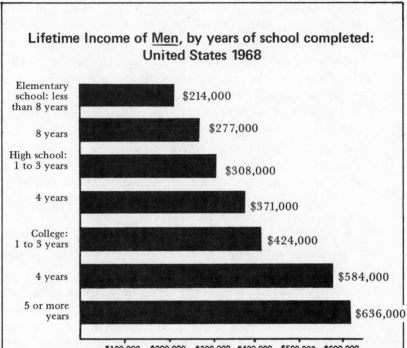

Lifetime Income of <u>Men</u>, by years of school completed: United States 1968

Elementary school: less than 8 years	$214,000
8 years	$277,000
High school: 1 to 3 years	$308,000
4 years	$371,000
College: 1 to 3 years	$424,000
4 years	$584,000
5 or more years	$636,000

$100,000 $200,000 $300,000 $400,000 $500,000 $600,000

We used to see a lot of charts like this, but we don't see them very often any more. First of all, it cries out for a companion chart for Women. And *that* would be depressing. Secondly, education is having a lessening impact on lifetime earnings. A study recently reported by the National Institute of Education showed that in 60% of the cases, level of income could not be correlated with the amount of education.

work. Sometime ago, there was a letter to the editor, in one of the newspapers I read, which summed this up in a particularly eloquent way. The writer reported how, at the age of 21, he had bought himself a diploma in psychology. Then he added:

"I worked with that fake degree for 12 years, mainly in homes for emotionally disturbed and delinquent children. Generally, I worked in government run institutions. My credentials were never questioned. And the children in those institutions were delivered to far worse persons than I. After 12 years of working in institutions for emotionally disturbed children, it is my firm conviction that the children who recover do so in spite of, rather than because of, the 'highly competent staff.' It is an in joke in this field that the staff of those homes are usually more disturbed than the children. A person who laughs readily, gets along well with people, likes animals, appreciates art, and has generous but firm notions of what is right and wrong is a lot more competent to deal with disturbed children . . . In my 12 years, . . . not once did a psychiatrist or psychologist or anyone else talk about setting a good example of cheerful, considerate, fair, industrious behavior, about being the sort of decent person after which a child would want to pattern himself or herself. Such persons are important, not the furnishings or the degrees."

If from your education, you learn to be these things, the fact that you do not have a degree will not diminish your valuableness in any way. The only thing it will do (in this dim-witted world of ours) is make it more difficult for you *to get hired initially.* You will, consequently, have to pay more attention to your job-hunting strategies, and make sure that yours is carefully planned and carefully executed. What that means, we shall see in our next chapter.

We turn now to the tenth (and last) purpose of education:

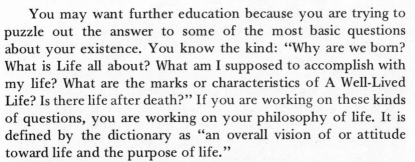

"I want to develop
my philosophy of life." □ 10

The
tenth
'possible
reason'
for
taking
further
education

You may want further education because you are trying to puzzle out the answer to some of the most basic questions about your existence. You know the kind: "Why are we born? What is Life all about? What am I supposed to accomplish with my life? What are the marks or characteristics of A Well-Lived Life? Is there life after death?" If you are working on these kinds of questions, you are working on your philosophy of life. It is defined by the dictionary as "an overall vision of or attitude toward life and the purpose of life."

You may think of this as a search for answers to the kinds of questions posed above. Or you may think of it in another way: as somewhat akin to humor. Let us look at two examples of humor, which appeared in Herb Caen's column in *The San Francisco Chronicle*. Prior to the presidential elections of 1976, then-President Ford appeared twice in California, during both of which times an attempt was made on his life. Shortly thereafter, a notice appeared in Mr. Caen's column: "President Ford today conceded California."

Another time, the heiress-fugitive Patricia Hearst was finally arrested—after a long search for her—in the city of San Francisco. It turned out she had been in the city for a number of days prior to her arrest. Following the arrest, Mr. Caen quoted a man as saying: "Isn't that just like today's kids? In town for two weeks, and she doesn't even phone her parents."

Now, what is the essence of the humor in both cases? *They take an event (or events) and put it in a larger context or perspective.* The event of attempts on the President's life is put into the larger context of the whole national election. The event of Patricia Hearst's hiding is put in the larger context of the whole "youth-culture."

A philosophy of life is akin to humor in precisely this aspect: *it attempts to establish a Larger Context in which the daily events of your life may be viewed and thus given perspective.* This may, or may not, sometimes lend humor to those daily events. But it always gives them perspective, as to their importance, and relationship to other things.

The kinds of further education which can help you formulate your philosophy of life more clearly are obvious:

- All those courses which deal with the learnings, lessons and values of the past, viz., *the classics, literature, history, civilization* and the like.
- All those courses which deal with *the history of values, philosophy or religion.*

But there are others. In order to be clear as to what they are, we need to be clear as to what the elements of a philosophy of life are. In workshops conducted by the National Career Development Project, these were some of the elements that were identified. You might check off the ones you especially want help with:

Elements In A Philosophy of Life

MY VIEW OF, OR BELIEFS ABOUT:

1. ☐ reality—   what is it, what's included, how do I apprehend it?
2. ☐ the universe— how it was made, by what or whom, and why
3. ☐ the earth—   its place in the cosmos, why there is life on earth, what it is meant to do or be
4. ☐ nature—   how it functions, what the relationship of its parts are to each other, including humanity, what its purposes are
5. ☐ reverence for life—
                      what it means, what it includes, how I act it out
6. ☐ life—   what it is, how it works, what makes it work better
7. ☐ time—   my beliefs about it, how it controls people, how it frees people, how I relate to the past, to the present, and to the future

8. ☐ concept of womankind/mankind—

who are we in the universal scheme of things, what are we at our worst, what are we at our best, what helps us to be at our best, i.e., most humane?

9. ☐ God—

whether there is One, what He/She/It/They/is/are like, relationship to us, difference this makes in our lives?

10. ☐ death—

its nature, its purpose, how we can best embrace it, is there life after it?

11. ☐ values—

what am I committed to? what would I be willing to die for? what am I willing to live joyously or enthusiastically for? what keeps me from committing suicide? what is the purpose of life? what is freedom? what is security? what is Peace of Mind, and how do we find it? what is Power? what comprises happiness for me? what comprises love? how should people behave toward each other? what kinds of beauty do I need in my life? what degree of truth do I need in my life? what degree of ethicalness or integrity do I need in my life? how do I think goodness is rewarded? how do I think evil gets its due? what is my hierarchy of values?

12. ☐ symbols—

what do I think about symbols, and their importance? which ones are the most important to me? in marriage? in love? in friendship? in the world?

13. ☐ self-awareness—who am I? what makes me different from other people? what do I share in common with other people? what are my strengths? what are my weaknesses? what is my value and worth as a unique individual? what am I looking for? how do I deal with my limitations? how do I deal with my strengths? how do I want

people to remember me? where do I start *acting?* what do I love the most? what do I fear the most? what do I worry about the most? what would I like most to be? what would I like most to do? what makes me feel good about myself? what do I want to be remembered for, after I die?

14.   □ awareness of others—

who have been, or who are, Significant People in my life, and how have they affected me? why are they significant for me? where have I come from—culture, history, family, religious or ethnic roots? who do I copy, emulate, follow, or want to be like? who am I instinctively drawn to? who am I instinctively repelled by? what sorts of relationships do I seek to establish? how do I relate to people? how close to others do I want to be? who remembers me, and how do I think they remember me? am I an isolationist, and if so, how? what do I hide from? how do I reconcile my individuality with the rights and needs of others? how do I deal with others' strengths? with others' weaknesses? what is my attitude toward the family? my family? when I am committed to others, how do I act out that commitment? how do I deal with others' values or ethics if they differ from mine? where do I stop compromising? where is my personal cut-off line? what do I expect of others? what do I buy into? what do I resist? what is the relationship between self and society? what is giving, and what is receiving?

15.   □ things—

how do I relate to things? to food? to housing? to clothes? to other possessions? to car? to TV? what things are

essential to my life? how close to things
do I want to be? which things? how do I
feel about money? how do I feel about
civilization? how simply do I want to
live? or how complexly? what kind of
life-style do I believe is best? how do I
feel about progress? change? growth?

16. ☐ other realms and beings—
what other kinds of reality and life do I
think there are in the universe, besides
life on earth? how do we or can we relate
to that, or to them? what kinds of activities in my own life, religious, psychic,
meditative or other, do I feel their existence calls for?

Looking at this list, you may feel that what we have here is not
so much a philosophy of life—which we could write up, and
summarize right now—as a list of the eternal questions which we
as individuals never quite resolve, and have to keep working on
as long as we live. Well, first of all these elements as listed here
are the sum total of *two hundred* people's opinions, so it *is* a
more comprehensive list than any one individual might draw up.
But, secondly, you *do* keep working out your philosophy of life
for as long as you live, and any statement that you draw up
along the way may be like one single frame from a motion
picture of a moving gazelle.

So, anyway, whatever elements you checked should give
you some clue as to where to start, in terms of Kind Of Courses,
and the like. If you checked a number of things, and you don't
know which one you want to begin with, then (you guessed it)
use the prioritizing device in Appendix A of this book, to put
the elements in some order of priority, first.

THE TEN PURPOSES OF EDUCATION:

Well, there you have it. Whether you are eighteen or eighty,
whether you are thinking just about some weekend workshops,
or of going to college, this list—and explanation—of the ten
purposes of education should help you to define exactly *why*

you want this further education. If you haven't been filling out the Checklist on page 116 as you went along, through the ten, then now would be a good time to go back and do that. Use the prioritizing exercise in Appendix (well, you know by now). Put the reasons that grab *You* in order of priority, and you're ready to seek that education with some real sense of Mission and Meaning. Which will put you way ahead of those who just go to school without any sense of purpose or goals—playing smorgasbord, and frittering away the four years or the semester or the weekend.

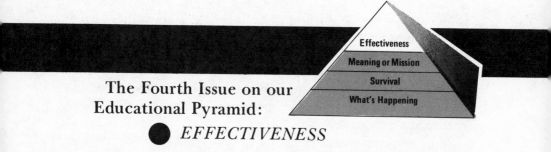

The Fourth Issue on our Educational Pyramid:
⬤ *EFFECTIVENESS*

Each time you choose some further formal education—be it college or a weekend seminar—you are faced with the three issues we have been looking at (at length): What's Happening, Survival, and Meaning or Mission. And this fourth one: Effectiveness. In common jargon, this is "How am I doing?"

Effectiveness is so frequently confused with Evaluation, that it is important—at the outset—to mark the differences between these two concepts. So here is a brief Table, that may help:

Effectiveness Vs. Evaluation

1. Is an issue or question posed by you, regarding your life or activities: — "How well am I doing?"	1. Is an issue or question posed by others regarding your life or activities, "How well is he or she doing?"
2. Self-directed. You choose what, how and when.	2. Other-directed. It is done by others *for* you (or, as is often the case, *to* you).
3. It is done at the times that meet your needs.	3. It is done at times that others decree, or else it is done in season and out of season, whether you want and need it or not.
4. The things you want to measure are chosen by you, from within you. You measure yourself by your self-chosen standards or criteria.	4. The criteria for evaluation are chosen from Out There— whether you are compared with other people (e.g., other students) or some norm, model or standard.
5. Regardless of whether you overestimate or underestimate, the measurement you take of your own effectiveness does end up telling you about you.	5. The orientation, filters or biases of The Evaluator(s) always affect the design of their evaluation of you, leaving open the question of how accurately it reflects You. In the end, the evaluation may tell more about the evaluators than it does about you.
6. It keeps you focussed on the fourth level: Effectiveness (on our pyramid of issues).	6. Because evaluation by others is so commonly connected with decisions (to flunk, or pass; to promote, or fire) it frequently concentrates your attention on the second level of our pyramid: Survival, instead of on the fourth level.

The above comparisons are generalizations, to be sure. Moreover, the comparisons fade when the word "evaluation" is used in certain phrases (like: self-evaluation), because then it means virtually the same thing as our first column, labeled "Effectiveness" above. Nonetheless, I think the comparisons are helpful and important, because they make it very clear that even in the absence of any formal evaluation by others, *you* still need to wrestle with this whole issue of Effectiveness. A weekend seminar that you attend, for example, which has no built-in evaluation (i.e., no grades or certificates) still has those inevitable questions surrounding it: "Was this seminar effective in giving me what I was looking for?" And: "Was I effective in milking this seminar for everything that it was worth?"

The comparisons also make it very clear that even where there is formal evaluation (i.e., grades, or marks are given), you still need to *supplement it* with your own program for getting at the issue of Effectiveness. I would like to suggest three tests for use in such a program.

Effectiveness Test No. 1

Did the seminar, workshop, course or
instruction that I just took, fulfill the objectives
or goals that I defined before I took it?

Your ability to wrestle with the issue of Effectiveness, as here presented, is directly proportional to the degree to which you wrestled with the earlier issue of Mission or Meaning. If you are going to make judgments about a particular educational experience that you have had, you can—of course—just ask yourself, "Well, how was it?" But for anything more definitive than that, you have to have certain criteria. And these are derived from the goals or objectives that you set for your education in the previous section. If you know *why* you decided to take this seminar, workshop, course or instruction, and *what* you were looking for, then — and only then — can you evaluate the experience, as to its Effectiveness. It works out like this:

I said *I wanted* *to take* *this course* *or workshop* *or seminar* *because* ↓	**My Own View** **of the Effectiveness** **of this** **Experience**	*I will* *check* *here if I* *feel it did* *accomplish* *that* *goal* ↓

☐ 1. I want to enlarge my mental, emotional and/or spiritual horizons. ☐

☐ 2. I want to learn how to learn, and how to think clearly. ☐

☐ 3. I want to learn the virtues and the limits of knowledge; what
we can know and not know. ☐

☐ 4. I want to learn reading, or writing, or arithmetic. ☐

☐ 5. I want to develop myself in relationship to others. ☐

☐ 6. I want to learn how to cope with change and with constancy—
especially when there is too much or too little of either. ☐

   7. I want to find further 'food' for

☐   a. my mind, and/or ☐

☐   b. my heart, and/or ☐

☐   c. my will ☐

☐ 8. I want to have a chance to meet people (with similar interests). ☐

   9. I want to pick up / polish up the required skills that I need for:

☐   a. a particular field or line of work in which I need accreditation. ☐

☐   b. a particular job (present, or contemplated) ☐

☐   c. a particular role that I have, or want to have in life. ☐

☐ 10. I want to develop my philosophy of life. ☐

If any of the above Goals or Objectives were only partially realized, this is What I Still Need To Get From Somewhere

_____

_____

_____

_____

You don't, of course, have to be this systematic or formal about it. You can just raise some questions in your head, if you want. Indeed, it must be emphasized that Effectiveness is a continuous issue or question, which you can raise for yourself *at any time you choose* along the way—unlike Evaluation by Others, which is traditionally done At The End of a particular period, or At The Conclusion of a course (e.g., a report-card). Because the issue of Effectiveness can be raised by you all along the way, you can make "a mid-course correction"—as they say (shades of flying). For example, if you feel a particular course is not giving you what you had hoped for, you can sit down and talk with the instructor in the middle of the course, while there is still time to do something about it—either in class, or in private study.

Should this book fall, by accident, into the hands of someone who is an instructor or teacher, let me point out that there are two strategies which you can adopt that will facilitate your students dealing with the issue of Effectiveness. First of all, you can have the students discuss what they want to get out of the whole experience, right at the beginning of your seminar, workshop, or course. You can divide them into small-groups (of six to eight students each) and let them help each other draw up a written statement, for himself or herself, as to what each wants to get out of the course. If such statements then are shared with

TEACHING TALENT REGRESSES

Christopher Michael Clark, researcher, has found that learning to teach is harder than learning to learn. Clark experimented with experienced teachers on how their teaching methods improve as time progresses, reports *Education Daily*.

He found that teaching techniques usually improve on the second day, but fail to further improve on succeeding days. In some cases, the teaching method may even deteriorate.

Clark theorized either the teacher doesn't know how to react to feedback from the students or the teacher needs more background information on student abilities.

The study *The Effects of Teacher Practice on Student Learning and Attitudes in Small Group Instruction*, Technical Report No. 47, is available from the Stanford Center for Research and Development in Teaching, School of Education, Stanford University, Stanford, Calif., 94305.

the instructor, namely you, you will have a much better chance of designing a seminar, workshop or course that really meets the needs of your students. Moreover, if any of the goals or objectives drawn up by individual students are unrealistic—given the limited time-frame or your limited expertise—you can say so at the beginning, and not allow unrealistic expectations to flourish and abound. Or you can suggest private study, reading or research, which will get at the things that individual is desirous of learning. Secondly, during your seminar, workshop or course you can use "feedback sheets" at regular intervals, asking every student to tell you what's going right for them, in the course, and what's going wrong for them—*while there is still time for you to make changes or* adaptations *that will be helpful,* and will make the educational experience more Effective *for those students.* (Incidentally, if this book didn't just fall into your hands, but some student slipped it under your door with a book-mark inserted in the book at this point, maybe somebody's trying to tell you something?)

Here's a form of feedback-sheet, which we have found is very popular with students:

FEEDBACK SHEET
FOR THE INSTRUCTOR OR TEACHER

---

1. The tool/idea/insight which I found most helpful ☐ so far
   was: ☐ today
   ☐ this week

2. The thing which still puzzles me or that I still want us to deal with is:

3. An idea/tool that I have discovered, which I think might help the rest of the class, is:

4. My overall impression of this course/seminar/workshop thus far is:

5. In terms of my own goals for this course/seminar/workshop, my feeling so far is:

6. Any other comments:

Effectiveness Test No. 2

Did the seminar, workshop, course or
instruction that I just took, help me toward
a lifestyle of continuous action/reflection?

Imagine, if you will, two women sitting in a particular class, or course. When that course is finished, the first woman says, "Well, I certainly learned a lot — in terms of my own goals or objectives. I'm very glad I was here." And that is the end of The Learning Period in her life, until the next time that she takes a class or course — maybe next semester, maybe five or ten years from now. The second woman, when the course is finished, also says, "Well, I certainly learned a lot — in terms of my own goals or objectives." But then she adds, "I've learned how to turn my whole life into a classroom, and how I can learn from every

day's experiences. I've learned how to learn continuously." So, the class or course is just the beginning of The Learning Period in her life. Of these two women, which one do you think has more effectively profited from that class or course? Well, naturally, the second one.

The same truth applies, of course, to your life and mine. Our education in formal classroom or workshop is patently most effective when it issues into daily learning from our everyday life. The way for this to happen is that we contract a hunger and thirst to *build in* to everyday's schedule both Time for Action and Time for Reflection. Because every day has lots of activity in it anyway, this actually means in practice trying to find daily Time for Reflection. Such reflection is a form of meditation, but a very particular form. It is reflection *upon* the day's activity. It is a Playing Back in the mind of all the experiences of the day, in order to examine them for their teachings. It is a questioning of those activities and experiences; either "What did I learn from each of these?" or "What did I learn from all of this, today?"

There are many ways in which this questioning can be phrased. It can be phrased in terms of your philosophy of life, or your chief values. Suppose, for example, you see life as a pursuit of either Truth, or Beauty, or Perfection. You might then look at each experience during a particular day, to ask: What did this teach me about Beauty? What did this teach me about Truth? What did this teach me about Perfection? Alternatively, the questioning during your Time of Reflection can be phrased in terms of subjects which you recently studied. Suppose you recently took a seminar on human relations. You might then examine each day by asking: "What did I learn about human relations today?" Similar questions can be framed out of any other subject you may have studied, so that—in truth—each day thereafter continues to teach you about the subject you *began* studying in class. The mark of how effective that class was, for you, lies precisely in the fact that the class was The Beginning of your study and understanding of that subject, rather than The End—as is true for altogether too many students.

This last is the product and consequence of our having taken a Model of what Man and Woman were able to be, and dividing it into two. We talk (you were just doing it over breakfast this morning, right?) about Active Man versus Contemplative or Meditative Man. Or we talk about Active Woman versus Thoughtful (i.e., Thoughtfilled) Woman. And we hold that some people are Active. Period. And others are Contemplative or Thoughtful. Period. The one type devotes all their life to nothing but activity. The other type devotes all their life to nothing but contemplation and thinking. As in a cloister or monastery. Or in a think-tank. Or university.

Most of us—in the United States at least—tend to opt for the activity model. So much so that even when we sit down in a classroom to study, we see that as just another *activity*, rather than as an invitation into an entirely different world—the world of *reflection or contemplation*. In consequence, when the course is ended, we breathe a sigh of relief that this activity is finished, so that we can now go on to another activity. Hence the feeling that the class or course was The End of our learning about that subject.

> Many men go fishing all of their lives without knowing that it is not the fish they are after.
> Henry David Thoreau

Only when we reunite this divided Model, and hold this truth to be self-evident: that Action and Reflection were meant to be united in *each* of us, do we perceive a class or course as A Beginning of learning. And the test of its effectiveness, how much we carry on the learning daily, through both Action and Reflection.

Some of us may find it difficult to reserve the time for reflection, in the midst of our very busy days. But the time can easily be found. We have only to think of the times when we are inevitably by ourselves—driving, waiting for a bus, waiting for a meal to be served, the twilight time before falling asleep, the time while we are doing our morning ablutions, and getting dressed, etc. That time can be well used. Instead of daydreaming, Reflection. Reflection upon our activities and action of the previous twenty-four hours, to see what learnings were there.

If you want to approach this more systematically, and you have a half hour or so that you can find each day for it, *writing down* your thoughts and learnings is a great way to go (Or, if you are artistically-inclined, and words aren't your strong suit, *draw* some of your learnings.) An aid for those who like to write is Ira Progoff's very thorough and helpful book on how to keep an Intensive Journal. (Ira Progoff, *At a Journal Workshop,* 1975, $12.50, from your local library, bookstore, or Dialogue House Library, 45 West Tenth Street, New York, N.Y. 10011.) In sum, use whatever means helps *you* toward a lifestyle of continuous action/reflection.

Effectiveness Test No. 3

**Am I balancing my educational experiences
with time also for the world of Work and for
the world of Play or Leisure?**

You're eighteen. Or twenty-four. Or thirty-seven. Or fifty-two. Or sixty-five. Or seventy-eight. You're taking some form of further formal education. And that's just great—for all the reasons we have seen. But is education becoming a box for you—is it becoming all you do? Or are you trying to build a more reasonable balance in your life, between education, work, and play or leisure? Throughout your life. That's the ultimate test of effectiveness, on the educational pyramid.

And having said that, it's time to go on to look at the world of work.

Chapter Three Footnotes

1. Digest of Educational Statistics, 1974. pp. 1ff.

2. The Condition of Education, 1976. p. 226.

3. *Ibid.*, p. 18.

4. *Ibid.*, p. 184.

5. *Ibid.*, p. 184.

6. Adapted from The Condition of Education, 1976, Chart 1.9.

7. Compiled by Philip Zimbardo, in a cross-cultural study. Reported in the *San Francisco Chronicle*, May 23, 1975. Since published in a remarkable book entitled: *shyness: what it is, what to do about it,* by Philip G. Zimbardo. 1977. Addison-Wesley Publishing Company, $5.95, paper.

8. This whole subject of andragogy is of great interest to many people. If you are one of them, the basic references are: *The Adult Learner   A Neglected Species,* by Malcolm S. Knowles. 1973. If your library doesn't have it, it's available from: Gulf Publishing Company, P. O. Box 2608, Houston, TX 77001; *Self-Directed Learning: A Guide for Learners and*

Teachers, by Malcolm S. Knowles, 1975. Available from: Association Press, 291 Broadway, New York, NY 10007. $4.95; *A Trainer's Guide to Andragogy; Revised Edition,* by John D. Ingalls. Foreward by Malcolm S. Knowles. 1973. Available from: Superintendent of Documents, U.S. Government Printing Office, Washington, D.C. 20402. Catalog No. HE 17.8:AN2/973, $3.10, paper; *Teaching Human Beings: 101 Subversive Activities for the Classroom,* by Jeffrey Schrank. 1972. Beacon Press, Boston. $3.45, paper.

9.   For further reading in this fascinating field, see: *The Psychology of Consciousness,* by Robert E. Ornstein. 1972. The Viking Press. $8.95, clothbound. Also out in paperback; *The Nature of Human Consciousness: A Book of Readings,* edited by Robert E. Ornstein. 1973. The Viking Press, 625 Madison Avenue, New York, NY 10022. Also out in paperback.

10.   This technique was invented by John C. Crystal, of McLean, Virginia and New York, NY. It is described in detail, in *Where Do I Go From Here With My Life?* by John C. Crystal and Richard N. Bolles. 1974. Available from: Ten Speed Press, 900 Modoc St., Berkeley, California 94707. $9.95, paper.

11.   The history of skills work revolves around the names of Sidney A. Fine, John Holland, Bernard Haldane, and John C. Crystal. Other significant contributions to the theory of skills and their identification have been made by such people as C. Heinz, Elliott Jaques, Wilfred Brown, and Eleanor Gilpatrick (of the Health Services Mobility Study).

12.   For further explanation of the theories of Sidney A. Fine in their *pure* form, see: "Vocational Counseling Skills Today and Tomorrow" by Sidney A. Fine, Ph.D., in *Vocational Guidance Quarterly,* April 1974; "Three Kinds of Skills: An Approach to Understanding The Nature of Human Performance," by Sidney A. Fine. A paper delivered to the 75th Annual Convention of the American Psychological Association, in 1967, and summarized in the *Proceedings, 75th Annual Convention, APA, 1967; An Introduction to Functional Job Analysis: A Scaling of Selected Tasks From the Social Welfare Field,* by Sidney A. Fine and Wretha W. Wiley. 1971. Methods for Manpower Analysis, No. 4, from W. E. Upjohn Institute for Employment Research, 300 South Westnedge Avenue, Kalamazoo, Michigan 49007; *Functional Job Analysis Scales: A Desk Aid,* by Sidney A. Fine. 1973. Methods for Manpower Analysis, No. 5. From W. E. Upjohn Institute for Employment Research (address above).

13.   This chart, from the *Dictionary of Occupational Titles,* is shown here as adapted by Sidney A. Fine in the last two works listed immediately above.

14.   When it comes time to decide *where* you're going to go get those skills, it would richly repay you to take some time to read the series that ran in *Fortune* Magazine, the October and December 1975 issues and the January 1976 issue, entitled "Education for the World of Work", parts I, II, and III. See your local library.

At my present job,
the only enjoyment is breakfast,
morning break,
lunch,
afternoon break,
4:30,
and payday.
Most of the time my body is there
but my mind is in the past

shooting buffalo with Jim Bridger,
riding with Butch and Sundance,
flying with Red Baron in his Fokker Tri-plane
or anything that offers escape.
I can't wait until tomorrow so I
can have breakfast at McDonalds,
and after that
everything is downhill.
—*A Job-Hunter in New Jersey*

Chapter Four
Toward a Balanced Life:
Life-Long Working

As things are, presently, most of us spend the earliest years of our life doing little else besides getting an Education. As we go from Kindergarten on up through the succeeding grades, we work our way up the Educational Pyramid—sort of.

We learn how to figure out what's happening in school. And we learn how to survive. In the case of many of us, that's as far as we get by graduation time. But others of us do go on to figure out how to get some sense of meaning or purpose out of all that schooling. And a few of us even wrestle with the issue of how to be more effective with our learning. So, some of us not only survive, but prosper.

You would suppose that all of this would prepare us very well for the next World we are going into—namely, the World of Work. But, *au contraire, mon ami.* This is not the case. Witness the following rather disconcerting facts:

(1) Follow-up studies have been done of high-school students, to see what happens to them after they leave the World of Education. Some of these studies are impressionistic, written in popular form, such as *What Really Happened to the Class of '65?* by Michael Medved and David Wallechinsky (1976, Random House). Others are more comprehensive, and scientific,

such as the American Institutes for Research's *Project TAL-ENT* [1] which began its survey in 1960 with nearly 400,000 students; The National Longitudinal Study of the National Center for Education Statistics, which began its survey in 1972, with almost 23,000 students;[2] and the National Assessment of Educational Progress, which began its survey in 1973-74, with 100,000 people. The findings of the latter are typical:

High-School Students Found Unrealistic About Their Careers

HOUSTON

Many high-school students have unrealistic expectations about their careers, according to a study released here by the National Assessment of Educational Progress.

The survey, conducted in 1973-74, indicated, among other things, that 44 per cent of the the 17-year-olds wanted a professional career. According to census figures, only 20 to 25 per cent of all jobs are professional or managerial.

The study was designed to determine the level of "career skills and attitudes" among 9-year-olds, 13-year-olds, 17-year-olds, and adults between the ages of 26 and 35.

100,000 Questioned

More than 100,000 people were questioned in the survey.

Included were questions in such areas as self-evaluation, career planning, attitudes toward work, skills, and work habits.

The survey also found that:

▶ "People who were deficient in basic skills tended to be those who typically have more difficulty in finding employment—blacks, residents of impoverished communities, people whose parents had little education, and, among adults, people with little personal education and low family income."

▶ One-third of the adults and more than half the 17-year-olds had difficulty writing a job application or figuring a finance charge.

▶ Only 54 per cent of the 17-year-olds could give correct answers to five questions about the training needed for a specific job.

▶ Only 35 per cent of the 17-year-olds said they had spoken with a school counselor or adviser about their career plans.

Roy H. Forbes, director of the national assessment, said the survey was designed to provide basic data on the effectiveness of new programs of career education.

Many of those programs have been developed in the past several years as a result of the interest generated in career education during the early 1970's.

The survey will be conducted again in 1979-80 to determine how "career skills and attitudes" have changed, Mr. Forbes said.

The National Assessment is a federally financed project designed to judge the effectiveness of educational programs. It is operated under the auspices of the Education Commission of the States in Denver.

(2) Things don't get *that* much better for students who go on to Further Education, i.e., college. Again, various studies have been conducted—though not on as thoroughgoing a scale as the Longitudinal Studies which are following-up high school students after graduation.[3] Colleges—as a general rule—show little curiosity as to what happens to their graduates. The most outstanding exception to this rule is Jack Shingleton's Placement Services Office at Michigan State University, which publishes—*every year*—a detailed report, listing every student who graduated, his or her major, if they got hired, where they got hired, and what their job title is.[4] Last year revealed a 14.04% unemployment rate, indicating that—at the very least—graduation does not immediately lead to employment. The World of Education does not just glide into the World of Work.

And no wonder. It *is* (as they say) a whole new ball game. You have to start up the Pyramid all over again:

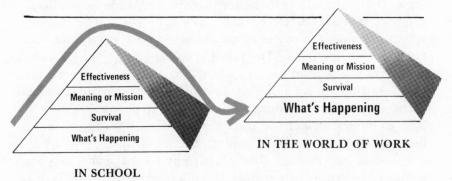

IN SCHOOL

IN THE WORLD OF WORK

To be sure, the issues remain basically the same. So, *if* you were conscious of The Tools you were using to survive and prosper in the World of Education, you can easily take the very same tools and transplant them to the World of Work, where they will likely serve you in just as good stead. You may, indeed, do this instinctively; and therefore the World of Work turns out to be 'your cup of tea' just as the World of Education or Schooling was. But for most of us, this is not so. We have to find new ways of coping, new tools, for this new world, along with the rest of our peers. And the first issue that we tackle, whether we are aware of it or not—and most of us are not; even to be *aware of what the issues are* is to be way ahead of most people,—is:

The First Issue on our "Working" Pyramid:
● *WHAT'S HAPPENING*

The most common way in which we go about gathering information concerning the World of Work is by simply *wandering*. We typically begin in our teens with almost any entry-level job that happens to present itself, or that we chance to hear about. It may be a job at McDonald's or a job delivering newspapers, or being a waitress, or whatever. The content of the job—for the purposes of information-gathering—is largely irrelevant. The point is to experience, for the first time in our lives, the fact that somebody outside our family (or maybe within) values us enough to pay us money in exchange for our time, our talents, and our labor. The point is to experience for the first time some of the artifacts of the World of Work: showing up, being on time, being able to take orders, being persistent about getting a job done, learning how to relate to people in this new role of server, helper, or whatever, learning how to relate to authority, enduring some discipline, and so forth.

In that job, through that job, and by means of that job, we gather our first bit of personal data about this first issue on our pyramid: WHAT'S HAPPENING in this new world. Or, to put it another way, lacking any other way of gathering the information, we use the Job itself *as an information-gathering system.* Sure, it's chancy and haphazard. Sure, if we run into a very untypical, bad situation, it's liable to give us distorted ideas about the World of Work for years to come. Nevertheless, if no one has told us any better, more systematic way to go about gathering information, this is better than Nothing. Some people may tell us (usually our family or our best friend), "Hey, why do you stay in such a crummy job?" The answer—though we probably can't put it into words—is that we value the job for what it is teaching us about the World of Work in general. Some people may admonish us, "You don't know what you're look-

Percentages of 9- and 13-year-olds who have participated in various activities	9 year olds	13 year olds	
	51%	81%	babysat
	33	62	baked cake or pie
	84	93	washed dishes
	62	65	built something out of wood
	63	80	repaired bicycle, wagon or skates
	80	91	painted an object (not a picture)
	33	49	ordered something from catalogue
	68	91	used card catalogue in library
	86	97	wrote a letter

Types of Jobs Most Often Held by 17-year-olds	Percentages citing each job	
	40%	service—includes babysitting, waiter/waitress
	11	clerical
	11	laborers
	5	farm laborers
	6	operatives
	5	sales
	4	craftsmen
	4	other

Tables from The First National Assessment of Career and Occupational Development Report No. 05-COD-00

ing for." But in a larger sense we do — or at least an unconscious part of us does — instinctively. We are trying to find out What's Happening in this New World.

After our first job has served its purpose, we move on. What kinds of jobs we get into thereafter, and how long we stay in them, is determined by many factors. Some of us settle down, relatively quickly, to one kind of job or another. Others of us wander a great deal. One man I know, for example, has held the following jobs:

> Magazine sales
> Lawn-care (cutting grass, trimming hedges,
>   cultivating flowers)
> Door-to-door cookie sales

Delivering newspapers
Milkman's helper
Soda fountain & drugstore clerk
Ditch-digger
Stock clerk in a department store
Salesperson in a department store
Steel mill floor sweeper
Foundry-worker
Chainman (working under a crane)
Carpenter's helper
Library clerk
Botanical garden worker
Night manager and clerk in a liquor store
Staff person in a teenage recreation center
Community-center group worker
Assistant manager in a variety store
Food product demonstrator
Life insurance salesman
Service manager in a department store
Office manager
Purchasing agent
Sales manager
Production manager
Advertising manager
Factory manager
Commissioned traveling salesman
Manufacturing consultant
Time study/layout consultant
Furniture showroom manager
Teacher
Counselor
Fighter pilot

Beneath such wandering, something is happening. Willy-nilly, in *order* or out of order, we learn how to deal with all the issues on our pyramid of concerns. We learn not only WHAT'S HAPPENING, but also how to SURVIVE in the World of Work, and how to find some sense of MISSION OR MEANING, and how to be EFFECTIVE. In one sense, each job that we hold gives us some information about all four issues—though in varying degree. However, in another sense each job deals primarily with just one of the four. And our work history can—at least in retrospect—be categorized accordingly:

- ●Those jobs I had which were useful primarily for what they taught me about the World of Work
  - ●Those jobs which I took just to survive; and/or which taught me how to survive
    - ●Those jobs which gave my life a sense of meaning or mission
      - ●Those jobs which were useful primarily for what they taught me about how to be more effective

The preceding list, for example, might be evaluated in some fashion such as this:

Primarily Dealing with What's Happening	Primarily Survival Type Jobs	Primarily Dealing with Finding Meaning	Primarily Dealing with Effectiveness
magazine salesman	ditch-digger	fighter pilot	office manager
lawn-care	stock-clerk	staff person in	sales manager
door-to-door	salesperson	recreation center	production
cookie sales	steel mill floor	community center	manager
delivering papers	sweeper	group worker	advertising
milkman's helper	library clerk	assistant manager	manager
soda fountain &	botanical garden	service manager	factory
drugstore clerk	worker	manufacturing	manager
foundry-worker	night manager	consultant	time study/layout
chainman	food product	furniture show-	consultant
carpenter's helper	demonstrator	room manager	
traveling salesman	life insurance	teacher	
	salesman	counselor	
	purchasing agent		

EXERCISE: If you have already had a number of jobs, try listing all the jobs you have ever held — full-time or part-time. Then divide them according to which of the four categories listed above you think each job *primarily* helped you with. When this is all done look over the four lists and then write down any Reflections or Learnings that strike you, as a result.

This, then, is the way that most of us learn about the World of Work, and how to survive—or even prosper—in it. The problem, of course, with this method is that *it takes so darn long*. You can find yourself learning only at age fifty, things which you wish you had known at age twenty-five. Moreover, the learnings acquired by this haphazard method are largely unsystematized, and usually devoid of any organizing principles. All of this helps to make the World of Work feel like a box, to so many people. And—sad to say—many many people are willing to live with this feeling, because they do not feel up to the effort, energy and time that would be required to change it.

But what about those of us who *want* to get out of this box-like feeling? We are going to need some Systematic way of getting at the four issues on the pyramid of our concerns, usable at any age. And if it is truly Systematic, it will dramatically shorten the time required for us to 'get a handle' (at least) on each of these four issues. Consequently, it is to this *alternative* way of learning—this *Plan B*—that we will now turn.

What's Happening—Plan B

When you try to get a systematic overview of What's Happening in the whole World of Work, the first thing that will strike you is The Overwhelming Amount of Information that exists concerning that world. I mean, there are over ninety million people in the U.S. labor force, over thirteen million employers, and over 20,000 different jobs described in the Labor Department's *Dictionary of Occupational Titles (1965 Edition)*—just for openers. Faced with this Overwhelming Amount of Information, there are three options open to you.

a) You can set yourself the task of trying to master *all* of this information—if you have the illusion that your mind is basically like a computer. You can take out every single book from the library that has anything whatsoever to do with jobs. You can haunt your local guidance, placement or career-planning office. You can read constantly, memorize endlessly, day and night, until you have sold yourself the fantasy that you are absolutely up-to-date on just about everything that is happening *out there* in the World of Work. Of course, by that time your brain may feel like scrambled eggs, and you may not be able to make any sense out of all that information. But still, you will *feel* tremendously expert. Of course, if this option doesn't seem attractive, alternatively:

b) You can give up trying to master *all* the information about what's happening in the World of Work, and settle instead for knowing a few facts about the most popular career fields. You can read *The Occupational Outlook Handbook* or *Occupational Outlook for College Graduates* or some other popular summary of selected occupations for which the demand is anticipated to be greater than the supply. You can, in other words, allow your knowledge of What's Happening to be relatively limited or constricted. Instead of knowing a little about a whole lot of things (as above), you will end up knowing a whole lot about a few things. Of course, if this bothers you—because you remember Confucius said *Never choose a card, except from a full deck* (didn't he)—then you will want to ask, What else have you got? That leads to your third option:

c) You can try to deal with *all* of the information concerning What's Happening out there, not by digesting that information necessarily, but by finding some Organizing Principles or Categories into which all such information fits, or can fit—as you pick it up. This option turns out, in the end, to be a great deal like trying to master all the information that exists concerning our country, by using a map of the United States. Once you have drawn the map, and divided the country into its fifty States—with their principal topography, cities and history duly noted, you are ready to deal with any information that may come to you thereafter, concerning the U.S. You can locate that information within the proper State or States, and thus relate it to what you already know. The States therefore become your "organizing principles" or "categories". In a similar fashion, you can approach all the information that exists regarding the World of Work by first seeking out comparable Organizing Principles. Needless to say, once you have decided to adopt this approach, your problem will be *which* Organizing Principles to choose, since there is almost no end to the kinds of principles that different vocational experts have proposed. There are three major schemata however, which stand out above all the others, so let us look at each of these in turn:

(1) The First Organizing Principle: *Data, People and Things* All the jobs in the world deal either with Data (numbers, words, ideas, or other kinds of information) or with People, or with Things (tools, machines, vehicles, nature, and so forth). In most cases, jobs deal with all three, in varying degree. Consequently, it is possible to use Data, People, and Things as Organizing Principles, under which you can group all that is Happening in the World of Work. The grouping can be very simple. For example, suppose you are a high school student going out on field trips to visit various people at their work. After your trips, you could set down your impressions of the various jobs you looked at, under the following three headings:

Jobs Which Deal Primarily with Data	*Jobs Which Deal Primarily with People*	*Jobs Which Deal Primarily with Things*
for example:	*for example:*	*for example:*
key punch operator	teacher	auto mechanic
file clerk	counselor	farmer
sewing machinist	athletic coach	truck driver
bookkeeper	minister/priest/rabbi	tree surgeon
typist	politician	watch repairer
proofreader	funeral director	dishwasher
accountant	entertainer	taxicab driver
cashier		painter

There would, inevitably, be some problems with such a simple classification. Where, for example, do you put an airline ticket agent? S/he is dealing with People all the time. But the job also involves endless handling of Things (pens, ticket folders, computer keyboards, tickets, money, checks) and constant dealing with Data as well (flight numbers, arrival and departure times, seat assignments, gate numbers, ticket prices, etc.). So, the question is, which category is *primary?* Unavoidably, different people will come up with different answers as to where they think a particular job should be placed in the above categories. If this difference of opinion occurs within a classroom or group situation, it can be the source of some lively and illuminating discussion, as each student is asked to explain and defend why s/he put a particular job in a particular category. But if you are working on this all by yourself, it can lead to great perplexity. For the truth is, many jobs belong in all three categories. This was, not surprisingly, the conclusion reached by Sidney Fine and his co-workers, when they were doing their preliminary work on the *Dictionary of Occupational Titles,* 1965 edition (now superseded by a 1977 edition). Consequently, all the jobs listed in the D.O.T. were categorized by *the degree to which (and the level at which)* they were involved with Data *and* People *and* Things. So, you see, this Organizing Principle can end up being rather complex—though still helpful. If you want to explore it further, I recommend that you read;

What Color Is Your Parachute? Chapter Five. (1981 Edition) Ten Speed Press, Box 7123, Berkeley, California 94707. ($6.95 +.50 postage and handling.) "An Introduction to Functional Job Analysis: A Scaling of Selected Tasks from the Social Welfare Field," by Sidney Fine and Wretha W. Wiley. (September 1971). Available from: The W.E. Upjohn Institute for Employment Research, 300 South Westnedge Avenue, Kalamazoo, Michigan 49007. ($2.00)

And, if you *really* are ready to tackle the biggie, there is:

The Dictionary of Occupational Titles itself (1977 Edition). Department of Labor. Get this in your local library.

(2) The Second Organizing Principle: *Occupational Clusters*
During recent years, particularly with the rise (and sometimes
fall) of interest in "Career Education" (the relating of Education, especially K-12—Kindergarten through Twelfth Grade—to
the World of Work) there have been a whole series of attempts
to organize all information concerning jobs into 'families' or
'Clusters', according to the *field* in which a particular job is to
be found. For example, a typical series of Clusters goes as follows:

> *Agri-Business and Natural Resources*
> *Business and Office Occupations*
> *Communications and Media*
> *Construction*
> *Consumer and Homemaking-Related Occupations*
> *Environment*
> *Fine Arts and Humanities*
> *Health Occupations*
> *Hospitality and Recreation*
> *Manufacturing*
> *Marine Science Occupations*
> *Marketing and Distribution Occupations*
> *Personal Services Occupations*
> *Public Service*
> *Transportation*

You can find a number of variations on this list, in the literature
related to Career Education. There is no 'right', 'official' or
authorized list, per se; everytime one is about to be announced,
it gets revised, abridged, or abandoned (sounds like the title of a
new Italian movie). In any event, once you have this sort of list,
it serves as another kind of Organizing Principle for dealing with
whatever information comes to you thereafter, concerning the
World of Work. Every job can be classified, indeed every family
of skills can be classified, in one Cluster or another. If Occupational Clusters as an Organizing Principle appeals to you, you
may wish to get your hands on the following resources:

Career Interest Guide for Students. Available from: Educational Services, Northern States Power Company, 414 Nicollet
Mall, Minneapolis, Minnesota 55401. This is a more complete
'map' of Career Clusters, as seen from an industry's viewpoint.

For some evaluation of the whole concept of Clustering, see:

Career Education Survival Manual: A Guidebook for Career Educators and Their Friends, by Larry McClure. Available from: Olympus Publishing Company, 1670 East Thirteenth South, Salt Lake City, Utah 84105. See particularly the chapter entitled, "Clusterphobia, Or, Clusters' Last Stand."

(3) The Third Organizing Principle: *People-Environments* We have just seen that jobs can be described in terms of What You Deal With (data, people and/or things), or in terms of What Field You Work In (such as communications and media)—and that both of these concepts offer some Organizing Principles, by which we can deal with The Overwhelming Amount of Information that exists regarding What's Happening in the whole World of Work. But there is another principal way in which jobs can be described; and this also affords us a helpful Organizing Principle. With the great emphasis upon the importance of the environment in recent years, it has become increasingly realized that jobs are environments too. While there are many factors, within such environments, that could be catalogued, the most fascinating and most helpful factor turns out to be The People in that environment. Every job, except possibly that of being a full-fledged hermit, surrounds us with people to one degree or another. Moreover, these people-environments can be described in terms of certain principal types. Dr. John L. Holland, of Johns Hopkins University, has the best-defined, best-researched, and best-known such typology. He distinguishes six basic people-environments:

1. The Realistic People-Environment: filled with people who prefer activities involving "the explicit, ordered, or systematic manipulation of objects, tools, machines, and animals."

217

2. The Investigative People-Environment: filled with people who prefer activities involving "the observation and symbolic, systematic, creative investigation of physical, biological or cultural phenomena."
3. The Artistic People-Environment: filled with people who prefer activities involving "ambiguous, free, unsystematized activities and competencies to create art forms or products."
4. The Social People-Environment: filled with people who prefer activities involving "the manipulation of others to inform, train, develop, cure or enlighten."
5. The Enterprising People-Environment: filled with people who prefer activities involving "the manipulation of others to attain organizational or self-interest goals."
6. The Conventional People-Environment: filled with people who prefer activities involving "the explicit, ordered, systematic manipulation of data, such as keeping records, filing materials, reproducing materials, organizing written and numerical data according to a prescribed plan, operating business and data processing machines."

Taking these six types in hand, they are useful Organizing Principles for dealing with the whole World of Work. Returning to an illustration we used earlier, if you were a high school student going out on field trips to visit various people at their work, you could organize your impressions afterwards in terms of which people-environment was *dominant,* for each job you observed. It might come out looking something like this:

Realistic (Things)	Investigative	Artistic	Social	Enterprising	Conventional (Data Jobs)
farmer	scientist	musician	teacher	executive	accountant
carpenter	psychologist	writer	counselor	salesman	file clerk
bus driver	physician	dancer	bartender	lawyer	typist
auto-mechanic	researcher	singer	hairstylist	real estate agent manager	computer-programmer
			service representative		

Certainly, as with the Organizing Principle of Data-People-Things, problems would be encountered, in trying to classify certain jobs. And, ultimately, a more systematic and sophisticated use of this typology would be needed.

Most jobs need to be described in terms of three people-environments (one dominant one, and two lesser ones). Indeed, John Holland has done this for the 456 most-common occupations in our country. Your teacher or counselor can obtain this for you in:

> "The Occupations Finder", for use with *The Self-Directed Search: A Guide to Educational and Vocational Planning*, by John L. Holland, Ph.D. Available to professionals from: Consulting Psychologists Press, 577 College Avenue, Palo Alto, California 94306.

Or, in the absence of a teacher or counselor, you can get your hands on this yourself by ordering:

> *Making Vocational Choices: A Theory of Careers*, by John L. Holland. 1973. Available from: Prentice-Hall, Inc., Englewood Cliffs, New Jersey 07632 (that address is sufficient). $4.95 paper. Both "The Occupations Finder" and *The Self-Directed Search*, listed above, are reproduced in the back of this excellent resource. It also gives definitive explanations of John Holland's whole theory and typology, in his own words, together with the evidence for it.

If you want a *workbook* that deals with John Holland's theory and typology, and—further—relates it to Career Clusters and to the Data/People/Things principle, see:

> *Career Planning: Search for a Future*, by Gerald P. Cosgrave. 1973. U.S. readers can obtain this from: Consulting Psychologists Press, 577 College Avenue, Palo Alto, California 94306. $4.00 (plus $.51 postage and handling) There is also a supplement to it, called *Career Workbook: Projects to help in developing your career*. CPP has both for $5.50 (plus $.60 postage and handling). Canadian readers can obtain both books from: The Guidance Centre, Faculty of Education, University of Toronto, 1000 Yonge Street, Suite 30A, Toronto, Canada M4W2K8. Their price is $4.15 for *Career Planning* and $5.75 for both books.

Well, there you have it: three different systematic approaches to the problem of What's Happening out there in the total World of Work. You can choose whichever one you prefer (I personally like John Holland's *people-environments* much the best) or you can attempt to put them all together, in a three-dimensional map/picture/model of the whole World of Work, something like the following:

The Total World of Work

DEPICTED AS A *VERY* LARGE BOX

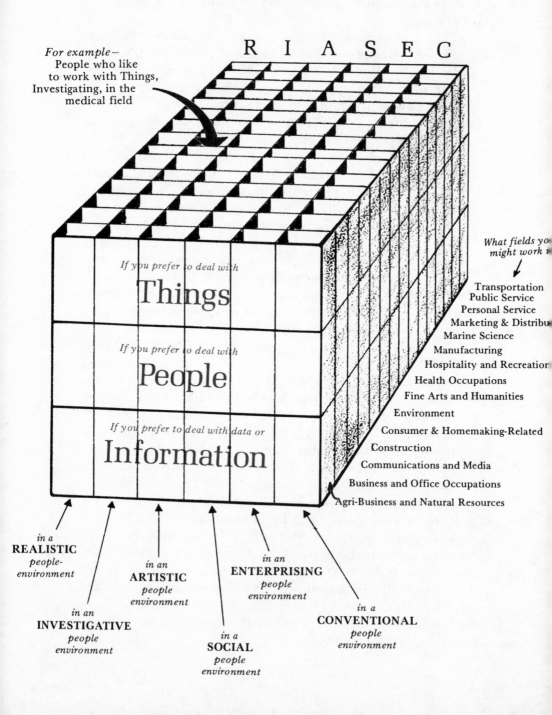

R I A S E C

For example—
People who like
to work with Things,
Investigating, in the
medical field

If you prefer to deal with
Things

If you prefer to deal with
People

If you prefer to deal with data or
Information

*What fields yo
might work*

Transportation
Public Service
Personal Service
Marketing & Distribu
Marine Science
Manufacturing
Hospitality and Recreation
Health Occupations
Fine Arts and Humanities
Environment
Consumer & Homemaking-Related
Construction
Communications and Media
Business and Office Occupations
Agri-Business and Natural Resources

in a
REALISTIC
*people-
environment*

in an
INVESTIGATIVE
*people
environment*

in an
ARTISTIC
*people
environment*

in a
SOCIAL
*people
environment*

in an
ENTERPRISING
*people
environment*

in a
CONVENTIONAL
*people
environment*

● The Point of All This is that you now have in your hands:

An overview   of the whole World of Work. It may seem like a very generalized, superficial one; but the truth is, some people work all their lives without ever knowing even as much as you already do.

A means of *deciding* what particular parts of that World you may want to investigate further. Either once and for all, or else again and again, you can use this sort of framework to cross off those parts of the World of Work that—at the present time—are not of interest to you. The parts that remain, then, will be the area upon which you will want to focus your information-gathering energies. For example, suppose that as you look at WHAT YOU DEAL WITH, you decide that you prefer to deal with Data. Suppose that among the TYPES OF PEOPLE-ENVIRONMENTS AT YOUR JOB, you prefer Investigative. And suppose that among WHAT FIELDS YOU MIGHT WORK IN, you prefer ENVIRONMENT. You would then need to deal with further investigation of the sorts of jobs that exist within those three categories: Investigating physical, biological or cultural phenomena, or the data resulting therefrom, in the Environment field. It sure does cut down the territory, as we used to say in the Old West. Information-gathering thus becomes a manageable task.

A means of *organizing* any new things you may learn about the whole World of Work, from hereon out. You now have a framework within which to place such information, and thus relate it to what you already know. If, for example, you meet someone who is an Accountant for a bunch of artists who do work for television, you can quickly put her or him in some perspective within the total World of Work, by realizing s/he works with Data (primarily) in an Artistic People-Environment, within the field of Communications & Media. So much for information that drops right into your lap, so to speak.

221

'DECIDED TO FINALIZE YOUR PLANS, TOM?'

What do you do when you have to go seeking the information—say, for your own life? The cardinal rule here is: *You Must Have Some Idea of What It Is You Want to Know.* That principle is so obvious, it is embarrassing to even mention it. But I have met so many people who set out to do their information-gathering, without the slightest idea of what it is that they want to know, that it seems not only worth mentioning, but worth *underlining.* So, here is a kind of check-list that you might want to take in hand when it is time to go *Information Shopping.*

An Information Shopping List

I want to know more about the _____ sector of Work:
☐ what kinds of jobs there are, in that sector; ☐ which of these will superficially* interest me, and why; ☐ what's attractive about the jobs that interest me; ☐ what's unattractive about them; ☐ what kinds of skills, traits, and interests these require; ☐ how people typically get hired in those jobs; ☐ what the pay and other rewards are; _____

☐ other: _____

_____

_____

*or greatly

So much, if you're interested in working for Someone.

If you're thinking more specifically about Working for Yourself —selling your own creations, or your own products, or your own services, your checklist will be a little different. It may look something like this:

An 'On-My-Own' Information Shopping List

I want to know more about how you make a living doing/selling _____

☐ what kind of demand there is for this creation, service, or product; ☐ where, in the geographical area that interests me, that demand is greatest; ☐ what the rewards are, for doing this; ☐ what the pitfalls are; ☐ how other people, in this line of work, got started;

☐ and: _____

_____

_____

223

You can, of course, embroider, expand or revise this list in any way you wish. It should, in the end, be completely *Your list.*

Once you know what it is you want to know, where do you go to find it? Well, there's practically no end of resources. But, when all is said and done, they tend to divide into two basic categories: (1) *Printed Stuff;* and (2) *People You Go Talk To.* We shall look at each of these in turn.

Information-Gathering From Printed Stuff

If you ever wander into the exhibit hall of the annual APGA (American Personnel and Guidance Association) Convention, you will simply not believe all of the career information materials — books, charts, pictures, audio-visuals, models, primers, pamphlets, games, wheels, videotapes, films, filmstrips, records, crafts, and the like — that are being produced by private industry, non-profit associations, and various arms of government, these days — most of them intended for groups, classes, schools, and in cost beyond the reach of the average inquirer.

But there is your local library which, if it is of any decent size, ought to have a sizeable number of books and pamphlets on various careers, all free for the using. Assuming you know what it is you want to know about, your reference or general librarian ought to be of considerable help in locating relevant materials.

In addition, if there is a college in your town—community college, four year college, or university—you should not over-look the library there, *and* the office of career counseling, career development, placement, or whatever it calls itself. The latter often has extensive career information materials, which you may browse through, free.

If you desire further information, the budget-minded information seeker can find inexpensive career literature from our beloved government. There is alot of it. If you want a list of what's available, write to:

U.S. Department of Labor,
Bureau of Labor Statistics,
Occupational Outlook Service, GAO Building,
Washington, D.C. 20212

Among the literature which you can order from the regional offices of the BLS, are:

(1) A series of pamphlets on careers which use:

ECOLOGY	SCIENCE
ENGLISH	SOCIAL SCIENCE
FOREIGN LANGUAGES	OFFICE JOBS
LIBERAL ARTS	OUTDOOR JOBS
MATHEMATICS	REPAIRMAN OR MECHANIC

(2) A series of larger pamphlets on careers which require different educational backgrounds:

"Jobs for Which A High School Education Is Preferred, but Not Essential"

"Jobs for Which Apprenticeships Are Available"

"Jobs for Which Junior College, Technical Institute, or Other Specialized Training Is Usually Required"

"Jobs for Which a College Education Is Usually Required"

Each of these gives the job title, a brief summary of the qualifications and training, the employment trend to 1985, and what pamphlets are available (at a cost of $.35 each) further explaining that particular occupation.

(3) A series on careers within the various agencies of the Federal Government. All of these are summarized in a bibliography entitled "Guide to Federal Career Literature," published by the United States Civil Service Commission, and available free from the Superintendent of Documents, U.S. Government Printing Office, Washington D.C. 20402 (Stock Number 0060-00791; remittance of $1.00 must accompany order).

(4) A series on forecasts of the hiring outlook for various occupations:

The Occupational Outlook Handbook. Contains the following information on 850 occupations: the nature of the work, the places of employment, training, employment outlook, earnings and working conditions, and sources of additional information. It costs $8. This is the big daddy of them all. If your library doesn't have it, and you can't afford the $8, there are excerpts or summaries from it, which you can either order directly from the BLS, or find in your library:

Occupational Outlook Handbook in Brief. $1.30

Occupational Outlook Quarterly. $4. per year. If you order it, make the check payable to Superintendent of Documents, Government Printing Office, Washington D.C. 20402.

All of the above, except where an address is given, can be ordered from the Bureau of Labor Statistics, U.S. Department of Labor's office that is nearest you:

BUREAU OF LABOR STATISTICS
REGIONAL OFFICES

Boston
1603 Federal Bldg. Government Center
Boston, Mass. 02203
Phone: (617) 223-6727

San Francisco
450 Golden Gate Ave.
San Francisco, Calif. 94102
Phone: (415) 556-4678

New York
Suite 3400
1515 Broadway, New York, N.Y. 10036
Phone: (212) 399-5405

Kansas City
911 Walnut St.
Kansas City, Mo. 64106
Phone: (816) 374-2378

Chicago
9th Floor, Federal Office Bldg.
230 South Dearborn, Chicago, Ill. 60604
Phone: (312) 353-1880

Philadelphia
P.O. Box 13309
Philadelphia, Pa. 19101
Phone: (215) 596-1154

Dallas
2nd Floor, 555 Griffin Square Bldg.
Dallas, Tex. 75202
Phone: (214) 749-3516

Atlanta
1371 Peachtree St. NE
Atlanta, Ga. 30309
Phone: (404) 526-5416

Certain States have taken alot of this information, plus a good deal of their own, and put it on computers. These systems (usually) do more than dispense information; they try to match it with the particular aptitudes, interests or needs of the individual inquirer. The computer information systems have such exotic acronyms as CIS (*Career Information System*)—and all its variants, usually with another letter in front of CIS, standing for the particular State—, SIGI (*System of Interactive Guidance and Information*), CBEOC (*Computer-Based Educational Opportunity Centers*), GIS (*Guidance Information System*), DIS-COVER, CVIS (*Computerized Vocational Information System*), ECES (*Educational Career Exploration System*), and the like. There is also the Federal system, OIS (Occupational Information System). So, if you live in Alabama, California, Colorado, Florida, Illinois, Iowa, Maryland, Massachusetts, Minnesota, New Jersey, New York, Ohio, Oregon, Pennsylvania, Tennessee, Texas, Washington or Wisconsin, there's a computerized system somewhere in your State. Ask at your local Employment Service office, or at a nearby college's placement office for information as to the job-information computer's location or locations. If that doesn't turn up where it is, write to the National Center for Educational Brokering, 405 Oak Street, Syracuse N.Y. 13203 (315/425-5275) or the National Occupational Information Service, Employment and Training Administration, U.S. Department of Labor, 601 D Street, N.W., Room 9122, Washington D.C. 20213.

In addition to Government publications and State Computer systems, there are commercial publishers, who put out alot of "briefs" about various occupations, with the cost for each one ranging between $.30 to $1.00. You can write and ask for their catalog or price-list:

> Careers, Inc.
> > P.O. Box 135, Largo, Florida 33540
>
> Chronicle Guidance Publications, Inc.
> > Moravia, New York 13118
>
> Science Research Associates, Inc.
> > 259 Erie Street, Chicago, Illinois 60611

Now, before we leave pamphlets, books, and computer print-outs, let's ask the $64,000 question about *Printed Stuff:* how reliable and trustworthy is it? Well, in addition to the fact that much of the information is too general, shallow and bland, all career information in general, and occupational forecasts in particular, have the following defects:

1.   *The Source of the Information is Often Biased.* Clearly the Bureau of Labor Statistics is not in a position to know the picture for every occupation, or every industry. Consequently, interviewers from the BLS have to turn to leaders of industry, or coordinating councils of one type or another, in order to find out what the picture is for that industry or that occupation. Now, suppose you are the person that the BLS turns to, and you know that there are probably going to be 170,000 vacancies in your industry next year. Will you tell the BLS that figure? What if you are in error? What if there turns out to be a need for 10- or 20,000 more than you had thought? You will then have a bad shortage. So what do you do? Well, naturally, you "overguess" a little bit. Or a lot. You are, after all, an advocate for employers, not for the job-hunter. So, if a few thousand job-hunters are attracted to your industry, and then can't find jobs, that's their problem, not yours. This is why, for example, the *Occupational Outlook Handbook* a few years ago was predicting a continued clergy shortage when, in fact, most Protestant denominations were long since aware that they had a clergy surplus. And so it was, and is, with most occupations or industries. It is safe to guess that because of "employer bias," less bodies are needed in any particular field than the OOH claims.

2.   *There Is a Time-lapse Built-in To All Forecasts.*

Let us depict the situation
in a given industry or occupation
by a pendulum:

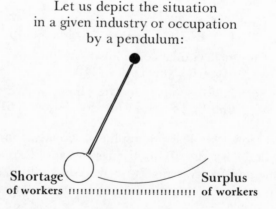

Shortage
of workers ⫿⫿⫿⫿⫿⫿⫿⫿⫿⫿⫿⫿⫿⫿⫿⫿ of workers   Surplus

The pendulum, for most occupations, is continually moving, swinging between shortage and surplus, or between surplus and shortage. The only imponderable is how fast it moves, or how slowly. Now, let us suppose that for a particular occupation the pendulum is in the position shown above, *at the time the Bureau of Labor Statistics gathers its information.* So, in the *Occupational Outlook Handbook* the BLS subsequently publishes the information that there is a vast shortage, for that field. In point of fact, however, it has taken a while for the BLS to get its findings into print, and during that time the pendulum has *moved.* It may have moved only slightly, because its movement is slow. Or it may have moved quite a bit, because the situation in the field is changing rapidly. In which event, though the OOH describes (in effect) the pendulum as first depicted, the actual situation *by the time the data gets published*—is as shown at the left.

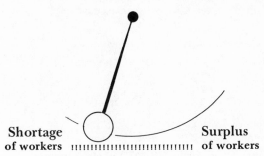

Shortage of workers ꞁꞁꞁꞁꞁꞁꞁꞁꞁꞁꞁꞁꞁꞁꞁꞁꞁꞁꞁꞁꞁꞁꞁꞁꞁ **Surplus of workers**

Typical users of the OOH, say high school or college students, will of course not know this. They will see the particular field-in-question depicted as one which has a vast shortage. So, they may well aim for that field. It will, however, take the high school senior or the college freshman some 4-5 years (in many cases) to finish his or her training for that particular field. By the time their training is completed, and they are ready to seek a job in that field, the pendulum may have moved dramatically, so that the situation *by the time they get there* is actually this:

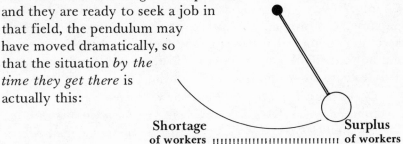

Shortage of workers ꞁꞁꞁꞁꞁꞁꞁꞁꞁꞁꞁꞁꞁꞁꞁꞁꞁꞁꞁꞁꞁꞁꞁꞁꞁ **Surplus of workers**

The compilers of the OOH are, of course, acutely aware of this Time-Lapse between data-gathering, publishing and completed training, and they try to deal with it by making long-range forecasts. But the longer the range, the more unreliable such forecasts become, sad to say. One vocational expert I know takes an occupational forecast film put out several years ago, and shows it to her audience. It is laughable. That is her commentary on the accuracy of forecasts. Her listeners can see for themselves that the predictions were way off the mark, in many cases. Incidentally, there is an introductory section in each edition of the OOH (called "Tomorrow's Jobs") which lists all the factors that may cause the forecasts to be wrong. But unfortunately, few people read this section, or take it seriously.

3. *There Is No Description of the Relationship between Supply and Demand.* All forecasts are based on the ratio between supply and demand, as follows:

JOB OPPORTUNITIES	PROSPECTIVE DEMAND-SUPPLY RELATIONSHIP
Excellent	Demand much greater than supply
Very Good	Demand greater than supply
Good or Favorable	Rough balance between demand and supply
May Face Competition	Likelihood of more supply than demand
Keen Competition	Supply greater than demand

Yet, in point of fact, occupational forecasters do not actually know how many people are preparing for a field or—what is even more to the point—switching over from another field. A case in point was Santa Clara County, California, several years ago. A vast number of electronics engineers found themselves out of work, and as a stop-gap measure, went into the related field of TV repair-work, resulting—as one observer drily put it—"in one TV repairman for every TV set in Santa Clara County." Even with occupations requiring a long period of preparation, forecasts are often wrong because although the OOH accurately pinpointed the vacancies that would be developing, it did not anticipate a great increase in the number being trained. This leads to anomalies like the following:

> *Occupational Outlook Handbook:* "*Employment opportunities for architects are expected to be favorable through the mid-1980's. Several thousand openings will occur annually due to very rapid growth of the profession. . .*"

MONEY Magazine, January 1977: *"Losers of the Year (1976) in Starting Jobs: Architects, who are lucky to get a job, since there are nearly three new architects for every opening in architectural firms."*

To illustrate this problem with a further example, an occupation which had the following pattern of projected vacancies, would be regarded as having excellent prospects

Number of Workers in Demand	1ST YEAR	2ND YEAR	3RD YEAR	4TH YEAR
	200,000	*207,400*	*215,000*	*223,000*

because of the increasing employment opportunities. Yet, suppose we toss in the other "missing ingredient"—the *supply* of those being trained for this occupation, each year, and because of an unpredicted dramatic increase, it ends up looking like this:

	1ST YEAR	2ND YEAR	3RD YEAR	4TH YEAR
Demand:	*200,000*	*207,400*	*215,000*	*223,000*
Supply:	190,000	207,000	220,000	235,000

Then we see that, during the 3rd and 4th years, this field does not have excellent prospects, by any means. In the absence of that second figure, "the missing ingredient", occupational forecasts are very difficult to evaluate. Yet this ingredient *is* usually missing, as you can see from the Architects' forecast quoted previously.

4. *Finally, The Forecasts Make No Allowance for Different Job-Hunting Behaviors.* In the introductory section (not often read) of the OOH, appears the following advice:

> *"The prospect of relatively few job openings should not prevent someone from pursuing a particular career. . . Even in occupations with relatively poor prospects, jobs are available because of the need to replace workers who leave the occupation. . ."*

Which is to say, there are openings for every job in the world. All that forecasts, such as those in the *Occupational Outlook Handbook,* can do is define "the degree of competition." Are there two people competing for every vacancy in a particular field; three people? Six? Ten? A hundred? That is all the forecasts really tell: the difficulty of getting hired. Fields with so-called "excellent" prospects are fields with little or no competition for vacancies; fields with so-called "poor" prospects are those with keen competition. What that adds up to is simply this: if a field which interests you has keen competition, that means that your job-seeking behavior *is more and more important.* It does not mean that you should avoid that occupation, unless you fear competition greatly. Properly thought of, therefore, occupational forecasts—when you use them to help you decide what fields or occupations to go into,—are actually forecasts of how important is the effectiveness of your job-hunting techniques. But little more than that.

The Moral
of all the preceding is simply this: *begin* with printed materials, to get a 'quick fix' on fields in general, and occupations that might be interesting to you in particular. But *take everything you read (or everything the computer prints out for you) with a grain of salt.* And in some cases, a whole bushel.

Then, it is time to go on to:

Information-Gathering From People You Go Talk To

All that we said in the chapter on Lifelong Education, about interviewing people for information (page 84) still applies. To recapitulate:

(1) If the idea of going out and talking to people makes your knees turn to jelly, and causes perspiration to break out on your forehead, you've got lots of company: over half the people in the United States, as a matter of fact.

(2) Interviewing for information means, emphatically, that you can take someone else with You. You can take someone who is more at ease with people, someone who is more verbal, someone who is more experienced, or whoever you wish. And you can let them start the interview, asking your questions for you, so long as:

    (a) You watch them to see how they do it, so that you are—in truth—using them as a model, and learning how you can do it yourself.

    (b) You chip in with your own questions, once the interview is going well.

(3) If you absolutely don't know *who* to go interview, concerning a particular subject or field that you want to know more about, go to the 'Switchboard People' or 'Resource Brokers' in your community. For your purposes, with respect to the World of Work, these are:

    (a) The head of the appropriate department or school, at your nearby community college or college/university.

    (b) The career counseling or placement office at that same college.

    (c) Your local chamber of commerce, or city hall (e.g., the tax man).

    (d) Your local librarian.

    (e) Anyone in the community whose business it is to find out information; e.g., the city editor at your local newspaper, or the head of a local resource-center or collective.

(4) Anytime you run into a dead end, which is to say, the person you are talking to just doesn't know (what it is that you want to know), *always* ask: "Who do you think might know?" You'd be surprised how people will *not* volunteer such information, until you ask them.

(5) Never believe anything just because one person tells you That. Never take one person's word for anything. *Always* talk to three sources; then make up your mind. If it comes out to be Two Against One, that does not necessarily mean you have to vote with the Two. Some intuition may tell you you trust the One more than you do the other Two. But at least the things which that One told you were "tested in the fire" of the Other Two's opinions. And that's worth alot.

Well, so much for our Recapitulation (with a little embroidering). This sort of Information-gathering—from people you go talk to—is relatively simple when the field or occupation you are trying to find out about is One of The Obvious Ones. But what do you do:

When You're Looking For
A Really Unusual Occupation

Suppose you're fresh out of high-school, or college, you've looked through the Occupational Outlook Handbook and nothing — absolutely nothing — looks interesting. Or suppose you're in your middle years or retirement years, by that time you feel as though You've Done It All, and you're looking for something *really* new, challenging, and stimulating. How do you go about finding out *that* sort of information? There are basically two routes you can take:

I. You can start with the occupation that you Like The Most (or Dislike The Least) on the list of all the familiar ones, and *identify one element* about it that you liked very much. Let us say, by way of example, you liked the fact that You Were Able To Work Outdoors. That's what made this particular occupation, or job, so attractive. Having identified that element:

A. You go to the library and try to find out all the obvious jobs which have that element in common. A pamphlet from the

Bureau of Labor Statistics, for example, would tell you that, in the case of "Being Able to Work Outdoors" (to one degree or another), there are the following:

agricultural workers
amusement park workers
animal trainers
archaeologists
athletic coaches
athletes
automobile service
    occupations:
    auto, bus, truck
    mechanics; gas
    station attendants,
    others
beekeepers
billboard erectors
boat-dock & boat-
    ride operators
    (recreation)
border patrolmen
bounty hunters
    (predatory animals)
bricklayers, stonemasons,
    marble setters, tile
    & terrazzo workers
caddies
campground caretakers
carhops
carpenters, painters
cement masons
cemetary workers
charter boat operators
circus workers
coast guardsmen
commercial fishermen
conservation workers:
    foresters, forestry
    aides, range managers,
    soil conservationists
construction inspectors
construction laborers
divers, scuba
dogcatchers
dredge operators
driving occupations:
    bus, truck, taxi,
    routemen
electric power industry:
    transmission & distri-
    bution occupations,
    customer service
electric sign servicemen
engineers: civil, mining

environmental scientists:
    geologists, geo-
    physicists, oceano-
    graphers
exterminators
farm equipment mechanics
firefighters
fish & game wardens
fishing & hunting guides
fur farmers & trappers
furniture movers
garbage or trash collectors
gardeners, grounds
    keepers
golf range attendants
guards & watchmen
highway construction &
    maintenance workers
ironworkers, machine
    movers, riggers
irrigation workers
landscape architects
life scientists
lifeguards
logging & lumbermill
    industry workers
mail carriers
merchant marine occupa-
    tions: officers,
    seamen, longshoremen
messengers
newspaper carriers
nursery workers
operating engineers:
    heavy equipment
    operators
park rangers & caretakers
parking attendants
parking meter collectors
parking meter servicemen
petroleum & natural gas
    production & proces-
    sing industry workers
police officers, state
    police officers
racetrack workers
railroad industry workers:
    bridge & building,
    signal department,
    track workers
ranch hands

recreation workers
rodeo performers
roofers, sheet-metal
    workers
sandblasters
sheepherders
shipyard workers
ski resort workers
steeplejacks
streetcleaners
surveyors
telephone craft
    occupations:
    linemen, cable
    splicers, phone
    servicemen
tour & sightseeing
    guides
tree surgeons
tree trimmers
tugboat and towboat
    workers
tunnel workers
vendors
well drillers
wildlife refuge workers
window cleaners
wrecking and salvaging
    workers
zookeepers

NOTE:
This list was put together
before the Bureau of the
Census revised titles to
eliminate those that
denote sex stereotypes.
In a word, women as well
as men should regard
every job listed as open
to them.

236

B. Once you've assembled this sort of list, choose from it that job or occupation which sounds the Most Attractive to you. You are about to play an information-interviewing game of Leap-frog. It works like this. You're trying to use several interviews to leap from the Known (i.e., this occupation which sounds the most attractive among the Obvious Ones) to the Unknown (i.e., some occupation you've never thought of, before), thus:

The Known.
(An obvious job that seems at least mildly attractive)

First information interview

Second information interview

Etc.

The Unknown.
(A non-obvious job that fascinates you)

The way you go about it, is this: you begin with someone who works at the Known Occupation you have chosen. Let us say you chose "Tree Surgeon." You would talk to an actual Tree Surgeon. You may already know one, among your circle of acquaintances. If not, try the Yellow Pages in the telephone directory. Or any of the "Switchboard People" listed on page 87. Once you find him or her, there are four *kinds* of questions for you to ask that Tree Surgeon (or whoever you choose):

---

1 — How did you get into this work?
2 — What do you like most about it?
3 — What do you like the least about it?
4 — Where else could I find people who *(here name the element with which you began:)* work out of doors, and
(here name any additional attractive elements that have become clear to you as your priorities, during the conversation with this person—perhaps when s/he was telling you what s/he did or didn't like about the job; for example:) and work with trees, but not in cutting them.

5 — *Optional question (if s/he didn't have any answer to 4 above):* Who do you think might know?

With this information in hand, you then go on (in your Leap-frog Information-Game) to one of the people s/he suggested. You ask the very same four (or five) questions there. Then on to the next person or type of person who has been suggested to you. Same questions. And so forth, until you strike (what is for You) paydirt. If you go down any false roads along the way, just backtrack and go on from there.

That's how you begin with *one element*—like Working Outdoors. What if it's more complex than that? That leads us to our second route:

You start by identifying *several elements* that interest you in whatever occupation (as yet undesignated) you might eventually want to choose. Let us say, for example, you were a liberal arts major in college, you are about to graduate, and you can't imagine what it is you want to do. If you do the kind of homework indicated in the third section of this chapter (MEANING OR MISSION), page 262, you list whatever interests you succeed in identifying for yourself. It would help, here, to take an actual example. Larry W. identified the following elements as of interest to him, in whatever job he might really want to seek:

> a love of counseling people
> an interest in psychiatry
> an interest in plants
> a love of carpentry.

The more elements you can identify, the better. You then take the elements and turn each one into a person or job-title, thus:

> a love of counseling people = a counselor
> an interest in psychiatry = a psychiatrist
> an interest in plants = a gardener
> an interest in carpentry = a carpenter

And, having done this, you ask yourself which of the persons you have now listed would be most likely to have The Largest Overview of the World of Work. Most often, though not always, this turns out to be synonymous with the question: Which of these persons took the longest to get his or her training? In the

238

case above, the psychiatrist wins, hands down. So you go to see him or her, and ask:

(1) Do you know of any occupation or specialty, that has all these elements in it: counseling people, psychiatry, plants, and carpentry?

(2) If you don't know, who might?

In this example, it would, of course, be difficult to find a psychiatrist in private practice who would be willing to talk to you, without charging you for the time; so, try a psychiatrist who works in a hospital, or for the county or city, or is in some department at your nearby community college or college/university.

Larry W. went about this information-interviewing, and discovered that there is a branch of psychiatry which uses plants in the therapy with extremely withdrawn patients, who are beginning to make contact with the world again, but are afraid—as yet—to deal with human beings. By giving those patients some plants to take care of, they gain the courage to feel that something needs them and will respond to their care. Thus Larry W. put all the elements together, except carpentry. Possibly he will use that to build the wooden planters for the plants.

In any event, you *can* find out What's Happening in the World of Work—at any age, in any place, by a skillful blend of "Written Stuff" and "People You Go Talk To." But because Only You know what it is you really want to know, Only You can really do this Information-Search to your own complete satisfaction. Anyone else will do it less thoroughly, less satisfactorily, because it is information for Your Life, not theirs. So, don't delegate this task. You can do it better than anyone else. And have fun, besides.

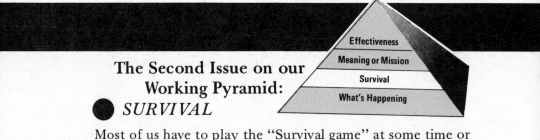

The Second Issue on our Working Pyramid:
● *SURVIVAL*

Most of us have to play the "Survival game" at some time or other in our life. Sometimes it is only when we are first getting started; then we have relatively smooth sailing ever thereafter, for the rest of our life in the World of Work. Othertimes some of us get to mid-life with relatively easy going up to that point, then suddenly we are laid off, and for the first time in our life we have to learn how to play "the game." In any event, for most of us, it is a sporadic episode in our life, and not our normal lot.

But there are others who—because of a situation forced upon them by heredity or circumstance—have to play the "Survival game" continuously and endlessly all their life. And they hate every minute of it. Or endure it with dull resignation.

And others still, there are, who play the "Survival game" endlessly not because they have to but because they want to. They see it as a challenge, a test of their wits, a throw-back to an earlier day when it was man and woman against the uncharted, untamed wilderness. There is for them an exhilaration in the very playing of "the game"—and winning.

No matter when it is played, continuously or occasionally, some prove to be very good at this "game." They seem to have been "born Survivors." Like the inflated rubber-balloon figure with weighted feet, every time they get tossed up in the air (as it were) they always seem to land on their feet.

Most of us, however, find that we are not very good at this "game" of being out of work and trying to survive. Particularly if we have a family to help support, we may find that neither unemployment benefits (while they last), nor food stamps, nor welfare is really sufficient. In which case—short of illegal activities—there is but one Survival avenue open to us. And that is, to hunt for a job. That's where the Survival game really becomes rough. For a lot of us.

How many? Well, that takes a little addition of three figures. You begin with

a) *The number of unemployed that the Federal Government will admit to.* In the most recent year that we have figures for (at this writing)—1975—the total was 7,830,000 of persons 16 years and over. This was the largest number of unemployed since the end of the great Depression (1930-1940), as we can see on the Table[5] on the next page *(remember to add 000 to each figure).*

Do remember please—in looking at these figures—that the Government has a very limited view (to put it charitably) of what constitutes an Unemployed Person. If you are out of work, but did some kind of part-time work recently, while looking for a full-time job, you are regarded as no longer Unemployed, no matter how little you received, by way of pay. Or if you are out of work, but you got discouraged, and didn't look for a job *during the last four weeks* you are regarded as no longer Unemployed; you have, from the Government's point of view, and I quote: "dropped out of the Labor Force." That gives us some clues, as to the other figures we need to add in, here:

b) *The number of people whom the Government counts as Employed, but who are in fact still playing the survival game because they are below the Federal poverty level.* The February 1975 *Jobs for Veterans Report* of the National Alliance for Businessmen commented: "If one counted those forced to take jobs paying below the federal poverty level, the unemployment

UNEMPLOYMENT—1900 TO 1975

[In thousands of persons 14 years and over for 1900 through 1960. In thousands of persons 16 years and over for subsequent years. Annual averages.]

Year	Unem-ployed	% of civilian labor force	Year	Unem-ployed	% of civilian labor force	Year	Unem-ployed	% of civilian labor force
1900	1,420	5.0%	1925	1,453	3.2%	1951	2,099	3.3%
1901	1,205	4.0%	1926	801	1.8%	1952	1,932	3.1%
1902	1,097	3.7%	1927	1,519	3.3%	1953	1,870	2.9%
1903	1,204	3.9%	1928	1,982	4.2%	1954	3,578	5.6%
1904	1,691	5.4%	1929	1,550	3.2%	1955	2,904	4.4%
1905	1,381	4.3%	1930	4,340	8.9%	1956	2,822	4.2%
1906	574	1.7%	1931	8,020	16.3%	1957	2,936	4.3%
1907	945	2.8%	1932	12,060	24.1%	1958	4,681	6.8%
1908	2,780	8.0%	1933	12,830	25.2%	1959	3,813	5.5%
1909	1,824	5.1%	1934	11,340	22.0%	1960	3,931	5.6%
1910	2,150	5.9%	1935	10,610	20.3%	1961	4,714	6.7%
1911	2,518	6.7%	1936	9,030	17.0%	1962	3,911	5.5%
1912	1,759	4.6%	1937	7,700	14.3%	1963	4,070	5.7%
1913	1,671	4.3%	1938	10,390	19.1%	1964	3,786	5.2%
1914	3,120	7.9%	1939	9,480	17.2%	1965	3,366	4.5%
1915	3,377	8.5%	1940	8,120	14.6%	1966	2,875	3.8%
1916	2,043	5.1%	1941	5,560	9.9%	1967	2,975	3.8%
1917	1,848	4.6%	1942	2,660	4.7%	1968	2,817	3.6%
1918	536	1.4%	1943	1,070	1.9%	1969	2,831	3.5%
1919	546	1.4%	1944	670	1.2%	1970	4,088	4.9%
1920	2,132	5.2%	1945	1,040	1.9%	1971	4,993	5.9%
1921	4,918	11.7%	1946	2,270	3.9%	1972	4.840	5.6%
1922	2,859	6.7%	1947	2,356	3.9%	1973	4,304	4.9%
1923	1,049	2.4%	1948	2,325	3.8%	1974	5,076	5.6%
1924	2,190	5.0%	1949	3,682	5.9%	1975	7,830	8.5%
			1950	3,351	5.3%	1976		

Note: Beginning 1957, certain limited changes have been made in definitions of employment and unemployment with the result that each month about 200,000 to 300,000 workers, formerly classified as employed, were counted as unemployed. On the basis of old definitions, unemployment in 1957 averaged 2,693,000.
See *Current Population Reports*, Series P-57, No. 176.

rate would be triple the official rate." That means that approximately 15,660,000 are below federal poverty level (which, in 1974, was $5,038 a year for a nonfarm family of four). The Government claims there are only 5,100,000 *families* below poverty level—since families having two wage earners, each of whom is working below poverty level, will often come out above the level when both salaries are added together.[6] To avoid argument, we will here take the lower figure: 5,100,000 still playing the survival game, in spite of their being employed part or full-time. Now, to the two figures arrived at thus far, we must add:

c) *The number of people whom the Government counts as Dropped Out of the Labor Force, but who—in fact—still want a job.* The Government has told us how many this was in 1975, as seen from this Table:[7]

Job Desire of Persons Outside the Labor Force, By Sex, 1975 Annual Averages
(THOUSANDS)

LABOR FORCE STATUS (Age 16 and Over)		Total	MEN	WOMEN
Civilian noninstitutional population		151,268	71,403	79,865
In civilian labor force		92,613	55,615	36,998
Not in civilian labor force		58,648	15,787	42,861
DO NOT WANT A JOB NOW		**53,452**	**14,145**	**39,307**
Current Activity	going to school	6,291	3,191	3,100
	disabled	4,789	2,554	2,235
	keeping house	31,334	219	31,115
	retired	7,851	6,428	1,423
	other	3,187	1,753	1,434
WANT A JOB NOW		**5,196**	**1,642**	**3,553**
Reason for	school attendance	1,439	736	703
not looking:	ill health, disability	672	299	373
	think cannot get a job	1,082	359	722
	16 to 19 years old	178	88	90
	20 to 24 years	167	57	110
	25 to 59 years	539	106	433
	60 years and over	198	109	88
	white race	776	258	518
	negro and other races	306	101	205
	home responsibilities	1,109	29	1,109
	other	894	219	646

Note that detail may not add to totals because of rounding.

Remember, the above figures are in thousands, so we need to add -000 to each. Thus the total number of people *outside the labor force* who want a job now is 5,196,000. We can presume they want a job because they are finding it difficult to survive, even though: 1,439,000 are in school; 672,000 have ill health or a disability; and 2,003,000 have home responsibilities or

243

"other" reasons, which preclude job-hunting at the present time. That still leaves a *minimum* of 1,082,000 who want a job, but are not looking for work simply because they have become convinced that there is no work—and so, are playing the Survival "game" with a vengeance.

Taking all three of the above figures, we are left with the following:

	Minimum	Maximum
Technically "Unemployed"	7,830,000	7,830,000
"Employed" below poverty	5,100,000	15,660,000
"Outside labor force" but want a job	1,082,000	5,196,000
TOTAL:	14,012,000	28,686,000

i.e., somewhere between fourteen million and twenty-eight million people are at the Survival level, in the World of Work. And the point of this statistic, so laboriously arrived at, is that *if you are wrestling primarily with the issue of Survival, on your "Working" Pyramid, you have lots and lots of company.* Enough, in fact, to fill eighty thousand Super Bowls. I want to emphasize this, because one of the most disheartening factors in wrestling with the issue of Survival is the feeling that you are virtually alone, in this. You are not.

Apart from welfare, living off one's family, or illegal activities, the key to Surviving—for most people—is the ability to find a job. Indeed, there would be no problem with Survival at all,

—IF there were an equal number of job-seekers and Jobs-Available.

—IF anyone could do any job.

—IF employers would hire anyone who was even remotely capable of doing the job, regardless of age, experience, training, color, handicaps, or whatever.

—IF we had an Employment Office system that was capable of linking up every job-seeker with every available job.

In point of fact however, we have many problems with Survival

—BECAUSE there are *apparently* not as many Jobs-Available as there are job-seekers. The fact that fourteen *million*—not fourteen hundred—people are wrestling with the need to find a better job and better-paying job in this country, should tell us something. It suggests a monumental *dysfunction in our society,* either in its ability to produce jobs, or in its ability to link them up with job-seekers, or both.

—BECAUSE jobs require certain skills—even though these are usually over-stated by people who are doing the hiring—and not everyone can do every job. More about this, later.

—BECAUSE we have lots of prejudice in this country. And every kind of prejudice—against the young, against the old, against minorities, against women, against ex-offenders, against ex-addicts, against ex-psychiatric patients, against short people, against the handicapped, against people with education, against the rich, against the poor, or whatever—can be indulged, subtly or openly, during the hiring process, no matter how many laws are passed. To illustrate this, it was revealed recently *(The Chronicle of Higher Education,* October 11, 1976) that the Equal Employment Opportunity Commission, set up to combat job discrimination facing women and members of minority groups

- had a backlog of 120,000 cases,
- with an average waiting period of two years before settlement,
- with 89% not receiving relief, even after settlement,
- resulting in the General Accounting Office's conclusion that the EEO Commission had had only a "minimal effect" on the discrimination.

As a consequence of the above prejudices, the job-hunt turns out to be an obstacle course, of the first order. First you're too *Young;* a minute later (as it seems) you are too *Old.* First only *Whites* need apply; a minute later (historically speaking) only *Minorities* need apply ("we've got to fill our quota—sorry"). First you're *Underqualified* ("when you've got more experience, come back and see us. Well, nō, I don't know how you're going to get that experience, when nobody will hire you"); a minute later you're *Overqualified* (that's "employer-ese" for: "I'm scared that if I hire you, since this job doesn't take advantage of all your training and experience, you'll leave me the first time you see something better"). First only *Males* are being hired ("Sorry, lady, all our secretarial positions are filled"); then only *Females* are being hired ("Sure, buddy, I'd like to hire you, but I've got some government contract, and I'm under the gun to hire more females—fast"). First only *High-Paying Positions* are available ("Man, if you were a company vice-president, I could place you tomorrow."); then only *Low-Paying Positions* are available ("I'm afraid your salary demands are too high for us to meet"). And so forth.

What all this adds up to (he said, facetiously) is that there is about one hour in your whole life that you are "hirable." More seriously, what this all adds up to is that our whole Hiring Process is a mess, and compares favorably with the haphazard process by which we choose a mate.

—BECAUSE we do not have a linkage system between job-seeker and Jobs-Available—least of all in the person of the U.S. Employment Service. As you will note from this Table,[8] in

INDIVIDUALS SERVED BY THE U.S. EMPLOYMENT SERVICE:	Fiscal 1975 (thousands)	Fiscal 1974 (thousands)	% Change
New and renewal applicants	15,035	13,307	13.0%
Job openings received	7,889	9,851	−19.9%
Placed in jobs*	3,138	3,334	− 5.9%
Counseled	884	982	−10.0%
Tested	710	854	−16.9%
Provided with reportable service**	7,727	7,652	1.0%

*   Includes short-term placements of three days or less.
**   Reportable services include placement jobs, enrollment in training, referral to jobs, WIN appraisal interviews, referral to training, enrollment in orientation, referral to supportive services, job development contacts, testing and counseling.

Fiscal 1975, out of 15,035,000 applicants to the Employment Service, 3,138,000 or 21% were placed in jobs—*if you include jobs which lasted three days or less.* This means the placement rate was even more dismal if such jobs were excluded. How

dismal? Well, it gets down to a placement rate of 13.7% as you will see from this summary of a survey done by the Census Bureau, of ten million job-seekers, in 1972:

USE AND EFFECTIVENESS OF JOB SEARCH METHODS: Method:	% of total job-seekers using this method	* Effec-tive-ness Rate
Applied directly to employer	66.0%	47.7%
Asked friends: . . . about jobs where they work	50.8%	22.1%
. . . about jobs elsewhere . .	41.8%	11.9%
Asked relatives: . . . about jobs where they work	28.4%	19.3%
. . . about jobs elsewhere . .	27.3%	7.4%
Answered newspaper ads: local	45.9%	23.9%
. . . nonlocal	11.7%	10.0%
Private employment agency	21.0%	24.2%
Federal/State employment service	33.5%	13.7%
School placement office	12.5%	21.4%
Civil Service test	15.3%	12.5%
Asked teacher or professor	10.4%	12.1%
Went to place where employers come to pick up people	1.4%	8.2%
Placed newspaper ads: local	1.6%	12.9%
. . . nonlocal	.5%	**
Answered ads in professional or trade journals . . .	4.9%	7.3%
Union hiring hall	6.0%	22.2%
Contacted local organization	5.6%	12.7%
Placed ads in professional or trade journals	.6%	**
Other	11.8%	39.7%

* Effectiveness Rate Percentage was obtained by dividing the number of jobseekers who found work using the method, by the total number of job-seekers who used the method, whether successfully or not.

** Base less than 75,000.

Source: Occupational Outlook Quarterly, Winter 1976.

Reversing the above "effectiveness rates" so that they are stated in the form of "ineffectiveness" (20% effectiveness equals 100-20, or 80% ineffectiveness), we see that The "Official" Job-Hunting Apparatus in this country comes out as follows:

1. Private employment agencies (fail to place 75.8 people out of each 100 who turn to them for help in finding a job)
2. Newspaper ads (fail to place 76.1 out of each 100 who try to find a job through them)
3. Union hiring halls (fail to get a job for 77.8 out of each 100 people who go there)
4. School placement offices (fail to place 78.6 out of each 100 who try to find a job through them)
5. The Federal (U.S. Employment Service)/State offices (fail to place 86.3 out of every 100 persons who try to get a job through them)
6. Civil Service (fails to yield a job for 87.5 out of every 100 people who try for a job there)

All in all, not exactly a record calculated to inspire you with confidence.

No wonder, then, (at this writing) the average length of time it takes to find a job is 115 days, or four months. And, in many cases, it takes far longer—up to two years. This means that when we are out of work, we have to wrestle with Survival for quite some time. Inevitably, this takes its toll, physically and mentally. In a study prepared by Professor M. Harvey Brenner of Johns Hopkins University for the Joint Congressional Economic Committee, every rise in the unemployment rate in this country has been followed by increases in "seven indicators of social stress": homicide, suicide, deaths from cardiovascular and kidney disease, deaths from cirrhosis of the liver, total number of deaths, admissions to mental hospitals, and the number of people sent to jail for crimes. There are varying 'time lags' between a rise in unemployment and these stress consequences—suicides peak a year after the rise, while fatal heart attacks peak three years later—but Professor Brenner has concluded that the consequences (or, as he more cautiously puts it, the associations) with each one per cent rise in unemployment currently, when it is sustained for six years is as follows:[11]

Each 1% Rise = Approximately One Million
Additional Persons Out of Work —

and, *36,887 additional total deaths*
20,240 additional cardiovascular (heart) deaths

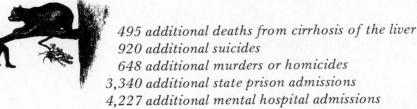

495 additional deaths from cirrhosis of the liver
920 additional suicides
648 additional murders or homicides
3,340 additional state prison admissions
4,227 additional mental hospital admissions

If the rise in the unemployment rate of some 3% (since 1970) is sustained for six years, the above table should be multiplied by three.

It should be further pointed out that women bear a disproportionate share of this kind of stress from playing the Survival 'game' as an unemployed person. In a study done by Rachelle Warren, of the Institute of Labor and Industrial Relations, funded by the National Institute of Mental Health,[12] unemployed women suffered almost four times more stress (evidenced by headache, depression, and insomnia) than unemployed men—probably because they felt they had no one to turn to. Whereas unemployed men usually have the support of their spouses, unions, former co-workers, and so forth.

Survival is, consequently, no joking matter. Sometimes the issue is literally that. And since job-hunting is the core of the problem, clearly what we need are some

---

Rules For Survival Job-Hunting

FIRST RULE FOR SURVIVAL JOB-HUNTING:
☐ **Use as many different methods as you can.**

Since no one method is fool-proof—even the best method, applying directly to an employer, fails to work for more than half (52.3 out of every 100 people who use it, to be exact)—it comes down to a kind of 'Las Vegas Mentality.' Namely, if you're going to play the slot machines, play as many different ones as you can, in the hope that one of them at least will pay off.

SECOND RULE FOR SURVIVAL JOB-HUNTING:
☐ **Invest the most time in those methods that work the best.**

They turn out to be, in order: applying directly to employers—face to face at the factory, place of business, or wherever; private employment agencies; answering local newspaper ads; asking friend about jobs where they work; and asking relatives about jobs where they work.[9]

THIRD RULE FOR SURVIVAL JOB-HUNTING:

☐ As much as you physically can, go face-to-face with people—rather than inserting a piece of paper (i.e. your resume) or an instrument (i.e., your phone) between you and them.

As a friend of mine once said, "Remember, paper is an insulating material." So are instruments, like the telephone. Paper turns you into a monologue, and the telephone deprives you of any response except the verbal. When you go face-to-face however, you can see their eyes, their face, and hands—and whatever it is that these are 'saying'—as well as hear their voice. All of this applies to your contacts with your Contacts (friends, relatives, etc.) as well as to your contacts with employers.

FOURTH RULE FOR SURVIVAL JOB-HUNTING:

☐ If your problem is that of even getting an interview for a job, you will have to work harder on Alternative Methods of the Job-Hunt, which ignore the question of whether or not a place has a vacancy. In other words you will need to have a Plan B.

When people wrestling with Survival have tried in vain to get a job—they can't even get in for an interview—they traditionally go one of three routes thereafter:

a) They go back. They search the past history of this country, to uncover some jobs that used to be popular and necessary. For example: blacksmith, stone carver, chimney sweep, stained glass designer, bookbinder, quill pen maker, and so forth.

b) They stand still. In a word, welfare. It is a Godsend for some people who absolutely have no alternative. It has become virtually a way of life for others, who do have an alternative.

c) They go into uncharted futures. Some people take occupations that already exist, and do new things with those occupations. Women, for example, have been (at long last) "invading" jobs once regarded as exclusively the perogative of men: police officers, telephone repairpersons, crafts jobs, and the like. Just as men have been invading fields once regarded as exclusively the prerogative of women: flight attendants, secretaries, etc. Another uncharted future is finding new ways to relate jobs to each other. Dr. Jessie Hartline, a specialist in banking and finance at Rutgers University, for example has proposed that two housewives band together and agree to clean each other's house for wages—in other words, that they hire each other, for $35. a day or whatever the proper wage would be. They would then each be employers, and would have to contribute an additional sum (as any employer does) to Social Security and the like. This, however, would qualify each for such benefits as workmen's (sic) compensation, disability insurance, health and medical protection, and Social Security. Other uncharted futures include identifying new needs of society, and rushing to meet them. A nationwide canning lid shortage, for example, such as hit the U.S. in the summer of 1975, provided an opportunity for enterprising persons to round up or produce such lids. Earlier, the gasoline shortage produced a rash of enterprising services (car-sitting for people tired of waiting in the long gasoline station lines) and products (devices to prevent gasoline from being siphoned out of automobile tanks, etc.). Such crises are always striking this country, in one area or another, and many enterprising souls—unable to find the traditional job—have put on their thinking-caps, and found Survival by helping people deal with those crises.

In addition to these three traditional routes that Survivors take, there is the option of looking askance at the whole traditional method of job-hunting, and opting for Alternative Methods. The Alternative Methods are described in our next section (on MEANING OR MISSION) and at great length in *What Color Is Your Parachute?*

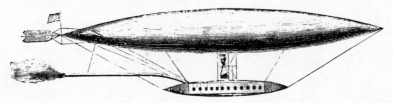

☐ **If you have no trouble getting interviews, but nothing ever comes of them, work on your Interview Techniques.**

Not being able to get in for an interview is one kind of problem; getting in, but not being able to get the interview to lead anywhere is another. Here is a checklist of things which cause employers to decide NOT to hire people. If you're clear about that, you can then decide to do the opposite.

Reasons for Not Getting Hired by An Interviewer	Things Which Will Improve Your Interviewer's Impression of You
1) Your posture is terrible, when you stand. And when you sit, you slump in the chair. You never look the interviewer in the eyes. Your handshake is as limp as a dishrag.	☐ Stand erect. When you sit, don't slump down in the chair. Look the interviewer in the eyes. Shake hands with a firm, but not overbearing, grip.
2) Your appearance is not clean and neat. You look sloppy.	☐ Look well-groomed. Wear the best-looking clothes you have. Clean fingernails. Hair neat.
3) During the interview, you talk the entire time about yourself—your needs, your likes and dislikes, and your demands.	☐ Divide the time you are speaking 50–50 between talking about yourself, and talking about the company or organization—asking questions about what it does, etc.
4) You obviously know nothing about the company or organization, and have spent no time trying to find out about it.	☐ A day or a week before your interview, go to the Personnel Office *solely* to pick up the company's annual report. Ask for anything else that is in print about what it does. Read the report. Underline things you like about it. Jot down any questions you have. Take the report, and your notes, with you when you go on the interview.
5) You demonstrate during the interview that you don't know how to get along with people, because you clash even with your interviewer.	☐ Treat your interviewer with neither too much respect nor too little. Don't interrupt him or her. Don't appear argumentative or belligerent.
6) During the interview, you demonstrate annoying personal habits: chewing gum, chain-smoking, etc.	☐ Be on your very best personal behavior. If you're nervous or scared, tell the interviewer so. He or she can identify with *that*. Talk about it, rather than just acting it out.
7) You make unrealistically-high salary demands.	☐ If this is truly survival job-hunting, and you're desperate, you have relatively little negotiating power about salary. Acting as though you do is not going to endear you to the interviewer.

8) The last reason for not getting hired by a particular interviewer is rarely talked about, but is crucial for you to know: You may be talking to an interviewer who has No Power to hire you. He or she *only* has the power to Screen you out. (Otherwise he or she has to pass you on 'upstairs' to the person who really does have the power to hire.) So, he or she is sitting there *looking* for reasons to screen you out. If this is true, the odds are ninety to one that you are talking to an interviewer in the personnel department.

☐ Try to avoid the personnel department at any cost. If there is no way for you to avoid it, and you find you are getting screened out, i.e. he or she is not passing you on 'upstairs' for a further interview, ASK WHY you are being turned down. This is your perfect right, if you ask it politely, gently, but firmly— and in the spirit of wanting to improve your impression at the Next Place you go to.

Now, I do want to emphasize that the above rules about Interviewing Techniques apply only to this one kind of job-hunting: Survival Job-Hunting. The requirements are: you are desperate. You are having trouble finding a job. Employers seem to have all the power. You have no time, or you have no motivation, to sit down and do some heavy thinking and detailed homework about Yourself. If any of these things are not true, then you ought to be looking very hard at the dramatically-different way of going about the job-hunt that is described in our next section (on MEANING OR MISSION). But then, you are no longer doing Survival Job-Hunting.[10]

☐ **If you are truly at the desperate/survival level, be willing to take ANY job TEMPORARILY, so long as the job is something you can handle.**

Many job-hunters *talk* as though they were doing Survival Job-Hunting, when in reality they are rather choosy about what jobs they will accept and what jobs they will not accept. *This shows that they are really at the "Meaning or Mission" level, on the Pyramid of Issues, and—consequently—ought to be using the tools, exercises, and approach that are described there.* If, however, you *are* at the survival level, use the Federal/State and private employment agencies to help you find honest work of any sort. You'd be surprised at how many different jobs you are capable of doing. According to some vocational experts, 1/3 of all the jobs in the Dictionary of Occupational Titles can be done by anyone who can read, write, compute, pick up and lay down things, and drive an automobile. 1/3 of all jobs can be done with some amount of on-the-job training, i.e., without further schooling. And 1/3 of all jobs require some kind of education, pre-entry training, or credentialing before the job can be obtained.

So, you *can* do—at the minimum—some seven thousand different jobs (there are approximately twenty-one thousand titles in the D.O.T.). Some of these may be very unappetizing to you, but — in a pinch — you may not want to be very choosy, for a period of time. If you are in a time-bind, money-bind, or any other kind of a bind, take what you can get.

Only, take care about these three things:

a) If the job really is unappetizing, 'way beneath you', and that sort of thing, label it clearly in your mind as 'temporary and stop-gap.' Don't for a moment make peace with it in your mind as something permanent and inescapable.

b) The more this job seems to have no purpose, meaning, or whatever for you, the more you should use your evenings, weekends, etc. to define your purpose and meaning in life—and what a job would look like which had such purpose and meaning. (See the next section, on Meaning and Mission.)

c) Thus the present unappetizing job will itself assume a purpose: "this job was to help me survive, bring in some bread, and buy time for me to get about my Plan B." And that may help you live with it, at least for a while.

SEVENTH RULE FOR SURVIVAL JOB-HUNTING:

☐ If nothing is turning up, and you're really down to rock bottom, run — not walk — to those agencies and centers which are very experienced in dealing with Survivors (that group, mentioned earlier, which plays the Survival 'game' endlessly, not because they have to but because they want to). Hunt for such agencies and centers diligently, and when you find them, pick their brains for all they're worth.

Here is an information search, again—but then, the whole job-search is little else than a hunt for information. The principles, by now, should be clear (unless you've been leaping around in this book, like the proverbial grasshopper). First, find the Switchboards or Resource Brokers—those who know who might know. In this case, your information centers might be:

> *the local 'underground' or 'counter-culture' or*
> *'peoples' newspaper—or its staff (phone them);*
> *the local 'underground' or 'peoples' bookstores,*
> *and such directories as they may carry (e.g.,*
> *"The People's Yellow Pages", etc.);*
> *the local 'peoples' radio stations;*
> *the local Legal Aid Society, and its staff;*
> *the local college newspaper, and the college*
> *counseling staff or placement staff;*
> *bulletin-boards in laundromats near college campuses.*

Such 'Switchboards' as these should be able to give you clues as to the actual agencies and centers that you are looking for. The simple criteria that distinguishes the latter are: 1) Do they see themselves truly as advocates for the job-hunter or Survival client? and 2) Are they really experienced? The types of places you may eventually come up with are: advocates for women, affirmative action centers, urban leagues, special centers for particular groups (welfare mothers, the handicapped, minorities,

257

etc.). If they know such things as how best to leave a job so as to be qualified for unemployment benefits, how to put together temporary expedients (like, running a day care center in your home), how to get employers to take a chance on you when you finally do get that job interview (like, offering to work the first five days without compensation so the employer can take a look at the quality of the work you do—if he or she will not otherwise hire you, because your training or experience look weak), then give them high marks. If they *aren't* familiar with such matters, go look for another agency or center. Your ultimate goal here is to find a place where someone who is new to the whole Survival 'game'—namely, You—can pick the brains of those who are old hands at it. Unfortunately, what we tend to do in our society is create groups where someone who is new to the Survival 'game' is put in with a whole lot of other people who are also new to the Survival 'game.' It's comforting, but it's not always helpful. You, on the other hand, are presumably looking for both comfort and helpfulness. Another strategy: if you have to go on welfare, or whatever, strike up conversations with others in line there. Get whatever helpful hints they have.

BEGGAR CAN EARN $17,000, TEST SHOWS

NEW YORK— A beggar can earn about $17,000 a year simply by panhandling, according to a survey conducted by a newspaper here.

The New York Post assigned one of its reporters to ask for spare change during a single eight-hour day.

Despite New York's highly-publicized financial woes, the reporter, Gene Weingarten, collected $48.96.

At that rate, a panhandler would take home $12,729 a year—equivalent to a gross salary of $17,100. *Zodiac News Service. 10/27/75*

If you're living out in Timbuktu, somewhere, and there absolutely isn't any such person or agency within 200 miles of you (Survivors do tend to congregate in urban areas, or out in remote wildernesses), there are always books. Not a whole lot of help—but better than floundering totally on your own. Go to your local bookstore (or stores) and browse in the paperback section, to see what kind of survival books have been put out lately (the list keeps getting added to, virtually every week). If you can afford, buy what looks like the most useful one to you. If you can't afford, finish the research there at the bookstore, then go to your local library and see if they have the title or titles that intrigued you the most.[11]

EIGHTH RULE FOR SURVIVAL JOB-HUNTING:

☐ <u>Pay particular attention to your main relationships— family or otherwise—during this whole period.</u> Under the strain of job-hunting, and the preoccupation of Survival, some good relationships get neglected, go down the drain—unnecessarily.

New studies are published every year, demonstrating the effect that joblessness has on the breakdown of marriages, etc. I cited, in *What Color Is Your Parachute?*, the fact that one major job-counseling firm found that 75% of their clients had been in, were in, or were about to be in some kind of marital separation, or divorce. In another study (of executives) it was found that between the ages of thirty-four to forty-two, 80% were hit by a job crises and/or marriage crisis.[12] But we surely do not need studies, to convince us that joblessness and living on the level of Survival—particularly if this is a new experience—exert a severe strain on any relationship. Hopelessness, depression, low energy, idleness, and other consequences of joblessness *can* cause you and your main relationship to find new solace, comfort and strength in each other's love. On the other hand, they can— when accompanied by irritability and the like—tear a relationship apart. It is necessary, therefore, to pay a great deal of attention to your main relationships, and invest more time in them—not less—during this time. So that, in retrospect, this period will turn out to have been a blessing, not a curse.

☐ **When (or if) you do get a job, don't assume the issue of Survival is all taken care of. You ought then to expend as much energy on not getting fired, as you did on the problem of getting hired.**

(Yeah, I know it would be nice if it turned out we had ten rules—it's such a nice round number. But nine is all it takes). The problem of holding on to your job is a real one. "Last hired, first fired", as the saying has it, reminds us that getting hired is not the end of our worries. It pays to stay alert, to put it mildly. Books keep coming out, on this subject—like:

Jobkeeping: A Hireling's Survival Manual by David Noer. 1976 Chilton Book Company, Radnor, Pennsylvania. $7.95. An excellent writer, who knows his stuff. The best book out, on this subject. Out of print—but see if your library has it.

John C. Crystal also has a very realistic and helpful section on how to survive after you get the job, in *Where Do I Go From Here With My Life,* 1974, Ten Speed Press, 900 Modoc Street, Berkeley, California 94707. $9.95. pp. 241-245, 150-159.

Clearly, *somebody* (some authors and publishers, at the very least) thinks this is a real issue, and one that the public is willing to listen to some advice about.

Apart from books, one way of surviving-after-you-get-the-job is to ask your fellow-workers what the secret of surviving in that place is. Workers who have been there for awhile *always know.* They've seen people fired, and they know why. We have asked a number of workers this question. The way we put it, was: "Given the world of work as it presently is, what do you think is the secret or key to surviving and holding onto your job?" These were the answers the workers gave:

1. *Know 'what the hell' is going on at all times.*
2. *Make sure the ones who "count" are comfortable with you.*
3. *Don't stand still. Work to improve your own productivity.*
4. *Stay alive — vibrant.*
5. *Check out with your supervisor each new task or assignment to be absolutely sure you understand exactly what he wants, or she wants.*
6. *Do assigned work thoroughly.*

7. Don't rock the boat.
8. Stay visible, know when people aren't buying you.
9. Stay current and well-informed in your field.
10. Stay beyond the cutting-edge; take risks.
11. Be willing and able to move, change, grow.
12. Stay flexible, able to respond to new demands.
13. Have a life outside the job.
14. Know what you are willing to do to hold onto the job, and what you are not willing to do. There are some things that no job is worth.
15. Hold on to your sense of personal worth, dignity and freedom, at all costs. No matter how others treat you, don't you disvalue yourself.
16. Work on your life/work planning. Have a 'plan B.'
17. Keep your parachute strapped on at all times; be ready to use it.

One key to survival not mentioned above, though emphasized by both Bernard Haldane and John Crystal, is to keep a log or diary of all the things you accomplish on the job, or all the things you are even indirectly responsible for; see our later section on "Effectiveness," for further details.

The Third Issue on our "Working Pyramid: ● *MEANING OR MISSION*

Effectiveness
Meaning or Mission
Survival
What's Happening

The average person today spends from twenty three to forty years in the World of Work—as we can see from the following table:

LIFE AND WORKLIFE EXPECTANCY AT BIRTH, FOR MEN AND WOMEN, 1900-70

Year	Life Expectancy		Worklife Expectancy		Nonwork Years	
	Women	Men	Women	Men	Women	Men
1900	50.7	48.2	6.3	32.1	44.4	16.1
1940	65.7	61.2	12.1	38.1	53.6	23.1
1970	74.8	67.1	22.9	40.1	51.9	27.0

Sources: Seymour L. Wolfbein, *Changing Patterns of Working Life* (Washington: U.S. Dept. of Labor, Office of Manpower, Automation, and Training, 1963), and Howard J. Fullerton, Jr., and James J. Byrne, "Length of Working Life for Men and Women, 1970," *Monthly Labor Review,* February 1976, pp. 31-35.

Note I did not say "average man", for one of the most striking aspects of the World of Work in recent years has been the advent of women into the labor force. As you can see from the chart on the facing page:

In 1954, men (twenty years or older) represented 65.5% of the labor force, while women (twenty years or older) represented only 28.2%. By 1974, those figures had become 55.3% and 35%, respectively, while today (1978) there are thirty nine million women workers, and they represent 41% of our total labor force.

What all of this means is that men and women alike have a long time to plan for, in the World of Work and beyond.

COMPOSITION OF LABOR FORCE AND UNEMPLOYED

Members of Civilian Labor Force and Unemployed
Persons, 16 Years of Age and Over, by Color, Sex and Age,
as Percentage of Civilian Labor Force
and of Unemployed Persons, Respectively, Selected Years

	1954		1959	
	% of labor force	% of unem- ployed	% of labor force	% of unem- ployed
White men 20 years plus	59.4	46.6	57.2	42.4
White women 20 years plus	24.4	22.3	26.1	22.4
White teenagers 16–19 years	5.5	12.0	5.9	14.0
Nonwhite men 20 years plus	6.1	11.0	6.1	11.7
Nonwhite women 20 years plus	3.8	5.9	4.0	6.1
Nonwhite teenagers 16–19 years	0.8	2.2	0.7	3.4
All whites	89.3	80.9	89.2	78.8
All nonwhites	10.7	19.1	10.8	21.2
All men 20 years plus	65.5	57.6	63.3	54.1
All women 20 years plus	28.2	28.2	30.1	28.5
All teenagers 16–19 years	6.3	14.2	6.6	17.4

	1964		1974	
	% of labor force	% of unem- ployed	% of labor force	% of unem- ployed
White men 20 years plus	55.0	36.4	50.0	30.5
White women 20 years plus	27.3	24.1	30.4	27.7
White teenagers 16–19 years	6.6	18.7	8.6	22.1
Nonwhite men 20 years plus	6.0	9.0	5.3	7.1
Nonwhite women 20 years plus	4.3	7.5	4.6	6.4
Nonwhite teenagers 16–19 years	0.8	4.3	1.1	6.2
All whites	88.9	79.2	89.0	80.3
All nonwhites	11.1	20.8	11.0	19.7
All men 20 years plus	61.0	45.4	55.3	37.6
All women 20 years plus	31.6	31.6	35.0	34.1
All teenagers 16–19 years	7.4	23.0	9.7	28.3

Note: 1974 data are for June. Other years are national averages.

Sources: 1974 data *Monthly Labor Review,* August 1974; other years, *Manpower Report of the President,* 1966

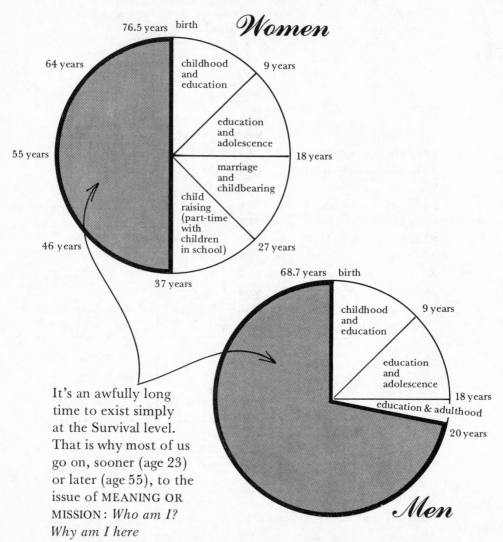

It's an awfully long time to exist simply at the Survival level. That is why most of us go on, sooner (age 23) or later (age 55), to the issue of MEANING OR MISSION: *Who am I? Why am I here on earth? What do I really want to accomplish with my life? What will give it some real purpose and meaning? Do I have any sense of mission or 'driveness' about any cause or any need in our society?*

Good questions. The only wonder is, that it takes us so long to get around to dealing with them. The Procrastinators' Club (see insert) has a lot more members than it thinks it does.

READY... SET...
PROCRASTINATE!

PHILADELPHIA (AP) — Last week was National Procrastination Week. Obviously this announcement should have appeared sooner but, frankly, nobody got around to writing it.

This is not a put on. Or put off. There really is a Procrastinators' Club of America, Inc. Its annual "week," set aside for the purpose of doing nothing, is actually the first week in March, though it is traditionally observed the second week.

If that is confusing, puzzle it out later.

That's the doctrine of the PCA: never do today what you can put off until tomorrow. Its slogan is "Procrastinate Now!" Les Waas, the PCA president, says it's the only sensible way to live.

"It's surprising how many problems become less important, even disappear, if you postpone them," he said, yawning.

"People who rush around and never relax and get all worried about being on time are people who die early. Then they are referred to as the late Mr. so-and-so. Why not be late while you're alive!"

Les Waas is 50, slight of build, with sandy hair, a matching mustache and no ulcers. He became president of PCA in 1956, when he and a few other unhurried Philadelphians organized the club.

"I'm still president," he said, "because we haven't gotten around to holding our 1957 elections yet.

"When we hold them, just think, I might be defeated. That would mean I haven't been president all these years. That's all right with me because it can get to be a nuisance."

As president, Waas had led club members on trips to Italy to see the show at the Circus Maximus, to Holland to relieve the boy with his finger in the dike, to London's Whitechapel Bell Foundry, where the Liberty Bell was cast, to complain about the crack.

"We met Douglas Hughes, who is the co-owner of the foundry," Waas said, "and pointed out the shoddy workmanship.

"He said the bell would have to be returned in its original carton. He blamed the crack on ignorant colonials who didn't know how to work it. He said the colonials were the crackers—and that we were crackers too."

The club also arranges an unbusy schedule of activities closer to home so its 2,000 dues-paying members can participate. Paying dues on time, incidentally, incurs a 5-per-cent penalty.

"I really think we have close to a half million members," Waas said. "They just haven't gotten around to joining."

To join, prospective members fill out a form which arrives in an envelope marked "open later." Right now the 1973 membership drive is in full swing.

"A good year to join," Waas said. "One of our most inactive.

"That's the beauty of kicking the habit of punctuality. You get to see how things turn out before you commit yourself. We always celebrate New Year's Eve some time in June, to see if the year was worth celebrating."

One of the PCA's most successful projects was its demonstration against the war of 1812.

"That was a real procrastinator's war," Waas said. "It began after England had corrected the conditions that caused it and its last battle was fought after the treaty was signed. That's our kind of war."

The club also names a Procrastinator of the Year. Well, most years it does.

It honored one fellow for his world's record overdue library book. It honored Philadelphia's Methodist Hospital for not placing its cornerstone, dated 1968, until 1972. It honored the postmaster general.

In the current (1976) issue of its publication, "Last Month's Newsletter," the club also named the winner of its 1958 essay contest on "How Procrastination Has Helped Make Life Better." Winner was Mrs. Walter Treftz. Her entry: "I'll Write Tomorrow."

There's lots more to tell about the Procrastinators' Club of America. Maybe another time.   *Sunday, March 13, 1977*

Some procrastination could, of course, be stamped out if we had more of these in our society:

If you've been saying to yourself, "Well, sure I'll do some life/work planning and figure out how to get a really meaningful job for myself. I'll do it as soon as I get a 'round tuit'," your troubles are over.

This illustration is a 'round tuit'. If you cut it out and keep it handy, you should have no difficulty in doing your life/work planning or life/work designing of a meaningful job, for you've finally gotten a 'round tuit.'

Of course, it *may* be that your difficulties consist of something more substantial than procrastination. You may not get around to designing a meaningful job for yourself, because you think that it would be an exercise in futility. Suppose your telephone rings at this point. On the phone is some friend, and in the course of the conversation you tell her or him what you are reading (namely, this book). "It says that I can find a job which has both meaning and a sense of purpose to it." Immediately a guffaw will greet your ears. "Well, of course," your friend will reply, "*everyone* would like a job like *that*. But, to quote *The Washington Post* and a lot of other experts, 'There simply are not enough good jobs to go around to everyone who thinks he or she deserves one.' Come *on*, Charlene (or Charlie)."

Very plausible. And if true, then of course the whole issue of jobs with meaning comes down—in the last analysis—to this: a few people are lucky, and find such jobs; most of us are

unlucky, and must settle for what we can get. (If you feel the sweet sickening aroma of the Victim Mentality in the air, go back and reread pages 49-53.)

In the National Career Development Project, we have amassed a lot of evidence that—on the contrary—people of every imaginable background, age, sex, race, education, and skills can deliberately set about to find a job that gives them a sense of meaning and mission in life, and succeed at finding it— *provided* only that they are willing to devote a lot of hard work to the planning thereof, and provided they do not believe the myths concerning the job market that are so pervasive in our society. These myths, incidentally, are very widespread and widely-believed. And no wonder. We hear these ideas from our childhood so frequently and so convincingly, that we think "Well, of course, they *must* be true." But they are Myths in the old sense of that word: "old wives tales" (or "old husbands tales"), no more to be believed than some of the information we picked up "on the street" about sex. There are seven such myths. Let's take a hard look at them:

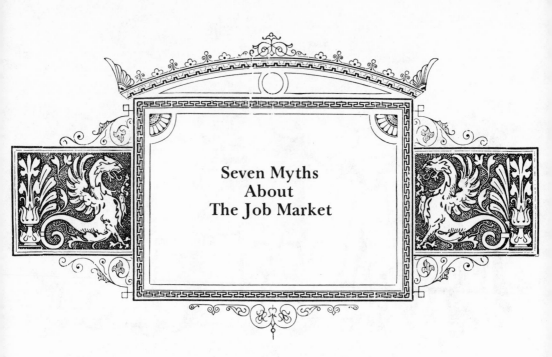

Seven Myths
About
The Job Market

MYTH **1** THERE ARE COMPARATIVELY FEW JOBS
'OUT THERE,' ESPECIALLY WHEN THE
'LABOR MARKET' IS TIGHT.

The truth is: there are probably at least two million jobs 'out there' at any given moment. A survey conducted by the National Federation of Independent Business, when the 'job-market was 'tight', revealed that small businesses *alone* had one and a half million vacancies (San Francisco Chronicle, December 11, 1974); never mind, big businesses. If you are going to be job-hunting, your problem is not that of canvassing too-few possibilities, but too-many.

MYTH **2** IF YOU CAN'T FIND A JOB THAT PROVES
THAT THERE ARE COMPARATIVELY FEW
JOBS 'OUT THERE.'

The truth is: there is a vast difference between existence (on the one hand) and communication (on the other). YOU exist, for example, but what percentage of the people in your city or town know that? So too with jobs. If you can't find a job, that proves nothing about its existence. It only says something about the rotten Communication 'system' our country has devised, regarding job vacancies. How rotten? Well, a study done some years ago — allegedly by The Conference Board, and funded by the Ford Foundation—, *and* a study done last year by Toni St. James of the federal/state Employment Service (in California) both came up with an identical conclusion: between 75-80% of the job-vacancies which exist at any given moment are NOT advertised or otherwise communicated through ANY of the agencies or places that a job-hunter traditionally turns to: viz., newspaper ads, civil service notices, federal/state employment agency, private employment agencies, computer job-banks, etc.

MYTH **3** **MOST PEOPLE, WHEN IT IS TIME FOR THEM TO GO JOB-HUNTING, BASICALLY KNOW HOW TO DO IT,**

The truth is: there are two basic ways to go about the job-hunt, one of them infinitely more effective than the other. [13] But most people only know about the relatively ineffective way: which depends on resumes, employment agencies, etc. Resumes, on an average, only produce one invitation to come in for an interview, per every 245 resumes that a company receives. Only half these invitations—according to the same survey[14] —were responded to, probably because a few highly-skilled individuals received the bulk of the invitations; so, in fact, only one interview *actually* took place for every 490 resumes that an average company receive. Furthermore, the average company conducted three interviews before it made a job-offer, which works out to one job-offer for every 1470 (490 times three) resumes a company receives. That means 1469 disappointed resume-senders, for every resume-sender who did finally secure the offer of a job. Conclusion: resumes are tremendously ineffective ways of digging-up a job. But this is all that most job-hunters know, about how to go about the job-hunt, *because job-hunting is not taught in most high schools and most colleges of this country— so job-hunters are thrown back upon what they've been able to pick up by word of mouth among their peers, or from some of the terrible job-hunting books that bookstores and libraries are filled with.* When this 'plan' doesn't work, 99 job-hunters out of 100 have no 'plan B' to fall back on.

MYTH 4 **THERE ARE A NUMBER OF PLACES THE JOB-HUNTER CAN TURN TO FOR HELP, THAT HAVE THE JOB-HUNTER'S BEST INTERESTS AT HEART.**

The truth is: the quality of help offered by these places is hampered by one minor little detail: they have only a very *limited* idea about what jobs are available. How limited? Well, an FTC study, released in 1968, revealed that the average private employment agency finds jobs for only 5 out of every 100 people who walk in their doors. A more recent study, this time of newspaper ads, revealed that in two 'typical' cities (San Francisco and Salt Lake) 75-85% of *all* the employers in those cities did not hire *anyone* through want-ads during the *entire* year. Of course, newspapers continue to publish ads *anyway,* and private employment agencies continue to make a profit *anyway* —because there are *enough* employers who use them both, to permit them to survive (or even thrive). But it *is* the employers, and not the job-hunters, who support them and therefore their loyalty is —in the first instance and the last—to the employers. The basic interest of these places which supposedly have the job-hunter's best interests at heart, is—starting with a job-vacancy as The Given—trying to find some job-hunter to match *that,* even if the job-hunter has to be pushed and shoved into a somewhat different shape, in order to match that Given. What the Job-hunter is hoping for, of course, is some place which will take *the job-hunter* as The Given and then try to find a job which matches him or her—even if that job has to be pushed and shoved into a somewhat different shape. *That* sort of place is, needless to say, infinitely more difficult to find. Though, college placement offices and Life/WORK Planning courses do indeed begin by taking the job-hunter as The Given: not to be folded, spindled, or mutilated.

MYTH 5 **EMPLOYERS ARE IN THE DRIVER'S SEAT, SO FAR AS THE WHOLE JOB-HUNT PROCESS IS CONCERNED.**

The truth is: admittedly, employers have a vast amount of power. Namely, the power to hire and the power to fire. What they are unhappy about, as you will discover if you talk to

270

them at length is *how often* they have to use these two powers. In a word, they have high employee turnover, because it is so hard for employers to find dedicated, competent employees who can really do the job and love to do the job. Without such employees, every employer is going to fail—because he or she can't possibly run the whole business, factory, organization, or whatever by himself or herself in most cases. And most employers are as perplexed about how to find such employees, as job-hunters are perplexed about how to find good employers. In other words, *employers are as much a victim of the communication problem cited in Myth #2, above, as job-hunters are.* When a job-interview finally takes place—i.e., when employer and would-be-employee meet—both are equally desperate (in many cases). The employer only has the *illusion* that he or she is in the driver's seat.

MYTH 6 JOB-HUNTERS MUST PASS EMPLOYERS'
SCREENING (OF THE RESUME, APPLICATION
BLANK, TEST, AND/OR INTERVIEW) AND
THE JOB-HUNTER'S ONLY HOPE IS EITHER
EXPERIENCE OR CREDENTIALS.

The truth is: it is equally a part of the whole job-hunt process, that an employer must pass the job-hunter's screening. The trouble is: while almost all employers do this screening (mentally, or process-wise) *before* they hire, most job-hunters postpone this screening until *after* they have been hired. Proof of this is to be found in a survey[15] which revealed that of all those placed in a job by the Federal/State employment agency in one geographical area, 57% were *not* to be found at that job within one month following. Obviously, job-hunters don't know how to conduct their screening before getting hired, so they do it afterwards ("this is a lousy job; I think I'll quit"). Admittedly, these are probably blue-collar jobs, for people without college training. The mark of a college graduate is that he or she usually takes five years to do the screening, i.e., to make up his or her mind that "this is a lousy job; I think I'll quit." Employers' screening, of course, is not that much more accurate. Employers keep concentrating on the job-hunter's past (his or her experience or credentials)—whereas obviously the only thing that can

271

possibly be of interest is the job-hunter's present and future (see pages 125 and 126 in the 1978 edition of *What Color Is Your Parachute?*).

MYTH **7** THE PERSON WHO GETS HIRED IS THE ONE WHO CAN DO THE JOB BEST.

The truth is: we received a letter from a man who applied for a particular vacancy, and was hired. He reported that, due to an organizational fluke, he found in his files all the applications for that vacancy—and as he studied them, he realized that a lot of the applicants were much better qualified for the job than he was. *But he knew how to get hired; and they did not.* This is absolutely typical, throughout the world of work—as you have good cause to know, if you will only reflect upon some of the people you have seen in certain jobs, and the thoughts you had at the time about their incompetency. Yet they got hired. In the world of work then, this is the truth: the person who gets hired is not *necessarily* the one who can do the job best, but the one who knows the most about how to get hired.

Wrestling with Meaning or Mission

The two things which finally goad us into dealing with this issue are *usually* Worker Dissatisfaction; or Finding the Traditional Job-Hunting Method Doesn't Work No Matter How Hard We Try. Actually, under these two broad headings are alot of different groups of people, and *each* group assumes that it has a Unique Problem which needs a Special Manual or Approach. Thus, if those assumptions were correct, we would need to have the following Manuals (I said, IF they were correct, we would need):

I. Manuals on Job Dissatisfaction
   A. A Manual for Executives Who Want To Change Careers
   B. A Manual for Executives Who Want To Know How to Restructure or Improve Their Present Job
   C. A Manual for Workers Who Want To Change Careers
   D. A Manual for Workers Who Want to Start Their Own Business
   E. A Manual for Workers Who Want To Know How To Restructure or Improve Their Present Job
   F. A Manual for (So-called) 'Housewives' Who Want to Find Volunteer Activities Outside to Supplement Their Activities in the Home
   G. A Manual for 'Housewives' Who Want to Find Part-time Work
   H. A Manual for 'Housewives' Who Want to Enter the Labor Market (or World of Work) Full-time

II. Manuals on Ways Around the Traditional Job-Hunting Method, When It Doesn't Work, No Matter How Hard We Try
   A. A Manual for the Teenager Who Cannot Find Work
   B. A Manual for the High-School Graduate Who Cannot Find Work
   C. A Manual for the Liberal Arts College-Graduate Who Cannot Find A Job in His or Her Field
   D. A Manual for Members of Minority Groups in This Country Who Cannot Find A Job in Their Field
   E. A Manual for Members of Minority Groups in This Country, Who Cannot Find The Kind of Job They Want, Because of Prejudice

F. A Manual for 'Housewives' Who Have No Credentials or Experience in the World of Work (As They Suppose)
G. A Manual for Ex-Offenders Who Cannot Find Work Because of Employer-Prejudice About Their History
H. A Manual for Ex-Addicts Who Cannot Find Work Because of Employer-Prejudice About Their History
I. A Manual for Psychiatric Out-patients, Who Cannot Find Work Because of Employer-Prejudice About Their History
J. A Manual for the Handicapped Who Cannot Find Work Because of Employer-Prejudice About Their Abilities.
K. A Manual for Alcoholics Who Cannot Find Work Because of Low-Motivation
L. A Manual for Middle-Aged Job-Hunters Who Cannot Find Work Because of Employer-Prejudice About Their Age
M. A Manual for Short Male Job-Hunters Who Cannot Find Executive Jobs Because of Employer-Prejudice About Their Height
N. A Manual for Retired Persons Who Cannot Find Work Because of Employer-Prejudice About Their Age
O. A Manual for Female Job-Hunters Who Cannot Find the Proper Wage That Their Expertise and Position Entitle Them To, Because of Employer-Prejudice About Their Femaleness
P. A Manual for Welfare-Recipients Who Cannot Find Work Because of (Supposedly) Few "Marketable Skills"

That's alot of separate manuals! And (unfortunately) somebody somewhere has in fact produced any kind of manual that you can point to in the list above . . . . with possibly the exception of the manual for short male job-hunters (some reader doubtless will write me—my address is in the back of this book—to let me know there even is a manual like *that*).

What's unfortunate about that fact is that ALL OF THE PROBLEMS ABOVE HAVE THE SAME SOLUTION, AND THEREFORE ALL THAT IS NEEDED IS ONE MANUAL. We (in our culture) like, of course, to hide this from folks. We like to put women job-hunters altogether with one another (but with no-one else), and have them talk about "the problems that are unique to women." And we like to get alot of retired people who are job-hunting, together in one room, and have them talk about "the problems that are unique to retired people." And so forth. Why? Well, for one thing it creates more jobs for professionals in this field. If each group needs its own separate room, and its own separate process, then each group needs its own separate leader. Voila! Jobs are created for job-counselors. (I did not say: for their clients. Poor clients!) Then, for another thing, it is not yet well known in this country that the varying problems listed above all have a common solution. Each job-hunting group does assume that its problems are unique; and counselors sometimes 'buy in' on these assumptions unwittingly and without thinking.

The best known example of such an assumption is the one about: "women are grossly underpaid in this country (very true) *and they are the only ones who face that kind of wage discrimination*" (tilt). Several years ago I did a survey of male campus ministers in the nine Western States, and discovered that these men—with at least seven years' education beyond high school—were making an average annual salary of $7200. So, women are indeed grossly underpaid in this country. A lot of men are grossly underpaid, too. Therefore whatever remedy the women need, alot of men need also. And so it goes. Job-hunters are not naturally divided into tribes; nor should they artificially be.

Okay, then, we all need only *one* manual in order to know how to find a job that will avoid the myths, and give our lives a sense of Meaning or Mission. But it would take a complete *manual* to deal with that subject; no mere "half a chapter" will do. Since that manual has already been written—well actually two manuals have already been written, and their names are (don't tell me you guessed it already) *What Color Is Your Parachute? A Practical Manual for Job-Hunters and Career-Changers,* and the more comprehensive *Where Do I Go From Here With My Life? A very systematic, practical, and effective life/work planning manual* which my good friend John C. Crystal co-authored with me, inasmuch as it describes the system which he invented,—and since so many of you are familiar with one or both of these, it would be idiotic to reproduce here what you already know.

I will, therefore, content myself with merely jotting down some "Late Learnings"—things which, since the writing of *Parachute* and *Where,* we have learned (from our workshops and counseling of job-hunters) need especially to be underlined and stressed. I will jot these down in briefest form, assuming that you are familiar with the two manuals just alluded to, and will understand these as footnotes. (Or finger-notes, as the case may be.) However, in the event that you are *not* familiar with either of the two works cited, for you we have a series of cartoons so that this section shouldn't be a total loss. On we go, then, to:

OUR "MISSION AND MEANING" CARTOON BOOK
WITH FOOTNOTES AND UNDERLININGS

The secret of changing careers and/or finding a job and work that will give you a sense of Mission and Meaning, consists in the following steps:

I. Remembering	V. Researching
II. Factoring	VI. Naming
III. Prioritizing	VII. Finding—Linking Up
IV. Focusing	VIII. Always a 'Plan B'

I. Remembering

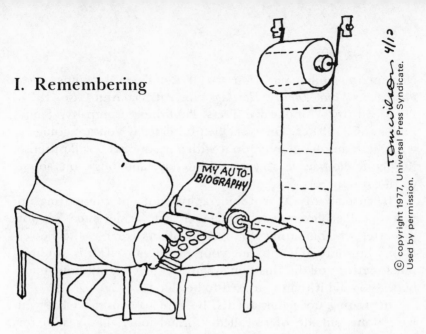

Our learnings have been (and your learnings may be):

The autobiography is by far the most effective way of Remembering; but the majority of people lack the self-discipline to do it.

Selected episodes from different periods of one's life, describing "peak achievements", takes much less time, so this is an infinitely more popular method of Remembering; but it is less effective than the autobiography.

The autobiography is receiving a lot of push these days under various names—autobiography, journal, diary, oral history, etc.—for reasons other than skill-identification. It will not surprise you that Alex Haley's *Roots* gave a lot of impetus to this movement. It is being pushed as a means of:

- integrating all of one's experiences, and hence one's self-concept;
- preserving one's feelings and thoughts;
- helping to pass on family history to future generations;
- making up for the fact that people write fewer day-by-day diaries these days, and fewer letters recounting their personal lives.

For these broader uses of the autobiography, the most helpful sourcebook is *At a Journal Workshop: The basic text and guide for using the Intensive Journal,* by Ira Progoff. 1975. Dialogue House Library, 45 West Tenth Street, New York, NY 10011. In both hardcover and paperback. For a simpler more elementary guide, see *How to Write Your Autobiography, Preserving Your Family Heritage,* by Patricia Ann Case. 1977. Published by Woodbridge Press Publishing Company, Santa Barbara, CA 93111. One very helpful clue: if you are going to write your autobiography, do it with a partner who will promise to phone you at least every third day, and bug you about getting it done.

If, instead of the autobiography, you opt for writing up your "peak achievements", remember that "achievement" is not a matter of comparing yourself to others (that is the Power *motif*) but only of comparing yourself to yourself. It is not how much better you did this thing than anyone else, but how much better you did it than you used to be able to.

In writing up achievements, be sure to consider what you have done outside of so-called "formal jobs," i.e., search for achievements in your home, your marriage and family relation-ships, your professional and personal groups outside of work, your community and volunteer activities, your social life, your religious life, your intellectual and aesthetic life, and in your recreational life.

People are habitually too brief in writing up achievements, or autobiography. To guard against this, each time you describe something you did, ask the question, "What did I have to do—or what did I do—in order to make this happen, or in order to make this achievement come off?"

You like inspirational quotes, on this subject of remember-ing? Okay, here are my two favorites: "Experience by itself simply means you are growing older. Experience that is looked at and evaluated provides clues that can be the wellspring of growth into your potential." (Bart Lloyd) And: "Self-esteem and good feelings come from remembering past achievements and strengths. They come from realistically taking stock of oneself. But good feelings, in themselves, do not contribute to learning unless the data generated from them are directed toward some future goal." (Ullik Rouk)

One final learning: if you can't write, get a tape recorder (they are dirt cheap these days) and talk into it. Get someone who knows how to type, to transcribe your taped talking onto paper later. If you not only can't write, but are also tongue-tied, have someone interview you in the presence of the tape recorder.

II. Factoring

"What can she do? Well, she can consolidate, separate, correlate, annotate, evaluate, calculate, delineate, estimate, tabulate, act up and go ape."

(FACTORING: Breaking a Larger Thing Down Into Its Simpler Elements)

Our learnings have been (and yours may also be) that:

Factoring is the general activity of breaking a larger thing down into its simpler elements, and may be performed with any number of objects, e.g., factoring your favorite geographical spot into its constituent components (good weather, uncrowded, etc.) or factoring your favorite partner (good conversationalist, nice sense of humor), etc. When factoring is done with "peak achievements" or an autobiography, it is more specifically called "skill-identification."

If you don't like the word "skills", there are a number of other labels floating around—from which you can choose, e.g., "motivated skills", "strengths", "demonstrated abilities", "beauties", "career resources", etc.

In the particular kind of factoring called "skill-identification" or whatever, you are going back over your autobiography or your series of peak achievements, in order to break them down into their simpler elements, i.e., the skills it took to do them.

Skill-identification is, at first, merely a kind of 'brainstorming'. You put down whatever occurs to you. Later, you can go back and clean up the labels. This is particularly true of "free-floating" skill-identification (i.e., that which is done without any lists, as in Trioing—see pages 66, 67, 68, 69, 70 and 72 in *Where Do I Go From Here With My Life?* Note that what is called "personal traits or qualities" on pages 72 and 73, we are here calling "self-management skills").

If you feel you are bad at skill-identification, get two other friends and form your own Trio, until you get the hang of it.

If you need warm-up practice, take a simple everyday activity (like driving an automobile) and run it through the skills list we gave you earlier (pages 169-176).

You will note that the aforementioned list is *primarily* of "functional" skills. If you wish to inventory your "work-content" skills (sometimes also called "specific-knowledges" skills), here is a framework on which to do your brainstorming— or to record the information already set down in your autobiography:

a) My Work-Content Skills: Where I Picked Them Up

List All The Schools or Places of Formal Learning, That You Have Attended, So Far In Your Life	List All The Jobs You Have Held, Together with Any Pre-Job or On-the-Job Training Programs	List All Your Leisure Time Activities (Whatever You Did When You Weren't In School Or At Work)
Be sure to include schools, colleges, conferences, workshops, books, cassettes, etc.	*Be sure to include volunteer jobs as well as those for which you were or are paid, and part-time as well as full-time, etc.*	*Be sure to include activities 'out on the street', clubs you belonged to, church or synagogue work, hobbies, crafts, amateur interests, recreational activities, therapies attended, etc.*

280

When you are done with that inventory, then fill in the following chart, using the list you just made to "tickle your memory".

b) My Work-Content Skills a.k.a. (also known as) My Specific Knowledges a.k.a. My Special Knowledges

The Degree of Skill I Possess (in my own estimation) ↓	Knowledges I Picked up In School Or In Courses	Knowledges I Picked Up At Work Or On The Job	Knowledges I Picked Up Out On The Street Or In My Leisure, At Hobbies, Etc.
	e.g., languages, psychology, etc.	*names of things, tools, processes, etc.*	*about cars, antiques, survival, etc.*
Rather Elementary			
More Advanced			
Very Advanced or Absolute Mastery			

When you are done with the above inventory, *circle* those knowledges you still enjoy so much that you would like to be able to use them in your *Future (Work or Leisure)*. Pick the 3, 5, or 10 that are most important to you, and prioritize them, in order.

exceptional unique
challenging mastery
strong dynamic versatile
responsive attractive highly
sophisticated artful
earning respect diplomatically
innovative readily repeatedly
perceptive responsible
deeply concerned discretion
unusually good grasp broad outstanding
new and improved driving
natural creative tactful acuity
with candor enjoying challenge
enjoying pioneering quickly adept competent
vigorous uncommon leading penetrating
greatly contributed toward enjoying lifelong
bringing new life humanly oriented challenge initiative
warm aware accurately extensively highest outgoing
patiently urgently exceptionally broad
thinks on her feet thinks on his feet well trained
open-minded firm deep insight expert talented
high-level empathy
participative
calm diverse
sensitive
imaginative
foresight
kind

If you wish to also inventory your Self-Management Skills (and we hope you do), simply use the list on page 145 as a kind of questionnaire—"Do I have. . . ?" Jot down on a separate piece of paper the ones you believe you possess, and for each one give some examples of the kinds of situations where you believe you have demonstrated that skill. If the list on page 145 isn't long enough for you, additional ideas may be found on page 211 in *Where Do I Go From Here With My Life?*

If you want to know (somewhat plaintively) if there is *any* other way to do skill-identification besides writing an auto-biography, or writing up your peak achievements, the answer is "Of course". You can take the list of skills on pages 158-161, but re-title the two columns where you put the check marks, so that they now read: "I feel I possess this skill" and "I feel I possess this skill more than most of the population". Then check off whichever column is true—so far as you are concerned —for each skill. Or leave it blank if you feel you don't possess the skill at all. If you draw a total blank as to which skills you have, get a friend, a loving mate, or anyone else who knows you very well, to help you check it off. When all done, go back and —for every skill you checked—try to list at least two examples of situations or achievements in which you used that skill, and demonstrated that you have it. Or get your friend to help you do that. One problem with this approach: it isn't as thorough as The Other Way (you know what I mean) by a long shot. Whole bunches of your skills will be left, unnoticed, by the wayside. But if you just can't do The Other Way (and you did try), then this is obviously better than nothing.

You've written down (i.e., identified) a particular skill that you have, but as far as you can see, it locks you into only one occupation? Then you've probably put it into "work-content" language. Take it out of that language. Say you taught Sunday School. "Skilled at Sunday-School teaching" is *very* limiting. But: "skilled at interpreting universal truths in terms of every-day experience" is not. So, when a skill-identification gets too "locked in", ask yourself what larger skill is *this* a particular example of?

If you've got the skill out of "work-content" language, into "functional skill" language, and you still don't see what possibilities for The Future it has, try listing Five Different Settings (or Ways) in Which This Skill Can Be Used.

Even as Writing Your Autobiography has a raison d'etre beyond work related considerations, so does skill-identification. When s.-i. is done in Trios (see above) it is a *superb* means of helping to raise your self-esteem—whether or not you are job hunting or career changing.

III. Prioritizing

AFTER 'MAKING A BUNDLE' WHAT IS YOUR NEXT MOST IMPORTANT OBJECTIVE IN LIFE?

Our learnings about what needs to be underlined, are:

Anytime you have gathered information (about yourself, or about the world-out-there), it is *crucial* to prioritize it. Unprioritized, you have ten things (let us say) and it is not necessarily at all clear which you could let drop (if you had to) and which you want to hang onto, at all costs. Prioritized, the ten things are now in order of importance to you.

This is particularly true of skills. You *must* prioritize them. Otherwise you just have a bunch of unorganized information. You can prioritize any way you want to, but the best method is outlined in Appendix A of this book.

Before using Appendix A, it is terribly useful to take all your skills and put them into 'families' or 'clusters'—as John Crystal calls them. It is for example very difficult to prioritize 500-700 skills (the average number that people turn out to have), but relatively easy to prioritize 12-15 or 20 'families' or 'clusters' of skills. This is assuming the 500-700 have been 'clustered' into 12-15 or 20 such 'families.' If you're working off of the instrument we call "The Quick Job Hunting Map"— *The Beginning Version* on pages 163-176 plus Appendix D of this book, or *The Advanced Version,* which is Appendix A in the 1978 (and subsequent) editions of *What Color is Your Parachute?*—your skills are already 'clustered' for you. If you're inventing your own designation for your skills (as in Trioing), you will have to do your own clustering. Instructions are on pages 214-219, 74-84 in *Where Do I Go From Here With My Life?* P.S. Some people in career education circles do not like the word 'clusters' to be used with regard to skills, preferring to reserve it for their more limited usage as applying to occupations only. Tsk, tsk.

Before doing clustering (or prioritizing, for that matter) some people have found it *very useful* to do the following process: Write each skill on a separate sheet of paper. If you took it off "The Quick Job Hunting Map"'s list, you may also want to put a shorthand symbol at the bottom of each piece of paper, as to what 'cluster' it came from. Then make four piles, and distribute each piece of paper (i.e., each skill you have) into one of these four piles:

Pile I: "Can't Live Without"
Pile II: "Never Want To Do Again, If I can Help It"
Pile III: "Really Like"
Pile IV: "Eh" (for borderline liking or borderline disliking)

You *may* then want to prioritize Pile I all by itself (dividing it first into families or clusters), then "padding it out" with skills from Pile III, that fit with the prioritized families of your favorite skills. Finally, you may want to take the skills from Pile IV and Pile II, and arrange them in order, within a small box, say, going from "hate the least" to "hate the most"—for the future, in case you ever need to come up with additional skills for any particular family or cluster. At which point, you can go to the *front* of that small box, or filing drawer. (Our thanks to Phyllis Bailey, for this whole idea.)

Please note that the *Beginning Version* of "The Quick Job Hunting Map" and the *Advanced Version* have entirely different clustering systems. A third one is found on pages 215-216 (Section III, A.) of Appendix J, in *Where Do I Go From Here With My Life?* (Hereafter referred to as WDIGFHWML?) A fourth clustering system is suggested by John L. Holland's typology, viz., 1. Organizing Facts; 2. Influencing Others; 3. Creating Art; 4. Solving Problems; 5. Helping Others; and 6. Making Things (or The Body) Work. The 'code', in order, for the above is CEAISR. (Holland devotees will understand immediately; the rest of us can go on the the next cartoon.)

IV. Focusing

'HAVE YOU DECIDED WHAT PART OF THE
COUNTRY YOU'D PREFER WORKING IN?

Things we have learned to underline about this part of the process are:

As outlined in "The Quick Job Hunting Map" (see Appendix D), and in WDIGFHWML?, pages 224, 22ff, 36ff, 42ff, 84ff, you will greatly facilitate finding work that gives you a sense of Meaning and Mission if you focus on exactly Where it is that you want to use your skills. And this focusing has at least six parts to it:

1. Focusing on the values, purposes or goals that you want your skills to serve.

2. Focusing on the subject matter you want your skills to work on (this matter is defined by your preferred Special Knowledges or Work-Content skills).

3. Focusing on the kind of people-environment that facilitates your doing your best work.

4. Focusing on the relationship with those people that you work best in (member of a team, leader, follower, or independent)—i.e., what level of responsibility you desire or need.

5. Focusing on the particular working conditions that facilitate your doing your best work (these are defined by your Self-Management skills, as well as by a prioritized summary of your most distasteful past working conditions).

6. Focusing on your preferred geographical location where you would do your best work, together with a second and third back-up, in case.

These are principles of exclusion, just as I explained earlier on page 74 (see the diagram there).

☞ Ways of getting at No. 1: *Focusing on the values, purposes and goals that you want your skills to serve* include:

● the popular exercises called "values clarification"—for which there are a *million* (would I exaggerate?) texts, notably *Values Clarification: A Handbook of Practical Strategies for Teachers and Students,* by Sidney B. Simon, Leland W. Howe, and Howard Kirschenbaum—who are indebted in turn to the work of Louis E. Raths (1972, Hart Publishing Company, NY); these same authors have (naturally) written follow-up works, individually.

● meditating at length about what's wrong with the world today, aided in your meditation by such books as *Systemantics: How Systems Work and Especially How They Fail,* by John Gall (1977, Quadrangle, The New York Times Book Co., Three Park Avenue, New York, NY 10016, $6.95, hardcover) and/or *How Things Don't Work,* by Victor Papanek & James Hennessey (1977, Pantheon Books, a division of Random House, Inc., NY, $4.95, paper).

● the exercises in WDIGFHWML?, on the pages alluded to above, dealing with Your Philosophy of Life (see also pages 187-191 of this book), What Needs Doing (see also Appendix E at the end of this book), Your Ultimate Life Goal, and What You Would Like to Accomplish.

● the exercises in chapter five of *Parachute,* and in "The Quick Job Hunting Map" (see Appendix D at the end of this book).

☞ Ways of getting at No. 2: *Focusing on the subject matter you want your skills to work on,* essentially involves defining and then prioritizing your Special Knowledges or Work-Content Skills, as I indicated earlier (pages 280–281).

☞ Ways of getting at No. 3 include Holland's "Party Exercise", pages 126-128 in this book, and Crystal's exercise, pages 44-47 in WDIGFHWML?, dealing with "types of people I hope I never have to work with again." This exercise incidentally is done in the same step-by-step fashion as the "Distasteful Living/Working Conditions" exercise, pages 185-186 in WDIGFHWML?

☞ Ways of getting at No. 4, in focusing down, include:

● defining your preferred working level. Do you prefer to be a member of a team, a leader, a follower, or independent? (Generally speaking, the "Party Exercise" on pages 126-128 *may* give a clue: if your preferred corner is S, that suggests teamwork; E, leader; C, follower; and A, independent. I and R are ambiguous. There are, needless to say, endless exceptions to the above generalizations.)

● defining your preferred salary level. If you basically want to be a follower, but desire a salary of $50,000 a year, there is what we call a *slight inconsistency* here.

'They don't pay much where I work—
but man, what prestige!!'

Generally speaking, if you want/need $50,000 a year, you are going to have to be an independent or a leader, in order to get it. (Unless you know the President, and you're his brother or sister.) So salary *defines* level, to some degree. For help in getting at this see chapter seven in *Parachute,* and pages 86-89, 140-143, 222-223 in WDIGFHWML?

Incidentally, if you are involved in career change, and you wonder how much of an increase over your present salary you could ask for without your ultimate employer finding it unreasonable, executive search people (at this writing) report it takes a 25 to 40% increase to lure someone from one company to another. Thus it is reasonable for you to ask for 25-40% more than

> A wealthy woman asked a famous millinery designer to design a hat for her. He placed a canvas form on her head, and in eight minutes with a single piece of ribbon, he created a beautiful hat right before her eyes.
>
> The matron was delighted. "How much will that be?", she asked.
>
> "Fifty dollars," he replied.
>
> "Why, that's outrageous," she said, "It's only a piece of ribbon!"
>
> The milliner quickly unraveled the ribbon and, handing it to her, said, "Madame, the ribbon is free!"
>
> —Abigail Van Buren

you previously made, and still be regarded as within the bounds of 'normality'.[16] You can of course ask for more than that, but then you must be prepared to justify it.

● doing a thorough survey of your chosen field to see what 'the going rate' is for the level of responsibility that you desire/ want/need. Or what the level of responsibility is, for the salary you have determined you desire/want/need, in your preferred geographical area (salaries sometimes vary widely from one section of the country to another, for the same job).

☞ Ways of getting at No. 5 include:

● defining your distasteful living/working conditions, based on your past experience and/or pet hates. For detailed instructions as to how to do this, see pages 22-23, 185-186, in WDIG-FHWML?

● defining your Self-Management Skills (as we saw earlier, under "Factoring"), and then analyzing each skill to see what it suggests about the kind of job you ought to have, e.g., "spontaneity" suggests you ought not to seek a job where you would be working in a rigid, pre-restricted environment.

☞ Ways of getting at No. 6, *focusing on your preferred geographical location,* are fully described in pages 187-193, 36-37 in WDIGFHWML?

V. Researching

'I was just doing a little research on the company before my interview!'

Our learnings, or the things we have learned that need to be underlined, are:

It is tremendously important to do a *Practice* Survey first, on subject matter unrelated to the job questions that you will later be researching. Directions for this Practice may be found, briefly described, at the end of "The Quick Job Hunting Map" (Appendix D, at the back of this book). For greater detail, see the description by John C. Crystal (who invented this exercise) on pages 187-196, and 28-33 in WDIGFHWML?

For the kinds of subject matter that people have chosen to interview *for Practice,* the following examples may be instructive: owning and operating a small printing shop; churches in transition; the 'Big Brother' organization; a traveling columnist; a wedding shop; woodworking or cabinet-making; community arts programming; mind-control and psychic healing; sex education; old furniture repair; non-traditional education; chess sets in history; contemporary graphics; emergency medical services; cross-country skiing; African sculpture; sewing; women's centers; building backyard garden waterfalls; the U.S. Weather Bureau; jail programs for women; backpacking; photography; recording studios; natural foods and health; car maintenance; community theatre programs; adoption agencies; erotic art posters; leisure counseling; Japanese culture; learning to fly; how white school districts deal with the needs of black students; what it's like to own your own business; self-contained life support systems; how TV stations decide which news to put on the air.

In a nutshell: any organization, activity, hobby, or issue *that is of great interest (not to say, fascinating) to You,* is legitimate subject matter for your Practice Survey.

Both in the Practice and in the later Informational Survey (See Appendix D), you need not only people who are doing the thing you are interested in, but people who know what people are doing the thing you are interested in. We call the latter "informal information centers," or "switchboards" or "Resource Brokers. Examples of such Resource Brokers are: taxi drivers, hotel doormen, policemen, newspapers, library research staff, bankers, people in the appropriate federal, state or county agencies; TV Action Line staff; secretaries; phone operators; churches, synagogues, ministers, priests and rabbis; YMCAs, YWCAs, YMHAs, etc.; shop owners; waitresses; bus drivers; hotel clerks; and so on.

Further ideas for Practice Surveys may be found in such books as the *Yellow Pages of Learning Resources,* edited by Richard Saul Wurman, and available in your bookstore or from the publisher, The MIT Press, Massachusetts Institute of Technology, Cambridge, MA 02142, $1.95, paper.

It is *crucial to understand* that you can go out on both the Practice Survey and the Informational Survey *with someone else,* as we stressed earlier on pages 84-85. Indeed, we recommend it, especially if you regard yourself as shy. The Practice Survey, like the Autobiography and the subject of Skill-Identification, has a use beyond job hunting. It is an excellent way of building up your self-esteem, and for this purpose, it is useful even outside a job hunting context.

Directions for doing your real Research or Informational Interviewing (once you are done with Practicing), may be found:
● in this book: the four principles described under the World of Education (pages 74-89) also apply here, to the World of Work. As does the Map (Appendix D).

● in *Parachute:* chapter six in the 1981 edition (or later). This is especially detailed and helpful.

● in WDIGFHWML?: pages 52-65.

Anytime you are not finding out what you want to know, write out on a piece of paper just exactly what it is that you are trying to find out. It may be that you are not getting the answers you need because you are not posing the question clearly. So, restate it to yourself, first of all. Read it to your mate, partner, best friend and see if they think it's clear.

A useful questionnaire when you're starting out, and trying to find information about a particular field or kind of job, is to ask the person you are interviewing:

☐ How did you get into this (field or job)?

☐ What do you like best about it?

☐ What do you like least about it?

☐ What do you like or dislike about this city, town, or area?

☐ What do you like best about the kinds of people who work here?

☐ What do you see as the purposes, goals and values that this place serves?

☐ What subject matter is used here, and what special knowledges are needed here?

☐ What about the working conditions here—what are they like?

☐ What about your level of responsibility and salary?

Some of these questions you may prefer not to ask out loud, but to ask of yourself silently, as you listen and observe.

P.S. *No interview is over until you have sent a thank-you note.*
No interview is over until you have sent a thank-you note.
No interview is over until you have sent a thank-you note.

This means, while you are there, asking the name, title, and address not only of the person you are interviewing, but also of the receptionist or secretary that you met on your way in (they deserve thank-you notes, too).

VI. Naming

'I know of a perfect job for a man interested in cleaning up the country!'

Our learnings and underlinings about this step in the process:
What you have in essence done is taken your job history apart, and broken it down into its most basic elements. You are now in the process of putting it back together again. To help you understand this, let us take another look at the diagram that we saw earlier in this book (page 141) while we were muddling through the World of Education:

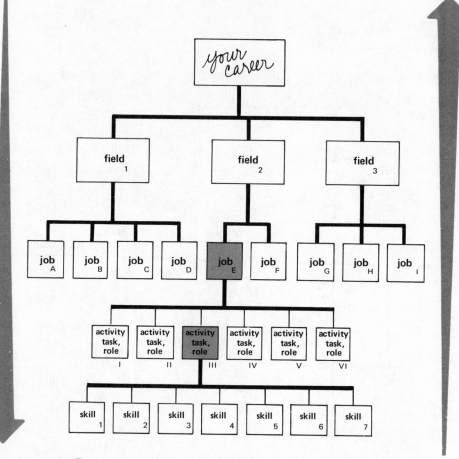

For simplicity's sake only the sub-components of one *job*, and of one *activity* are diagrammed here. The picture actually spreads over a wide area when filled in.

In order to construct a picture of That Job which will give you a sense of Meaning or Mission, or in order to change careers (it is the same process), you begin by going *down* this diagram, as indicated by the arrow on the left-hand side. You dismantle your career, as it were, into the fields that have made it up, thus far. Then you dismantle those fields into the jobs that comprised them. Then you dismantle the jobs into the activities, tasks or roles that, in turn, comprised *them*. Finally, you break down those into the elemental skills that made them up. So far, well and good. But then, you see, having remembered, factored, and prioritized all this (Steps I, II, and III in this section), you proceed back *up* the diagram, as indicated by the arrow on the right-hand side. Taking your prioritized inventory of skills in hand, you proceed to the next level, which involves your defining what activities, tasks and roles you want to use your skills with in the future (this is the Step we called No. 4, Focusing). And then you proceed up to the next level, to find out what kind of job or jobs would let you use these skills with those activities, tasks or roles that you have identified as your favorites. Which brings us to the present steps (No. 5, Researching, and No. 6, Naming).

John Crystal's warning (page 97, first column, 225-230 in WDIGFHWML?) about not trying to use a "job title" as the Name of the thing you are aiming at, should be taken very seriously. As he says, "It is [only] *sometimes* advisable. . ." Generally, your naming should be more general. See his examples in the pages cited above.

The essence of the Naming, that is your object at this stage of the process, is to name the job you are aiming at as:

- a particular kind of "post" (usually the words in front of "post" describe the Special Knowledge you most want to use, e.g., a human development post);

- in a certain kind of organization (the kind you like best, as uncovered in the previous step: Researching);

- which wants certain skills (here you name the functional skills that came out highest on your prioritized inventory).

VII. Finding—Linking Up

"Well, here's <u>my</u> list. I have three bosom buddies, four good buddies, four dear friends, eight friends, thirty acquaintances, forty-four nodding acquaintances, twenty-one contacts, and five enemies."

Our learnings and underlinings, for whatever help they may be to you, are:

The key to this whole business of finding and linking up is Contacts.

Contacts.

 Contacts.

A contact is *anyone* you know, or who knows you. It makes no never-mind whether they are in business (that's a *business* contact, a more rarefied species) or not. If you say, "But I don't have any contacts, " you thus prove you don't understand the word. (See the cartoon, above: he doesn't, either.)

Contacts are more fully explained in the following sources:

- **WHY** you need them: WDIGFHWML? pages 197–198,
  page 38, last column, page 39, first column
- **WHERE** to find them: WDIGFHWML? pages 198–199
- **HOW** to compile a list of them: WDIGFHWML? pages 38, 40
- **WHEN** to use them: *Parachute*, chapter 6;
  WDIGFHWML? pages 120, 122, 124–133

The process of linking up can be done haphazardly and randomly (just going from contact to contact), or systematically. The latter approach is commonly called "Targeting," and has been carried to its most complete form by John Crystal. He explains the systematic process of Targeting in WDIGFHWML? pages 200-201, 42-44, 52-60, 63, 65, 102-115, together with some pages already cited (120-133).

The going from contact to contact is called "Remembrance and Referral", and was invented by Bernard Haldane. He explains it in *How To Make A Habit of Success* (1975, Warner Books, Inc., 75 Rockefeller Plaza, New York, NY 10019, $1.95, paper), pages 124-145, and (more completely) in his latest, written with Jean Haldane and Lowell Martin, *Job Power Now! The Young People's Job Finding Guide* (1976, Acropolis Books Ltd., Colortone Building, 2400 17th St., NW, Washington, D.C. 20009, $3.95, paper), pages 67-90.

During this process of Finding and Linking Up, the question of a resume will inevitably arise. *Generally speaking,* a resume (if used at all) is something that should be *left behind,* not sent on ahead, of any interview you have. Resumes are more fully treated, in *Tea Leaves: A New Look at Resumes,* by Richard N. Bolles. (From: Ten Speed Press, P. O. Box 7123, Berkeley, CA 94707, 50¢, plus 25¢ postage and handling.) Resumes are called by many names, and sometimes change form altogether; for example:

◆ *functional resume:* see *How To Make A Habit of Success* (cited above), pages 147-177.

◆ *job power report:* see *Job Power Now!* (cited above), pages 41-66.

◆ *statement of where you are going:* see WDIGFHWML?, pages 235-237, 118-121.

▶ *qualifications brief:* see *Who's Hiring Who,* by Richard Lathrop (1977, Ten Speed Press, P. O. Box 7123, Berkeley, CA 94707, $5.95, paper), pages 61-121.
The last two works cited above are the best, and most helpful.

In this whole process of Researching, Naming, Finding and Linking Up, there are (we would remind you) *three* kinds of interviews. These are summarized at the end of "The Quick Job Hunting Map,"—see Appendix D at the back of this book.
For more information on the third kind of interview, the linking up one (commonly called the Hiring Interview), see:
* WDIGFHWML?, pages 132-145 (excellent!),
* *Parachute,* chapter seven,
* *Who's Hiring Who,* pages 172-189.

The final bugaboo for most women and men, in this Linking Up process (linking you up with the job that will give you a sense of Meaning and Mission), is the *minor* little matter of salary negotiation, which comes (hopefully) at the conclusion of a Hiring Interview that went well. For:
* *an overview,* see *Parachute,* chapter seven, in the 1981 (or later) edition.
* *detail on simple salary negotiation,* see *Who's Hiring Who,* pages 90-97.
* *detail on complex salary negotiation,* see WDIGFHWML?, pages 86-89, 140-143.

VIII. Always a 'Plan B'

Learnings,
   learnings,
      learnings:

You've done all the steps above (let us say), and there is one organization that looks *very promising.* But, please have a plan B as an alternative to that plan A; and *work on plan B at the same time.*

You've found a name for the kind of job you're looking for, that will give you a sense of Meaning and Mission. And that name is a job title, which looks like it wraps it all up. But, please have a plan B: another job title, just in case the first one runs out of gas.

Your area of geographical preference looks as though it has alot of promising opportunities; so it seems as though it's going to be easy to locate there. But, please have a plan B, in case it doesn't.

"Plan B" is just another way of saying: Never never put all your eggs in one basket. (Confucius say, you may wind up with egg on your face.)

SPECIAL PROBLEMS IN FINDING A JOB
WHICH GIVES YOU MEANING

As I said earlier (pages 273-275), there are always those who feel that there are many 'special problems' in finding meaningful work—by which they mean: "certain groups of job hunters have special problems." Part of this feeling, I am afraid, arises from a confusion between *form* and *substance.*

All of us instinctively feel better about someone who addresses us very personally by name. If that someone is a speaker or writer, we cease to hope he or she will address us by name, but we are pleased, touched, flattered and/or moved when he or she is at least addressing him- or herself very personally to 'our tribe', as it were. "You women out there," or "you elderly people out there," etc. This is a matter of *form.* And form is admittedly of some importance in creating rapport, conveying empathy, and increasing understanding. ("Gee, s/he really knows the kinds of problems that I face.") However, form is not the be all or end all. For, beyond form, is the matter of *substance.* Someone can address himself or herself very specifically to 'your tribe', and still give absolutely lousy advice and incredibly inept solutions.

Ideally, each of us would prefer a book that—from the point of view of 'our tribe' is excellent in both *form* and *substance* (or content). In this imperfect world, however, such books are few and far between. Consequently, we often have to choose between books, counselors, etc., which are *excellent in form* (they talk to 'our tribe' specifically) *but poor in substance* (they don't really know how to help us with our special problems) AND/OR books, counselors, etc., which are *poor in form* (they don't address themselves just to 'our tribe') *but excellent in substance* (they do know how to help us with our special problems). Unhappily, too many people opt for the former, rather than the latter, inasmuch as we live in an age that is all too easily hypnotized by *form.*

Parachute lists any number of resources in its Appendices B and C (1981 edition, or later) designed to help with special problems. There you will find helps for high school students, college students, women, minorities, executives, mid-life changers and the elderly, clergy, military, the self-employed, etc.

But in the end, where substance is concerned, you will

discover that no matter what problem you begin with, that you consider is true only for 'your own tribe', the key to solving it will turn out to be somewhere in the eight steps outlined above: Remembering, Factoring, Prioritizing, Focusing, Researching, Naming, Finding-Linking Up, and Always Having A Plan B.

And if you are a counselor or professional in the life/work planning field, hell-bent on finding new or better tools for your particular clients, whatever you invent (and more power to you) I think you will discover, inevitably, that they are tools which are better ways of getting at precisely the eight steps outlined above.

Verily, verily, when it comes to finding a job with meaning, upon these eight steps hangeth all the losses and the profits.

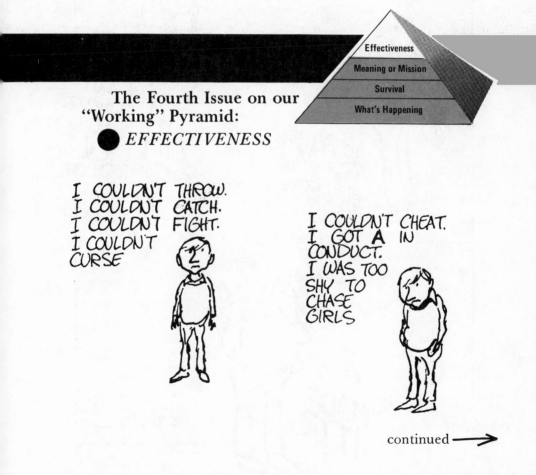

Effectiveness
Meaning or Mission
Survival
What's Happening

The Fourth Issue on our "Working" Pyramid:
● *EFFECTIVENESS*

I COULDN'T THROW.
I COULDN'T CATCH.
I COULDN'T FIGHT.
I COULDN'T CURSE

I COULDN'T CHEAT.
I GOT A IN CONDUCT.
I WAS TOO SHY TO CHASE GIRLS

continued ⟶

Well, not exactly, At least not by those criteria. Okay, then, how *do* you measure your effectiveness in the World of Work? It *is* you who must measure it, not someone else—as was pointed out earlier (pages 16, 192-194).

How you measure your effectiveness will be largely determined by what you are trying to accomplish or do or be, in the World of Work. For example, if you are trying to get to the very top of your profession, you will conclude you are effective or not by how near you are to that goal. If, on the other hand, you are a waitress and darned proud of it, and your only goal is to be the best waitress that you can possibly be, you know—*Earth-Mother in Disguise*—, then you will conclude you are effective or not by how good you are at doing precisely that. Again, if your goal is to be the first woman to break into management in a particular field that was dominated previously entirely by men, your conclusions about your effectiveness *so far,* will depend on how close you are to your goal. This leads us to the first law concerning Effectiveness in the World of Work: only you can set the *criteria* by which you measure your effectiveness.

But, things being what they are, the criteria that various people choose tend to divide into certain 'families' or groups. The first such set is suggested by the various ways in which we judge our TIME USE (pages 13-14): just

> Why should we be in such desperate haste to succeed, and in such desperate enterprises? If a man does not keep pace with his companions, perhaps it is because he hears a different drummer. Let him step to the music which he hears, however measured or far away.
> Henry David Thoreau,
> *Walden*, Chapter XVII, conclusion

keeping busy, vs. enjoying what we are doing, vs. having a sense of immediate or ultimate achievement.

A second set of criteria is suggested by the work of David McClelland[17]. He has contended in the past for the importance of three basic motivations: the achievement motivation, the power motivation, and the affiliation (or relationship) motivation. More recently he has added to these a fourth: the motivation of love.

Putting these together, and noting an overlap—achievement appears in both sets of criteria—we end up with the following second law concerning Effectiveness in the World of Work: we *tend* to evaluate our own effectiveness by one or more (or all) of the following *kinds* of criteria:

- how busy we are able to keep.
- how much we enjoy our work.
- how much of a sense of achievement or accomplishment our work is giving us.
- how much of a sense of power our work is giving us.
- how much our relationships at work (with fellow staff and/ or clients) are satisfying our affiliation needs.
- how much our work fits in with our need to love and/or our need to be loved.

Let us look at each of these, in turn.

CRITERIA
FOR MEASURING
MY OWN EFFECTIVENESS
IN THE WORLD OF WORK

I am effective to the degree that I am able to keep busy.

This is the most common way that people deal with the issue of effectiveness. Millions of workers, students, home-makers, politicians, professionals, etc. give no more thought to the issue of their effectiveness than this: I sure am keeping busy. Indeed, so busy that they have no time to wrestle with this issue. Morning to night, morning to night, their time is spoken for. Mention the issue to them: "Do you think it is important to sit down and reflect upon where all of this is going?" they reply, "Well, sure, but I just don't have time."

If this criteria (busyness) ever does get taken to a higher level, it usually involves figuring out if there is a better way of keeping busy. "I mean, I had five things I was supposed to get done yesterday, and I only got to two of them. What's more, they were the two least important tasks." At which point, we are ripe for some "time management" training. If that's where you are, my friend, the most popular book in the field is *How To Get Control of Your Time and Your Life* by Alan Lakein (1973, Peter H. Wyden, Inc./Publisher, 750 Third Avenue, New York, NY 10017, available in most bookstores, hardcover or paper); but there are also others.[18]

2 *I am effective to the degree that I enjoy my work.*

This is the next most popular way of evaluating our job or our work, for we all want a job that is at the very least enjoyable. (Except for those whose favorite college course was Masochism 102.) In the literature, this is called "worker satisfaction", or—more commonly—"worker dissatisfaction".

Reams of prose have been written about worker dissatisfaction. For anyone who wants to familiarize herself or himself with 'the literature', you could do no better than to start with *Work in America* (Written by a Special Task Force to the Secretary of Health, Education and Welfare, administered by—my friends—the W.E. Upjohn Institute for Employment Research. MIT Press, Cambridge, Massachusetts 1973.) followed by *Where Have All The Robots Gone? Worker Dissatisfaction in the 70s* by Harold L. Sheppard and Neal Q. Herrick (1972, The Free Press, A Division of the Macmillan Company. Also out in paperback). Then if you want to flesh this all out with living people, read *Working* by Studs Terkel (1974. Avon Paperback, New York $2.25).

For me—inevitably—it is not prose but poetry that captures boredom and dissatisfaction best. The piece on the next page is from a journal on assemblyline life, by Jim Campbell of the Detroit Industrial Mission.[19]

Worker dissatisfaction, or job dissatisfaction as it is more broadly called, is not—however, confined to factory workers. A survey of 2,821 executives (by the American Management Associations) turned up the following facts: 52% "found their work, at best, unsatisfying"; 50% have changed jobs in the last five years or are considering changing jobs and fields; 30% believe that business activities adversely affected their health during the preceding five years.[20]

The Gallup Poll is always publishing results which show that worker dissatisfaction is relatively low, in the country as a whole. This is at wide variance with other people's conclusions, such as Myron Clark, past president of the Society for the Advancement of Management, who says that 80% of all American workers are *under-employed* and hence (we may presume) dissatisfied.[21]

Easy, tedious work—
50 thousand ashtray doors and
100 thousand screws!
Childish, foolish, serious banter
As monotonous as the line—
Are these men—and women—
These workers of the world?
Or is it an overgrown nursery—
This factory—this automobile mill—
With children—goosing, slapping
Boys, giggling, snotty girls—
And the teacher with white shirt and tie.
40 rules to uphold, the power
To suspend or expel—
"Whistle-to-whistle you work,
No horseplay—This shit's got to stop—"
What is it about that entrance-way,
Those gates to the plant? Is it
The guards—the showing of
Your badge—the smell?
Is there some invisible eye
That pierces you through and
Transforms your being? Some
Aura or ether, that brain and
Spirit washes you and commands,
"For eight hours now you shall be different."
What is it that instantaneously makes
    a child out of a man?
Moments before he was a father,
    a husband, an owner of property,
A voter, a lover, an adult.
When he spoke at least some listened.
Salesmen courted his favors.
Insurance men appealed to his
    family responsibility.
And, by chance, his church sought his help.
The PTA his support, the United Fund his
    participation,
The Legion his opinion.
He was calm, refined, mature.
But that was before he shuffled past the guard,
Climbed the steps,
Hung up his coat, and
Took his place along the line.
50 THOUSAND ASHTRAY DOORS AND
100 THOUSAND SCREWS.
The austere general foreman marches by,
    his sober eyes seeing all.
The whistle blows, the day shift gleefully
    plunges for the time clock towards which
    with guilty glances at the foreman they
    have been furtively edging for the last
    45 seconds.

The line continues inexorably to wind amid
    a chaotic yet reasoned morass of air hoses,
    racks, drawers, trash barrels, boxes,
    screws, stock, and human beings.
The adventures since yesterday are recounted.
Then a pause. The clowns take over.

It's goose your buddy time. It's hand
    wrestling time.
It's argue about who passed the gun
    down and who didn't time.
It's history of sexual exploits time.
    It's flip coins time.
It's break time. It's showdown poker time.
It's look at the sunset time.
It's Chevrolet vs. Ford time. It's threat of
    a drag race time.
It's screw-you time. It's play the numbers time.
It's what's wrong with the Tigers time.
It's lunch time.
It's what the hell's the foreman up to time.
It's rumor time. It's check-pool time.
It's what would I do if they laid me off time.
It's Cadillac is better than Chrysler time.
It's screw the union, screw the company time.
It's look at the women time.
It's lay plans for changeover time.
It's break time.
It's goddam my legs are tired time.
It's someday I'll get out of this goddam
    factory time.
It's the hell you will, you'll be here till
    you die time.
It's complain about your wife time.
It's puzzle about your two-year-old time.
It's dream about the sweepstakes time.
It's buy me a coffee time.
It's work ahead so we can get the hell out
    of here quick time.
It's sneak toward the clock time.
It's quitting time.
It's show your lunch box to the guard.
A squeal of rubber, a cloud of dust, and
    Hyde becomes Jekyll.
1088-825 becomes Lester Johnson Morton,
    citizen-husband-father.

    —James M. Campbell
    Reprinted with permission
    from the Winter 1974 issue of
    LIFE AND WORK, vol. 14, no. 4,
    Detroit Industrial Mission

Such dissatisfaction, or failure to enjoy our work, may be minor, major, or terminal. We (that's not an author's "we"—I mean the National Career Development Project) continuously ask people if they enjoy their work, and if not, why not. Here are the kinds of answers we have been receiving:

Working Conditions We Find Annoying

☐ A bad boss (insensitive or overbearing or lacking confidence in his/her employees or indecisive or delegating insufficient authority to accomplish a task or uptight "x" type (McGregor's distinction) management style or incompetent or thoughtless or lack of constructive communication or oversupervising or not giving complete information about what's going on or laying out false 'team rhetoric' or laying out unclear, unthinking, unreasonable, conflicting or changing accountability criteria. ☐ Too long a commute, and/or difficult access to job-site. ☐ Hot stuffy working conditions, rooms without windows, poor ventilation ☐ Too many people in the same space, bull-pen offices, cramped quarters ☐ No quiet space ☐ Being stuck in the office all day, being confined to desk ☐ Inflexible hours, rigidly observed ☐ Working in neutral or hostile working-space ☐ Unclear job description ☐ Male chauvinistic environment; women treated as second-class citizens ☐ No sense of purpose ☐ Too much pressure, constant deadlines, and crash programs or tasks ☐ Not having control of our own work ☐ Not allowed to experiment and try new things ☐ Frenzied work patterns ☐ Regimentation ☐ No challenges ☐ No sense of working on a team ☐ Meetings held for no significant purpose ☐ Dissatisfied co-workers, who won't do anything beyond the minimum ☐ No friends among co-workers; too much rudeness, lack of tact, or oversensitive ☐ Being asked to work past the time we're supposed to be able to leave ☐ No opportunity to talk with people ☐ Having no time for reflection; emphasis on action, action ☐ Never being able to see concrete results of our work ☐ Incompetent co-workers ☐ Chronically-returning clients ☐ Too severe dress code ☐ Coffee not readily available ☐ Dishonest, false, or hard-sell representation of company or product ☐ Not being given recognition, appreciation, or chance for advancement ☐ Never being given feedback, OR, being subject to too many evaluators ☐ Being asked to do tasks we hate (e.g. accounting, for some) ☐ Too much paper work; record-keeping at the expense of people-helping ☐ Having always to go through established channels ☐ Not being given enough resources or resource persons ☐ Power struggles within the company ☐ Economic cliff-hanging about future; no job-security ☐ Underpaid ☐ Co-workers' personal agendas consistently blocking group goals and action ☐ Unhealthy competition among co-workers: game-playing, back-stabbing ☐ Extreme noise and constant interruptions ☐ Building set in ugly part of town, or way outside of town ☐ Not being given a chance to grow on the job ☐ Everyone having to pick up the pieces behind a certain inadequate person, rather than having him/her replaced ☐ Lack of fairness and justice in way employees are treated ☐ Bureaucratic philosophy insensitive to human need and variability ☐ Discrimination regarding age and credentialing ☐ Underutilization of employees' skills ☐ Never being involved in the decision-making process ☐ Supervisors who use 'underlings' as whipping posts for their own personal incompetency ☐ Being held responsible for policy made by others ☐ A company without a social conscience in any way, shape or form ☐ Lack of safety (security) ☐ Subject to constant humiliation or being made to feel stupid ☐ Unwillingness to allow for human failure ☐ Inconsiderate time-consuming co-workers or supervisors ☐ Meaningless routine busy-work ☐ Co-workers all of the same sex ☐ Refusal to admit, and/or deal with, conflict ☐ Thing-centered or computer-centered organization (rather than people-centered) ☐ Things done a certain way because 'they've always been done that way'; no rationale for procedures or willingness to experiment ☐ Lack of opportunity to create or implement new ideas ☐ No parking for employees ☐ No privacy ☐ Performance problems *not* dealt with ☐ Closed administration, secrecy ☐ Lack of nearby convenient personal services (e.g., banking, etc.) ☐ Nearby smokers, to non-smokers ☐ Having to answer disagreeable, boring or senseless phone calls ☐ Clock-watching co-workers, who will not carry out their assigned tasks ☐ Late starting meetings ☐ Too many rules ☐ No scheduled time for review, evaluation and future planning; no focus on future ☐ Inaccessibility of the administrative staff ☐ Inequality of pay ☐ Facility and equipment limitations ☐ Slow response to Affirmative Action or Equal Opportunity ☐ Too little vacation, or too rigid vacation patterns ☐ Forced transfers, and no control over geographical location ☐ Lack of variety in work ☐ Organizations more concerned with quantity than quality of service ☐ Organizations more concerned with profits than with people (especially employees) ☐ No travel, or great restrictions on travel to conferences, etc. ☐ Whatever you do, it's never enough ☐ Having to hustle money for own or organization's support ☐ Having to play roles contrary to our own values, to satisfy the organization ☐ Excessive reporting system; having to prove worth over and over ☐ Given false promises or expectations, at outset of hiring, that are never fulfilled ☐ Minorities treated differently from the rest of the workers ☐ Discriminating against 'singles' ☐ Unsanitary working conditions ☐ Competition between units of the same enterprise ☐ Employees criticized or ridiculed by superiors in front of others ☐ Restroom facilities inconvenient ☐ Water fountains inconvenient ☐ Distinctions carefully made between professionals vs. secretarial (or other) support staff; latter being treated as 'a frill' ☐ Sabre-rattling, annually, just to stir up troops' insecurity ☐ Working for an organization that buys cheap toilet paper (rough) ☐ Working for an organization that can't fire incompetent employees ☐ Age discrimination ☐ Night work ☐ Someone else taking credit for our work, particularly those over us ☐ Knee-jerk administrative decisions ☐ Being always talked down to; not being taken seriously ☐ An autocratic administration masking under democratic noises ☐ Tight budgetary control; treasury-hounding ☐ Memos dealt out to everyone because memo-issuer doesn't want to confront the one or two people for whom memo is really intended ☐ Non-supportive staff situations ☐ Antagonistic supervision ☐ Lack of recreational facilities ☐ Organization making social demands outside working hours ☐ Inescapable commercial background music played all day ☐ Too much bitching!!! or griping!!!!!

Having digested this list, we can understand better perhaps what is meant by 'worker dissatisfaction'. The list is so long and intimidating! Of course it can be reduced to more manageable terms; but I will leave this to you to do. I will simply point out that almost everything on this list can be put on one of the parts of an octagon that looks something like this:

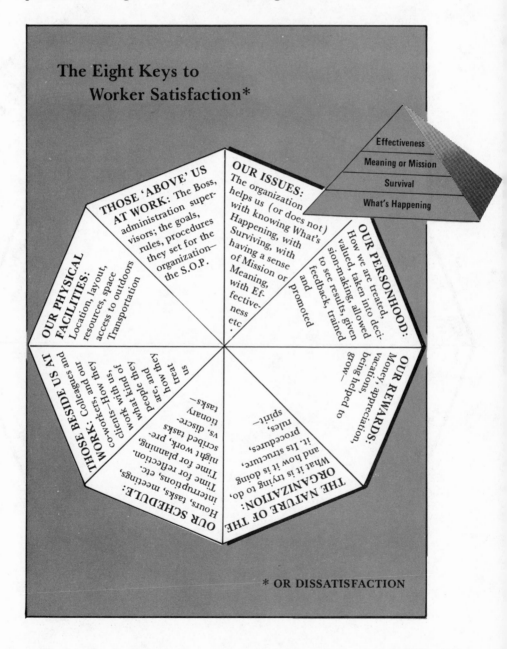

The Eight Keys to Worker Satisfaction*

Effectiveness

Meaning or Mission

Survival

What's Happening

THOSE 'ABOVE' US AT WORK: The Boss, administration supervisors; the goals, rules, procedures they set for the organization—the S.O.P.

OUR ISSUES: The organization helps us (or does not) with knowing What's Happening, with Surviving, with having a sense of Mission or Meaning, with Effectiveness etc.

OUR PHYSICAL FACILITIES: Location, layout, resources, space, access to outdoors Transportation

OUR PERSONHOOD: How we are treated, taken into decision-making, allowed to see results, given feedback, trained valued, and promoted

THOSE BESIDE US AT WORK: Colleagues and co-workers, and our clients—How they work with us, what kind of people they are, and how they treat us

OUR REWARDS: Money, vacations, appreciation, being helped to grow—

OUR SCHEDULE: Hours, tasks, meetings, interruptions, etc. Time for reflection. Time for planning, night work, prescribed tasks vs. discretionary tasks—

THE NATURE OF THE ORGANIZATION: What it is trying to do, and how it is doing it. Its structure, procedures, rules, spirit—

* OR DISSATISFACTION

309

To help you get a better sense of how much you enjoy, or don't enjoy, your work, you may want to make up your own octagon, and fill it in with whatever 'bugs' you about your present job, and/or past jobs you have had:

My Own Dissatisfactions in The World of Work

PRESENT OR PAST

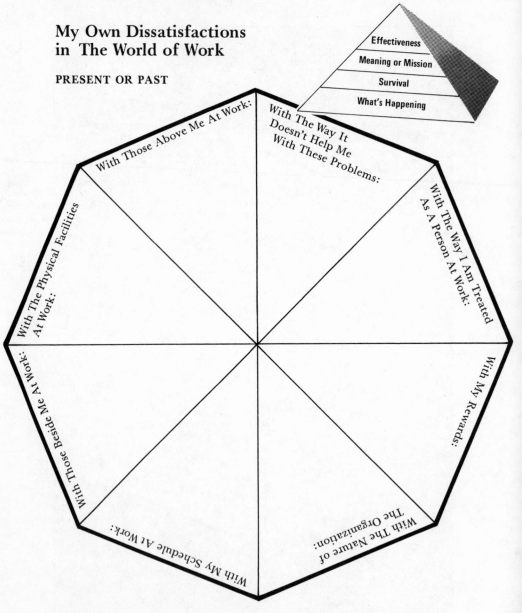

Effectiveness

Meaning or Mission

Survival

What's Happening

With Those Above Me At Work:

With The Way It Doesn't Help Me With These Problems:

With The Way I Am Treated As A Person At Work:

With The Physical Facilities At Work:

With My Rewards:

With Those Beside Me At Work:

With The Nature of The Organization:

With My Schedule At Work:

If this octagon, thus filled out, is so depressing that you conclude you have just got to go find another kind of work, *halt*. Don't put this exercise down, just yet. It can yield some genuine help to you in seeking that job. The way to do this, as John Crystal has so insistently taught us all, is to turn the negative statements concerning (what we hope will be) our past into some positive descriptions concerning the future job we would like to find—that *would* be enjoyable. The method for doing that is as follows:

My Own Dissatisfactions in the World of Work, Present or Past	*What I Would Like To Have In Any Future Job*
EXAMPLES:	
Not being given a chance to grow on the job.	A chance to grow on the job.
Too many people in the same place.	Sufficient room for me to feel I have my own space, adequate for spreading out in order to do my job.
No opportunity to talk with people.	Reasonable opportunities during the day to talk with people.
Oversupervised.	A reasonable amount of authority and supervision over me, leaving me some leeway to exercise my own judgement.

You will note from the above examples (out of our workshops) that sometimes the right hand column is merely the opposite of the left-hand column. But not always. In the last example, as you can see, the opposite of "oversupervised" was not "no supervision"—but rather the median that you see stated above, in the right hand column.

You may wish to a) prioritize, using Appendix A, the factors from each section on your octagon of "My Own Dissatisfactions", first; e.g., first prioritize all the factors under "My Own Dissatisfactions With Those Above Me At Work." Then go on to prioritize all the factors on "My Own Dissatisfactions With The Physical Facilities At Work." And so forth. Once done, with all eight lists, go on to b) take the three most important factors, in priority, off the top of EACH of the eight lists, yielding 24 factors in all—the most important twenty-four to you. Be flexible here. If the first five factors under "With Those Above Me" are more important to you than *any* of the factors under "With The Physical Facilities," then use those five, and just take one factor from the Physical Facilities list—thus giving you the six from the two lists that you were striving for, in the first place. When you have the most important twenty-four factors, you should list them on the left hand column (above) and then put each one into a Positive form for your right hand column. Thus, you will have a head start in developing your picture of what would be *for you* an enjoyable job.

Of course, using the octagon to measure how enjoyable your work is doesn't necessarily lead to the conclusion that you should change jobs. You may conclude that you are happier at your work than you thought you were, and that you are a very lucky woman, or man. Now, on to the next criteria of effectiveness:

3 *I am effective to the degree that I can achieve or accomplish something that has some meaning to it, for me.*

Only you, of course, can define a meaningful accomplishment *for your own life*. This has been lampooned in the famous (anonymous) chart on the facing page.

To help you define what it is that you are trying to achieve, there are various aids. Edward L. Adams, Jr., Ph.D. has designed an interesting "Achievement Planning Calendar," which helps you list—for each month—whatever work-improvement, self-improvement, people-relationship, self-management, community, and recreational projects you would like to aim toward achieving; not to mention dealing with meeting deadlines and such, that others have laid on you.

There is an infinite *variety* of possibilities by which the achievement-oriented individual can measure her or his effectiveness. But there are also *common denominators,* one of which is that *every* achievement-oriented person is discontent with his or her effectiveness "rating." The person we saw earlier whose goal is to keep busy will ask, "Am I keeping busy?" and if the answer is Yes, well That is That. Likewise, the person whose goal is to

Performance Effectiveness Ratings

	FAR EXCEEDS JOB REQUIREMENTS	EXCEEDS JOB REQUIREMENTS	MEETS JOB REQUIREMENTS	NEEDS SOME IMPROVEMENT	DOES NOT MEET MINIMUM REQUIREMENTS
Quality performance:	Leaps tall buildings with a single bound.	Must take a running start to leap over tall buildings.	Can leap over short buildings only.	Crashes into buildings when attempting to jump over them.	Cannot recognize buildings at all.
Timeliness performance:	Is faster than a speeding bullet.	Is as fast as a speeding bullet.	Not quite as fast as a speeding bullet.	Would you believe a slow bullet?	Wounds self with bullet when attempting to shoot
Initiative performance:	Is stronger than a locomotive.	Is stronger than a bull elephant.	Is stronger than a bull.	Shoots the bull.	Smells like a bull.
Adaptability performance:	Walks on water consistently.	Walks on water in emergencies.	Washes with water.	Drinks water.	Passes water in emergencies.
Communication performance:	Talks with God.	Talks with Angels.	Talks to self.	Argues with self.	Loses arguments with self.

enjoy will ask, "Am I enjoying my work?" and if the answer is Yes, that is the end of the effectiveness issue—for the time being, at least. But the person who asks, "Am I achieving?" will never let the matter rest, just because the answer comes back: Yes. S/he will always go on to ask, "How could I do better?", for—as David McClelland has pointed out[17],—the *sina qua non* of strong achievement motivation is the urge to improve and do things better.

● Thus, if you are predisposed to measure your effectiveness in terms of achievement, primarily, you will always want to know *how to improve your effectiveness.* Since there are about a million studies on this subject, here is a summary of some of the major findings and recommendations:

1. believe in the possibility and desirability of change in almost everything, including Yourself;
2. think continuously in terms of action-consequences-results;
3. look at everything with a view toward improving it or doing it better;
4. make your own assessment of situations, with perhaps auxiliary help from others— but never leave assessment entirely in the hands of others;
5. strive to distinguish those situations in which you have some control;
6. assume some personal responsibility for improving those situations, rather than leaving the outcome solely to chance, or solely in the hands of others;
7. set higher goals for yourself, strive to excel; the goals should be moderately difficult but potentially achievable—where you have a 1 in 3 chance, at least;
8. wherever possible, set specific time-lines regarding the means by which you intend to try to achieve your goals; have a greater "future-perspective";
9. take initiative in the situations you have identified, exhibiting energy, drive, and decisiveness;
10. on the other hand, don't try to run the whole show by yourself; choose colleagues wisely and delegate tasks to them confidently;
11. acquire a reputation for complete integrity; always keep your word;

12. take moderate risks, be ready to try something new, regardless of your background or training; seize opportunities that come your way, and be willing to take a little gamble;[22]
13. keep at your goals, exhibiting persistence, persistence, persistence, and patience;
14. when you run into an absolute dead end, seek new and alternative means for improving the situation;
15. continuously broaden your acquaintances, in your own and related fields; join professional, trade or civic groups where you will run into influential people;
16. continuously seek concrete feedback from people around you as to how you are doing; this feedback is *crucial* to your improving your effectiveness;
17. continuously seek advice as to how *they* would handle the situations you face, or how they would use the skills that you have;
18. seize every opportunity for additional training, particularly when it is offered by your employer;
19. when you are in a stressful situation, or need help, seek it from the most expert people you know or can find — not from people who are "just friends";
20. see something enjoyable in every job you do; be amiable, exhibit as much of a sense of humor (particularly about yourself) as you can; draw people to you, particularly during stressful times or situations;
21. promote your boss in every way you can; be as loyal to her or him as you can be; whisper not a word of criticism, even in confidence, that you would not want rebroadcast; (you may be unwittingly talking to the office parrot);
22. keep a diary of every single achievement you accomplish, or help to accomplish;
23. be more concerned with achieving success, in doing things better or in improving a situation, than in merely compiling a record of having always avoided failure;
24. see "doing better" as your ultimate reward, with money as only a symbol of that — never an end in itself.

Now, all of the above may sound like advice from *Poor Richard's Almanack,* or kindly aphorisms from your Wise Old Aunt Sarah; but, in point of fact they are summaries of studies which endeavored to discover what distinguished achievers from non-achievers, and the successful from the unsuccessful. (See McClelland's writings,[17] for further details about some of these, at least.) If you want to increase your effectiveness as an achiever, don't just read this list. Memorize it.

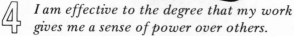

4   *I am effective to the degree that my work gives me a sense of power over others.*

With this criterion, we come into new territory. For, everyone who judges their work by the earlier criteria of busyness, enjoyment or achievement, will cheerfully admit that fact. But "power over others"? That is something else, again. We have entered into the hidden kingdom, where people will not only not admit this need to others; they will often not admit it even to themselves. Oh, to be sure, politicians and such will. But what about the haughty waiter or waitress in some French restaurant, who secretly delights in hearing the customers mispronounce the menu, and *in correcting them.* Or what about the Federal clerk in some unemployment insurance office, who acts as though every cent dispensed belongs to her (or him) personally, and who seems to delight in forcing the unemployed worker to grovel for awhile. The need of such clerks and waiters for power is very clear to everyone except themselves. Their clients and customers know, even if they do not, how much that need affects their effectiveness. Put them in another job, where they do not have any such power, and they will—likely as not—feel totally misused and misplaced.

We need to differen-
tiate perhaps between
unreasonable power over
others, and reasonable.
McClelland has distin-
guished[17] these characteristics of reasonable (my
term, not his) power:

● is not so concerned
with improving his or her
daily work performance;

> "It has always seemed strange to me," said Doc. "The things we admire in men, kindness and generosity, openness, honesty, understanding and feeling are the concomitants of failure in our system. And those traits we detest, sharpness, greed, acquisitiveness, meanness, egotism and self-interest are the traits of success. And while men admire the quality of the first they love the produce of the second."
> —John Steinbeck, *Cannery Row*

● is concerned with having an impact on others;

● is concerned with getting attention;

● is concerned with getting recognition;

● wants to control channels of communication;

● regards money as important, because it buys possessions which enhance his or her prestige.

Such power is reasonable to the extent that our whole society is dependent on such persons—seeks them out, nurtures them, rewards them, and seeks to replicate them. It calls them "leaders." To paraphrase John Steinbeck, we love what they produce. So, if you recognize this need for power over others to be your need,—and it *is* a need which many of us have, in one degree or another—the presence or absence of such power in a particular job may give you a clue as to why you do or don't feel effective there.

5 *I am effective to the degree that my work is satisfying my need for affiliation—i.e., for relationships.*

There are a lot of workers who love the work they have to do, but who detest the people that they have to do it with. And there are a lot of workers who find their work very boring, but who tolerate that boredom because they work with (as they say) "such a great bunch of people." In both cases, the people-environment at work is what makes or breaks that particular job.

Indeed, this is a factor which has become increasingly important since the late 1960s at least. More and more people seem to be coming into the World of Work, dismayed by the old business ethics of achievement and power, but really 'turned on' at the idea of working with kindred souls. For them, the people-environment at work is not merely one of the things which make Work attractive: it is the only thing.

And while this may seem to be a question of What makes work enjoyable?, it does, in the end, turn out indeed to be a question of Effectiveness. For we are all most effective when we are doing that which we most enjoy.

If, in your self-evaluation, you conclude that you're miserable because of the relationships you have at work (or the lack of them), the first thing you're going to need to examine is whether or not you ought to change your whole line of work. Certain jobs pre-determine the kind of people you're going to be surrounded by, that's for sure. For example, if you love being surrounded by artistic types, and you've chosen computer programming as your field, you can twist and push and shove your job six ways to Sunday, and it still won't give you an artistic people-environment. So, you will need to do some homework (pages 126ff), decide what kind of people you *do* want to be related to at work, get Holland's book (pages 217-219 tell all about it), and in his Appendix E (pages 136-141 in *his* book) he has told you where in the 1965 edition of the *Dictionary of Occupational Titles* (20,741 job titles) you will find the people-environments that you prefer. (There is, as I said earlier, a newer edition of the D.O.T., published in 1977, but many authors and researchers are still working out of the 1965 one—so be sure to ask for *that* edition when you go to your local library.)

Within these broad "people-environments", however, there are still "personality-types" that can make a job absolutely miserable. It matters little whether they are your co-workers or your clients. If you're clear about what these types are, you *may* be able to choose a job where you mostly avoid them. And even where you can't avoid them, it helps to have a clear picture of them—so that you'll *know* ahead of time that they are "energy-drainers", who lower your effectiveness, *or* present you with your most dramatic challenge. That way, you won't wonder why you're tired after being with them.

We have discovered that groups of individuals with varying backgrounds display a surprising unanimity about the kind of person who 'turns them off'. As you read down the list, you may wish to put a checkmark in front of the descriptions which are also true for You.

I Dislike Working/Playing With People Who Are
OR
I Find My Own Effectiveness Is Decreased
When I Have To Deal A Lot With
People Who Are:

- ☐ authoritarian
- ☐ closed
- ☐ apologetic
- ☐ exhibiting a low self-image
- ☐ aggressive
- ☐ abusive
- ☐ dull
- ☐ wishy-washy
- ☐ disorganized
- ☐ a sloppy dresser
- ☐ chain-smoker
- ☐ lazy
- ☐ a loud mouth
- ☐ always dropping the ball
- ☐ highly political
- ☐ defensive
- ☐ untruthful
- ☐ devious or manipulating
- ☐ overly formal
- ☐ snobby
- ☐ condescending
- ☐ overly dependent
- ☐ pushy
- ☐ manifesting little self-insight
- ☐ uncooperative
- ☐ inconsistent
- ☐ demanding
- ☐ little people who try to be big people

- ☐ unethical
- ☐ rude
- ☐ uninterested
- ☐ people who don't enjoy people
- ☐ overly pious
- ☐ hard-sell people
- ☐ legalistic
- ☐ complainers
- ☐ gushy people
- ☐ single-minded
- ☐ gossipers
- ☐ brown-nosers
- ☐ bad breath
- ☐ overbearing or dictatorish
- ☐ savage (ruthless)
- ☐ glory hogs
- ☐ clock-watchers
- ☐ dwell on unimportant details
- ☐ workaholics
- ☐ sexist
- ☐ racist
- ☐ closed to new ideas
- ☐ curt
- ☐ blamers
- ☐ non-riskers
- ☐ chauvinists
- ☐ hypocritical
- ☐ too serious
- ☐ filthy

- ☐ 'company' people
- ☐ moody
- ☐ indefinite
- ☐ bigots
- ☐ rigid
- ☐ controllers
- ☐ egotists
- ☐ irresponsible
- ☐ tardy
- ☐ prying
- ☐ arrogant
- ☐ pretentious
- ☐ touchy-feely
- ☐ low self-disclosure types
- ☐ rednecks
- ☐ filled with 'military mentality'
- ☐ sour-puss
- ☐ unjust

Additional descriptions of 'people-types' that turn you off:

_____
_____
_____
_____
_____
_____

The preceding list is in a *negative* form, for a reason. John Crystal has pointed out that most of us tend to store the lessons we learned from our Past, in this fashion. So, when we are trying to go back to that storehouse, and get our 'memory-banks' to 'cough up' what they know, they will usually produce more data if addressed by a question in a negative form ("What kind of people turned you off?"), than in a positive. Thus, if you are working individually, you might begin with the checklist on the previous page, and then after having checked off those items *which are true for you,* add any additional items which occur to you —in the space provided. If you are working in small groups (6-8 people), you can produce your own group list with the question: "What kind of people, in the past, have turned you off, caused you to feel bad about that job, and/or decreased your effectiveness?"

I recently read this line in your newsletter. The line was an extract from an earlier letter by Jerry Salny in which he was trying to persuade members to attend the Mensa functions [an organization for people whose I.Q. is in the top 2% of the population]. He said, "You may run into a dud and find Mensa not of interest to you. On the other hand. . ."

Now right there you have the reason I don't attend many Mensa functions. I happen to be the dud people keep running into. How would you feel about it? I can't help it that I'm a dud. I am not a dud from choice. It is a matter of genetic heritage and environment. My whole family are duds. I was trained for duddery from birth. I am ashamed of being a dud but I can't help it.

How do you think I feel when I see a group of jolly nonduds looking at me out of the corners of their eyes and I know they're saying, "There's that dud our new members keep running into and getting turned off of Mensa. If it wasn't for him we'd have a much larger group."?

Well, I guess there's no help for it. I've thought about forming dudSIG but I probably couldn't stand the crummy duds who would join.

*The MENSA Newsletter
of Northern New Jersey*

When, however, it comes time to think about the Future, the mind works best in terms of *positives*. At least for most of us, this is true. Therefore, the lessons from our Past (in their negative form) need to be redeemed and recycled into a positive form. We have discovered this is best done by simply taking the 'negatives' and *translating* them into positive form—whether you are working individually, or in a group. It works something like this:

I Have Learned From The Past, That My Effectiveness Is Decreased By People Who Are:	Therefore, In The Future, I Will Try As Much As I Can To Surround Myself With People Who Are:
manipulative	direct and honest
boring	stimulating
buck-passers who won't do their share	share the work
always serious	showing a sense of humor
missionary-types	accepting of differences
incompetent	competent
undependable	dependable
rigid	flexible
highly competitive	cooperative/supportive
afraid to try things on their own	trying to work independently
compulsive	calculated-risk takers
insensitive, crude, cruel	appreciates feelings, the arts, etc.
excessively critical	positive reinforcers of others
easily manipulated	autonomous, self-actualized
inefficient	efficient
heavy work-ethic people	valuing some time for reflection
'smart-asses': laughing at me	humane: laugh with me
gossipers	non-gossipers
talking about themselves continually	spending at least half their time listening
fanatics	reasonable
pessimists	optimists
very slow workers	moderately-paced workers
superficial	genuine, sincere
authoritarian	democratic
abusing their own body	healthy, well-groomed
know-it-alls	still learners
indecisive	decision-makers
flippant party-persons	gutsy-enough to be who they are
stubborn	open-minded
undisciplined	self-disciplined
nasty	polite, considerate
non-communicative, secret	direct, and up-front
self-pitying, chip on shoulder	self-empowered
wishy-washy	people with convictions
seductive	able to see others as whole persons
pushy, force decisions	allows flexibility, space
arbitrary	fair
drowningly sympathetic	empathetic
arrogant	humble
marshmallows	assertive
angry all the time	peaceful inside
suspicious	trusting
sullen	happy
cold-water throwers	facilitators
third-person types [she feels]	people who own their own feelings
messy	neat
take too long to say what they mean	able to be succinct and to the point
perfectionist, unaccepting of failures of others or of self	accepting of humanity and limitations of self and of others

As we saw earlier, with "Work Dissatisfactions", the 'future statement' is often The Opposite of 'the past' one, but this is not always the case. For example, take:

judgmental . . . . discriminating

The thing that is wrong with being judgmental is not that a person's critical faculty is being exercised, but that it is being exercised *excessively*. So, the positive form of that is *an appropriate use of the critical-faculty* (which is "discriminating"), not suspension of all critical-faculties (which the obvious "non-judgmental" would imply).

When you are all done with this exercise, you will probably have a rather long, even intimidating, list. If this is the case, it may be helpful to you to choose out the ten factors which are most important to you (the ten characteristics which, in the Past, have turned you off the most; and their "Future" translations, as above).

I AM MOST TURNED OFF WHEN I AM AROUND PEOPLE WHO ARE	I AM MOST HAPPY WHEN I AM AROUND PEOPLE WHO ARE
1	1
2	2
3	3
4	4
5	5
6	6
7	7
8	8
9	9
10	10

Having composed, and prioritized, these lists, you now have—in the left hand column—a portrait of your own principal energy drainers, those people who most lower your effectiveness (or present you with your greatest challenge), and—in the right hand column—the kinds of people you most prefer to be surrounded by, or to serve, because they make you happiest. At which point, you are potentially the most effective. Especially if being in good relationships is, for you, the *sina qua non* of effectiveness.

Before we leave this criterion, I would like to suggest you look over the right hand column above, to see which of these descriptions seem to you to be true of You yourself. Check them off. And then be sure to highlight them at your job, and in any future interviews when you go looking for another job. I mean, if these things are important to you about *Them,* it is reasonable to think that these things may be important to them about *You.*

6 *I am effective to the degree that my work fits in with my need to love and/or my need to be loved.*

Well, at first sight, that may seem to be expecting too much of one's job; but wait. I have a story to tell. My best friend died a couple of months ago. He was a dear, dear man, and also a very wise man. His name was Stan Rodgers. Shortly before he died Stan and I had lunch with a colleague of mine. During our conversation together, we fell to talking about our various adventures, since we had last met. And I told of a speaking engagement I had recently kept in another city, where I had been treated rather poorly. As I thought. The man who invited me had not met my plane, had left no word at the hotel where I was to be staying, and on and on and on I went in cataloguing his omissions. "You know," Stan responded when I had finished my tale, "you are talking about a series of what I would call 'rituals' that he failed to perform. And often in this life we get preoccupied with such rituals. But the question we are asking, in *all* such rituals and *beneath* all such rituals is, 'Does he really love me?' So the important point of your story, it seems to me, is not that he failed to perform the rituals, but that he left you with the feeling that he didn't really love you or care about you as a person."

A couple of days after this luncheon conversation, Stan died —suddenly, abruptly, without warning,—of a massive heart attack, leaving me with the feeling of an incredible void. As I thought about the source of this feeling, I remembered an incident some ten years earlier. Stan and I were working for the same employer, when all of a sudden—with a month or so warning—I was fired. As luck would have it, shortly after this news became public and while I was still on the job, it fell to Stan and me to conduct a workshop together. I arrived late, and with a very bemused glance bordering on mischief, Stan explained that they had all just finished an exercise in which each had drawn on a blackboard a picture of where he, or she, felt their life to be, at the moment. And would I now please do the same? So, I went to the blackboard, and quickly drew a picture of a bird in flight. "Now," Stan said, "you have to explain what you've drawn." I responded that I had drawn a bird because, as they all knew, I had just been fired, and the future seemed filled with infinite possibilities: I could fly almost anywhere. I was free. At the same time, however, I was filled with anxiety about where it would all lead. And so, the bird had a double meaning: for me, as a Christian, it was also the symbol of God's Holy Spirit, and the pledge that God was with me wherever it all led. When I was done with the explanation, Stan nodded, while the mischief just grew in his eyes. "Now it's my turn," he said, and he stepped to the blackboard. First the picture: he drew a saddle on the back of the bird. Then the explanation: "Wherever you go," he said, "I go."

That incident, remembered on his death, seemed to me to be symbolic of our whole relationship. Beneath all the rituals of our friendship together,—sometimes observed, sometimes unobserved—, Stan always left me with the feeling that he really loved me and cared about me as a person. Particularly when the chips were down. And I think for many of us, this is the main issue of our work. As we look back over the various jobs we have had thus far in our lives, we search our memories for the persons who, like Stan, conveyed to each of us the feeling that we were appreciated, valued, and cared for as a person; or, in a word, loved. If there were such persons at the jobs where we were, or if there are such persons at the job where we presently are, we have an entirely different feeling about that job than would otherwise be the case. Beyond busyness, enjoyment, accomplishment or power, our work has helped fulfill our need to be loved.

And to give love. Hopefully, somewhere in the country today, someone else is trying to recall who it was that made their job a special joy; and it is your name that they come up with, as the person who made them feel loved. For, we all need not only to receive, but also to give. Ann Landers (bless her heart) published a definition of success some time back, which captures this beautifully. It is reproduced at the right.

What Is Success?

To laugh often and love much;

To win the respect of intelligent persons and the affection of children;

To earn the approval of honest critics and endure the betrayal of false friends;

To appreciate beauty;

To find the best in others;

To give of one's self without the slightest thought of return;

To have accomplished a task, whether by a healthy child, a rescued soul, a garden patch or a redeemed social condition;

To have played and laughed with enthusiasm and sung with exaltation;

To know that even one life has breathed easier because you have lived;

This is to have succeeded.

Ralph Waldo Emerson

Now, in dealing with this criterion of success, or effectiveness, it is crucial—it seems to me—to recall Stan's point: that we often have a great deal of difficulty in thinking or talking about love at work, so we fall to talking about rituals instead. "Do you know, he thanked everyone at the banquet except me—and I put in *hours,* working on that thing." "She seems to just take me for granted around here. Boy, will she be sorry when I give her my notice."

And so it goes. We talk about being slighted, ignored, overlooked, passed over, taken for granted. We talk about promises broken, credit not given, responses not forthcoming, letters unanswered, phone calls unreturned, anniversaries not observed, contributions not acknowledged, engagements not remembered, appointments not kept, punctualities not honored, gratitude gone unspoken, ideas not sought, opinions not solicited, advice not kept. But these are all, in the end, rituals. Easy to talk about. What we really mean—not so easy to talk about—is that, beneath all these rituals, and because of all these rituals unobserved, we don't feel that the significant persons at our work (usually our bosses) really love us. And, whether we can talk about it or not, whether we can even admit it to ourselves or not, this is one of the primary factors that—for many of us— helps us to work at our best. So, in making a checklist regarding your effectiveness, be sure to meditate upon this factor. How loved do you feel at work? How much love do you give?

Effectiveness Odds & Ends
or, Meditations of a LIFE/work Planner
While Shaving

● If Promotion, Advancement, etc. are of the *slightest* concern to you in your present job, it is *crucial* for you to keep a daily, or weekly diary about your work, and what you accomplished — as we mentioned earlier. Why you need to do this is very simple:

when it comes time to discuss a raise, promotion or advancement, you need to be able to substantiate your claim that you have contributed a great deal to the organization. Dredging up year-old memories, at that point, simply won't do. Too vague. And if you depend on your boss to have done this catalog of your accomplishments, for you, you will deserve what you get. Bernard Haldane was the first to popularize this technique (see his *How To Make A Habit of Success,* Warner Books, 75 Rockefeller Plaza, New York, NY 10019, $1.95 paper, plus 35¢ mailing and handling. Pages 178-199). John Crystal discusses this and other matters in an excellent section in his (our) *Where Do I Go From Here With My Life?,* entitled "How to Survive After You Get That Job," pages 150ff. Richard Lathrop has some additional ideas in *Who's Hiring Who* (Ten Speed Press, Box 7123, Berkeley, CA 94707, $5.95 paper), particularly in the chapter entitled *"Double* your pay with your present employer" *(that* should sell), pages 199ff. Beyond these three primary sources, there are new books coming out virtually every month on this subject. For example, *how to negotiate a raise* by John J. Tarrant (1976, Pocket Books, 1230 Avenue of the Americas, New York, NY 10020. $1.75 paper, plus 35¢ mailing and handling).

● It may be that Promotion, Advancement, etc. are *not* of the slightest concern to you. New concepts of success are becoming more popular— concepts which emphasize

> O money, money, money,
>   I am not necessarily one of those
>   who think thee holy.
> But I often stop to wonder
>   how thou canst go out so fast
>   when thou comest in so slowly.
>   —Ogden Nash

that unlimited growth, onward and upward, is not an unqualified good. See *The Limits to Growth, A Report for The Club of Rome's Project on the Predicament of Mankind* by Donella H. Meadows, Dennis L. Meadows, Jorgen Randers, and William W. Behrens III (1972, New American Library, P. O. Box 999, Bergenfield, NJ 07621. $1.75 paperback, Signet); *Mankind at The Turning Point: The Second Report to The Club of Rome* by Mihajlo Mesarovic and Eduard Pestel (New American Library, Inc., address above); and *Small Is Beautiful: Economics as if People Mattered* by the late E. F. Schumacher (1973, Harper &

Row, Publishers, Inc., 10 East 53rd Street, New York, NY 10022. $2.45, paper). As all of this is applied to the life of the American worker, it means that many are renouncing the traditional career ladder of their profession, and—after a fling at the executive suite or whatever—are dedicating themselves to the old crafts, to working with their hands, and to something closer to subsistence-type living. One magazine has called this trend "Downward mobility," and that has become a criterion by which some people at least are measuring the effectiveness of their "career". As they get on in years, the smaller their aspirations, the more beautiful.

● Effectiveness or success is a judgment, ultimately, upon your total life, not just upon your life at work. "Many people," says Lotte Bailyn, a researcher at M.I.T., "make the mistake of dividing their lives into two parts—job and family. They don't consider that both actually happen in the same human being." As a consequence, success on the job is often purchased at the expense of failure with the family. Keeping your eye on both: your job and your family, continuously, is a much more difficult process. But any lesser concept of success will ensure A Hollow Victory. For assistance, there are the following books: *The Pursuit of Loneliness: American Culture at the Breaking Point* (Revised Edition) by Philip Slater (1976, Beacon Press, Boston. $2.95, paper) a superb book!; *The Hazards of Being Male: Surviving the Myth of Masculine Privilege* by Herb Goldberg, Ph.D. (1976, Signet Books, The New American Library, Inc., P. O. Box 999, Bergenfield, NJ 07621. $1.75, paper); *Blue-Collar Marriage* by Mirra Komarovsky (1967, Vintage Books, A Division of Random House, New York. $2.95, paper); and *The Divorce Experience* by Morton Hunt and Bernice Hunt (1977, Mc-Graw-Hill Book Company, 1221 Avenue of the Americas, New York, NY 10020. $8.95, hardcover). Remember, what we are talking about in all of these pages is LIFE/Work. *Work* is the smaller concept; *LIFE* is the larger.

> Let us stop equating work with earning a living, but rather think of it as an important component of making a life.
>
> —Ralph C. Weinrich,
> *Michigan Business Review*

How Do You Know When You've 'Arrived'?

Among the readers of every book, there are always Perfectionists—people who are not content with the ordinary definitions, but who want to strive for a higher goal. Faced with this subject of *Effectiveness in the World of Work*, they will of course have mere disdain for the earlier checklist. They want to know: what does Elegant Effectiveness look like? Well, who knows? But if I had to take a crack at it, I would hazard a guess that Elegant Effectiveness involves building a better balance or blend of Learning, Working and Playing (or Re-creation) in your life. It seems to me there are two ways of going about this. We can call them Elegant Effectiveness I, and Elegant Effectiveness II.

Elegant Effectiveness I: at this beginning level, you attempt to build a better balance in your life between Learning, Working and Playing. That is to say, each of these three elements occupies its own separate time frame—"now I am Learning, now I am Working, now I am Playing"—but you move toward the goal of giving them "equal time" as it were. We talked about this much much earlier (pages 46-49, 53-55). Two interesting phenomena are happening in the world of work, designed to help make this happen. One is called "Job-Sharing." You choose some partner and the *two* of you apply for one full-time job. For those who do not financially require full-time salaries, this is an ideal way to increase your options and at the same time have more opportunity for Learning and Playing. Since one out of every five American wage earners is a part-timer,[23] the popularity of this Job-Sharing is bound to grow. The organization to write to, if you want more information about the concept, is NEW WAYS TO WORK, 457 Kingsley, Palo Alto, CA 94301. The other phenomenon that is giving people more flexibility about balancing Learning, Working and Playing, is called "Flexitime." It is a method of permitting employees to pick their own work hours, within a 40-hour a week minimum. For further information, there is the government pamphlet *Flexitime,* published by the U.S. Civil Service Commission, and available from the Superintendent of Documents, U.S. Government Printing Office, Washington, D.C. 20402. 65¢. Or, if you want to go delve in your local library, there is "New patterns for working time" by

Janice Neipert Hedges, which appeared in the *Monthly Labor Review*, February 1973 issue. In addition to Job-Sharing and Flexitime, there are other experiments: the Four-Day Work Week, the Three-Day "Workend," etc. These are described in: *4 days, 40 hours, Reporting a Revolution in Work and Leisure*, edited by Riva Poor (1970, Bursk and Poor Publishing, 66 Martin Street, Cambridge, MA. $5.00, paper); and *More Time-wealth for You!* A Realistic Way Out of the American Rat Race Through Split-Week Living, by Millard C. Faught, Ph.D. (1969, Pyramid Books, 757 Third Avenue, New York, NY 10017. 75¢, paper).

Elegant Effectiveness II: at this advanced level, the three elements — Learning, Working, and Playing — are not seen as occupying separate time frames, but as *three different aspects of every time frame.* Here we are not talking about balancing, but about blending. Your work becomes such fun for you, that you aren't sure any longer whether to call it "work" or "leisure". Perhaps a new word is needed, like *leis-work.* Moreover, you are at the same time always learning so much, that it is really *learn-leis-work* for you. There are individuals, already, who have learned how to do this. And I would say that they have indeed taken Effectiveness to its highest level. The rest of us mortals need to take the goal more seriously. It *is* worth striving for.

The question arises often as to how all of this applies to The Employer. Effectiveness then becomes the subject of Evaluation, and we have included an Appendix F at the end of this book, in order to deal with that. (Employees can eavesdrop, too.)

Chapter Four Footnotes

1. *The American Citizen: 11 Years After High School,* by Sandra Reitz Wilson and Lauress L. Wise. June 1975. American Institutes for Research, P. O. Box 1113, Palo Alto, California 94302. $7.75. There are a number of other Project TALENT reports available from the AIR.

2. National Longitudinal Study of the High School Class of 1972. "Comparative Profiles One and One-Half Year After Graduation." NCES 76-220. And: "Changes in Attitudes One and One-Half Years After Graduation." NCES 76-227. Available from: Superintendent of Documents, U.S. Government Printing Office, Washington, D.C. 20402. $1.25, and 35¢ respectively.

3. One exception to this is Project TALENT's report (address above) entitled, *Post High School Education and Career Development,* by W.M. Yen and D. H. McLaughlin, which examines the effects of 4-year college, junior or community college, and noncollege training on salary, job satisfaction and employment rate. Other studies done, not on as thorough a scale, include: The SAM (Student Accountability Model) Project of the California Community Colleges, 1238 S Street, Sacramento, CA 95814; "A Follow-Up Study of Chabot College Technical-Vocational Career Graduates of 1975" by Charles V. Gebhardt, III; "Career Patterns of the Illini Graduate Class-Urbana"; and probably a hundred others that I haven't heard of.

4. "Placement Services Follow-Up Report", Jack Shingleton, Director of Placement, Michigan State University, Placement Services, Student Services Building, East Lansing, Michigan.

5. Source: Employment and Training Report of the President, 1976. Catalog No. L 1.42/2:976, Superintendent of Documents, U.S. Government Printing Office, Washington D.C. 20402. $5.20.

6. *Ibid.*

7. *Ibid.*

8. *Ibid.*

9. *Union hiring halls* and *school placement offices* are omitted from our list here, because they are avenues only open to a particular kind of job seeker (i.e., union members, and college students). Three out of four workers in this country are not union members.

10. For additional tips on Interviews you may wish to get your hands on: "How To Get and Keep The Right Job," from: Carnation Company, Public Relations Department, Carnation Building, 5045 Wilshire Boulevard, Los Angeles, CA 90036. Free. And: "Making the Most of Your Job Interview," from: New York Life Insurance Company, 51 Madison Avenue, New York, NY 10010. Free. Very thorough. "You and Your First Job!" from: Personnel and Industrial Relations Association, Inc., 1730 West Olympic Boulevard, Los Angeles, CA 90015. Free.

11. And if your unemployment lasts for sometime, there are books to help you with that, too. Cf. *The Unemployment Handbook: A Practical, Comprehensive Guide to Your Legal Rights,* by Peter Jan Honigsberg, J.D. (1975, 1976, Ballantine Books, available from Ballantine Mail Sales, Dept. LE, 201 E. 50th Street, New York, NY 10022, $1.00. Order No. 25320) Or: by the same author, *Your Legal Guide to Unemployment Insurance,* 1975, available from Golden Rain Press, P. O. Box 2087, Berkeley, CA 94702, $3.35.

12. This study was reported in the *San Francisco Examiner,* October 31, 1975, and in the *Washington Post,* December 28, 1975.

13. As explained in the church pamphlet (tract) called "Take Heart: A Word to the Unemployed," Forward Movement Publications, Publisher, 412 Sycamore Street, Cincinnati, Ohio 45202, 25¢; as well as in *What Color Is Your Parachute?*, chapters two and three.

14. Done by *Electronic Design* Magazine, August 2, 1970, page 63ff. This and the immediately following statistics are taken from a pamphlet entitled *Tea Leaves: a new look at resumes,* by Richard N. Bolles; available from Ten Speed Press, Box 7123, Berkeley, CA 94707, 50¢ plus 25¢ for postage and handling.

15. See *Parachute,* 1981 edition, pp. 27, 36

16. *Moneysworth,* September 29, 1975 issue.

17. "Must" reading, for those not familiar with McClelland's work, includes: *Human Motivation: A Book of Readings,* by David C. McClelland and Robert S. Steele (1973, available in your bookstore, or order directly from the publisher, General Learning Corporation, Box 2345, Morristown, NJ 07960. $7.80, paper); *Power: The Inner Experience,* by David C.

McClelland (1975, available in bookstores or directly from the publisher, Irvington Publishers, Inc., 551 Fifth Avenue, New York, NY 10017.) A workbook in these theories is also available: *Motivation Workshops: A Student Workbook for Experiential Learning in Human Motivation* by David C. McClelland and Robert S. Steele (1972, from the publisher: General Learning Corporation, address above. $5.95, paper).

18. Other books on time management: *The Time Trap: How to Get More Done in Less Time* by R. Alec Mackenzie (1972, McGraw-Hill Paperbacks, 1221 Avenue of the Americas, New York, NY 10020. $2.95, paper); *How to Get More Done In Less Time* by Joseph D. Cooper (1971, Doubleday and Company, Garden City, Long Island, New York, $7.95, hardcover); *The Management of Time* by James T. McCay (Sixth Printing, January 1977, Prentice-Hall, Inc., Englewood Cliffs, NJ. $2.95, paper, U.S.A. $3.50, paper, Canada); and others, appearing at the rate of about once a month, it seems. See your library or bookstore.

19. The Mission, sad to say, went out of existence in the Spring of 1978. If you are interested in other books relating to assemblyline work and its boredom, recent works include: *Auto Work and Its Discontents* by B. J. Widick (1976, Johns Hopkins University Press, $2.95, paper); and *Clockwork: Life In and Outside an American Factory* by Richard Balzer (1976, Doubleday, New York, $10.00, hardcover).

20. The *Wall Street Journal,* May 29, 1973.

21. The *Washington Post,* May 18, 1975.

22. If you want some help with this whole subject of "taking more (manageable) risks", there is: *Risking* by David Viscott, M.D. (1977, Simon & Schuster, Rockefeller Center, 1230 Avenue of the Americas, New York, NY 10020. $7.95, hardcover); and: *A Guide to Personal Risk Taking* by Richard E. Byrd (1974, AMACOM, 135 West 50th Street, New York, NY 10020. $12.95, hardcover).

23. *Family Circle* Magazine, March 1, 1978., p. 144.

Note found in a floating bottle:
"Help! I'm a twenty-five year old
imprisoned in a fifty year old body."

Chapter Five
Toward a Balanced Life:
Life-Long Leisure or Playing

ell, we've spent a chapter on Education or Learning, and a chapter on Working, so normally this is where you would expect a chapter on Retirement to appear. That's the way it goes in our culture: Education, Work, Retirement—the Three Boxes. First an "orgy" of learning, then an "orgy" of working, and finally, an "orgy" of leisure.

"Retirement" is the title we give to the orgy of leisure, in our culture. Accordingly, you would expect this chapter to be a careful dissertation on some such subject as How To Enjoy Full-time Leisure During Your Sunset Years. There are, however, three problems with that expectation. First, if you've followed the *argument* of this book thus far (Heavens, you're not a *Page-Flipper* or a *Chapter-Skipper,* are you?) you will know that LIFE/work Planning has as one of its main goals, *Lifelong* Leisure. This means (among other things) that Leisure is not to be saved up until you are a "senior citizen" but is to be indulged in, throughout your whole life. Thus, if this *were* a dissertation, the subject would have to be How To Enjoy Leisure During Your Early Years, Your Middle Years, and Your Later Years. Such guidelines as this chapter will contain, are meant to be applied at *any* age and at *every* age of your life.

Secondly, you will also know by now that the other goals of LIFE/work Planning are *Lifelong* Learning, and *Lifelong* Working (although, to be sure, by arguing that "Working" means "working at something you *love* to do", we have almost redefined the word from the sense in which it is commonly used —as virtually synonymous with "drudgery"). Now, "Lifelong" means just what it says: namely, extending itself into the period commonly termed "Retirement." And so, from this point of view, Retirement is a meaningless term. If you—during the years after sixty, say—are still engaged in a balanced life of Learning, Working and Playing, just as you were in your earlier years, then in what sense have you "Retired"? Retirement normally alludes (in its most specific sense) to a disengagement from Work or (in its more general sense) to the beginning of our disengagement from Life. Which is why Death (the completion of that disengagement) often comes so abruptly and early to those who do indeed *retire*, and just sit around the house.

Thirdly, if you are persuaded by our viewpoint that the so-called "Retirement Period" of your life ought to be a balance of Learning, Working, and Playing, then you will perceive without my saying it (but I will anyway) that this chapter can't cover *Retirement* because this whole book is A Retirement Manual. Just as this whole book is a Youth Manual, and a Young Adult Manual, and a Mid-Life Manual. Once you take Learning, Working and Playing out of their *boxes,* and aim your life at Lifelong Learning, Lifelong Working and Lifelong Playing, then the strategies needed *at any one age* are the strategies needed *at every age.*

But, of course, the majority of people have not taken Learning, Working and Playing out of their boxes yet. And so, they approach "Retirement" relatively traditionally. In view of this fact, it is appropriate to pause briefly here—before talking about Lifelong Leisure and Playing—in order to consider:

A Few Notes About Retirement

If you consider Retirement a very separate period from Learning, or Working, then of course the World of Retirement confronts you all over again with *The Pyramid.*

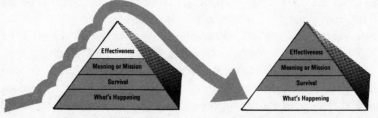

In The World of Work   In The World of Retirement

And no matter how skillfully you may have mastered the Issues in the World of Work, it is a whole new ball game when you enter the World of Retirement. In this bright new world, you have to figure out all over again just exactly What is Happening, and how you Survive, and what will give you a sense of Meaning or Mission in *this period,* and how you can make it the most Effective. The *answers* you found earlier (in the World of Work or in the World of Education) won't help very much here; but the *tools* will, for they are the same tools. But first:

FOR AN OVERVIEW OF YOUR TIME USE

See Pages 46-58, in Chapter Two.

How To Deal, In the World of Retirement, with What's Happening

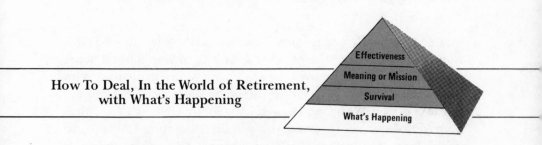

The tools for doing this will be found (for your review) on
a) pages 74-77, 84-89 in Chapter Three
b) pages 221-224, 233-240 in Chapter Four
c) Practice and Informational Interviewing
   at the end of Appendix D.

What these tools boil down to, as you will no doubt recall, is a combination of Talking with People, and Using Printed Resources.

What are you trying to find out? Well, of course, what this strange new world—the World of Retirement—is going to be like (if you are not there yet) or is like (if you already are there). It's a matter of preparing yourself, or of speeding up the period of acclimation to this New World.

Most of us have a wide variety of opportunities to talk to people in retirement, long before we ourselves reach that blessed

estate. We usually waste such time, by settling for talking with
them about the weather or what's on TV, or our mutual aches
and pains. You will be wise beyond your years if, instead, you
use every chance you have to interview older people—who are
already in the World of Retirement—about what it's like, thus
preparing yourself to avoid the pitfalls that they fell into, to
profit from the lessons that they learned, and to use the tools
that they found or find most helpful. What kinds of questions
to ask them? Well, principally adaptations of the questions we
saw earlier. You might ask them: What are you enjoying the
most about this period of your life? What are you enjoying the
least? What do you wish someone had told you about Retirement before you ever reached Retirement? What is the greatest
problem that you face, or have faced—and how are you dealing,
or did you deal, with that problem? What resources and places
for help—or what ideas—have you found the most helpful to
you during this period of your life? And: like that. You'll be
amazed at what you learn.

There is no need at all to enter the World of Retirement as a
stranger. You can enter into it as into a World you have spent
years learning about and visiting in the imagination of your
heart. It all depends upon your taking the management of this

Learning into your own hands, rather than depending upon Someone or Something Else (the personnel department at your place of Work, or whatever) to do it for you. In this program of your own Self-Directed Exploration concerning the World of Retirement, you will of course want to supplement your personal interviewing of people, with some additional exploration through books and articles—i.e., printed stuff. Here is a *sampler* of some helpful books:

ON THE GENERAL SUBJECT OF AGING

Passages: Predictable Crises of Adult Life, by Gail Sheehy. 1974. Bantam Books, Inc., 414 East Golf Road, Des Plaines, IL 60016. $2.50, paper.

The Seasons of A Man's Life by Daniel J. Levinson and Charlotte N. Darrow, Edward B. Klein, Maria H. Levinson and Braxton McKee. 1978. Alfred A. Knopf, New York. $10.95, hardcover.

In 1945, there was only one person in the World of Retirement (and receiving Social Security benefits) for every 35 people in the World of Work. In 1977, that ratio had decreased to 1:3.2. If things continue as they are, by the year 2025 there will be one person in the World of Retirement for every two people in the World of Work. [1]

"The Middle Years: Neither Too Young Nor Too Old" by A. J. Jaffe, A Special Issue of *Industrial Gerontology,* September 1971 from: The National Institute of Industrial Gerontology, The National Council of the Aging, 1828 "L" Street, NW, Washington, D.C. 20036. $1.50 from: Bureau of Applied Social Research, Columbia University, 605 West 115th Street, New York, NY 10025.

The Inner World of the Middle-Aged Man by Peter Chew. 1976. Macmillan Publishing Company, Inc., 866 Third Avenue, New York, NY 10022. $8.95, hardcover.

The Coming of Age by Simone de Beauvoir. 1972. G. P. Putnam's Sons, 200 Madison Avenue, New York, NY 10016. $10, hardcover.

ON RETIREMENT SPECIFICALLY

If you go into a bookstore, and just browse, you will find books about Retirement that range from the simplistic to the profound. That old rule: *Caveat emptor*—Let the Buyer Beware —is essential to remember, in this field.

Still, in even the worst of them there are some interesting facts or ideas. Such as, the size of the World of Retirement (there are 23 million people who are age 65 or older), the number of new 'senior citizens' each year (300,000+), the percentage of persons over 65 who are not in a nursing home or institution (95%), the percentage of persons over 65 not in an institution, who report relative freedom from any chronic activity-limiting health problems (82%), and such.[2] So, you may want to go down to your friendly neighborhood public library and borrow any books that look even remotely interesting and helpful. *Take Notes!* You will find they help to organize your picture of What's Happening in the World of Retirement, once your reading or browsing is completed.

Down in your local bookstore these days, you will find books like the following:

A Good Age by Alex Comfort. 1976. Crown Publishers, Inc., One Park Avenue, New York, NY 10016. $9.95, hardcover.

The Retirement Book: A Complete Early-Planning Guide to Finances, New Activities, and Where to Live by Joan Adler. 1975. William Morrow & Company, Inc., 105 Madison Avenue, New York, NY 10016. $9.95, hardcover.

The Retirement Threat by Tony Lamb and Dave Duffy. 1977. J. P. Tarcher, Inc., Publishers, 9110 Sunset Blvd., Los Angeles, CA 90069. $7.95, hardcover.

How to Enjoy Your Retirement by John Sunshine. 1974. AMACOM, A Division of American Management Associations, 135 West 50th Street, New York, NY 10020. $7.95, hardcover.

How To Avoid The Retirement Trap by Leland Frederick Cooley and Lee Morrison Cooley. 1972. Popular Library, New York. $1.50, paper.

Ready or Not: Planning Your Successful Retirement by Lowell Ledford and Jeanne Brock. 1977. Manpower Education Institute, 127 East 35th Street, New York, NY 10016. Available from: Walker and Company, 720 Fifth Avenue, New York, NY 10019. $3.95, paper.

They are, as I said, of unequal value. (That's as tactful as I know how to be.) Moreover, the above list is only a *partial sampler,* since new books are constantly appearing. So go, browse, buy what looks irresistible—or tell your children what you want for Christmas or your next birthday.

But *puhlease,* check out anything you may find in printed stuff by going and talking to actual live people—amongst your friends, neighbors, volunteer groups, church or synagogue—who are in the World of Retirement. Asking them: Have you found this to be true? (whatever "this" is) may save you a whole peck of trouble, down the road. If you alternate between reading (printed stuff) and interviewing (live Retirees or Senior Citizens), you'll soon be able to tell the wheat from the chaff.

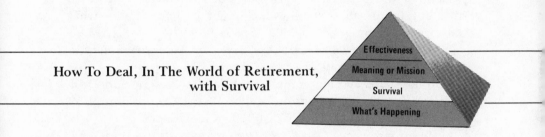

How To Deal, In The World of Retirement, with Survival

Survival, as I said earlier (pages 11-13) tends to be a whole *family* of issues. This is never more true than during your time in the World of Retirement. Let us look, briefly, at that family:

PHYSICAL SURVIVAL

This is the question of your health. And *that* is the whole province of exercise, medicines and doctors. The basic decision you have to make, concerning this survival issue, is not whether you will be healthy or not. But whether, healthy or otherwise, you will see this as:

a) an area of your life that you just deliver completely into the hands of doctors and other 'experts'; OR

b) an area of your life that you keep entirely in your own hands, without any recourse to doctors or other 'experts'; OR

c) an area of your life that is the joint responsibility of both yourself and your doctors.

Assuming you opt for the latter decision, there are a number of helpful aids (i.e., books) on the market, that you may want to take a look at, and—in some cases—purchase. The ones which I have personally found helpful are:

How To Be Your Own Doctor—Sometimes by Keith W. Sehnert, M.D. with Howard Eisenberg. 1975. Grosset & Dunlap, Publishers, $4.95, paper (U.S.A.), $5.95, paper (Canada). William Nolen has said, "If you choose to have one self-help medical book in your home, this ought to be the one." I agree heartily.

The Essential Guide to Prescription Drugs: What You Need To Know for Safe Drug Use by James W. Long, M.D. 1977. Harper & Row, Publishers, Inc., 10 East 53rd Street, New York, NY 10022. $8.95, paper. There are several books out on this subject; this is my favorite. I believe that some such book as this is an essential home companion for anyone who ever takes prescribed drugs, inasmuch as our doctors are rarely able to spell out for us all the things we ought to know about what they are prescribing.

The People's Pharmacy: A Guide to Prescription Drugs, Home Remedies and Over-the-Counter Medications by Joe Graedon. 1976. A nice complement to the Prescription Drug book. Avon Books, a division of The Hearst Corporation, 959 Eighth Avenue, New York, NY 10019. $3.95, paper.

Symptoms: The Complete Home Medical Encyclopedia, edited by Sigmund Stephen Miller. 1976. Thomas Y. Crowell Company, 666 Fifth Avenue, New York, NY 10019. $17.95. (Why not get your children or friends to give it to you for Christmas or your birthday, if this is beyond your budget). This book lists the different parts of the body, and then the various symptoms therein that may have caused you to dive for this book. It gives you a description of the various diseases that may be causing the symptom, so you can evaluate how rapidly you need to get thee to a doctor or to the emergency room at your local hospital.

> If you haven't got charity in your heart, you have the worst kind of heart trouble.
> —Bob Hope

Now, I list these books here—under Retirement—but it will be obvious to us all that they are useful at *any* time of our lives. Physical survival is not, after all, just an issue in our old age, or senior citizenhood. The better part of wisdom would be to buy these books (or ones like them) at as young an age as you can, supplementing them with:

Man's Body: An Owner's Manual by the Diagram Group. 1976. Grosset & Dunlap, Publishers. $6.95, large size. Bantam

Books, Inc., 666 Fifth Avenue, New York, NY 10019. $2.25, small size.

Woman's Body: An Owner's Manual by the Diagram Group. 1977. Grosset & Dunlap, Publishers. $6.95, large size. Bantam Books, Inc. (address above). $2.75, small size.

Whenever it does get down to a matter of literal physical survival for you, and neither doctors nor drugs are able to offer any hope, it is important to remember that there are healing methods which we know relatively little about, these days; but we are learning. Meditation, yoga, metaphysical healing are not to be lightly dismissed:

The Body Is The Hero by Ronald J. Glasser, M.D. 1976. Random House, New York. $8.95, hardcover. Great title: What caused the healing? Doctors didn't do it. Drugs didn't do it. The body is the hero.

The Path of Action by Jack Schwarz. 1977. E. P. Dutton, 201 Park Avenue South, New York, NY 10003. $3.50, paperback. After seeing what Jack Schwarz can do with/to his body, you've *got* to be interested in whatever is going on in his mind.

Beyond Biofeedback by Elmer and Alyce Green. 1977. Delacorte Press/Seymour Lawrence, 90 Beacon Street, Boston, MA 02108. $10.95, hardcover. On the potency of the human mind and will, once it has sufficient information.

The Miracle of Metaphysical Healing by Evelyn M. Monahan. 1975. Parker Publishing Company, Inc., West Nyack, New York 10994. $8.95, hardcover.

There are many other good books in this area. Try interviewing other people to see what they've found helpful, try browsing your bookstore, then see if your local library has the titles you're interested in.

FINANCIAL SURVIVAL

Whenever industry or government runs pre-retirement seminars for its employees, those seminars tend to focus upon finances. A very important survival issue, in the World of Retirement. Actually, however, it does not first appear in that World; it dogs our heels all of our lives.

Financial survival breaks down into three compartments:
a) how to manage what money you have;
b) how to search for additional funds;
c) how to find essential services at low cost, or for free, when your money simply will not stretch far enough.

As to the first, managing what money you have, there are a number of helpful pamphlets, books, and other resources. These are listed in a most helpful, omnibus bibliography entitled, "Planning for Retirement: A Bibliography of Retirement Planning Literature", obtainable without charge from the American Association of Retired Persons and the National Retired Teachers Association. Write to: NRTA-AARP Library, 1909 "K" Street, NW., Washington, D.C. 20049. This bibliography, incidentally, lists not only resources dealing with financial survival (Social Security, Savings, Budgeting, etc.), but

The Economic Nightmare

If you are elderly *and poor*, retirement can be what Sylvia Porter calls "an economic nightmare." 15.7% of all elderly are dramatically poor—living below the poverty level. If they live alone, or with non-relatives, their situation is likely to be much worse. 50% of all such elderly receive incomes under $3,000 per year, and 83% of them receive less than $6,000 per year. Elderly couples fare somewhat better, but not all that much: 20% of them still receive less than $4,000 per year, and 75% of them receive less than $10,000 per year.

The familiar artifacts of life after 65, for many people, include: substandard housing or dramatically rising property taxes; inflation eroding the purchasing power of pensions, savings and Social Security payments; Medicare covering only 60% of the total health care costs; and heaven-knows-what-else the next time you look around.

Social Security's limitation on outside earnings—where you lose $1 of benefits for every $2 you earn over a set limit (in some cases as low as $3,240 a year)—has doubtless contributed toward the depressing fact that currently only one out of five men, among the elderly, is still working, and only one out of twelve women. In 1960, one out of every three men over 65 was working, and in 1950 almost one out of every two.[3]

also resources dealing with physical survival, legal survival, and other aspects of Retirement. One of the best on money managing is *Rosefsky's Guide to Financial Security for the Mature Family* by Robert Rosefsky. 1977. Follett Publishing Company, 1010 W. Washington Blvd., Chicago, IL 60607. $7.95, hardcover.

The second matter, that of searching for additional funds, is a grave matter if you are not working. But, throughout these pages, we have been espousing the LIFE/work Planning ideal of *Lifelong* Working. And, except for those confined to institutions, or suffering from some chronic health problem, the need for additional funds can be *partially* or fully met by holding to this goal. Starting your own small business, or finding employment, ought not to be super-difficult *provided* you use The Alternative Method of Job Hunting—outlined in Appendix D, and on pages 262ff. And that you follow it *religiously,* so to speak. Your age is, in this method, close to An Irrelevancy. In The Other Method, however, you know—the traditional way that everyone normally goes about looking for a job—your age almost certainly will be held against you. Unless you just exude Charm. I know of a woman who went into a small store in upper Michigan which incidentally sold books, and idly asked as she was making her purchase, "Do you sell a book entitled *What Color Is Your Parachute?*" "No," they replied, "is it a comedy book?" "No," the woman said, "though it has some humor in it. Actually, it's about your Self, and how you can figure out who you are and what you want to do." "Well, did it help you?" they asked. "Yes," she said, "I did all the exercises and I figured out that I'm a lovable slob. Do you know anyone who would want to hire a lovable slob?" To make a long story short, the store manager offered her a job on the spot. This woman, incidentally, was 62 years old, and had never held a job in her life.

Our third—and last—matter under Financial Survival, is (needless to say) the matter of a Plan B: what do you do when you cannot find any additional funds, and the money you have simply will not stretch far enough? For The Mature Family, the Senior Citizen, the Retiree (take your choice from among a whole bunch of disagreeable labels) there are directories of resources, such as:

The Older American's Handbook by Craig & Peter Norback, with Bernard E. Nash, Consulting Editor. 1977. Van Nostrand Reinhold Company, 450 West 33rd Street, New York, NY 10001. $8.95, paper. It lists resources and services in such areas as housing, food, transportation, employment, mental health and counseling, medical and nursing care, legal services, in-home services, telephone reassurance, etc.

There are financial guides on how to make your dollars s—t—r—e—t—c—h, that are apparently written primarily for the young, but are useful at any age. Some of the best known are:

Champagne Living On A Beer Budget: The Updated Insiders' Guide To Living Better For Less by Marilyn and Mike Ferguson. 1968, 1973. Berkley Medallion Books, 200 Madison Avenue, New York, NY 10016. $1.95, paper.

Getting The Most For Your Money: How to Beat the High Cost of Living by Anthony Scaduto. 1970. Paperback Library, Coronet Communications, Inc., 315 Park Avenue South, New York, NY 10010. 95¢, paper.

How To Live On Nothing (Updated and Revised) by Joan Ranson Shortney. 1971. Pocket Books, A Division of Simon & Schuster, Inc., 1230 Avenue of the Americas, New York, NY 10020. $1.50, paper. Has a great chapter on "How to Make Something Out of Nothing."

And, *of course:*

Sylvia Porter's Money Book: How To Earn It, Spend It, Save It, Invest It, Borrow It—And Use It To Better Your Life. 1975. Doubleday & Company, Inc., New York. $14.95, hardcover. Also out in paperback. For all ages.

From a LIFE/work Planning point of view, the moral of all this is very clear: you aren't the first person to have to wrestle with the issue of financial survival, other people have been there before you. You can profit from their experience and from the lessons that they learned, either through interviewing the people all around you, or through reading the books which other financial survivors have thoughtfully written.

It is rare to meet a person who hasn't at some time or other in their life, feared that they were headed for a mental breakdown. Heralded by the universal cry: I don't think I can take any more of this. There are, throughout life, a number of crises which normally put a great deal of pressure on us: pressure that is not so much physical or financial as it is emotional. So, this issue is—again—not an issue solely of Retirement, by any means. But, in Retirement things do tend to come to a head, particularly in personal relationships. Some couples find the World of Retirement (in its traditional definition of "no more working") an absolutely idyllic time, when life allows them at last to savor each other without interruption or deadline. The housewife who deeply loves her husband, but felt for years that his work was really his wife, and she only his mistress, now may have him exclusively to herself, in a kind of luxurious re-honeymoon.

But for some other couples, it is not so. This World of Retirement may become a nightmare for them both, as they suddenly awake to the realization that they were able to tolerate each other in marriage precisely because they spent the majority of each day apart, at their separate places of work. Age will not necessarily deter them from separation or divorce, once this realization hits home. I remember asking a sixty-seven year old woman, in the midst of a divorce which she initiated, why she had not decided simply to live out the rest of her years in what had—for fifty years—been at least a *tolerable* relationship. She replied, "Well, the man is a tyrant, and during the years that he worked, he could take it out on all his employees. But now that he has retired, and sits around the house all day, he has only me to order around—and I don't like it one bit. I figure I have a number of years still remaining in my life, and I don't know why they should be ruined by my living any longer with him."

From the point of view of LIFE/work Planning, the principles for dealing with emotional survival are the same ones that we were just looking at, in the section on financial survival. Namely: you aren't the first person to have to wrestle with these experiences, other people have been there before you, and you can profit from their experience and the lessons that they learned—either through talking to people who have been through

347

it, or by reading what such people have written. A *sampler* of the latter includes:

Shifting Gears: Finding Security In A Changing World by Nena O'Neill and George O'Neill. 1974. Avon Books, Mail Order Department, 250 West 55th Street, New York, NY 10019. $1.95, paper, plus 25¢ for handling and postage (must accompany order).

Married, Etc. A Sourcebook for Couples by Roberta Suid, Buff Bradley, Murray Suid, Jean Eastman. 1976. Addison-Wesley Publishing Company, Jacob Way, Reading, MA 01867. $5.95, paper.

The Divorce Experience by Morton Hunt and Bernice Hunt. 1977. McGraw-Hill Book Company, 1221 Avenue of the Americas, New York, NY 10020. $8.95, hardcover.

Women in Transition: A Feminist Handbook on Separation and Divorce by Women In Transition, Inc. 1975. Charles Scribner's Sons, 597 Fifth Avenue, New York, NY 10017. $6.95, paper.

> To love. . . is to be vulnerable. Love anything, and your heart will certainly be wrung and possibly broken. If you want to make sure of keeping it intact, you must give it to no one, not even to an animal. Wrap it carefully around hobbies and little luxuries; avoid all entanglements; lock it up safe in the casket or coffin of your selfishness. But in that casket—safe, dark, motionless, airless — it will change. It will not be broken; it will become unbreakable, impenetrable, irredeemable.
>
> *—C. S. Lewis*

Creative Divorce: A New Opportunity for Personal Growth by Mel Krantzler. 1974. A Signet Book, New American Library, P. O. Box 999, Bergenfield, NJ 07621. $1.95, paper, plus 25¢ for handling and mailing costs.

Divorce and After: An Analysis of the Emotional and Social Problems of Divorce edited by Paul Bohannan, with a number of contributors including Margaret Mead. 1970. Anchor Books, Doubleday and Company, Inc., 245 Park Avenue, New York, NY 10017. $1.95, paper.

Learning to Love Again by Mel Krantzler. 1977. Thomas Y. Crowell Company, 10 East 53rd Street, New York, NY 10022. $7.95, hardcover.

While divorce or the loss of a primary, loving, supportive relationship by whatever cause (including death), is the most dramatic event to confront us with the issue of emotional survival, it is hardly the only one. You may face many other causes of acute stress.

Whatever the nature of the problem that is bothering you, there are three rules that seem to be of universal help:

(1) Take the initiative in dealing with the problem. Don't just sit there, waiting for God to prove that He (or She) loves You. Don't count on someone else seeing your plight and coming to rescue you. Don't count on the problem just going away. In keeping with the basic principles of LIFE/work Planning, it is important for you to understand that this is *your* life, and no one cares quite so much about what happens to that life as you do. It is crucial that you reach out, even if it takes all your strength to do so.

(2) Recruit every acquaintance, friend and family member that you possibly can, to be a member of an Emotional-Support Community for you. Let them know that you are going through a difficult time. Tell *the best of them*—the ones in whom you have the most confidence—a brief summary of the *history,* and a detailed account of the *feelings* you are experiencing; as for the rest of them, spare them the gory details. You don't want them to start running when they see you coming. Self-pity and repetitious details have, in the past, alienated people who would otherwise have been glad to have been emotionally supportive to the self-pitier. It is sufficient to tell anyone other than the ones in whom you have the most confidence, "I am going through a rough time, and your friendship and emotional support mean a great deal to me during this time."

(3) Any time someone in your Emotional-Support Community says that they have been through a rough time, don't just leave such statements with a murmur of sympathy. Think of them as fellow members of Emotional-Survivors Anonymous, and ask them what ideas, techniques or supports they found most helpful when they were going through *their* rough time. You'll be surprised at the mind-boggling, life-saving ideas and experiences that you may pick up just from the people around you.

When the three steps, above, are faithfully followed, but you are still having a perilous time emotionally, then you probably need to get so-called expert help. I say "so-called" because the use of the term "expert"—in contrast with "amateur"—needs a lot of reexamination, these days. The question must always be: "expert at what?" If a man or woman is expert at a particular therapy, that's fine; however, a particular therapy is only a *means* toward an end. The end, presumably, is Living. Or, if you prefer, Living Victoriously. Consequently, what any of us *really* wants when we are wrestling with emotional survival is someone who is an Expert at Living. And once you have said that, the problem of identifying who is an amateur and who is an expert becomes much more difficult. The little old lady next door, wrapped in her simple housecoat, may be more of an Expert at Living than the well-dressed learned-looking therapist sitting in his or her professional-looking office. But, on the other hand, it may be the therapist who is more of the Expert at Living, than the little old lady next door. You're going to have to do your own intelligent questioning of both, before you can decide. One thing, however, is for sure: you can't decide the issue simply by their *labels* (housewife, therapist).

Further guidance in this matter may be found in *What Color Is Your Parachute?* 1981 edition, pages 268–273. Now, supposing you live somewhere where no therapist of any kind, nature or persuasion is to be found for hundreds of miles? Well, there are always books. If there is *any* emotional problem you face, that someone hasn't thought to write a book about, just wait until next week.

From a LIFE/work Planning point of view, the key issue in all of this is that you are in charge of your life, but you don't have to work it out all by yourself. From a Retirement point of view, the key issue is the temptation we all face, in one degree or another, to increasingly disengage ourselves from the outside world and from outside relationships as we grow older. In a word, Don't.

The best defense against emotional disaster is a good offense: a balanced life, even in the so-called 'Retirement Years', of Learning, Working, and Playing—which will help to keep you engaged with Life and in relationships with others whom you can talk with, touch, support—and be supported by, emotionally.

Reflections of A Marvelous Spirit
On The Subject of Aging

At 86, Rosie and I live by the rules of the elderly. If the toothbrush is wet, you have cleaned your teeth. If the bedside radio is warm in the morning you left it on all night. If you are wearing one brown and one black shoe, quite possibly you have a like pair in the closet.

Rosie has aged some in the past year, and now seems like a woman entering her forties. She deplores with me the miscreant who regularly enters our house in the middle of the night, squeezes the toothpaste tube in the middle, and departs.

As for me, I am as bright as can be expected, remembering the friend who told me years ago, "If your I.Q. ever breaks 100, sell!"

Like most elderly people, we spend happy hours in front of our TV set. We rarely turn it on, of course.

I walk with a slight straddle, hoping people will think I just got off a horse. I considered carrying a riding crop but gave it up—too ostentatious.

I stagger when I walk and small boys follow me, making bets on which way I'll go next. This upsets me; children shouldn't gamble.

On my daily excursions, I greet everyone punctiliously, including the headrests in parked, empty cars. Dignified friends seem surprised when I salute them with a breezy "Hi!" They don't realize I haven't enough breath for some huge two-syllable word of greeting.

My motto this year is from the Spanish: "I don't want the cheese, I just want to get out of this trap."

When we are old, the young are kinder to us, and we are kinder to each other. There is a sunset glow that irradiates our faces, and is reflected on the faces of those around us. But it is still sunset.

—The late Bruce Bliven

This means various things to various people. For some, it means maintaining a living two-way relationship with God — or however you describe the Spiritual Center of the universe — conceived to be a "who" rather than a "what", and regarded as being a living, thinking, caring, moral Being. Others, who deny belief in such a Being, may still be concerned about spiritual survival in the sense of "the basic *I* whom I know myself to be," surviving through all the varying experiences of life unchanged in its basic *essence*. For still others, "spirit" has a very symbolic meaning only, as in the phrase "she has a very generous spirit." And for them, spiritual survival means that life should not turn a generous spirit into a mean one, nor an honest spirit into a warped one, and so forth.

Each of these different definitions of spiritual survival requires of course a different remedy, when survival is at stake. At one extreme, the remedy is religious counseling or religious workshops, meditation, prayer, and the like. At the other extreme, the remedy may be that of quiet reflection and inventory.

There seem, however, to be three common denominators behind all successful spiritual survival:

(1) *The search for unity.* The late Gordon Allport used to emphasize how much this search for unity was behind all religious or spiritual impulses. It is essentially the desire not to leave Reality distributed into a bunch of different baskets, as it were, but to see an inter-relatedness and connectedness between *everything*. It is the desire to be unified, first of all, in the Self. Then to find unity amongst all of one's experiences, and finally to find unity in the universe. "Hear, O Israel: the Lord our God is one Lord."

(2) *The search for a larger context* in which to view one's life. We spoke of this earlier (page 187), when we were discussing a philosophy of life. People who survive best, spiritually, seem to be those who are able to take any random experience that happens to them and put it into some kind of larger perspective. Tied to this ability, as I noted earlier, is usually a keen sense of humor about oneself.

The Unity of Creation

We need another and a wiser and, perhaps, a more mystical concept of animals. We patronize them for their incompleteness, for their tragic fate of having taken form so far below ourselves. And therein we err, and greatly err. For the animal shall not be measured by man. In a world older and more complete than ours they move finished and complete, gifted with extensions of the senses we have lost or never attained, living by voices we shall never hear. They are not brethren, they are not underlings; they are other nations, caught with ourselves in the net of life and time, fellow prisoners of the splendour and travail of the earth.

The Outermost House, by Henry Beston

(3) *The search for meaning.* I remember listening, some years ago, to a doctor as he recounted a search which he and some of his colleagues had conducted to find out why some patients healed faster than others. The search was conducted at a New York City hospital, with pairs of patients who had undergone basically the same surgery. In each pair, one healed faster than

the other. The researchers tried to see what the fast healing correlated with. They tried matching it with age, health, beliefs, optimism, faith—no correlation was found between any of these and the rate of healing. Then one day, through a fluke, the researchers got the idea of trying to match it with "sees or believes there is some meaning to everything that happens to him or her". Bingo! The correlation was virtually perfect. The more the patient believed that there was no such thing as a meaningless experience, the faster the patient healed. Thus, spiritual survival seems to require that there be some meaning to everything that happens, even if that meaning is not evident to us at the time that we are going through the experience.

Well, there you have the family of survival issues: the physical, the financial, the emotional, and the spiritual. Issues which are *Lifelong,* but which seem to come to a head when we enter the World of Retirement. If, in the Spirit of the best LIFE/work Planning, you've mastered the tools for solving these issues earlier in your life, Retirement will be much easier. But, if not, it's never too late to learn.

How To Deal, In The World of Retirement, with Meaning or Mission

Effectiveness
Meaning or Mission
Survival
What's Happening

In the literature on retirement, an oft-quoted statistic is that those who make no plans for their retirement years receive on an average just thirteen Social Security benefit checks, and that seven out of ten of them die within two years.[4] Patently, we are talking about men predominantly—accustomed or addicted to work all their life, deriving from that work some sense of importance, and then suddenly deprived by Retirement of both the work and the sense of self-worth. Their wives however have been in a different case, where the home was *their* work-place and the cradle of their self-worth. They do not enter the World of Retirement so dramatically as their husbands. Indeed, in some sense, they never retire. Their life cycle looks something like this:

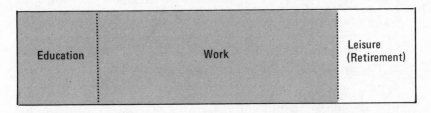

Education | Work in The Home and Community (Marriage)

Leisure

Children are born — Children all grown

in contrast with the traditional pattern we have been discussing:

| Education | Work | Leisure (Retirement) |

However, as many vocational experts have observed, the greatest change in the World of Work during the last decade or so, has been the dramatic influx of women into the marketplace—now thirty-nine million strong, or one out of every two women. It will be interesting to see if they too go through the same withdrawal symptoms (withdrawal from a sense of Meaning to their lives) when they enter the World of Retirement *en masse.*

In any event, from the statistics above (and others like them) it would appear that for those who have been working outside the home, finding some sense of Meaning and Mission for your life after Retirement is not really optional. If you want to keep on living, some sort of LIFE/work Planning is quite literally a matter of life or death.

The sense of self-worth, the finding of some Meaning for your life during your time spent in the World of Retirement, may occur in a number

> Forget how old you are and keep on planning — just as though you're going to keep on living. The one thing that keeps you going is to have an objective. You should have ambitions, and work to fulfill them. Then you can forget those actuarial tables and life expectancy statistics.
> — Rodney Jones, at the age of 101

of different ways. It may be that you will find such Meaning or Mission in leisure activities, or in educational activities. But most generally, it is found in some sort of Working—whether that working be voluntary or for pay, by oneself or in company with others, as an employee or as a boss.

Man Hates Inactivity

OWOSSO, Mich. (AP)—Fred Hayes is out of work and job hunting. He says he isn't "chomping at the bit" about working again but would rather not sit around "twiddling my thumbs." Mr. Hayes is 92 years old, and says: "I haven't got time to squander."

Not surprisingly, to any experienced LIFE/work Planner (and if you've plodded through this book thus far, you *are* now experienced), the *tools* for getting at identifying a sense of Meaning and Purpose for your life in Retirement, are the very same tools that we have already seen in "Lifelong Working". They will be found, for your review, on pages 262ff, and in Appendix E.

There are a number of special resources which exist to help senior citizens find volunteer and paid work, incidentally:

Mature Temps, currently located in Los Angeles, San Francisco, Washington, D.C., Chicago, Baltimore, Boston, New York City, Philadelphia, Plymouth Meeting, PA, Dallas and Houston.

Senior Community Service Employment Program. In virtually every county in the country, you can find it in your phone book, or through your local Department of Aging.

SCORE (Service Corps of Retired Executives), with more than 5,000 volunteers aiding small businesspeople through 200 chapters around the country. Contact: ACTION, Attn: SCORE, 806 Connecticut Avenue, NW, Washington, D.C. 20525.

The Foster Grandparent Program, with more than 4,000 volunteers working in forty-one states plus Puerto Rico. Contact ACTION (address above) for information.

RSVP (Retired Senior Volunteer Program), doing volunteer work in communities. Contact ACTION (address above) for information.

Resources in addition to the above often exist on a state, county or community level. Contact your local Commission on the Aging—by whatever name it is known—for additional listings. (The commissions themselves are listed in *The Older American's Handbook* by Craig and Peter Norback.[5])

Geriacracy

(A COUNTRY RULED BY THE ELDERLY)

25% of our current population is over the age of 60. By the year 2000, that figure will read 33%. Currently, 10% of our population is over the age of 65. In 1900, there were only 3 million such persons. In 1975, 22 million. By 2030, that figure will be 46 million—according to present predictions. The elderly will control one third of the vote in the country.

This growing influence of the elderly will certainly influence marketing trends in America, with more and more attention being paid to things which the elderly need. And with the elderly showing up more and more in commercials, as on TV. There is also likely to be more political organizing of the elderly, although of course—since the people over 55 years of age in this country comprise as many as three generations (if you're 55, your parents could be 75, your grandparents 95)—it will be difficult to find unity among them. But doubtless attempts will be made. We will see more self-consciousness on the part of the elderly, and more of such organizations as Maggie Kuhn's Grey Panthers. See: *Senior Power: Growing Old Rebelliously* by Paul Kleyman. 1975. Glide Publications, 330 Ellis Street, San Francisco, CA 94102. $3.95, paper. And: *Why Survive? Being Old in America* by Robert N. Butler, M.D. 1975. Harper & Row, 10 East 53rd St., New York, NY 10022. $5.95, paper. Ultimately, the maturity of "senior power" will be shown in elders fighting not merely for their own rights, but equally for the rights of others. As Maggie Kuhn has well said: "Older persons have freedom, freedom to think, reflect and act. We are free to be involved in large issues and controversies. We are free to fight against the forces that oppress other minorities deprived of freedom and selfhood. We have nothing to lose and nothing to fear by being so involved."

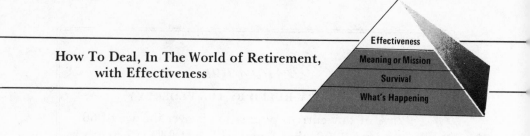

How To Deal, In The World of Retirement,
with Effectiveness

Effectiveness
Meaning or Mission
Survival
What's Happening

Effectiveness Exercise #1:
THE LIFE REVIEW

Effectiveness, as I have said *ad nauseam,* is the natural *instinct* of the individual to pause, look back, and ask, "How am I doin'?" This looking back is usually confined to the rather immediate past. But in Retirement, the looking back embraces all of one's life. It is the innate tendency of age to trot out memories from all different periods, childhood, teenage, when the children were born, when the children were growing up, etc.

Research by the National Institute of Aging in Washington has found that systematizing this reminiscing into some kind of 'life review' of one's entire past assists the elderly in gaining "a sense of the wholeness and meaning of their lives", in having a happier 'old age', and a more peaceful death.[6] From LIFE/work Planning's point of view, this is your self taking management of a process which nature will willy-nilly cause to happen anyway— for, how often have we been told that as we die, our whole life passes before our eyes?

There are three ways of doing the 'life review'. . . at any age:

1 *Write it.* This is essentially the autobiography, diary, or journal, that we described on page 277.

2 *Tell it.* You can speak your life-review into a tape recorder, in a kind of monologue. Or you can have someone interview you, again within the hearing of a tape recorder. The interviewer can be one of your grandchildren, or someone you know who is in college. (Some college classes have been assigned the task of interviewing elderly Americans, in order to get a better understanding of their own life cycles.) Your church, synagogue or temple may be able to put you in touch with a volunteer who would be glad to help you do your 'life review'.

3 *Draw it.* There are many ways to do this—at any age—but one of the most helpful is in terms of Decisions. The pictorial goes like this:

Below is a line, divided into time-segments, which you are asked to consider as representing your life:

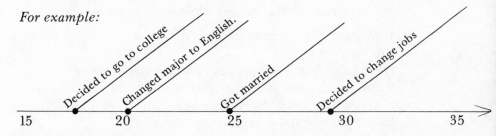

For each decision you made about something important in your life, put a dot.
From that dot, draw a slanted line upward. On that slanted line, write the decision that you made.

For example:

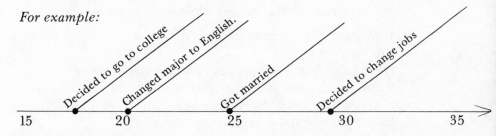

Now, to dramatize for yourself the force of that decision, from each dot draw a slanted dotted line downward, and write what might have happened IF you hadn't made that decision, but rather its opposite.

For example:

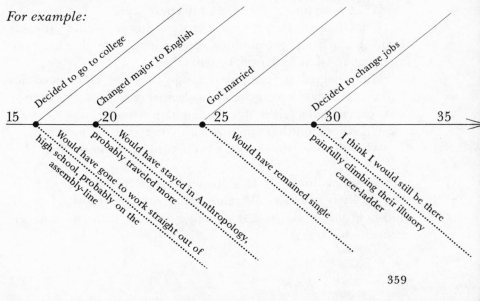

Every dot on that line of life————————————————————→

represents your freedom. For, as I said earlier, no one is free unless s/he has at least two things to choose between. This diagram is a reminder of how free you have been in your life; which is to say, how often you had at least two things to choose between. Thus, it is a picture of the (possible) Change in your life.

It is also however a picture of the Constant thread to your life—the common denominators, the constant values that ran through all of your decisions. Some of these common denominators may strike you instantly. Others may only become clear to you after some examination of the pictorial, and meditation upon it.

Here are some questions that may help your meditation:

What moments on the Life Line stand out in sharpest detail, to your memory?

What faces from your past can you see most clearly?

Whose voices can you hear most vividly? (from among your family, classmates, playmates, colleagues, lovers, idols, rivals)

Which of these did you trust the most?

Which of these did you want to be most like?

What were the events which moved you the most deeply?

What were the experiences which molded or affected you the most?

What were the scenes of your greatest sadnesses?

What were the scenes of your deepest joys?

What helped to preserve Constancy in your life? (people [who?], lack of geographical movement, few deaths, your memory, religion, isolation, or what?)

What helped to preserve Change in your life? (need for adventure, risk-taking, geographical movement, societal change, divorce, changing faiths, deaths, aging, or what?)

What decision that you made do you regret the most?

What decision that you made do you feel happiest about?

So much for your Life Review. Write it, tell it or draw it. But do it. It can turn idle reminiscing into constructive Review, and help you better to get a handle on how Effective you feel your life has been.

Moreover, if you do not wait for your last years before you do this sort of Life Review, but do it at younger ages, the Review can help you to see what new directions you may want your life to go in. Thus employed, the Review may begin with your past; but ultimately it will help to shape your future.

[ ] My eyes have been bequeathed to

(Or to the nearest Eye-Bank)   PLEASE NOTIFY PROMPTLY

[ ] My body has been bequeathed to

(Or to the nearest medical school)   PLEASE NOTIFY PROMPTLY

[ ] If for any reason my body is not accepted by the medical school it is
to be cremated as soon as possible and with the utmost simplicity. Services
will be held after. Written authorization will be sent promptly by the next of kin.

Signed _____ Date _____

Endorsed _____ Date _____
              (NEXT OF KIN)

If you want your body to benefit a living stranger after you are done
with it (i.e., after you have departed this world) you can will your eyes
or kidneys — to give sight or life to someone. Get a Uniform Donor's
Card and instructions from The National Kidney Foundation,
116 East 27th Street, New York, N.Y. 10016. If you want to will all
of your body to science or to a medical school, the national clearing-
house is: The Living Bank, P.O. Box 6725, Houston, Texas 77005,
telephone 715-528-2971. Write to them to secure a form (to be
returned to them) and a Uniform Donor Card (to be kept in your
wallet or purse).

All of the foregoing has dealt with *what* decisions we have made. But, as we get older, one of the Effectiveness issues which often arises more and more insistently is *how* we make decisions. This is a very important issue. Most books and courses on decision-making act as though each of us makes our decisions totally by ourselves, totally alone, and totally outside the context of relationships. In real life, that is not so. We tend to be in relationship with others, or at least One Significant Other—as Sociology majors say—who get involved in our decision-making, even as we get involved in theirs. In reviewing our effectiveness, particularly as we get older, we may muse more and more upon this issue of *Decisions For Two*. So, let us turn now to:

Effectiveness Exercise #2:
SHARING THE DECISION-MAKING

Not terribly long ago, the expectation in most families was that the major decisions affecting the family's life would probably be made by the husband/father, or—more accurately—by his job. Not only was the patriarchal model dominant in our culture, but most wives/mothers did not work outside the home at that time, and hence their wishes were regarded as less of a priority. Out of this period came the familiar decision-making pattern of The Trade-Off. The husband/father, for example, would come home and say, "Well, we've got to move to Pittsburgh; the firm just transferred me." Feeling guilty, then, over having made such a major decision unilaterally, without the wife/mother having any say in it, the husband/father would consequently yield to her for whatever the next decision might be. Something like: "Well dear, *you* decide what movie we should go to next Friday." When, over the years, it finally came time for the husband/father to retire, *if* the couple had the freedom to choose their place of retirement, and *if* they could not agree on which area of the country to move to, one partner would frequently defer to the other: "Well, Alice, over the years you've not had much say about where we lived, so now it's your turn at last." Thus, the Trade-Off pattern of decision-making (first it's your turn, then it's mine) persisted even into Retirement.

With the arrival, in the last decade, of the Women's Liberation movement in this country—a long overdue arrival, we might add—more and more this Trade-Off pattern of decision-making has been called into question. The wife/mother and husband/father are urged, rather, to make joint decisions in which both are involved and in which both have a voice, from the beginning of their relationship.

Moreover, such joint decision-making has become necessary at an earlier and earlier age in the family's life together, with the tremendous influx of women into the marketplace. Now both husband and wife are workers, and both of their jobs at times may seem to dictate where they should live. They may be living, let us say, in Denver, where the husband has a very fine job, but the wife only a so-so one. Then the wife is offered a *fabulous* job in Dallas. Should they uproot themselves from Denver, and go job hunting anew in Dallas, in order that the wife may accept the fabulous offer? Ah, that is the question.

There are, unhappily, no easy answers. Much may depend, for example, on whether or not the husband has mastered the Alternative Method of the Job-Hunt. If he has, then he may feel very confident about his ability to turn up something good in a strange new city. Much depends also upon the dynamics of the relationship—whether the husband and wife see themselves genuinely as a partnership, or whether they are highly competitive with one another. But, even assuming good will between the two, and even assuming they are both strongly committed to the joint decision-making model, one of the major problems they still face is *the lack of decent tools for getting at joint decision-making.* The only tool most couples know, when faced with a conflict in joint decision-making, is that of Compromise. And this is being, more and more, found wanting.

In Retirement then, or earlier—often much, much earlier—couples are testing their effectiveness by the degree to which they have sought and found better tools for *joint* decision-making. So, let us see what some of these better tools are. By way of illustration, let us consider a typical couple trying to decide where it is, in this country, that they want to retire to. We shall call them Ted and Alice. Ted wants to retire to Aspen, Colorado. Alice wants to retire to Santa Monica, California. Typically, if they are committed to joint decision-making, they will try to resolve their conflict by means of Compromise. They will probably settle on Phoenix, Arizona as their retirement place—*because it is halfway in between Aspen and Santa Monica.* Thus, neither Ted nor Alice will get what they really want, and they'll be suffering equally. Compromise indeed!

The Fastest Growing Retirement Counties in the United States

The 206 counties with 15% or more net in-migration of persons 60 years and older between 1960 and 1970. *Source: Bureau of the Census.*

The better tools for arriving at a joint decision, we have already seen. They were outlined at the bottom of page 276. I will list them here in only slightly different order:

Factoring, Remembering, Prioritizing, Focusing, Researching, Naming, Finding-Linking Up, and: Always a Plan B.

Now, let us see how these tools can be helpful in resolving Ted and Alice's dilemma. *Factoring* suggests, first of all, that they need to get beneath the Label of "Aspen" and "Santa Monica", by breaking that Label down into its component parts. In the case of a geographical location, this means they must ask themselves "What is it that I like about That Place?" When they do this, the list may come out looking like this:

	Ted's List	Alice's List
	(What I Like about Aspen)	*(What I Like about Santa Monica)*
	skiing	nearness to the ocean
	cold weather	warm year-round weather
	snow	variety of culture nearby
	small community	good public transportation
	lots of culture: music, etc.	access to metropolitan area
	trees, evergreen, etc.	immediately accessible medical
	clean air	care
		good newspaper

A good beginning. Now, the next tool—*Remembering*—suggests that this list of factors ought not to be restricted simply to Aspen and Santa Monica, but that it ought to be expanded, to include *all* the places that each of them has ever lived. Or, to be more exact, the list should be expanded to include the *factors* they each liked about those places. It might come out looking, then, like this:

	Ted's List	Alice's List
	(What I like about any place I Have Ever Lived)	*(What I like about any place I Have Ever Lived)*
	skiing	nearness to the ocean
	cold weather	warm year-round weather
	snow	variety of culture nearby
	small community	good public transportation
	lots of culture: music, etc.	access to metropolitan area
	trees, evergreen, etc.	immediately accessible medical
	clean air	care
	place for gardening	good newspaper
	good adult education program	aesthetically pleasant physical
	active churches	environment
	community services for all	TV with lots of stations to
	variety of cultures in the	choose from
	community	public parks
	friendly people—easy to make	good restaurants
	contacts	space to keep pets
	good discount stores	sense of identity to the
	a place with a history	community
		good museum
		moderately-paced life
		casual dress styles

(If Ted and Alice had any difficulty in thinking about such factors, they could refer to the suggestive list in Appendix E, page 190, of WDIGFHWML?) When this list is as complete as they want it to be, the next tool—*Prioritizing*—tells them what they need to do with this information. Using the prioritizing

tool found in Appendix A of this book, they need to ask themselves "Which of these factors is most important to me? Which
is next most important? Etc." Or, to put it more exactly in the
language of Appendix A: "If I could only have one of these
factors, which would be most important to me to have?" When
such prioritizing is finished, Ted and Alice's list may come out
looking something like this:

Ted's List *(My preferred geographical factors, in their order of priority for me)*	Alice's List *(My preferred geographical factors, in their order of priority for me)*
1. trees, evergreens, etc.	A. warm year-round weather
2. friendly people—easy to make contacts	B. aesthetically pleasant physical environment
3. clean air	C. public parks
4. good adult education program	D. casual dress styles E. good newspaper
5. skiing	F. nearness to the ocean
6. small community	G. variety of culture nearby
7. good discount stores	H. good public transportation
8. active churches	I. immediately accessible
9. snow	medical care
10. place for gardening, etc.	J. good restaurants, etc.

Once their lists are thus prioritized, they know what is important
to them and what is not, what they are willing to do without
and what they are not willing to do without. Consequently, an
intelligent conversation can take place between them concerning
What Is Possible.

At this point, the next tool—*Focusing*—suggests what to do
with this prioritized listing. They need to focus this whole
dilemma by bringing their lists together, *in the order of priority,*
and building a new united list. The way to do this is simply to
take the first item off one list, then the first item off the other
list, and so forth. In the above case, it would come out looking
like this:

Ted's and Alice's List
Of Preferred Geographical Factors
(We Want To Live In A Place That Has:)

A. warm year-round weather
1. trees, evergreens, etc.
B. aesthetically pleasant physical environment
2. friendly people — easy to make contacts
C. public parks
3. clean air
D. casual dress styles
4. good adult education programs
E. good newspaper
5. skiing
F. nearness to the ocean
6. small community
   etc.

The virtue of this new list is that, unlike Compromise, each partner's priorities are getting honored. Now to the next tool: *Researching.* Ted and Alice's problem at this point is a simple one: "What community or communities would give us all of, or most of, these factors?—beginning with the ones at the top of our joint list." This is clearly a problem of Research—using friends, the library, and so forth, to discover the answer to that question. I might mention also that there are computer services which— for a fee— will make a stab at doing this for you.[7] Your goal, in all this research, is to come up with some Names of communities—even as the next tool, *Naming,* suggests. In Ted and Alice's case, this means the Name of communities which would give them, first of all, warm year-round weather, secondly trees, evergreens, etc. The two most limiting or conflicting factors on their joint list—namely, skiing and nearness to the ocean—suggests some place or places in California, halfway between the ocean and the mountains where there is skiing. Not all that difficult to find. Certainly not as difficult as one might at first think. The researching will uncover all that.

The result of this entire process will be Ted and Alice's discovery of a place which honors each partner's genuine priorities. In other words, authentic joint decision-making will have taken place—*not only because they had the will to make such decisions, but also because they had the proper tools.*

The final two such tools that were on our list, are *Linking Up,* and *Always A Plan B.* These are pretty self-explanatory, at this point. "Linking Up" means, once your target community has been identified, subscribing long distance to its newspaper, writing to its Chamber of Commerce indicating your intention to move there and asking for as much information about the community as they have, and—in general—using your contacts. "Always A Plan B" means having a second community that you are researching, naming, and linking up with, in case something goes wrong with your first choice. You Know What I Mean.

I trust that it is clear by now that this whole Ted and Alice episode was designed to illustrate how we may enter upon joint decision-making at any time in our life, with *any* issue. Factoring, Remembering, Prioritizing, Focusing, Researching, Naming, Finding-Linking Up, and: Always A Plan B, are the keys. The better we get at such joint decision-making, the more effective we will feel ourselves to be—in relationships.

But suppose—just suppose—that you are not in an active living-together-with-someone relationship. You will then, inevitably, raise some very different questions under the general canon of Effectiveness. They may run somewhat along the lines of: "How effectively am I, who had always lived with someone, coping now with my aloneness?" While that may seem like a question which arises primarily in Retirement, and primarily for women—who traditionally outlive men, in our culture—in actuality this question is getting raised by both sexes, at younger and younger ages. So, let us look at:

Effectiveness Exercise #3
LEARNING TO REACH OUT

We have been speaking, throughout this book, about the three main worlds we all live in: the World of Education, the World of Work, and the World of Retirement. And how, each time we move our way up the Pyramid of Issues—What's Happening, Survival, Meaning & Mission, and Effectiveness—all over again.

There are, however, worlds within these worlds. And Aloneness is one of them. If you have been accustomed to living your life with another, thinking of yourself as a couple, sharing decision-making —and then suddenly by accident or design, by your own hand or another's, you are precipitated into the

unfamiliar (by now) state of Singledom again—it is indeed a new world. And you have to work your way up the Pyramid of Issues (wearily or wholeheartedly) once more: "What's Happening— in Singledom." "How to Survive—in Singledom." "How to Find Meaning & Mission — in Singledom." And "How to Be Effective — in Singledom."

Since we are here talking about Effectiveness, it is the last issue (mentioned above) that we want to deal with. For openers, there is—as virtually every philosopher in the world has observed—a vast difference between *loneliness* (the longing to be with someone) and *aloneness* (the state of Singledom, or Solitariness—with which one may be content or even delighted). Loneliness is *the pits*. Aloneness is—well, whatever you make of it. Down through the ages there have been people, not necessarily weird, who have greatly prized aloneness—creative thinkers, artists, craftspeople, writers, meditators, mystics, nuns, monks and other contemplatives. To which list, we must add: housewives surrounded by screaming children all day. And executives—male or female—tired of being endlessly surrounded by the maddening crowd. And—perhaps—yourself. From a LIFE/work Planning point of view, for all of the above citizens Aloneness is not to be fled from, but sought, *because it is part of their ideal working/living/playing environment, when they do their best and are at their most effective level.*

Thus, if in Retirement or much earlier, by death, divorce, or separation, you who were accustomed to thinking of yourself as "a couple" suddenly find yourself as "a single", this is not necessarily fatal. The Aloneness that faces you may usher you into the most creative, and fulfilling period in your life. Everything depends upon your setting some (preferably written) goals down for yourself, as to what you hope the Aloneness will make it possible for you to do:

☐ create something you've long wanted to have the time
   and space to create;
☐ go visit people, or entertain people, you never had
   time for when you were a couple;
☐ do some reading you've never been able to get
   around to before;
☐ take some courses you haven't had time to take until now;
☐ indulge in museum visiting or other leisure activities
   you've never had time for;
☐ do some meditating, self-examination;
☐ catch up on your sleep, exercise, listening to music;
☐ all of the above;
☐ some of the above, plus other things.

With such a check-list, set forth beforehand, you will then be able to measure how well you have used your Aloneness to advantage.

By way of contrast, there is Loneliness. This is the judgment or feeling that Aloneness is *not* your ideal working/living/playing environment, by a long shot. But that, au contraire, being alone keeps you from doing your best or being your most effective Self. Some distinction needs to be made, at this point, between

370

mild Loneliness and *paralyzing* Loneliness. It is possible to keep on working/living/playing despite mild Loneliness, which comes in the shape of a vague discomfort or restlessness. Self-discipline, invoked to help you get past such restlessness and keep on doing what you want or have to do, may strengthen you in all kinds of positive ways. It is the old truth which the early Christians told, of how suffering can lead to resurrection. But this is not likely to be the case with paralyzing Loneliness—that Loneliness which can neither eat nor sleep nor laugh nor take enjoyment at the sound of music or the sight of sunset anymore, but is totally preoccupied with the unbearableness of this Being Alone. Such paralyzing Loneliness usually will not submit to being sublimated, transformed or transfigured. It demands that it first be fed, comforted and assuaged. In which case, you had better get out and Be With People—take courses, do volunteer activities, go down to the Church, Synagogue or Mosque, and seek out friendly faces, conversation, and touching, over a cup of coffee. Your spirit has decreed for you that only when you are With Others Again will you be able to work/live/play,—so, do it.

But what if you are Alone *and housebound*—by grief, infirmity or illness—and Loneliness sweeps over you? Then summon the world to you. Call the minister, priest, rabbi or shaman. Write at least one letter a day to someone, a different someone each day—and see if this Reaching Out does not begin to put you in touch again with those who care about you.

You know best whether Aloneness is the world in which you do your best, or Company is. Whatever it takes for you to be and do your best, the one fatal disease is to take no initiative on your part—but to wait for God, family, friends and strangers to prove they love you by coming to seek you. Forget it! If you are Alone, even more if you are Lonely, write this on your mirror, and in your living room, and over your kitchen stove: Reach out, Reach out, Reach out. As we have insisted throughout this explanation of LIFE/work Planning: the Management of Your Life is In Your Hands. What it is, or is not, what it becomes or does not become, is up to You. And no one else. Waiting for Someone Else to come and rescue you can turn out to be a vigil unto death. Hopefully, you have chosen Life.

RESOLUTIONS AS I GROW OLDER
So that people won't run, when they see me coming:

1. I promise myself that I will not contact the same person or the same few persons every day, but will reach out to as many different people as I can—so that no one ever says, "Oh, it's *him*, again—or *her,* again." This applies to the telephone as well as to personal visiting. And writing.

2. I promise myself that if I know my memory isn't what it used to be, I will keep a carbon copy of the letters I write, and a series of notes about the things I talk with each person about, on the phone, so that next time I'll know what I've already told them—remembering the aphorism that when we grow older, it's not that we forget our stories; we just forget who we've told them to.

3. I promise myself that in every conversation, on the phone or in person, I will *make sure* that at least half the time I let the other person talk; and that when I do talk about me, it will be about the positive things in my life, not the negative: my joys, rather than my aches and pains.

4. I promise myself that each time others have finished telling me something, I will take time to respond—I mean *really* respond—to their story and their feelings, before I rush on to talk about me. I will avoid at all costs giving the impression that I am just tapping my toes, waiting until it's my turn again.

5. I promise myself that I will live in the present, not the past; that I will not go on and on about how great life used to be, but will be myself a living example of how great life is—now. Toward this end, I will continually read, watch and learn—so that I always have new opinions about new subjects—that in the end, young and old alike will enjoy being with me, as much as I enjoy being with them.

—R.N.B.

P.S. The name of someone will probably pop into our minds, as we read this list; and we'll determine that we must copy it and send it off to them *immediately* (and anonymously? tsk, tsk!). If so, let us do ourselves the favor first of reading the list aloud to ourselves. Preferably in front of a mirror.

Effectiveness Exercise #4
BALANCING OR BLENDING
LEARNING, WORKING, & PLAYING

Well, sure, it is the same issue that surfaced at the end of the chapter on Education, and at the end of the chapter on Working —for it is, after all, THE ISSUE of this book: in your retirement, as before, have you built a balance of learning, working and playing? Or, better yet, have you learned to blend all three in each time frame—so that in each activity you feel like you are working, but your working is like playing, and your playing is filled with learnings? If you feel as though you have moved even partway toward that ideal, then you have indeed broken out of the Three Boxes of Life.

This is effectiveness indeed! The cultural expectation that your life should consist of first an orgy of learning, then an orgy of work or homemaking, and finally an orgy of leisure or playing, is very, very strong. To be able to resist that expectation, and substitute instead lifelong learning, lifelong working, and lifelong leisure or playing—that is effectiveness at its greatest. Effective retirement? you ask. Well, words are so easily made obsolete. In the face of lifelong everything, what is left to be called "retirement?" We may have to outlaw the word, someday, and call age 60, 65, or 70—and beyond—simply "The Third Stage (or Third Age) of Life."

And having thus abolished "Retirement" altogether, we may return to our original intent—which is to consider that altogether charming subject of

Lifelong Leisure
or Playing

We are never going to be able to discuss Leisure, unless we begin by defining our terms. Hokay? There is, first of all:

• *Non-working time:* this is whatever time you have, that is not spent in preparing for your work, getting to your work, doing your work, getting home from your work, and doing work at home. (Sometimes this "non-working time" is called "leisure," erroneously.) Then there is:

• *Personal care time:* this gets subtracted from "non-working time." It includes washing, getting dressed, doing exercises (sometimes), getting meals, eating, and so forth.

• *Sleep:* this gets subtracted from "non-working time." It refers to day sleep (naps) as well as night sleep. It is really a personal care item, but it gets classified separately in most discussions.

• *House and family care:* this gets subtracted from "non-working time." It includes shopping, running errands, cleaning, doing repairs, child care, housework, and so forth.

• *Leisure, free-time, unscheduled time:* three different ways of describing the time that is left over, after "personal care time," "sleep," and "house and family care" are all subtracted from "non-working time."

Now, with these terms clear, we can proceed to the main point of this chapter, which is: that leisure ought not to be 'saved up' for your retirement years, but ought to be consciously programmed into your whole life—in your youth, in your young adult years, in your middle years, and in "the third age"—which is normally called 'retirement'.

According to various studies, at any age the average person has *at least* thirty hours of leisure at his or her disposal, each week.[8] But if you talk to the man or woman on the street, you will find this figure greeted with mild derision: "Who were they interviewing, four year old kids?" And comments like that. We live in a culture which is Busy, Busy, Busy (as Billy DeWolfe used to say). A vast number of us, therefore, are absolutely convinced that we have virtually no leisure time at all—nor any prospect of such. And will say so, loudly. And, somewhat proudly. For, the Puritan roots of our history are still very much with us. Thus, by the Puritan view, To Work is virtuous, while To Be 'At Leisure' is. . . . . . . not. Therefore, those of us who can-claim that we don't have one single moment 'for ourselves' are slightly superior morally to those who do have time for leisure—or so the Puritans claim. Hence, at once the sadness and the fierceness with which some of us proclaim how Busy we are. To any and all who will listen. Busy, Busy, Busy. Living the virtuous life: a life in which, after completing our work, our errands, our household chores, our family business, and our personal care, there is no time left for anything but to cast our tired bodies on the bed, and so to sleep, perchance to dream, of how much we are put-upon in our lives, and yet how virtuous. All in all, a delicious victim-hood.

Clearly, this book's argument that a balanced life consists of lifelong learning, lifelong working, and lifelong leisure, is robbed of any meaning if indeed there are as many people in America too busy to find any time for leisure, as say they are.

But there is much reason to doubt this. There is that ancient principle, now spoken of as 'a law', which maintains that activities tend to expand so as to fill the time that is allotted to them. That is to say, if you give me a task to do, and then tell me that I have three hours to do it, I will tend to take three hours before that task is completed. Or, if I tell myself that I have three hours free this evening, except that I have to go do some errands first, those errands are very likely to take the full three hours that I supposedly had free.

But conversely, if I have three hours free this evening, except that I have to go do some errands,—*but I schedule my first two hours for some 'time for myself'—i.e., some leisure,* I will often be able to accomplish those very same errands in that third hour alone. Of course, I may move faster while I'm running the errands. And of course I will cut corners—like, not stopping to chat with those neighbors I meet for as long a time as I otherwise might have, or not doing as much price-comparing as I might have—but I will still get the basic tasks done, and the errands accomplished, within the time that I allotted—one hour, rather than three.

This leads to our first important principle regarding Leisure:

1 IF YOU FEEL YOU LEAD A VERY BUSY
LIFE, YOU ARE GOING TO HAVE TO
BLOCK OUT ON YOUR CALENDAR, AHEAD
OF TIME, SOME BLOCS OF TIME THAT ARE
RESERVED STRICTLY FOR YOUR LEISURE.[9]

The errands, the household chores, the personal care, are all going to have to get done within the time remaining. And, basically, they will.

Now, if the Puritan within you is still arguing—at this point— that thirty hours, or however many you may want to block out on your calendar, is just too much time to reserve 'for such a Selfish Activity' as Leisure, there is a fantasy which may help you deal with that Puritan Within You. Pretend that you have been told that you are dying. The doctor has just revealed to you that you have some disease which will be terminal, in two years. What would that news do to your sense of priorities about life? Would you not be aghast at the idea of leaving this life, so unsavored and so untasted? Would not the words ascribed to one Brother Jeremiah (page 377) strike you with particular poignancy? And would you not vow to reorder your life, immediately, so as to have more time to pick the daisies? Thirty hours, or whatever, reserved each week for your leisure, would seem precious little time to a dying woman or man. "Ah, well and good," you may say, "*if* I were dying, that would be true." But, the Fantasy replies, are you not dying indeed? Every day, your body grows older. Every day, more cells decay. The fact of your dying is certain. The only thing you do not know is When.

So, no matter how young or old you may be, it is as a dying man or woman indeed that you block out time on your calendar for Leisure. In order that you may truly live.

WHAT HAPPENED TO THE PYRAMID?

Having reserved time for your Leisure, the issue now—of course—is what to do with that time. In each of our previous chapters we laboriously worked our way up the so-called Pyramid of Issues. . . as you hardly need to be told, weary reader. You might legitimately expect, therefore, since we are now

I'd Pick More Daisies

If I had my life to live over again, I'd try to make more mistakes next time. I would relax. I would limber up. I would be sillier than I have been this trip. I know of a very few things I would take seriously. I would take more trips. I would climb more mountains, swim more rivers and watch more sunsets. I would do more walking and looking. I would eat more ice cream and less beans. I would have more actual troubles and fewer imaginary ones. You see, I am one of those people who lives prophylactically and sensibly and sanely hour after hour, day after day. Oh, I've had my moments; and if I had it to do over again, I'd have more of them. In fact, I'd try to have nothing else. Just moments, one after another instead of living so many years ahead each day. I have been one of those people who never go anywhere without a thermometer, a hot water bottle, a gargle, a raincoat, aspirin, and a parachute. If I had it to do over again, I would go places, do things and travel lighter than I have.

If I had my life to live over, I would start barefooted earlier in the spring and stay that way later in the fall. I would play hookey more, I wouldn't make much good grades except by accident. I would ride on more merry-go-rounds. I'd pick more daisies.

Nadine Stair, age 85

tackling the subject of Lifelong Leisure, that it is time to work our way up that Pyramid, once more. What's Happening in the World of Leisure. How to Survive in the World of Leisure. How to Find A Sense of Mission or Meaning in the World of Leisure. And: How To Be Effective in the World of Leisure. (Sigh) But— oh happy surprise—we are here abandoning the Pyramid. For a very good reason, incidentally, and not merely out of a desire to spare you from another climb.

The Pyramid of Issues is, after all, a summary of goal-directed activity. Of purposefulness. Even drivenness. (There's no such word? There is now.) And clearly there are people who tackle their Leisure time in precisely this fashion, just as they tackle their Education and their Work. It's all of one piece. Driven. We bury such people. Or at least nurse them through their heart attacks.

In a landmark book *(Type A Behavior And Your Heart,* 1974, Alfred A. Knopf, publisher) Meyer Friedman, M.D. and Ray H. Rosenman, M.D. made a tremendously persuasive case for their thesis that those who allow themselves to lead a 'driven' life, with a compelling sense of time urgency or 'hurry sickness' (as they call it) about everything, are laying up for themselves not treasures in heaven, but heart attacks on earth. If one would avoid such a fate, these good men argue, then we must aim for a change in our entire life-style—pervading the way in which we do *everything:* our learning and our work and our leisure. We must do everything more leisurely. Thus, leisure becomes an Adjective characterizing all of our life, rather than a Noun describing only some of it.

It is perhaps too much to hope that all of us will, as of tomorrow, drop the purposefulness and sense of urgency with which we go about our work and even our education. But it is surely not too much to hope that we will at least introduce An Alternating Rhythm into our lives, in that place which we call "our Leisure." *Here,* at least, we may drop our 'driven-ness' and our compelling sense of urgency. So that, if there is the *Yin* of the style with which we do our work and our education, there will be a very different *Yang* in the style with which we approach our leisure.

Thus understood, the second important principle of Leisure is:

2 THE MOST IMPORTANT THING ABOUT YOUR LEISURE TIME IS NOT WHAT YOU DO WITH IT, BUT THE SPIRIT WITH WHICH YOU APPROACH IT. BY MAKING YOUR LEISURE THE PLACE WHERE YOU PRESERVE A SPIRIT OF LEISURELINESS IN YOUR LIFE, YOU WILL NOT ONLY ENJOY LIFE MORE — YOU WILL ACTUALLY PROLONG IT.

The spirit with which you do the thing is what makes it Leisure; not the activity itself.

Now, we must admit that this is not as widely understood— in our culture—as we might wish. Again and again, you will hear people refer to certain activities as "Leisure Activities." Tennis, for example. Tennis is held to be a Leisure Activity—as though it were this, at the very center of its being. But, clearly this is not so. One person may indeed go out on a tennis court, play with great energy, and yet—withal—play Playfully, even Leisurely. In his, or her, case you will cheerfully acknowledge that Tennis is a Leisure Activity. But look at his or her companion. He plays as though *driven* by demoniacal obsession, needing to win in the worst way and at any cost, hence playing aggressively, combatively, even angrily. Watching him, it becomes very hard to maintain that in his case Tennis is still a Leisure Activity. To repeat: the spirit with which you do the thing is what makes it Leisure; not the activity itself.

This point is what brings us up short, when we try to pass beyond *the Spirit* of leisure to the question of how to spend our leisure. The answer: "Leisurely" does not quite satisfy. For, the question is: *What* can I do, leisurely? Clearly, a lot of people want some help with this. The Department of Commerce reports that only 58 out of every 100 people claim "a great deal" of satisfaction with how they spend their leisure time. Which means, of course, that 42 out of every 100 people want some help in this area. Maybe more. ("A great deal" of satisfaction may still be far from "complete" satisfaction.)

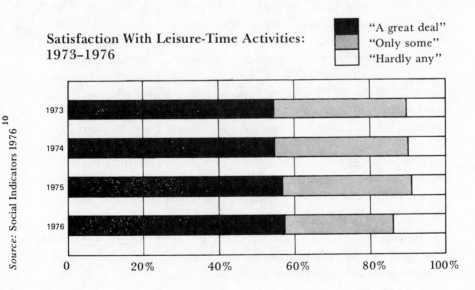

Satisfaction With Leisure-Time Activities: 1973–1976

"A great deal"
"Only some"
"Hardly any"

Source: Social Indicators 1976 [10]

379

The first answer one might give to those seeking some guidance as to what to do with their leisure time is: *Anything you want to do* (as long as it is not illegal, immoral or fattening). Anything? Anything. If (as we saw above) no activities are, by their very nature, Leisure Activities, it equally follows that no activities are, by their very nature, *not* potential Leisure Activities. If done in the right spirit: i.e., Leisurely.

Thus, every activity which we looked at in the chapter on Lifelong Working might with justice be repeated here, under Lifelong Leisure. The fact that some people make a living at it, does not rule it out as a potential leisure time activity—for someone else, and in a different setting. After all, some people make their living off tennis, too, and almost every other *so-called* Leisure Activity that you could name.

And so, we have come to our third important principle concerning Leisure:

3 **YOUR LEISURE IS WHAT YOU DO WHEN NO ONE IS TELLING YOU WHAT TO DO. EVERY ACTIVITY OF MAN AND WOMAN, THEN, CAN BE A LEISURE TIME ACTIVITY FOR YOU, SO LONG AS YOU CHOOSE IT FREELY, AND SO LONG AS YOU TRULY ENJOY DOING IT.**

Aye, there's the rub: "so long as you truly enjoy doing it." Out of the vast multitude of human activities, how do you go about determining just exactly what things you most enjoy doing, in your leisure? The choice would seem to be quite vast. Well, of course it is—if you look at activities. But beneath activities, there are skills. So, if you are in a quandary about what to do in your leisure, begin by considering what skills you most enjoy using. This will take you back *(l e i s u r e l y)* to page 127, there to find what skills-*family* you most preferred. Let us suppose it might have been "S". The skills described (briefly) there are: informing, enlightening, helping, training, developing, curing people, or working with words. There are three steps to take then with that list:

A. Which of those skills (or skills similar to them) are *your favorites?* (In our illustration above, it might turn out that your favorite is "working with words.")

B. In your work (at home, or in the marketplace) do you feel you get enough chance to use that favorite skill—or those favorite skills? If the answer is "No, I don't feel I get enough chance to use that skill," then you will want to look at Leisure-time Activities which will give you more chance to use it. Thus, you will be choosing it freely, and you will truly enjoy doing it. You have only to decide what kind of activity will let you use that skill. (In our illustration above, it might turn out to be: reading, filling out crossword puzzles, playing Scrabble, writing letters, writing poetry, stories, or a book, or talking with friends —or strangers; all of these activities involve the use of words— some playfully, some seriously.)

C. If, on the other hand, your answer is "Yes, I do feel I get enough chance to use my favorite skills at my work," then in your Leisure you may want to explore the principle of *Alternating Rhythms*. Instead of taking "a busperson's holiday" (i.e., doing in your leisure exactly what you do at your work), you may want to explore (leisurely) *the very opposite skills* from those you use at work. You find these by looking directly across the hexagon on page 127. (For example, if "S" were your preferred family of skills, as in our illustration above, and you felt you got adequate opportunity to use your "S" skills at your work, you would then look directly across the hexagon from "S", drawing as it were an imaginary line from "S" through the center point of the hexagon, which would bring you to "R"— and such skills as athletic ones, or mechanical ability, or working with plants, or animals, or objects, or machines, or tools. If among these, your favorite was—let us say—"working with tools," then you might decide to take up crafts or carpentry in your Leisure time. For one who works primarily with people all week long, this would be An Alternating Rhythm, indeed, in your life.)

The hexagon, as you may or may not have already divined, is a series of relationships as discovered by John L. Holland in his research. For example, if your preferred corner is "S" this usually means that you have had the most time and encourage-

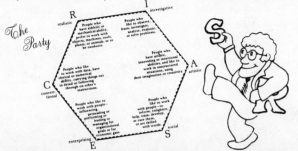

ment to develop "S" skills. Working our way around both sides of the hexagon simultaneously, it reads as follows: if you have had the time and encouragement to develop "S" skills, you are next most likely to have been given encouragement and the time to develop "E" and "A" skills, less likely to have been given the encouragement and the time to develop "C" and "I" skills, and least likely to have been given the encouragement and the time to develop "R" skills.[11] For the sake of shorthand, let us call your preferred corner "Your Oldest Skills," and let us call the opposite corner of the hexagon "Your Newest Skills." We can then formulate the fourth important principle concerning Leisure:

4 **IN DECIDING WHAT TO DO WITH YOUR LEISURE, "THE PRINCIPLE OF ALTERNATING RHYTHM" SUGGESTS THAT YOUR LEISURE COMPLEMENT YOUR WORK. . . IN WHICH CASE, LOOK AT YOUR OLDEST AND MOST ENJOYED SKILLS. IF YOUR WORK DOES NOT SATISFACTORILY EMPLOY THEM, CHOOSE LEISURE ACTIVITIES WHICH WILL. IF YOUR WORK DOES SATISFACTORILY EMPLOY THEM, THEN YOU MAY USE YOUR LEISURE TO EXPLORE YOUR NEWEST AND POTENTIALLY MOST ENJOYABLE SKILLS.**

Well, that should settle the matter of what you can do when no one is telling you what to do, which you may truly enjoy doing, and which you may choose freely, as your Leisure.

But what are we to say to the whimsical and free spirit—that broods within us all, though in some more than others—which doesn't want to be pinned down to just one kind of leisure activity, but wants to be as free as a bird to plunge into the Sea of Leisure, like a seagull, wherever and whensoever we choose—varying our Leisure Activities from Day to Day, and even from Hour to Hour. For such a soul and for such a spirit, clearly we need a sort of Leisure Map, just as—earlier, we had a Map of the World of Education (pages 68-69) and a Map of the World of Work (page 220, and Appendix C). Then, each time our Leisure rolled around (as we had blocked it out on our calendars) we could look at the Map, and choose something New to do. Well, of course, it would be very difficult to construct such a Map; but—nothing daunted—we will try.

Constructing A Map of Leisure Possibilities

To construct such a map, we first need a horizontal dimension and also a vertical dimension—not unlike *longitude* and *latitude* on a geographical map. That much is clear. What is not so clear, is what we should put on the horizontal and on the vertical measure. The following possibilities come immediately to mind:

a. We could classify all Leisure activities in terms of their pleasure level; thus:

Those Activities Which Give
The Least Pleasure

Those Activities Which Give
The Most Pleasure

The problem with this is that such a measure is highly subjective, e.g., one person may list "sex" as that which gives her or him the most pleasure, while another person may list "spiritual completeness" as that which gives her or him the most pleasure. Next.

b. We could classify all Leisure activities in terms of their emotional release; thus:

Those Activities Which Give
The Least Emotional Release

Those Activities Which Give
The Greatest Emotional Release

The problem, again, is the high subjectivity of such a classification. One person may find the greatest emotional release in some highly competitive sport, like football. Another person may find great release just by watching an emotional drama on TV. Let's try again.

c. We could classify all Leisure activities in terms of their degree of Adventure, or Risk-taking:

Those Activities Which Have The
Least Risk or Adventure To Them

Those Activities Which Have The
Most Risk or Adventure To Them

This is clearly moving away from the subjectivity of the earlier classifications. I mean, *everybody* would agree that mountain-climbing belongs over toward the right-end of the above spectrum. And that watching TV belongs over toward the far left. So, this is a possibility; but let us see what else we've got:

d. We could classify all Leisure activities in terms of the amount of Energy the activities *generally* require; thus:

Those Activities Which Require The
Least Expenditure of Energy

Those Activities Which Require The
Greatest Expenditure of Energy

Now, that's a very attractive classification. Not only is it relatively objective—i.e., most of us can agree that soccer takes more energy than walking along a beach, and therefore we can rather easily place activities along this continuum. But *also,* this is precisely the criterion most of us tend to use in making decisions about our leisure. We take into account how energetic we feel, how much we need to burn up energy, or to conserve it, before we decide what it is we are going to do. Moreover, it bears a certain correlation with the Risk-taking or Adventure continuum that we saw just before. Therefore, in a sense, we have here the best of both worlds—"c." and "d." So, *let's use it.*

It may help if we further refine this horizontal dimension to our Map, so as to indicate Degrees of Energy. I would argue for the following Degrees:

(1) "Killing Time" takes the least energy. It involves such activities as absent-mindedly watching TV.

(2) "Pleasure-seeking" or "Enjoying Yourself" takes a little more energy—as when you are trying hard to have fun at a party.

(3) "Celebrating" takes more energy still, as when singing lustily to celebrate your enjoyment of being alive.

(4) "Being Creative" or "Achieving Something" requires still more energy—sometimes physical, sometimes mental, most often both. And, finally:

(5) "Competing or Gaining A Sense of Power Over Someone or Something" requires the greatest expenditure of energy.

It all comes out looking like this:

LEAST ENERGY				MOST ENERGY
Spectator				*Participant*
Killing time	Pleasure seeking	Celebrating	Being creative, achieving something	Competing, gaining a sense of power over something or someone

Now, with the horizontal dimension of our Leisure Map locked up, we may turn to the vertical dimension. What shall we put there? Why not the other dimension of Leisure which we instinctively think of whenever we are trying to decide what to do—namely, the degree to which a particular activity can be done by ourselves, or the degree to which it requires the company of others?

It would come out looking something like this

SOLITUDE
Activities Done Alone

RELATIONSHIP
Activities Done With Others

It does not seem terribly useful to mark out degrees of Solitude, or degrees of Relationship—in quite the same way that it *was* useful to mark out Degrees of Energy. But it is interesting to note the Midpoint on this continuum. For want of a better name, I will call that Midpoint "Alone In the Midst of A Crowd." It is a most intriguing Leisure phenomenon. If you walk on a lonely beach by yourself, that is clearly a Leisure Activity which deserves the name of "Solitude." But what shall we say if you go by yourself to an art museum? You are, in a sense, alone. But all around you there is a crowd—not talking to you, or interacting with you in any real way (except to murmur, "Excuse me," or to exchange an interested glance)—and yet a crowd which makes its presence very much felt by virtue of the fact that *all of you share the same interests, and are engaged in the same activity.* This is the sort of thing which I think deserves the name of "Alone In the Midst of A Crowd." There are, in fact, a whole raft of activities which deserve this label.

And—since we are talking about midpoints,—let us cast a glance back at the horizontal spectrum (Degrees of Energy) that we settled upon, earlier. At its farthest left, we have the word "Spectator". At its farthest right, we have the word "Participant". How then might we label its midpoint? Well, clearly: Spectator-Participant. An example of a Leisure Activity which deserves this characterization would "gambling at a horse-race". To the degree you are watching the race, you are merely a spectator. But, to the degree that you have bet upon the race, and are therefore *involved,* you are also a participant. Spectator-Participant. A midpoint which is not merely half-way between two extremes, but a whole different genus, or species.

Well, so much for the horizontal and the vertical. Putting these two dimensions together, we begin to see the faintest outline of our Leisure Map:

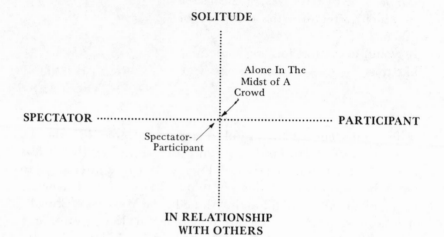

All Leisure activities which are done essentially by yourself, we may place above the horizontal line. So that, when the Map is completed, anything which appears above that line is—by definition—done by yourself. And all Leisure activities which are done with others, we may place below the horizontal line. So that, when the Map is completed, anything that appears below that line is—by definition—done with others. While Leisure activities which are done by yourself, but in the midst of a crowd, may be placed on or near the horizontal line.

Any activity which normally requires little energy, we may place toward the left-hand side of the Map—whether it be above, on, or below the horizontal line. Conversely, any activity which normally requires a lot of energy—so that you are no longer spectator, but participant—we may place toward the right-hand side of the Map. Neat! But there is one *minor little problem:* the same Leisure activity *could* be placed on the Map in several different positions. By way of illustration, let us look at "bicycling". There are a number of varieties of bicycling—namely:

Bicycling₁: aimlessly roaming around your street on your bicycle, just killing time for half an hour until someone shows up.

Bicycling₂: going by yourself on the back-roads, drinking in the beauty of the woods and the glory of the sunlight on the foliage.

Bicycling₃: going by yourself on a new ten-speed bike that you don't know how to ride; and keeping at it until you have mastered it.

Bicycling₄: going by yourself, and since seven miles up and down hills was the most you have been able to do, to date, you determine that this time you will go for ten miles over the same course.

Bicycling₅: the same as Bicycling₁ except that two of you —on your bikes—are aimlessly riding back and forth on your street, killing time until a third party shows up.

Bicycling₆: the same as Bicycling₂, except that two of you are with your bikes on the back roads, drinking in the scenery. Or four of you. Or a whole band of you.

Bicycling₇: you are taking the time to teach someone else how to ride a bicycle.

Bicycling₈: you are involved in a bicycle marathon race over a 75 mile course, with a trophy going to the winner.

Thus we see that we *could* place Bicycling on the Leisure Map in eight different positions: and it would come out looking like this:

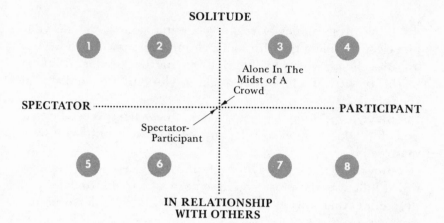

SOLITUDE

1   2   3   4

Alone In The
Midst of A
Crowd

SPECTATOR ⋯⋯⋯⋯⋯⋯⋯⋯⋯⋯⋯⋯⋯⋯⋯⋯ PARTICIPANT

Spectator-
Participant

5   6   7   8

IN RELATIONSHIP
WITH OTHERS

Unfortunately, that way lies madness; for, if we listed every Leisure activity eight times, our Leisure Map would be a hopeless mess. The only way it may be at all useful is if we list any particular Leisure activity only once—hopefully in its most popular form. And if we add the proviso that *if you see one of your favorite Leisure activities listed in one place on the Map, and you think it should be in another place, WRITE IT IN.* It's *your* Map, after all. If it isn't helpful to you the way it is, Change It. You are in charge of making this book yours, even as you are in charge of making your life yours.

I have placed on this Map—for starters—*a Sampler (only)* of the Traditional Ways in which people spend their leisure time. To put it more bluntly, although I said earlier that *all* activities can be leisure activities, I have here restricted myself primarily to those activities which our culture labels as "Leisure Activities." I must, however, repeat my earlier disclaimer: the spirit with which you do the thing is what makes it Leisure; not the activity in and of itself.

You will note that I have numbered the different sections of the Map—so that it will be easier for you to go back later and find something: Sections 1-4 represent Leisure Activities you do by yourself, placed in the order of the energy they require—from "least" (Section 1) to most (Section 4). Sections 5-8, on the other hand, represent Leisure Activities you do with others, again in the order of the energy they require—from "least" (Section 5) to "most" (Section 8).

And now, dear reader, here is our completed Map. Ta-Da.

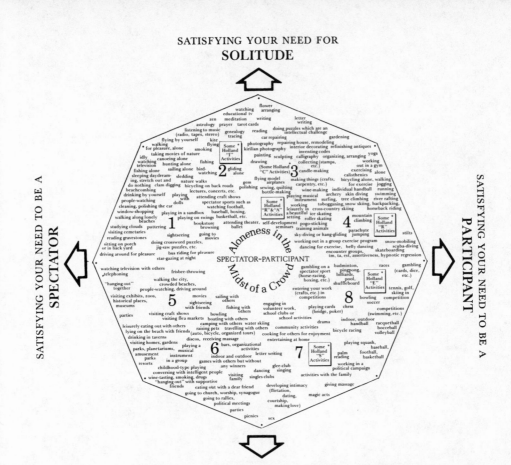

What's that? You say it is so small, you can't even read it? Picky, picky, picky. With this Map in hand, you are now ready to decide—on any given day, or at any given hour—between a vast array of *different* things that you can do in your Leisure. If you are one of those people who—like me—are addicted to Endless Variety, endless variety is what you can now have. Just decide—on any given day—whether you want to do your Leisure by yourself, or in the company of another (or in the company of others), and how much energy you want to expend. The possibilities are endless (well, almost).

What's that? It's a great idea, except you still can't read it? Okay, time for me to stop being playful, and give you the real Map (next page, please):

389

Leisure Map

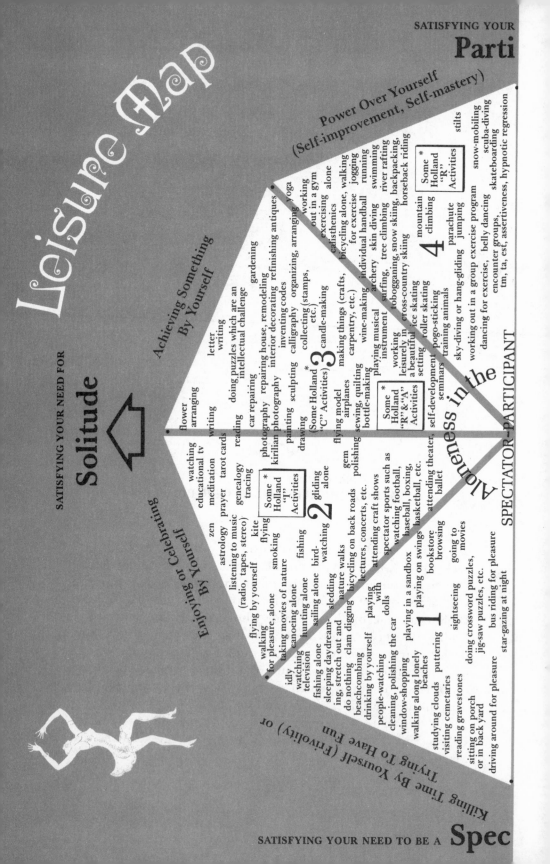

SATISFYING YOUR NEED FOR

Solitude

Power Over Yourself
(Self-improvement, Self-mastery)

Achieving Something
By Yourself

Enjoying or Celebrating
By Yourself

4

working
out in a gym
exercising   alone
calisthenics
bicycling alone, walking
for exercise   jogging
individual handball   running
archery   skin diving   swimming
surfing, tree climbing   river rafting
working   tobogganing, snow skiing, backpacking,
leisurely in   cross-country skiing   horseback riding
a beautiful   ice skating   mountain
setting   roller skating   climbing
training animals   parachute
pogo-sticking   jumping
sky-diving or hang-gliding
self-development   working out in a group exercise program
seminars   dancing for exercise, belly dancing
encounter groups,
tm, ta, est, assertiveness, hypnotic regression

stilts
snow-mobiling
scuba-diving
skateboarding

| Some |
| Holland |
| "R" |
| Activities |

3

gardening
refinishing antiques
interior decorating   remodeling
repairing house,   letter
inventing codes   writing
calligraphy   organizing, arranging   yoga
collecting (stamps,   doing puzzles which are an
etc.)   intellectual challenge
making things (crafts,   car repairing
carpentry, etc.)   flower
wine-making   arranging
candle-making   writing
playing musical   photography   reading
instrument   kirlian photography
sewing, quilting   painting   sculpting
bottle-making   drawing

| Some Holland |
| "C" Activities |

flying model
airplanes

| Some |
| Holland |
| "R" & "A" |
| Activities |

2

gem
polishing
bicycling on back roads
spectator sports such as
watching football,
baseball, boxing,
basketball, etc.
attending theater,
ballet

watching
educational tv
meditation   tarot cards
prayer
genealogy
tracing
astrology
zen

gliding
alone

| Some |
| Holland |
| "I" |
| Activities |

listening to music
(radio, tapes, stereo)
flying by yourself
walking   kite
for pleasure, alone   flying
smoking
taking movies of nature
hunting alone   fishing
canoeing alone   bird-
sailing alone   watching
sledding   nature walks
clam digging
beachcombing

1

going to
movies
bookstore
browsing
playing in a sandbox
playing on swings
playing   bus riding for pleasure
with   star-gazing at night
dolls
drinking by yourself
cleaning, polishing the car
window-shopping   sightseeing
walking along lonely
beaches   doing crossword puzzles,
puttering   jig-saw puzzles, etc.
visiting cemeteries
reading gravestones
sitting on porch
or in back yard
driving around for pleasure
studying clouds

idly
watching
television
fishing alone
sleeping daydream-
ing, stretch out and
do nothing

SATISFYING YOUR NEED TO BE A   **Spec**

Killing Time By Yourself (Frivolity) or
Trying To Have Fun

Aloneness in the   SPECTATOR–PARTICIPANT

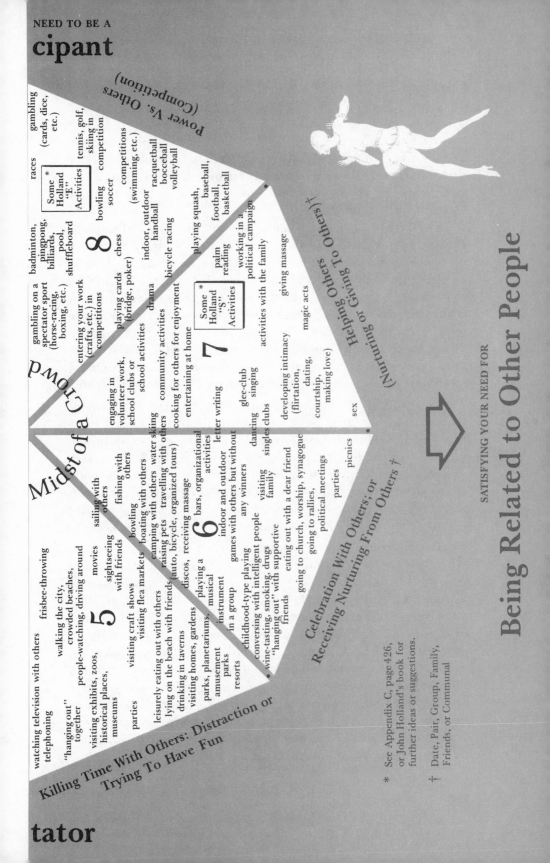

NEED TO BE A

cipant

tator

Power Vs. Others
(Competition)

Some Holland "E" Activities *

gambling (cards, dice, etc.)
races
tennis, golf, skiing in competition
competition (swimming, etc.)
bowling
soccer

badminton, pingpong, billiards, pool, shuffleboard
chess
indoor, outdoor handball
racquetball
boceball
volleyball
bicycle racing

playing squash, baseball, football, basketball

8

gambling on a spectator sport (horse-racing, boxing, etc.)
entering your work (crafts, etc.) in competitions
playing cards (bridge, poker)
drama

Helping Others or Giving To Others †
(Nurturing)

palm reading
working in a political campaign
giving massage
magic acts
activities with the family

Some Holland "S" Activities *

7

Midst of a Crowd

engaging in volunteer work, school clubs or school activities
community activities
cooking for others for enjoyment
entertaining at home

letter writing
glee-club singing
singles clubs
dancing

developing intimacy (flirtation, dating, courtship, making love)
sex

water skiing
travelling with others
fishing with others
boating with others
bowling
camping with others
raising pets (auto, bicycle, organized tours)
discos, receiving massage

bars, organizational activities
indoor and outdoor games with others but without any winners
visiting family
political meetings
going to rallies,
going to church, worship, synagogue
parties
picnics

eating out with a dear friend

watching television with others
frisbee-throwing
telephoning
walking the city, crowded beaches,
"hanging out" together
people-watching, driving around
visiting exhibits, zoos,
movies
historical places,
sightseeing with others
museums
parties
visiting craft shows
visiting flea markets
sailing with others

5

leisurely eating out with others
lying on the beach with friends
drinking in taverns
visiting homes, gardens
parks, planetariums,
playing a
amusement
musical
parks,
instrument
resorts
in a group

childhood-type playing
conversing with intelligent people
wine-tasting, smoking, drugs
"hanging out" with supportive
friends

6

Killing Time With Others: Distraction or Trying To Have Fun

Celebration With Others; or
Receiving Nurturing From Others †

SATISFYING YOUR NEED FOR

Being Related to Other People

* See Appendix C, page 426,
or John Holland's book for
further ideas or suggestions.

† Date, Pair, Group, Family,
Friends, or Communal

Games

The Map, as I said, is only a Sampler of the kinds of Leisure activities that are open to you. There are, for example, a tremendous variety of games and similar activities available to the devout Leisure variety-hunter, that are not all listed there. These games are of three varieties, and therefore belong to three different sectors on the Map:

First, there are the Games Which You Do Individually, Primarily As A Challenge To Yourself—these belong to Section 4, on the Map (though, of course, you *can* do many of these in competition with others, in which case they belong to Section 8): *solitaire, bilboquet, cat's cradle, magic squares, math puzzles, string puzzles, match games, construction puzzles, Victoria puzzle, Picking Cherries, Tangram, psychic exercises, pinball, computer-calculator games, mind games, body games, toys, puzzles, riddles, brain-teasers, mazes, shot-put, discus, hammer, high jump, javelin, hang-gliding, diabolo, yo-yoing, jump-rope, etc.*

Secondly, there are the Games Which You Do With Others, Where There Is Little Sense of Competition, But Only Enjoyment of The Thing In and For Itself—these belong to Section 6, on the Map: *the I-Ching, making-up stories, Simon Says, fantasy games, imagination games, clay-modeling, fingerpainting, play-acting, tinker-toys, Logo, blowing soap bubbles, train/car counting, spinning tops, aerobatics, sport parachuting, ballooning, and gliding, group roller or figure skating, marbles, hopscotch.*

Thirdly, there are the Games Which You Do With Others, Where The Sense of Competition Is Very High—these belong, of course, to Section 8, on the Map: *boxing, wrestling, judo, karate, kendo, aikido, fencing, darts, billiards, snooker, pool, skittles, bowling, court handball, jai alai, table tennis, volleyball, basketball, roller derby, chess, checkers, dominoes, lotto, cribbage, dice, roulette, backgammon, Scrabble, Monopoly, quoits, go, ma-jong, relay races, throwing, jumping, baseball, softball, rounders, cricket, lacrosse, field hockey, roller hockey, water polo, canoe polo, skibob racing, bobsleigh racing, horseshoe pitching, archery, shooting, bocce ball, badminton, croquet, golf, lawn tennis, squash, football, rugby, soccer, racing (car, stock car, sports car, sedan, motorcycle, moped, snowmobiles, etc.).*

Crafts

Another category of Leisure Activities, besides games, that is only incompletely represented on the Map is that of Crafts. These belong primarily in Section 3, on the Map, and a more complete catalog of them would go something like this: *Basketry, Beads, Candles, Ceramics, Doll-Houses, Dough Art, Embroidery, Enameling, Fabric Decoration, Felt, Foil, Glass, Jewelry, Knitting & Crochet, Lace Making, Leather, Macrame & Knotting, Marionettes, Metal, Miniatures, Models (Car, Train, Boat, Plane), Mosaics, Needlepoint, Netting, Paper, Paper-mache, Plastics, Puppets, Quilting, Rug Making, Spinning & Dyeing, Sticks, Textile Design and Construction, T-Shirt Transfers, Weaving, Wood (Carpentry, Woodcarving)—and some new crafts which will doubtless be invented by tomorrow.*

Guidebooks to Leisure

Whatever you choose—from the Leisure Map or from the above lists—I can guarantee you there is a book, somewhere, that tells you how to do it, or how to do it with greater enjoyment. Herewith, a *partial* list of some of the guidebooks to leisure:

The Whole Kids Catalog: For Adventure Seekers Of All Ages, created by Peter Cardozo, Designed by Ted Menten (1975, Bantam Books, Inc., 666 Fifth Avenue, New York, NY 10019. $5.95, paper). Somehow, leisure is assumed to be the exclusive possession of The Retired, while play is assumed to be the exclusive possession of kids. Hence it is writers for kids who put out the best materials for play, in adulthood.

The Second Whole Kids Catalog, same authors (1977, Bantam Books, Inc., address above. $7.50, paper.)

The Mature Person's Guide to Kites, Yo-Yos, Frisbees And Other Childlike Diversions by Paul Dickson (1977, New American Library, Inc., 1301 Avenue of the Americas, New York, NY 10019. $5.95, paper).

Games of the World: How to Make Them, How to Play Them, How They Came to Be, Edited by Frederic V. Grunfeld. (1975, Ballantine Books, Division of Random House, 201 E. 50th Street, New York, NY 10022. $7.95, paper).

The Way To Play: The Illustrated Encyclopedia of the Games of the World, by the Diagram Group (1975, Bantam Books, address above. $7.95, paper).

Craft Sources: The Ultimate Catalog for Craftspeople, by Paul Colin and Deborah Lippman (1975, M. Evans and Company, Inc., distributed by J. B. Lippincott Company, East Washington Square, Philadelphia, PA 19105. $5.95, paper).

The Catalog of Kits (How Anyone Can Make Anything by Ordering Do-it-yourself Kits Through the Mail), by Jeffrey Feinman (1975, William Morrow and Company, Inc., 105 Madison Avenue, New York, NY 10016. $6.95, paper).

The Catalog of Free Things, by Jeffrey Feinman & Mark Weiss (1976, William Morrow and Company, Inc., address above. $6.95, paper).

Mind Games: The Guide to Inner Space, by Robert Masters and Jean Houston (1972, A Delta Book, published by Dell Publishing Co., Inc., 1 Dag Hammarskjold Plaza, New York, NY 10017. $3.45, paper).

Put Your Mother On The Ceiling: Children's Imagination Games, by Richard De Mille (1973, Penguin Books, 625 Madison Avenue, New York, NY 10022. $2.95, paper).

Rules of The Game: The Complete Illustrated Encyclopedia of All The Sports of The World, by the Diagram Group (1974, Bantam Books, address above. $6.95, paper).

The Great Escape: A Source Book of Delights & Pleasures for the Mind & Body, by Min S. Yee and Donald K. Wright (1974, Bantam Books, address above. $7.00, paper).

The Pleasure Book, by Julius Fast (1975, Stein and Day, Publishers, Scarborough House, Briarcliff Manor, NY 10510. $8.95, hardcover).

In addition to these overall guidebooks or encyclopedias, there are books on individual pursuits that stretch in an unending pile, as far as the eye can see. You like paper? There is: *Pholdit,* by S. Goldberg (1972, Billiken Publications, Inc., P. O. Box 8564, San Jose, CA 95125. $2.00, paper). You like cards? There is: *Hoyle's Modern Encyclopedia of Card Games,* by Walter B. Gibson (1974, Dolphin Books, Doubleday & Company, Inc., 245 Park Avenue, New York, NY 10017. $3.95, paper). You like calculators? There is: *Games Calculators Play,* by Wallace Judd (1975, Warner Books, Inc., 75 Rockefeller Plaza, New York,

NY 10019. $1.50, paper). You like magic? There is: *Catalog of Magic,* by Marvin Kaye (1977, A Doubleday/Dolphin Book, address above. $5.95, paper).

You name it, you like it, there's a book about it. Go to your friendly neighborhood library, or bookstore, and see. But first: choose from the Leisure Map what it is you'd like to do. And— even better than a book—find *someone* who will show you how.

Thus, have we come to our fifth and final principle about Leisure:

5 **IF YOU LIKE TO EXPLORE AND DO MANY DIFFERENT THINGS IN YOUR LEISURE, USE A MAP (OF LEISURE) WHICH WILL CONTINUOUSLY REMIND YOU OF ALL THE POSSIBILITIES THERE ARE TO CHOOSE FROM. AND IN EXPLORING NEW FRONTIERS, FOR YOU, FIND A BOOK OR A PERSON WHO CAN GUIDE YOU IN YOUR INITIATION AND EXPLORATION.[12]**

And Now, In Conclusion,
A Word About Playfulness

When I think of the happiest and best people I know, or have ever known, one quality about them really sticks out. That is, while they enjoyed their Leisure, they never waited for their Leisure to come, before they enjoyed themselves. They seemed to be endlessly playing, no matter where they were, or what they were doing.

They were (and are) always listening for some sound with which they could play. Or looking for some sight with which they could play. Or searching for some person with whom they could play. They were always determined that the monotonous round of their daily appointed tasks would be transformed by the alchemy of their humor, and their light touch. I think of the bus driver who has all his passengers laughing, at the humor with which he calls out the stops. I think of the waitress, who has everyone adoring her, by the banter with which she greets their orders. I think of the mechanic at the neighborhood gas station, whom people always look forward to visiting, because of his kidding ways. I think of Shelly Berman's stewardess, who —when asked how long "this flight to Los Angeles" took— replied, "I don't know, we've never made it."

I think of the young lovers, making puns on words in ever more rapid crescendo, until they both fall, collapsed with laughter, on the grass. I think of the husband and father, walking through the living room on his way to some other part of the house who—upon hearing a march break out on the radio—turns his walking into a parody of silliness, that has his children and his wife watching, weak with laughter.

Clowns, you may say. The world is filled with clowns. Kids, you may say. Kids who have never grown up. Ah, Yes, and what a delicious compliment that is. Remembering That Man who said—two thousand years ago—"Except you become like little children, you cannot enter into the kingdom of heaven."

I can think of no more lovely a compliment than to say of a woman, "She is immensely playful." And there is no lovelier compliment that anyone can give to me, than to say, "He is a very playful man."

So, let us drink a toast to all those who refuse to let their playfulness be fenced-in solely within the compound of their Leisure time. But have allowed it to spill outside those bounds, into every compartment of their lives. Playful in the way they learn. Playful in the way they work. Playful in the way they make love. Playful in everything. Their whole life is their Leisure.

Let us drink a toast to all who have refused to leave their life in boxes. But have learned, or are learning, how to get out of them. With Lifelong Learning. Lifelong Working. And Lifelong Playing.

Yes, let us drink a toast to You.

Chapter Five Footnotes

1. "Life Cycle Planning" Summary of National Conference, New Strategies for Education, Work and Retirement in America, April 20-22, 1977, page 8.

2. *The Older American's Handbook* by Craig & Peter Norback, 1977, pages 1-2.

3. Statistics are taken from *The Older American's Handbook* (op. cit.); "The Realities of Retirement" by Sylvia Porter *(San Francisco Chronicle,* Sept. 10, 1973); and the *JSAC Grapevine,* Vol. 5, No. 5: "Old Age: Burden or Challenge?".

4. *Leaven,* the newsletter of the National Network of Episcopal Clergy Associations, Vol. VI, Number 14, June 1977, page 2.

5. If your library or bookstore doesn't have it, you can obtain it by writing to Van Nostrand Reinhold Company, 450 West 33rd Street, New York, NY 10001. $8.95, paper.

6. Reported in the *San Francisco Examiner,* June 4, 1977.

7. I am loathe to mention names, since services such as these have a lamentable tendency to go out of business Suddenly. However *Money* magazine—in its July 1976 issue—singled out Compare/USA, at 7482 South Delaware Street, Littleton, CO 80120, which for $9.95 would give you a list of 20 communities that most closely met your wants of priorities, and for $12.50 would give you those 20 cities' real estate agents, employment agencies, and chambers of commerce—with a full refund promised to any customers who were dissatisfied with their results.

8. See *Social Indicators 1976,* pages 483ff. Issued December 1977, by the U.S. Department of Commerce. Available from: Superintendent of Documents, U.S. Government Printing Office, Washington, D.C. 20402. Stock Number: 041-001-00156-5.

9. In speaking of reserving time for Leisure, let us take note of the fact that there are vast classes in our society who have no need to make such reservations: viz., the retired who have no work to do, *some* housewives or househusbands whose children are grown or in school, the unemployed, the idle rich, children, and *some* students. Let us also take note of the fact that there are some classes of persons who find it very difficult to ever reserve time for Leisure, viz., those who are leading regimented lives in various institutions, where their calendar is ordered by Another.

10. *op. cit.,* p. 504.

11. See *Making Vocational Choices: a theory of careers* by John L. Holland (1973, Prentice-Hall, Inc., Englewood Cliffs, NJ 07632. $4.95, paper), pages 23ff.

12. For further reading on the general subject and philosophy of Leisure, see:

The Psychology of Leisure: Research Approaches to The Study of Leisure, by John Neulinger (1974, Charles C. Thomas, Publisher, Springfield, IL).

Of Time, Work, and Leisure, by Sebastian de Grazia (1964, Doubleday & Co., Inc., New York).

Homo Ludens: a study of the play element in culture, by Johan Huizinga (1950, Beacon Press, Boston).

Work, Play and Worship in a Leisure Age, by Gordon Dahl (1972, Augsburg Publishing House, Minneapolis).

Leisure Counseling Techniques: Individual and Group Counseling Step-by-Step, by Patsy B. Edwards (1977, 511 N. La Cienega Blvd., Los Angeles, CA 90048. $9.00 — plus 6% for California residents). Lists current organizations engaged in leisure counseling, from whom additional information can be obtained.

"Career Planning for Leisure" by Theresa Ripley and Steve O'Brien, in the *Journal of College Placement*, Spring 1976 Issue, pages 54ff.

Toward A Society of Leisure, by Joffre Dumazedier (1967, The Free Press, Glencoe, IL).

"The Definition and Measurement of Leisure" by Philip H. Ennis, in *Indicators of Social Change*, Edited by Eleanor B. Sheldon and Wilbert E. Moore (1968, Russell Sage Foundation, New York).

Leisure: Theory and Policy, Edited by Max Kaplan (1975, John Wiley & Sons, Inc., New York).

Technology, Human Values, and Leisure, Edited by Max Kaplan and Phillip Bosserman (1971, Abingdon Press, Nashville, TN).

The Human Meaning of Social Change, Edited by Angus Campbell and Philip E. Converse (1972, Russell Sage Foundation, New York). Chapters on "Leisure" and on "Social Change Reflected in the Use of Time".

The Future of Work and Leisure, by Stanley Parker (1971, Praeger, New York).

It's not that I'm afraid of dying;
I just don't want to be there when
it happens.

Woody Allen

Epilogue:
Beyond LIFE/work Planning

I've often thought of putting a sign
Over my door,
The door to my office, that is,
And the sign would read:
"LIFE/work Planning isn't the answer
To everything."
True, as we have seen in this book,
It may help us deal, effectively,
With our learning, work, and leisure; but
Life is so much more.

Beyond LIFE/work Planning are relationships
With those people who are around us.
Beyond LIFE/work Planning is learning how to touch,
And to be touched,
To love
And to be loved.
For, Life consists in learning how to be open,
Growing, and playful.
Life consists in learning how to take
Initiative,
And how to respond to people
Tenderly, patiently, and lovingly.
Beyond LIFE/work Planning is learning
To endure
In whatever commitments we make,
And learning to endure
Despite adversity, sickness,
Suffering or pain.
For beyond LIFE/work Planning
Is Death.

Death is the end of LIFE/work Planning.
It is the queen of Unexpected Events,
Which knocks all of our plans
Into a cocked hat, as we say.
You were planning to do this or that
On the morrow,
But suddenly Death
Puts an end to all that

Planning.
Unexpected Events — aye,
There's a phrase for you.
For, nothing is more Expected
And Certain in all of this Life
Than Death.
The only question left hanging is
When?
Death is something you can think about
And plan for,
With the absolute certainty
That none of your planning and thinking
Will be wasted.
So, any LIFE/work Planning
That does not look beyond
LIFE/work Planning
Is partial and incomplete.
You need to think through, for yourself,
My friend,
Your feelings about Death —
Coming, as it does, as the capstone of Life
Work Planning.
Coming, as it does, as the capstone of
Your Life
Work Planning.
No one can do this task for you.
You must do it for yourself.
And: the earlier the better.
But, as a contribution toward that task
Of yours,
It may help some among You if I share
At this point
A personal word
Concerning my own thinking about Death.

Very well. I look at Death
From the point of view
Of a Christian. That is to say,
I am one of those men and women who believe
In Jesus Christ,
The Son of the Living God,
Crucified, dead, and risen.

An ancient litany of jargon, to be sure,
But jargon which for me has
Meaning beyond utterance.
It is not merely that I believe
This or that
About Him; but that I believe
In Him — an infinitely deeper thing,
As you know
When you move from believing this or that
About someone You love,
To believing in
Him or her.
Well, anyway, because I believe in
Jesus Christ, I think of Death
In perhaps a peculiar way.
Which is to say, I think of Death
In terms of an automobile. Well,
Why not? I am, after all,
A child of this Age
Of Technology.
So, imagine, I have said to myself,
Imagine a car maker coming out tomorrow
With this guarantee:
"If you buy this automobile,
No matter what happens to it,
In an accident,
No matter how badly it is wracked up
Or crushed, we guarantee
We will always be able to get you out
Alive,
From that twisted wreck,
Unscratched and unharmed."
Imagine, I have said to myself,
How we would all flock to buy
That car.
And yet, God has given us just such
A guarantee, not about a car
But about our body.
Death is God's guarantee:
"If you live out your life in
This body,
No matter what happens to it,
No matter how badly it is wracked up

Or crushed, I guarantee
I will always be able to get you out
Alive
From that damaged body,
With your soul completely
Unscratched and unharmed."
That is what I believe
About Death,
Because I believe in Jesus Christ.
I believe Death is a sign
Of Love,
To us.   From God.

And certainly I believe
Death is not the end.
But merely a Pause
At the entrance to a new Life
Which may
Or may not
In another dimension require
New LIFE/work Planning.
Yet, at this Pause,
That is to say, at this moment
We call Death, I believe
We must give
Account,
As managers of apartment houses do
When they are face to face at last
With the owner
Of that building; who was,
'Til then, only a Voice
On the telephone.
Christians, for ages, have called
This accounting "Judgment"
(Heavy, heavy),
Or "Stewardship" (a more palatable term),
But — for my purposes —
"Manager" will do.
I believe that You and I are managers
Only
Of all that we have —
Those gifts, those talents, those skills
— Functional, specific, self-managed —

That we have inventoried,
Prioritized, and used
Throughout this book,
And — hopefully — throughout our lives.
Managers only,
And hence accountable to Him
Or Her
Who gave us such gifts.

Seen from this perspective of Giving Account
At Death, Life
Work Planning is — in my view —
A Plan of Stewardship, or
A Plan for Managing
This apartment house of our body
And heart and mind,
To be sure that the gifts we were given
Get fully used
While yet we live
In this body.
All of this lends, to be sure,
Some kind of ultimate dimension to Life
Work Planning.
That pyramid of issues we have wrestled with
Throughout this book,
And throughout our lives,
Has more ultimate answers
— From my point of view —
Than any we saw
Thus far.
For, ultimately, the answer
(From a Christian's point of view)
To "What's Happening?"
Is: "God is at work in the world
And in Us."
Christians call it, if you care,
Revelation.
And ultimately, the answer
(From a Christian's point of view)
To "Survival"
Is: "God will help us to survive
All things,
Even Death."

*I have loved
the stars too fondly
to be fearful
of the night.*

—Epitaph on grave of
unknown astronomer

Christians call this
Salvation.
And ultimately, the answer
(From a Christian's point of view)
To "Meaning or Mission"
Is: "God is working His purpose out
In Us; and we must find
Not only what pleases Us
But also
What pleases Him."
Christians call it, for the record,
Discipleship, Calling, Vocation.
And ultimately, the answer
(From a Christian's point of view)
To "Effectiveness"
Is: "God and we together will judge
At Death how did we do."
Christians call this, as we have
Seen, "Judgement", or
"Giving Account".
Not that Christians have any monopoly
On these words
Or concepts.
Seekers from every nation
And creed may also embrace
Such terms.
I merely wish to point out
That if you believe,
Then the pyramid has some ultimate
Answers
Which we must seek
And find,
Without letting go
Of those more immediate answers
That we saw
Throughout this book.

I have spoken of Death
Thus far
In terms of two concepts:
Love, and Stewardship.
There is yet a third
(Christians are Trinitarians to the death),

And that is
Community.
Briefly stated: we are all in this
Together.
And that idea informs
And affects
Everything we do.
Those people all around you
Are mortals,
Who will die
In their good time,
Just as you and I will.
Die, and give their
Accounting,
Just as You and I will give
Ours. Hence, they need
Whatever we know
That will make their life better.
Thus, LIFE/work Planning
Can never be
An idea that we hoard
Only for ourselves,
A way to "beat out the competition",
And make sure that
"We get ours", regardless of what happens
To the rest;
LIFE/work Planning can never be
Merely a blueprint
For selfishness — though I am sure
There will be those, inevitably,
Who will see it as That,
And use it as That.
Unless, or until, they put Life
Work Planning in the context
And larger perspective of
Death.
But never mind the petty ways
In which LIFE/work Planning
Can be used.
Whatever others may do,
I hope that You and I
Will always see it in its largest
Use: as a tool to be mastered

First of all, in our own lives,
And then shared
In every way that we know how
With all those around us,
Who like us, will die
And give their
Accounting.
That is what happens when you set
LIFE/work Planning in the context
Of Death. At least that is how I
Perceive it,
For whatever usefulness that may be
To You.

If any of you think that the words above
Are written casually,
Or that what I believe was idly plucked
Out of the air,
Let me tell you that this is not so.
It is one of the ironies of life
That this very book
On LIFE/work Planning
Was set — by fate and circumstance —
In the larger context of Death,
Which fact informed
And affected
All that I have written
Here.
For, this book was only one week old,
That is to say, I had barely begun
Writing,
When — well, let me tell you about it,
In the words that I wrote
At the time:

He was my one and only brother.
He lived in Phoenix, and I in San Francisco,
Just an hour and a half apart, by plane.
We felt very close.
He was, like me, a writer.
He was, like me, a crusader.
But, unlike me, he had a courage
That filled me with awe.
Forty years ago, or more, we played
In the sandbox together,
And squabbled, and fought, and made up
As brothers do.
And I never dreamed that this boy
I lived with, for seventeen years,
Would grow up to be this man,
Whom I have thought of, for long,
And now always will,
Whenever the word *hero* is mentioned.
I do not mean to suggest he was a saint.
He wasn't that; in his personal life
He was all too human.
Yes, human to the core.
He could be angry, insensitive
And foolish,
As I too, have been — in abundance.
But when he went to this chosen work,
He was *Something Else*, as they say.

Last week, as he went about his work,
He was cold-bloodedly murdered,
In a monstrous way,
At the age of forty–seven,
Leaving behind a wife who called him *Don*,
And seven children (the youngest but six)
Who called him *Dad*.
I want to tell you about it,
Not simply because he was my brother,
But because — as John Donne said —
Everyman's death diminishes you and me,
And this man's death especially.

It began on Wednesday, the second of June,
When Don rose with a smile,
And put on his pretty blue leisure suit,

Because it was a special day —
His wedding anniversary. He went to work,
With plans to celebrate that evening,
With dinner and a movie:
All The President's Men, in fact —
A movie about two determined reporters.
Which was appropriate,
Because Don was a reporter too,
For *The Arizona Republic*.
But not your ordinary everyday reporter.
It was not in him just to be ordinary.
He was truly extraordinary.
Arizona Newsman of the Year, in '74 —
The best among one thousand in that State,
And earlier, nominated for the Pulitizer Prize
For his exposés.
His courage was awesome,
And so was his commitment to exposing
Wrongdoing, fraud, and corruption.
Truth was the flame that brightly burned
Beside the altar of his life,
And his devotion to it, at any cost,
Was total.
He did not fear the Mafia, or politicians'
Power. He had the freedom of the press,
And *the public's Right to Know* behind him.
Once given a tip,
He pursued it relentlessly,
Carefully building documentation upon
Documentation, lest by accident
He inadvertently libel the innocent.
His tape recorder ever by his side,
His integrity like a rock,
His passion for Truth widely known & feared,
His informants legion
Because they trusted only him.
He identified, by name, the organized crime
Figures moving into Arizona,
And by name, legislators involved
In conflict of interest.
Like some New Testament prophet
He took, as the text for his work,
There are men who love darkness,

Rather than light,
Because their deeds are evil...
But there is nothing that is hidden
That shall not be revealed.

He knew, of course,
The cost. They tapped his phone,
And his bank accounts.
Once, upon the witness stand,
For three days they tried to break him,
But he could not be broken.
They tried harrassments endlessly,
Political pressure, and libel suits
In never ending procession —
Sometimes for twenty million or so.
But he was proud of his documentation,
And when he heard of a new suit,
He was unafraid. As he once said to me,
"They've got to be kidding."
He was confident, cool and assured
Of his competency and professionalism.
In the midst of men (and women as well)
Who are content with their work
So long as they just keep busy,
He was an exceptional man
Who needed a mission in life,
And had found it,
Despite its danger.

But after a while, it got to him.
He grew tired of the pressure,
And even more of the public apathy
To the Truth that he gathered,
At so great a cost.
So he asked to be put out to pasture,
Of a sort; to go back to his beat
Covering the legislature. A relatively
Quiet job, where he hoped to find
Some peace.
The harrassments died down.
The libel suits ended,
His life became almost normal again.
"And," he said to me, "I sure like it
This way."

He no longer had to put a hidden piece
Of tape, across the hood of his car,
Nor examine it every morning to see
If it had been tampered with,
As was his wont before,
When death threats were part of
His daily life.

But, of course, he never could let go,
And some informants trusted only him,
So tips still came;
And with his calm professionalism
He had to follow each one up.
That is what they counted upon
When they decided to murder him,
That day.
Some men grew afraid that with Don
In the world, the scheme they were planning
Would soon be unmasked.
Or else, they smarted still
From the unmasking he had done, in the past,
And were only waiting until they knew
His caution was asleep.

And so, they set him up,
On his wedding anniversary,
As he went to the State capitol
In his blue leisure suit
To cover the legislature, that day.
They set him up, with the lure
Of a tip they knew he could not ignore.
They set up an appointment
At the Clarendon Hotel, in Phoenix.
It was an appointment they had no intention
Of keeping.
They only wanted him there to sit
In the lobby, for a while,
While they had his car, parked in back,
And the time, beyond his sight,
To stoop down beside his car
(For less than a minute)
And attach a bomb, gangland style,
Beneath the driver's seat.

Then their decoy phoned Don,
And told him to go on.
For it was a conspiracy,
And they wanted him to climb back in his car,
And start to back it out,
So that one of them, by remote control,
Could twist a model-airplane dial,
—Which he did—and thus blow Don away.

Pieces of the car
Went three stories high
As they set off the bomb, beneath his seat;
And Don should have died on the spot,
But he was six feet one
And of rugged physique,
With a heart as strong as his passion
For truth and righteousness.
And besides all that,
My brother's professionalism required of him
That he stay alive, if he could,
Long enough to press the truth
That only he knew,
Into the hands of another —
Like some Olympic and Olympian runner.
So, as he lay bleeding on the pavement
With his shattered legs and arms,
He coolly told the witnesses there
Just exactly who had set him up,
"In case," Don said, "I don't make it."

A professional is one who knows he is
A professional, to the end;
A hero is one who doesn't even know
That he is.
Thus Don gave police just the clue
That they needed
To start unraveling the conspiracy
That was taking his life
In this monstrous way;
So that his death might prove to be
The means of their undoing.

He took eleven days to die,
My brother who used to play
In the sandbox with me,
And even doctors wept as they watched
The incredible fight he put up
To live out his life
In *this* world, where Truth & Righteousness
Need every advocate they can find;
And Don was one of their fiercest and best.

No death in my whole life
Has moved me so much as this death.
I have seen death many times,
For I am not a reporter, but priest.
I have buried infant children
And patriarchs.
I have buried both stranger and foe
And closest friend.
I was with my Dad, in his dying and pain.
And I know that what the Scriptures say
Is true: *No man knows the hour
Of his death ... In the midst of life
We are in death, O Lord.*
So, that my brother died
When he least expected to,
Is not the point.
We must all, every morning,
Be able to say — as a miner once did —
"O Lord, if any must die this day,
Let it be me,
For I am ready."
My brother was a believer, indeed,
And that would have been his prayer,
I know.

Don and I both believed — and believe —
That God had a Son
Who was cruelly murdered,
In the prime of His life.
So I think The Center of the Universe
Knows well
This pain and grief that I feel.

The grief is not because I think
Don is no more; I know he is
—By faith, and by the stories I have heard
From those who died or almost died,
And came back that they might testify
How, when the body can no longer sustain
Its life, the soul within that body
Journeys outward
Toward the Brightest Light that it has
Ever seen. And there, in that Light
Waits a Figure of Love
With arms outstretched,
In a realm where there is incredible Peace;
And Truth & Righteousness reign.
So I believe Don is alive
In the profoundest sense,
Perhaps even reading these words
Over my shoulder,
And smiling.

Still, I have been weeping
Torrents of bitter tears
In my pain and my rage
At the manner of his death,
And the senselessness of this death
Of my brother, the hero.
I am enraged that beasts
Masquerading as men,
Too cowardly to do the deed themselves,
Could hire a hit man
To play with Don as though he were
Merely a model-airplane,
Diving to the earth.
Leaving his mother, his sister and me,
Seven children, a widow,
And a world that needed him so,
To contemplate what we all have lost,
And how we are diminished indeed
By this death
Of this man, my hero, my brother.

Don, I loved you; and love you still.
Thank God I told you that,
As you told me,
In our letters to each other,
Just last March.
I love you for many things.
Most of all, for your integrity & courage.
You knew that they could take your life,
But that was all that they could take.
Not your passion for truth,
Nor your hatred of corruption,
Nor your integrity,
Your courage,
Nor your love.
I love you for these things,
Which still burn bright in the world
And in my memory.
I know I will be seeing you again.
Til then:
Peace. Love. Shalom.

So may it be said of us all,
My friend;
So may it be said, at our death,
Of us
All:
That we lived a life filled
With Meaning and Mission,
And left this world richer
For our presence.

For Further Reading
Beyond LIFE/work Planning

On Death and Dying by Elisabeth Kubler-Ross, M.D. (1969, MacMillan Publishing Co., Inc., 866 Third Avenue, New York, NY 10022. $1.95, paper).

Questions and Answers On Death and Dying by Elisabeth Kubler-Ross, M.D. (1974, Macmillan Publishing Co. $1.50, paper).

Death The Final Stage of Growth by Elisabeth Kubler-Ross (1975, Prentice-Hall, Inc., Englewood Cliffs, NJ. $2.95, paper).

Life After Life by Raymond A. Moody, Jr., M.D. (1975, Bantam Books, Inc., 666 Fifth Avenue, New York, NY 10019. $1.95, paper).

Reflections on Life After Life by Raymond A. Moody, Jr., M.D. (1977, Bantam Books, Inc. $1.95, paper).

At The Hour of Death by Karlis Osis, Ph.D. and Erlendur Haraldsson, Ph.D. (1977, Avon Books, A Division of The Hearst Corporation, 959 Eighth Avenue, New York, NY 10019. $3.95, paper).

Living and Dying by Robert Jay Lifton and Eric Olson (1974, Bantam Books, Inc. $1.95, paper).

> *All of the above were either written by, or received the imprimatur of, Elisabeth Kubler-Ross, the scientist-saint (in my opinion) who has led the last decade's investigations into people's experiences of dying, death and mourning. All the above tend to report and/or reflect upon those investigations. The following books go further afield, ranging from thorough studies of certain aspects of death (such as suicide) to psychic phenomena.*

The Savage God, A Study of Suicide by A. Alvarez (1971, Bantam Books, Inc. $2.50, paper).

Visions of Heaven and Hell by Richard Cavendish (1977, Harmony Books, A Division of Crown Publishers, Inc., One Park Avenue, New York, NY 10016). Beautifully illustrated.

subtle body, Essence and shadow by David V. Tansley (1977, Thames and Hudson, 30 Bloomsbury Street, London, England WCiB 3QP. $7.95, paper). Beautifully illustrated.

Death is no longer a taboo subject among Americans, says a new insurance report. The report was prepared by the American Council on Life Insurance, a trade association representing firms with 90 percent of the industry's assets. It said Americans in general are becoming less inclined to treat the subject of death as a taboo. It cited the rapid growth of death education courses in high schools and colleges, describing one class in which students touch a dead body and visit a crematory; the increasing incidence of suicide among teenagers; and the extensive news coverage of Senator Hubert Humphrey's death and funeral.

The San Francisco Chronicle,
April 10, 1978

States of Consciousness by Charles T. Tart (1975, E. P. Dutton & Co., Inc., 201 Park Avenue South, New York, NY 10003. $4.95, paper).

Life Without Death? by Nils O. Jacobson, M.D. (1971, Dell Publishing Co., Inc., 1 Dag Hammarskjold Plaza, New York, NY 10017. $1.75, paper).

The Romeo Error, A Meditation on Life and Death by Lyall Watson (1974, Dell Publishing Co., Inc. $1.95, paper).

The Will To Live by Arnold A. Hutschnecker, M.D. (1966, Cornerstone Library Publications, Simon & Schuster, Inc., 630 Fifth Avenue, New York, NY 10020. $1.95, paper).

The Denial of Death by Ernest Becker (1973, The Free Press, A Division of Macmillan Publishing Co., Inc., 866 Third Avenue, New York, NY 10022. $2.95, paper).

Prioritizing

In our National Career Development LIFE/work Shops, we have discovered that each exercise a person works through turns up a number of factors that are important to that individual. And, that these factors do not make much sense or give much guidance to him or her, until the factors *are prioritized.* "This is the most important to me." "This is the next most important." "This is third." And so forth.

Sometimes this prioritizing can be done simply by intuition. Other times it can't be. The question, then, is "Do you have a Plan B?" The answer is Yes. Here is a prioritizing device adapted by Earl Lowell and myself from an instrument used by a research outfit in Syracuse, New York. You can use it again and again and again, in your Life/work Planning and Prioritizing. It works like a charm.

Step 1   Here's how it goes. Take your list of items that you want to put in priority order, and number each item. Let us say you have ten items. We'll take a menu, by way of illustration.

Item No. 1 — Fruit Cocktail	Item No. 6 — Brussels Sprouts
Item No. 2 — Escargot	Item No. 7 — Sourdough Bread
Item No. 3 — Roast Beef	Item No. 8 — Ice Cream
Item No. 4 — Mashed Potatoes	Item No. 9 — Chocolate Cake
Item No. 5 — Squash	Item No. 10 — Coffee

Step 2   You then prepare a number-grid in the following manner.

Take one and pair it with each of the other numbers by writing each other number beside it in a column, as in Column A below.
(There will always turn out to be one less pair of numbers than the total number of factors you are prioritizing.)
Repeat this with each succeeding item, dropping down one space each time.

A	B	C	D	E	F	G	H	I
1 2	—	—	—	—	—	—	—	—
1 3	2 3	—	—	—	—	—	—	—
1 4	2 4	3 4	—	—	—	—	—	—
1 5	2 5	3 5	4 5	—	—	—	—	—
1 6	2 6	3 6	4 6	5 6	—	—	—	—
1 7	2 7	3 7	4 7	5 7	6 7	—	—	—
1 8	2 8	3 8	4 8	5 8	6 8	7 8	—	—
1 9	2 9	3 9	4 9	5 9	6 9	7 9	8 9	—
1 10	2 10	3 10	4 10	5 10	6 10	7 10	8 10	9 10

Now, having built the grid in this fashion — regardless of how many items you have, you proceed to *use* it. Let me illustrate.

Step 3

You go to Column A, and take each pair there by itself. The first pair is 1 2 . You "hear" each pair asking, as it were: "If you could only have one of these two, which would you prefer?" The first pair, consequently, as you will see by referring back to the menu list, is No. 1 (fruit cocktail) "versus" No. 2 (escargot). That means the question is: "If you could only have fruit cocktail OR escargot, which would you prefer?" Whatever the answer, you *circle* the number corresponding to the item you prefer. Thus, if you prefer fruit cocktail, you circle the pair in this fashion: ① 2 . Whereas, if you prefer escargot, you would circle it this way: 1 ② .

Then you go on to the next pair in Column A: 1 3 . So now the question is: "If you could only have fruit cocktail OR roast beef, which would you prefer?" If your answer is, again, fruit cocktail, you circle it this way: ① 3 . But if it is roast beef, you circle it in this fashion: 1 ③ .

You go on to each succeeding pair in Column A, then Columns B, C, D, E, and F — until you have looked at every pair of numbers, referred back to the items from which the numbers were taken (and for which the numbers stand), and asked, "If you could only have one of these two, which would you prefer?"

When all the pairs have at least one (but no more than one) circle, your grid will look something like this:

A	B	C	D	E	F	G	H	I
①2	–	–	–	–	–	–	–	–
1③	2③	–	–	–	–	–	–	–
1④	2④	③4	–	–	–	–	–	–
1⑤	2⑤	3⑤	4⑤	–	–	–	–	–
①6	2⑥	③6	④6	⑤6	–	–	–	–
1⑦	2⑦	③7	④7	⑤7	6⑦	–	–	–
1⑧	2⑧	③8	④8	⑤8	6⑧	7⑧	–	–
①9	2⑨	③9	④9	⑤9	6⑨	⑦9	⑧9	–
①10	2⑩	③10	④10	⑤10	⑥10	⑦10	⑧10	⑨10

At this point you total up the number of times that each number got circled. In the preceding example, the totals are as follows:

Item No. 1 — 4 Times	Item No. 6 — 2 Times
Item No. 2 — 0 Times	Item No. 7 — 5 Times
Item No. 3 — 8 Times	Item No. 8 — 6 Times
Item No. 4 — 7 Times	Item No. 9 — 3 Times
Item No. 5 — 9 Times	Item No. 10 — 1 Time

You then rearrange the numbers in the order of the above priority (Item No. 5 got the most circles so it is first, No. 3 got the next most circles, so it is second, etc.) and — going back to your original list — put down the identifier with each number (No. 5 was squash, No. 3 was roast beef, etc.).

Item No. 5 — Squash
Item No. 3 — Roast Beef
Item No. 4 — Mashed Potatoes
Item No. 8 — Ice Cream
Item No. 7 — Sourdough Bread
Item No. 1 — Fruit Cocktail
Item No. 9 — Chocolate Cake
Item No. 6 — Brussels Sprouts
Item No. 10 — Coffee
Item No. 2 — Escargot

**I prefer these items
in this order of priority,
or importance,
or enthusiasm.**

You now have your list in its prioritized form. Your final step is to look it over, and see if your intuition tells you that there's something radically wrong with the order of priorities. If so, change your list. You are the final judge. The list — and indeed this whole exercise — was made to serve you, not you to serve it.

The only problem you can run into in this prioritizing is if two numbers end up with the same number of circles, i.e., in a tie. You can leave them tied, and simply list them both on the same line, in your final listing (Step No. 5 above). Or, you can take the two that are tied — let us say, in our illustration above, that both No. 1 and No. 9 turned out to have four circles — and you can look back on the original grid (Step No. 3 above) to the place where 1 and 9 are paired and see which one you circled there. It turns out to be No. 1 in Column A. Thus, in your final listing (Step No. 5) you would put 1 ahead of 9, thus breaking the tie.

Footnote, for those Working with Groups: If you ever need to get a group's opinion on a whole list of items, this is a very useful group exercise. Just have each individual in the group do the exercise individually, with his or her own grid, down through Step No. 4. Collect the results at Step No. 4 from each individual, and have a person with a calculator total up all the circles given to each number; e.g., suppose you are dealing with five people. The first circled Item No. 1 four times, the second circled No. 1 no times, the third circled No. 1 seven times, the fourth circled No. 1 two times, and the fifth circled No. 1 four times. The total for Item No. 1, then, would be 4 + 0 + 7 + 2 + 4 = 17. You end up then with the beginning of a group list for Step No. 4. The first item on that list now reads: *Item No. 1 got circled 17 times.*

In similar fashion, you total up the number of times each item number was circled by all the individuals in the group, and finish your group version of the list in Step No. 4. When done, you go on to Step No. 5. That is your Group Priority list. This is an incredibly accurate exercise, which is sensitive to the wishes of each member of the group, and yet places those wishes in the context of everybody else's. Wherever it has been used, it has engendered a lot of enthusiasm — not to mention respect for the leader's ingenuity!

Sample uses of this Prioritizing Device, in this book:

With the list of the various reasons why you want an education.
With the list of the philosophy of life items.
With the list of the skills you want to pick up.
With the list of the skills you already have.
With the clusters or families of skills.
With the individual skills listed under each cluster title or family name.
With your preferred geographical factors.
With your preferred people-environment factors or types.
With your list of values.
With your list of your Special Knowledges.
With your list of preferred working conditions.
With your list of organizations that you survey.
With your preferred leisure-time activities list.
With your list of books you'd like to read as follow-up.

The National Career Development Project

THE NATIONAL CAREER DEVELOPMENT PROJECT is designed to be a central clearing-house for the nation, of information concerning the job-hunt, career-change, and more effective ways of helping people identify what they want to do with their lives.

It does this through a nationwide network which sends the Project news about the latest research findings, magazine articles, newspaper clippings, and books, as well as personal experiences concerning the effectiveness (or ineffectiveness) of —

> public and private employment agencies • executive search and recruiters • newspaper ads • college placement bureaus • registers, job-banks, and clearinghouses • the use of resumes • how to identify skills • better ways of going about the job-hunt.

You are invited to be a part of this network by sending the Project copies of magazine or newspaper articles, details of your own experience, or news about books, related to any of the above (Research, NCDP, Box 379, Walnut Creek, CA 94596). Such information will benefit many people throughout the country.

NCDP publishes a newsletter about life/work planning which is sent every other month to 5000 professionals around the country who help others with the job-hunt, career-change, or identifying what they want to do with their lives, including campus ministers, college placement and career planning staff, counselors, decision-makers in the whole personnel world, and many others. Subscription is $10/year, for six issues. People wishing to subscribe should send their check made out to "National Career Development Project" together with their name and address, to

> NEWSLETTER ABOUT LIFE/WORK PLANNING
> National Career Development Project
> Box 379, Walnut Creek, CA 94596

Its director, Richard Bolles, conducts workshops and seminars to share our findings with professionals throughout the country. Each year, fifteen *Half-Day to One-Day Presentations* are given in various parts of the country, by invitation, usually to various meetings or conferences of professionals. Each year there are three *Four-Day Seminars* held in different parts of the country. Each August a *Two-Week Life/Work Shop* is devoted to helping professionals work all the way through a systematic life/work planning system.

NCDP creates needed resources when research indicates that there is an area where new or better material is definitely needed: These currently include three books by Richard N. Bolles *(What Color Is Your Parachute?; Where Do I Go From Here With My Life?* by John C. Crystal and R.N. Bolles; and *The Three Boxes of Life)*. Pamphlets by Richard N. Bolles include *Take Heart; The Essential Marks of Effective Career Counseling; The Quick Job-Hunting Map, Beginners Version and Advanced Version;* and *Tea Leaves — A New Look at Resumes.*

NCDP is a national program sponsored by United Ministries in Education in which eight denominations participate: American Baptist Churches in the U.S.A., Church of the Brethren, Christian Church (Disciples of Christ), Moravian Church in America, Presbyterian Church in the U.S., the Episcopal Church, United Church of Christ, and United Presbyterian Church in the U.S.A. The project was funded originally by a three-year grant from Lilly Endowment of Indianapolis.

The practical reason why United Ministries in Education became involved in this area was its perception of, and desire to respond to, a critical human need, as it saw people wanting better help in deciding what to do with their lives, but not finding it. The theological rationale for why U.M.E. became involved in this area was the Christian doctrine of stewardship, and our concern that the talents which God gave to every man and woman should not be (as it were) buried in the ground, but rather utilized to their fullest potential in the service of others.

Not often is the church known to have glimpsed a critical human need in time to be ready for addressing it in a substantive way at the critical moment. Our work in this area breaks that pattern. —Dr. Verlyn L. Barker, Past President, U.M.H.E.

The National Career Development Project
Box 379, Walnut Creek, CA 94596
Telephone 415-935-1865
Richard N. Bolles, Director

United Ministries in Education
American Baptist Convention
Valley Forge, PA 19481

Appendix C

Different Spokes for Different Folks

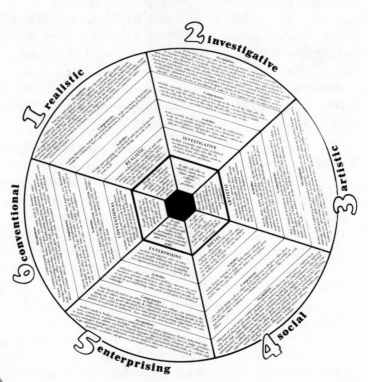

Instructions:
You are invited to cut out the next three pages
(along the dotted lines) in order to paste or
tape them together in the above formation.

See instructions on page 426.

1 realistic

Occupations

forester, industrial arts teacher, radio operator, auto engineer, mechanical engineer, mining engineer, vocational agriculture teacher, civil engineer, industrial engineer technician, aircraft mechanic, mechanical engineer technician, fish and game warden, surveyor, dental technician, architectural draftsman, electrician, jeweler, powerhouse repairman, tool & die maker, machinist, mechanic, stone cutter, locksmith, nuclear reactor technician, tree surgeon, piano tuner, typesetter, airconditioning engineer, ship pilot, instrument mechanic, motion picture projectionist, carpenter, tailor, typewriter repairer

Competencies

reading blueprints, repair and refinish furniture, make mechanical drawings, using the voltmeter, have a good mathematical and mechanical background

Activities

fixing and repairing of mechanical and electrical machinery, woodworking, metalworking, can work with tools well

REALISTIC

includes skilled trades, technical and some service occupations, people who have athletic or mechanical ability, prefer to work with objects, machines, tools, plants, animals—outdoors

People who have athletic or mechanical ability, work with objects, machines, tools, prefer plants, animals, outdoors—

2 investigative

Occupations

economist, internist, physician, anthropologist, astronomer, pathologist, physicist, chemist, production planner, medical lab assistant, tv repairer, biologist, osteopath, chiropractor, math teacher, natural science teacher, optometrist, psychiatrist, psychologist, medical technologist, bacteriologist, physiologist, research analyst, pharmacist, actuary, quality control technician, computer operator, geologist, mathematician/statistician, surgeon, meteorologist, agronomist, animal scientist, botanist, zoologist, horticulturist, natural scientist, oceanographer, biochemist, veterinarian, geographer, x-ray technician, administrator, dentist, tool designer, chemical lab technician, engineers such as aircraft, chemical, electrical, metallurgical, radio/tv, test; engineer aide, weather observer

Competencies

include scientific and some technical training in the use of the slide rule, the microscope and the different radioactive elements, can use logarithmic tables, can describe the function of the white blood cells, can interpret simple chemical formulae, can understand how a vacuum tube works

Activities

read scientific books or magazines, work in a laboratory, work on a scientific project, work on a chemistry set, solve math quizzes and puzzles, have taken courses in physics, chemistry, biology, and geometry

INVESTIGATIVE

include scientific and some technical occupations. People who like to observe, learn, investigate, analyze, evaluate or solve problems

People who like to observe, learn, investigate, analyze, evaluate, solve problems—

427

See instructions
on page 426.

③ artistic

④ social

ARTISTIC (Occupations)

photographer, women's garment retoucher, furrier, interior decorator, photolithographer (printer); music arranger, composer

foreign language teacher, philosopher, art teacher, literature teacher, writer, editor, advertising executive, critic, fashion model, advertising manager, radio program writer, entertainer, music teacher, dancing teacher, drama teacher, English teacher, drama coach, journalist-reporter

musician, orchestra conductor, public relations person, actor/actress, designer, interior decorator, jewelry designer, architect, artist, photographer, furniture illustrator

Occupations

Competencies

play a musical instrument, participate in two- or four-part choral singing, perform as a musical soloist, act in a play, do interpretive reading, sketch, draw, paint, sculpt, make pottery, design clothing, people so that they can be recognized, posters or furniture, write stories and poetry well

Competencies

Activities

sketch, draw, paint, attend plays, design furniture or buildings, play in a band, group, orchestra, practice a musical instrument, go to recitals, concerts, musicals, read popular fiction, create portraits or photographs, read plays, read/write poetry, take an art course

Activities

ARTISTIC

include artistic, literary, musical, innovating or intuitional abilities and like to work in an unstructured situation using their imagination or creativity.

include artistic, literary, musical, occupations, people who like to work in an unstructured situation using their creativity or imagination.

People who like to work with people—to inform, enlighten, help, train, develop, or cure them, or are skilled with words—

SOCIAL

includes educational and social welfare occupations, people who like to work with people—to inform, enlighten, help, train, develop, or cure them, or are skilled with words.

Activities

write letters, belong to clubs, help others with personal problems, like to make new friends, attend sport events, like to care for children, dance, go to parties

Competencies

can explain things well to others, feel competent with peers older than oneself, can plan a school or church function successfully, good judge of personality, enjoy working as a volunteer for benefit drives, like to work with others

Occupations

Director of social service, compensation advisor, dorm director, interviewer, employment rep, funeral director, job analyst, chamber of commerce executive, employee benefits approver, food serv. mgr., claim adjuster, production expediter, health & welfare coordinator, educational administrator, training director, historian, environmental health engineer, home service rep., community rec admin., counselor, business agent, extension agent, physical ed teacher, building superintendent, therapist, college professor, political scientist, sociologist, nurse, social and group worker, personnel director, food and drug inspector, teacher, minister, librarian, foreign service officer, history teacher

See instructions on page 426.

S enterprising

6 conventional

Occupations (Conventional)

certified public accountant, time study analyst, business keeper, auto writing machine operator, bookkeeping machine operator, estimator, time-(commercial) teacher, finance expert, accountant, credit manager, time-foreign trade clerk, office worker, payroll clerk, accounting machine operator, personnel clerk, sales correspondent, reservations agent, bookkeeper, cashier, secretary, medical secretary, library assistant, data processing worker, mail clerk, personnel secretary, proofreader

Competencies

operate business machines, file correspondence and other papers, use shorthand, can hold an office job, can type 40 words a minute, can do a lot of paper work in a short period of time, can post credits and debits, can keep accurate records of payments or sales, can use office equipment

Activities

type letters or papers, have typewriting, bookkeeping, business and commercial math usage, enjoy keeping records and files neat, can write business letters, can operate business machines of any kind.

CONVENTIONAL

include clerical and office occupations, people who like to work with data, have clerical or numerical ability, carrying things out in detail or following through on instructions

People who like to work with data, have clerical or numerical ability, carry out in detail, other's instructions

Occupations (Enterprising)

market analyst, banker, insurance underwriter, real estate appraiser, florist, industrial engi-neer, contractor, warehouse manager, salesperson—technical products, lawyer, judge, attorney, in-tv/radio announcer, admin. assistant, branch manager, director indus. relations, gov't official, in-surance manager, managers such as restaurant, office/traffic/personnel, director of production, etc., salary and wage administrator, labor arbitrator, securities analyst, systems analyst, personnel recruiter benefits, securities salesperson

Competencies

have been elected to an office in high school or college, can supervise the work of others, have unusual energy & enthusiasm, good at getting people to do things my way, good salesman, have organized a club or some group in presenting suggestions or com, bater, have acted as spokesman for a person in authority, have started my own business or service plants to a person in authority.

Activities

influence others, sell, discuss politics, operate my own business, people, attend conferences, give talks, supervise others, meet important people, lead of any group, participate in a political a group in accomplishing some goal, serve as officer for organizing or leading or managing campaign

ENTERPRISING

include managerial/sales occupa-tions, people-influencing or persuading or performing or leading or managing for economic gain or organizational goals

People who like to work with people—influencing, persuading, leading, managing for economic gain or organizational goals

431

Beginning Version

The Quick Job-Hunting Map

A fast way to help

*For the high school or college student,
or the housewife going back to work,
or anyone else entering the world of work
and facing obstacles in the job hunt.*

Richard N. Bolles
and Victoria B. Zenoff

Those readers who desire a more detailed skill-list than we have provided here, are referred to *What Color Is Your Parachute?*, in which the Advanced Version of the Quick Job-Hunting Map may be found. Or that version may be ordered separately as a 24 page booklet, 8½ x 11″, by writing directly to Ten Speed Press, Box 7123, Berkeley, California 94707. Enclose $1.25 plus $.50 postage and handling charge.

The *Beginning Version* of

The Quick Job-Hunting Map

by
Richard N. Bolles and Victoria B. Zenoff

INTRODUCTION:
What You Need Before You Go Job Hunting

You need to know that the traditional way of going about looking for a job—using want ads in the newspapers, private employment agencies, the Federal/State employment agency, job listings and the mailing out of resumes by the hundreds—is not very effective, for *most* of the people who follow it.

For example, in a recent study of a major U.S. city, it was discovered that only 15% of the firms in that city had hired *anyone* during the entire year, as the result of a want ad.*

For this, and other reasons, experts say that 80% of all the vacancies which occur in the work force (above entry level, at least) are never advertised through any of the avenues that job hunters traditionally turn to. And resumes are notoriously unsuccessful in turning up vacancies, for many if not most people.**

We need a better way of changing jobs, or of finding work for the first time. Especially because the average person has to go looking for a job up to fifteen times in his or her life.

What do you need to know, in order to be the most successful in your job hunt, and to arrive at a successful conclusion to your job hunt as quickly as possible? You need to know three things—which we have symbolized by the figures of

a) a cart;
b) a horse; and
c) a road.

---

* *A Study to Test the Feasibility of Determining Whether Classified Ads in Daily Newspapers Are An Accurate Reflection of Local Labor Markets and of Significance to Employers and Job Seekers.* 1973. Olympus Research Corporation, 1290 24th Avenue, San Francisco, CA 94122.

** For further background to this, and the whole Quick Job-Hunting Map, it is essential to read *What Color Is Your Parachute? A Practical Manual for Job-Hunters and Career-Changers*, by Richard N. Bolles (Ten Speed Press, 900 Modoc, Berkeley, CA 94707, $6.95). Also see: "Tea Leaves: a new look at resumes" from Ten Speed Press, fifty cents.

a) THE CART

You need to know that the most important thing about you to an employer (or to clients or customers directly) is not a recital of your past experience, not what field you were trained in, but what *skills* you have. This is the common denominator that you always take with you, no matter how many different organizations you may (or may not) have worked for, or how often you change careers. You *must* know, for now and all the future, not only what skills you *have,* but more importantly, what skills you have *and enjoy,* if you are to find a job, or change jobs, quickly and effectively.

b) THE HORSE

The skills you have and enjoy are like a cart without a horse, unless you know *where* you want to use those skills—i.e., what you want to hook them up to. Other people can help you here, by telling you what the possibilities are, but—in the end—this must be a self-directed search on your part. Only you can define and decide where you want to use your skills.

c) THE ROAD

The third thing you then need to know is *how* to identify the places where you would like to work, and how to get hired in one of those places. This step is the hardest step of all, *if* you have not spent any time on the preceding two questions. It is the easiest step of all, however, if you have done your homework on the WHAT (skills do I enjoy?) and the WHERE (do I want to use those skills?).

This Quick Job-Hunting Map, then, is devoted to helping you work through these three steps, to put together the information you need in order to go about your job-hunt quickly and

effectively. How long will your job hunt take? No one can say. It can be as short as a week or as long as nine months. A lot depends upon how hard you work at it, full-time, and on various other factors, principally Luck. What you are doing here is organizing your luck. One thing is sure: the time you invest in this Map will *greatly* shorten the time it takes for your job-hunt.

● FIRST, 'THE PARTY' EXERCISE

This will be found on pages 126-127. If you have not already done this exercise, it is important to do it now. Then, go on to

● YOUR SEVEN MOST ENJOYED
OR SATISFYING ACCOMPLISHMENTS

This will be found on pages 163-176. When this exercise is completed, you will be ready to consider

● WHERE YOU WOULD MOST ENJOY
USING THESE SKILLS

It's nice to 'stay loose' and be willing to use your skills any place that there is a vacancy, but — as we said on page 268 — vacancies are hard to discover. You are going to have to go out and canvass, or research, or interview, a particular area. The more you can cut this area down to manageable size, before you go out, by using some principles of *elimination* or *exclusion,* and the clearer a picture you can have in your own mind of what kind of place you want to use your skills in, the faster and more effective will be your search—to discover a vacancy, or even create your own job.

There are six principles of exclusion for narrowing down the area you need to focus on: *(Write answers on page 439.)*

1 Where would you most like to uncover a job, geography-wise? What city, rural area, county, or whatever, in this country or the world?

2 Where, in terms of the kinds of people you would like to be surrounded by? Here copy the answers you gave to The Party Exercise on page 127, for those answers were a description of people-environments that you prefer, as well as of skills. Add any other important descriptions—thinking of the kinds of people who have turned you off in the past, and then describing their exact opposites here.

3 <u>Where</u>, **in terms of what goals, purposes, or values do you want your skills to serve?** Two exercises will help here. Write out your answer (on a separate sheet of paper) to the question: What do I hope others will solve or change about this world, while I am still alive to see it? Brainstorm this with some friends of yours, if possible. Then, from this list select the five most important items (to you) and write a paragraph about each one of these five, as to why you would or would not like to be involved yourself, and in what fashion.

Don't disqualify yourself on the ground that your talents are too peculiar to fit this particular 'cause'. Remember, Pete Seeger was concerned about the pollution of the Hudson River, and his talent was not engineering but singing. Still he used his voice to sing about pollution there, and alert people to the need to do something about it.

Another exercise to get at this is: if you had $10 million and didn't have to work, what would you do with your spare time for the rest of your life? If it turns out to be simply gardening, or making and flying kites, then think about places which might pay you to do this (horticultural stores, or kite factories.)

Another version of the same exercise: if you had another $10 million and had to give it away, to what or to whom would you give it? To which causes, needs of our society, or unmet needs?

4 <u>Where</u>, **in terms of Special Knowledges you have picked up, that you still want to be able to use because you enjoy them?** Consider the school subjects you especially loved, languages you know and enjoy, or other special knowledges related to particular fields or professions that are still important to you, to be able to use in the future.

5 <u>Where</u>, **in terms of the particular working conditions you prefer?** Do you need a lot or very little of such things as authority/supervision, change, consistency, dress codes, opportunity for initiative, self-management at your work? If you have had experience already in the world of work, list the distasteful living/working conditions you have experienced, in the past, and then state these in a positive form for the future.

6 <u>Where</u>, **in terms of level, amount of responsibility, and (to put it another way) at what salary level?**

And now, to put it all together:

What my skills are

Enter answers here from pages 163-176.

My Strongest Skill is:

My Second Strongest Skill:

My Third:

My Fourth:

My Fifth:

My Sixth:

The segments of the illustration read:

#1 WHERE (GEOGRAPHY-WISE)

#2 KINDS OF PEOPLE I WOULD LIKE TO BE SURROUNDED BY

#3 MY SKILLS SERVING THESE GOALS, PURPOSES, AND VALUES

#4 USING THESE SPECIAL KNOWLEDGES

#5 WITH THESE PREFERRED WORKING CONDITIONS

#6 AT THIS LEVEL OF RESPONSIBILITY, SALARY

and–
Where I want to land
with these skills

Enter answers here from pages 436 & 437.

If you need additional space to write out the full answers
to pages 436 & 437, use separate sheets of paper
before entering a summary of
your answers here.

HOW TO FIND THE RIGHT PLACE
(Using Your Map)

There are three stages to this process of finding the place where you can use your skills, in the service of those values or purposes or needs of our society that you have decided upon:

1st Stage:
JUST FOR PRACTICE

At home, on vacation, or in the city where you live most of the year, or wherever, choose some hobby or enthusiasm or interest of yours—totally non-job-related, at best. Say, painting, skiing, music, gardening, stamp collecting, affirmative action for women, or whatever. Go visit someone—anyone—picked out of the yellow pages or from what somebody suggested to you, *and if you are shy take a friend with you, of course.* This is just for information. Just for information.

Ask the person you visit, who shares your enthusiasm (one hopes):

- How did you get into this work?
- What do you like most about it?
- What do you like the least about it? And:
- Where else could I find people making their living off this, or sharing this enthusiasm, in places I would not have thought of?

Then, go visit those people, and ask the same four questions. And so on, until you feel comfortable in talking to people who share your enthusiasm (most shyness comes from having to talk with people who don't share our enthusiasms). Practice this as long as you need to, until you feel comfortable with this stage.

2nd Stage:
JUST FOR INFORMATION

In the city or geographical area *of your choice,* now armed with the clues from your completed map on page 439, you need to go out as INFORMATION GATHERER, to discover all the places that fit the description on your map.

You start with the Chamber of Commerce, or the Yellow Pages in the phone book, or your friends (contacts)—anyone you know who can tell you. What you want to discover is just one place that is even *remotely* like the place you have described on your map. That's all you need. That place will lead you to others.

Example: one woman felt her most enjoyable (and effective) skills were with people, counseling them, in one to one situations face to face, in a place (she hoped) that was a private organization (as opposed to government or college), but was concerned enough about its employees to want to help them with their career development. So much for her "map".

The way she used this map was, in the city of her choice, to discover from her contacts (e.g., the alumni list from her college) where in that city was even *one* private organization that had a program of career development for its employees. (It turned out to be a bank.) Then to visit the officer in charge of that program to ask:

- how they got started in the program;
- what they were trying to accomplish with the program;
- how it worked;
- what its strengths and limitations had—so far—turned out to be. Then ask:
- where else in that city were similar programs, and who was in charge of them?

Her task then was as INFORMATION GATHERER ONLY, to visit each one in turn, and ask the same sorts of questions, until she had surveyed them all. Then to return to the two or three organizations whose programs she liked best, and tell them so — together with *why*, and the skills she wanted to use with them.

3rd Stage:
FOR HIRING, AT LAST:

One thing must be very clear about the two stages above: *you* are the Screener, and the employers or organizations you look at are the *Screenees* all during the first two stages.

If you forget this, you will lapse into the mentality of a Screenee early on, and every employer or organization that you visit will know it. Thereby you will lose whatever advantage you had, in this job hunt process.

But now, when you get to this third stage, when you are going back to the two or three places you already have visited in your second stage, which you decided fitted your description on the Map better than any other, now you are the Screenee. You are now, but only now, coming to visit them as job-hunter. Whether they have a vacancy or not is immaterial. You are going to seek out in each organization among your top three or so, the person who has the power to hire (not the personnel department), and you are going to tell him or her:

• what impressed you about their organization during your information survey (Stage 2).

• what sorts of challenges, needs or "problems" (go slow in using this latter word with sensitive employers) your survey suggested exist in this field in general, and with this place in particular—that intrigue you.

• what skills seem to you to be needed, in order to meet those challenges or needs in his or her organization.

• the fact that you have these skills (here use the information summarized on your Map, page 438).

For more detailed information about this third, or final, stage, see Crystal's book (below), or Haldane's, or Djeddah's.

BIBLIOGRAPHY
(if you want additional help)

What Color Is Your Parachute? A Practical Manual for Job-Hunters & Career-Changers
Revised, 1981. By Richard N. Bolles. $6.95 + $.50 for postage and handling, from:
Ten Speed Press, 900 Modoc, Berkeley, CA 94707; or at your local bookstore.

Where Do I Go From Here With My Life? by John C. Crystal and Richard N. Bolles.
$7.95 + $.50 postage and handling, from: Ten Speed Press, address above.

How To Make A Habit of Success by Bernard Haldane
$1.95 + $.35 for postage and handling, from: Warner Books, P.O. Box 690,
New York, N.Y. 10019

Making Vocational Choices: A Theory of Careers by John L. Holland
$4.95, from: Prentice-Hall, Inc., Englewood Cliffs, New Jersey 07632

Who's Hiring Who by Richard C. Lathrop. $5.95 + $.50 postage and handling,
from: Ten Speed Press, 900 Modoc, Berkeley, CA 94707;
or from: Who's Hiring Who, Box 3651, Washington, D.C. 20007

The authors gratefully acknowledge the
help of Gary Bolles and Joel Swetow
in preparing this version of The Quick
Job-Hunting Map.

What Needs Doing?

John Crystal invented the idea. The logic of it goes like this:

A. You can use your skills in a wide variety of places.

B. The problem is "Where?"

C. One way of getting at that problem is to remember that almost all of us see two worlds out there: The World As It Is, and The World As We Would Like It To Be.

D. There are a lot of people at work trying to change The World As It Is into The World As We Would Like It To Be. You could be one of them.

E. First, however, you have to develop your picture of The World As You Would Like It To Be, and break that picture down into its individual parts (or "atoms").

F. Most of us tend to just "freeze" when we try to do this, because we are looking at each part of the picture in terms of ourselves, and we are continually saying, "But I couldn't help change this," and "But I couldn't help change that." We are thinking so much about our own limitations (imagined or real), that our imagination dries up.

G. One way around this is to ask ourselves deliberately "What do I want to see *others* do, to help bring about The World As I Would Like It To Be? The minute you say "others", of course, you can endow them with every brainpower and every skill that you think you lack. Hence, your imagination gets freed up.

H. *After* you have thus freed up your imagination, you can come back to yourself, at the end. And bring this all home.

The fruits of this logic lie, then, in the way that John Crystal brilliantly formulated the question: "What do *you* think needs doing in this world, that you would like to see *others* accomplish —during *your* lifetime, while you are still alive to see it happen?

This exercise is to be found in *Where Do I Go From Here With My Life* by John C. Crystal (and yours truly), pp. 88-91.

It may help your own creative juices to hear what some other people think needs doing (these ideas are taken from the LIFE/work Shops run by the National Career Development Project):

1. Defeat cancer
2. Get rid of sexual and racial stereotyping and discrimination
3. Empower the whole country through LIFE/work Planning
4. Lick inflation
5. Eliminate hunger
6. Stop constant warring
7. Start low-cost living communities for lonely single-parent-families and the elderly
8. Improve day care
9. Lower the Western standard of living
10. Day care for elders
11. Develop an educational system that treats kids like human beings
12. Guaranteed anual wage
13. Up with andragogy, down with pedagogy
14. Clean air and water
15. Promote understanding of conflicting, opposing or differing viewpoints
16. Provide equal justice
17. Reorient our priorities regarding cities
18. Populate unpopulated areas
19. Elect a female President
20. Jobs for all
21. Equalize the world standard of living
22. Eliminate crime
23. Break down barriers between people
24. Eliminate America's 'consumerism-itis'
25. Eliminate victimless crimes
26. Encourage and support individuals' natural creativity
27. Develop the human mind to the fullest potential
28. World population stabilization
29. Fulfillment of all liberation movements of our time
30. Use of solar energy
31. Waste control from nuclear plants
32. Preservation of natural wildlife
33. Recycling waste
34. Preventative health care
35. Utilizing expertise of older people
36. Small/individual enterprises encouraged
37. Natural health-care programs
38. Way to remedy hangovers rapidly
39. Development of a meta-language (a universal, nonverbal, feeling language)
40. Equal opportunities for women
41. Universal multi-lingual and multicultural education
42. Eliminating the bottom level of Maslow's hierarchy (taking care of all peoples' survival needs)
43. Develop a limit of growth economy
44. Humanizing death and dying practices, particularly in medical profession
45. More creative use of parttime shared job ideas
46. Elimination of technological development for its own sake
47. Equal opportunities for all minorities
48. "Cleaner" politics
49. End physical abuse to children
50. An efficient rapid transit for the public

51. A cure for diabetes and baldness
52. End sexism in literature
53. Reduction of the cat and dog population
54. Sharing of money, skills and time
55. Increase the availability of information
56. Assist people in getting a better handle on their identity
57. Have people be more satisfied with their lot and not covet their neighbor's
58. Increase awareness of spiritual identity
59. Conserving energy resources
60. Unconditional love amongst the people of the world
61. Justice over expediency
62. Decreasing U.S. 'hogism' overconsumption per capita
63. End the drug problem
64. Climate control to avoid famine
65. Economical non-polluting transportation system
67. Break up mega-corporations
68. Small is beautiful
69. Eliminate organized crime
70. More family cohesiveness
71. End conflict between religious groups
72. Family education
73. Loving care of the dying
74. Humane corrections system for all offenders
75. Community facilities for the retarded
76. Abolition of capital punishment
77. Financial support for the arts and artists
78. Recycling of abandoned/burnt/marred/mauled housing
79. Five cent phone calls
80. Comprehensive tax reform
81. Built-in flexibility for change and fluid movement for people
    between the three boxes of life
82. Elimination of planned-obsolescence as a cultural norm
83. Meaningful retirement
84. Sexual equality
85. Elimination of violence through a nurturing environment, starting with infancy
86. Humanistic working conditions and environments
87. Six hour work day and flex-time
88. Marriage enrichment
89. People taking responsibility for themselves
90. Eliminate violence on television
91. Improve police relationships with citizens
92. Creative leisure programs
93. Eliminate or alleviate tedium at work
94. Non-interference of the U.S. in other nations' internal affairs
95. Control of multi-national corporations
96. Tangible ways of not exploiting the poor
97. Promote neighborhoods
98. Revise curriculums for all educational institutions toward life-long learning
99. Make better *widgets* (i.e., whatever it is that a person wants to make,
    help him or her to make better ones)
100. Control the growth of militarism

Now, I want to make several points about this list:

First of all, in its entirety the list is almost overwhelming. It reads rather like a blueprint for heaven—or for utopia at the very least. This list is, however, a composite of the brainstorming from seventy different people, working in small discussion groups of seven members each. So, the one hundred items represent seventy people's Visions of what they would like to see others do, within their lifetime.

Secondly, no one is necessarily expected to agree with all the items on this list. One should not look for consistency, from one item to another. These were the ideas of seventy *different* people, different in sex, age, race, background and values.

Thirdly, this list can be used in two different ways, depending on whether an individual is using it, or a group:

1. *If you are using it as an individual,* working by yourself, we suggest you might well go down the list and put a check mark √ in front of, say, five items which you feel are the most important to *You.* "These are the five things I would most like to see others solve, during my lifetime." As you check off these five, you may well think of others, not on that list. So, we have provided space here, for you to write them in:

My Own Additional Ideas About WHAT NEEDS DOING

6. ———————————————————————
7. ———————————————————————
8. ———————————————————————
9. ———————————————————————
10. ———————————————————————

2. *If you are using it as a member of a group,* we suggest that each member of the group read over this list to get some idea of how to go about the exercise. Having done this sort of 'priming of the pump', divide into small discussion groups of 3-8 members. We have found 6-8 is the optimum size. A 'recorder' should be appointed, to write down the members' ideas—preferably on a large sheet of paper, such as newsprint or shelf paper. Brainstorming should follow, each person throwing out (for the recorder to write down) one idea in turn, without any

criticism or evaluation of that idea, for the moment. When the brainstorming is completed, then each person in the group ought to read over the entire list. It may resemble our list of 100 items, above, at least in some respects. Or it may turn out to be entirely different. It all depends on who is in your group. From your group's list, you (and each other member of the group) should copy down in your own notebook, the five items that are most important to *You*. If you prefer to copy down ten items, that's okay. There is no magic number. Just keep the list manageable in size.

If you try this exercise, and when you're all done with it you're still just as puzzled as ever about where you want to use your skills, there is another way to get at the problem of "Where?"

It involves a fantasy about money.

Every one of us dreams what we would do some day if a huge windfall came our way. In the LIFE/work Shops run by the National Career Development Project, we have asked individuals of all ages and all walks of life this question: What would you do if you had $10 million and you were required to spend it on yourself? Some of the answers were predictable: buy a yacht, and that sort of thing. Surprisingly, however, some were rather altruistic. That is to say, the way in which some people would gain the most pleasure would be by spending the windfall on *others*. What emerged out of everyone's answer was: while the discussion began with money, it ended with Values. And everyone's values, in the end, dealt either with Truth/Ideas/Causes, or with Beauty/Pleasure/Emotions, or with Morality/Virtues/Ethics.

Here goes:

If I were given $10 million and I had to spend it on things related to myself, I would:—

1. buy a comfortable home with vistas of sunshine and sunsets, with sufficient privacy so that I could be naked, lots of land around, and quadraphonic sound in every room.

2. play a catalytic role in every activity I choose to support or be in.

3. lay back, relax, and dream.

4. travel 6-8 months a year, to old haunts in order to see how they are now, and to validate my own past.

5. devote myself to some innovative service that has a self-sustaining structure, and is influential (like Ralph Nader or John Gardner) for humane, fulfilling causes.

6. buy a yacht with my own crew to run it.

7. travel all over the world, getting to know different cultures and native people in each new place.

8. buy a school or a boat with electronic equipment for kids to operate, enjoy and learn from—staffed with experts in marine biology, film making, public speaking, etc.

9. build a team of experts to do research on human effectiveness, inviting in great minds to rest, talk and get recharged, then choosing one hundred of them to go teach others how to become great thinkers.

10. buy a glass house in a mountain area overlooking the ocean, whose inside and outside is closely integrated, with a large waterfall in the back yard, gardens, ponds, fountains that are lit at night, lots of color, bird life, with nice music, with a number of cottages nestled nearby.

11. build a swimming pool and give free lessons to the handicapped.
12. run for political office.
13. play the market.
14. develop shelters for child abuse victims, spouse-beating victims, etc.
15. establish a trust fund for my children.
16. buy impressionistic modern art.
17. give to my favorite causes, like the National Urban League, Sierra Club, Common Cause, NOW, etc.
18. try to find one person whose dreams aren't ever going to come true because of lack of money, and I'd make his or her dreams come true.
19. give it to cancer research.
20. support struggling, gifted artists.
21. write poetry, drama and essays myself.
22. buy a kangaroo ranch in Australia.
23. invest it, and use the interest to support ongoing projects.
24. hire researchers to go find people who need money, and then give anonymous $1,000 donations to them.
25. give to any group that could limit our cat and dog population.
26. build a permanent resource center for Indian women.
27. secure financially my father's farm, so that I could always go there.
28. give money toward the cure of diabetes, so that my wife could be freed of that disease.
29. pay off my debts.
30. hire a money manager.
31. continue my present work for free.

32. attend every major sports event wherever.

33. give weddings for my three daughters.

34. buy an asbestos suitcase, so that I could use it in this world or the next.

35. work at my same job, but only for 6 months each year.

36. upgrade the standard of living in the rest of the world.

37. provide seed money to encourage creativity around the world.

38. give toward the alleviation of hunger worldwide.

39. rebuild and revitalize inner-city homes and environments, provide jobs and training for the people presently living there.

40. do personal work with all top people in Bioenergetics and body movements.

41. learn to fly an airplane.

42. buy a professional sports team.

43. take professional dancing lessons.

44. help migrant workers.

45. figure out ways to stop the major negative impact of advertising, overcoming the 'data deluge' and helping people to take charge of their own life, without depending on 'better living through chemistry'.

46. establish a 'center for friends', and import friends for their presence.

47. go on a five-year cruise with friends.

48. go teach in poor rural areas.

49. buy a good-size airplane (a Lear jet) and travel.

50. set up a speaker's bureau of experts and personalities, available to me and my friends on short notice.

If you seek to answer this question (If I was given $10 million....) for yourself, there are two further steps to take, once you've jotted down your answers: (a) Go back over each answer and ask yourself, "Can any of these activities be done *now*, in some fashion, with existing resources?" (b) Then go back over each answer once more, and ask yourself, "Can I identify or develop resources over the next five years, that would enable this thing to be done, in some fashion?"

Hopefully, all of this will push you well along the way toward identifying not just a place where you could use your skills, but a place where you could use your skills *and* get a real sense of some Meaning and Mission for your life.

Evaluation
or The Issue of An Individual Worker's Effectiveness Looked At From The Employer's Point of View

SOME BEGINNING ABCs

You, as an employer, never see the individual as he or she really is. You only see them as they are when they are in your presence or within your sphere of influence. To put it another way, the moment you introduce yourself into the situation, you change the situation, sometimes slightly, sometimes drastically.

Evaluation, if it is done at all, should be a part of the regular order of daily life in your organization, as normal and taken for granted as breathing. If evaluation is not a regular procedure, and then is introduced suddenly, it has the effect of plunging those being evaluated into preoccupation with survival, thus:

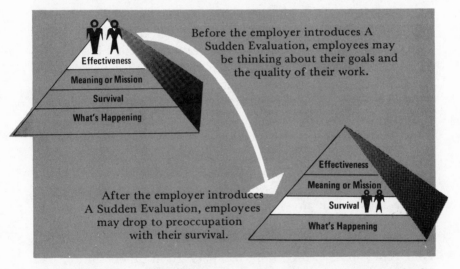

Before the employer introduces A Sudden Evaluation, employees may be thinking about their goals and the quality of their work.

Effectiveness
Meaning or Mission
Survival
What's Happening

After the employer introduces A Sudden Evaluation, employees may drop to preoccupation with their survival.

Effectiveness
Meaning or Mission
Survival
What's Happening

Anytime employees are reduced to preoccupation with the issue of their survival, you can be sure that they sense an evaluation is going on, whether or not it is called an evaluation. (Sometimes, as when the organization is to be closed down forever, it is an evaluation of the organization that they sense, not an evaluation of themselves individually.) When an evaluation is going on, panic sets in (i.e., even greater preoccupation with the issue of Survival) in direct proportion to the invisibility of the criteria by which the evaluation is being made. As, for example, when notice is served on *all* employees (or all in a particular group) that *some* of them will be terminated in the next six months, say, but no accompanying guidelines are revealed as to how it will be decided who gets elected for this honor.

Anytime employees are preoccupied with survival, efficiency is likely to drop, since the employees are no longer devoting their mental energies to the issues of work goals or work quality. Those who survive best at such times are those who are very secure, or those who can manufacture Appearances best—not necessarily those who do the best work all year round.

The Moral of All This: have evaluation as a regular procedure in your organization, or—if you must introduce it suddenly—be sure all the criteria for evaluation are identified, agreed upon and publicized *from the first moment the evaluation is announced.*

THE HEART OF THE MATTER

Evaluation should be a constant, regular procedure whereby:
a) an employer encourages *every* employee to keep his or her own record of achievements, on a weekly or monthly basis; AND
b) the employer ensures that each employee gets feedback *from others,* peers as well as supervisors,
- in the form or praise when he or she does well; OR
- in the form of Constructive Feedback aimed at the future (how to improve performance) rather than at the past (judgmentalness), when he or she does not do well.

In effect, this is a "Mr. Inside/Mr. Outside" or "Ms. Inside/Ms. Outside" process. It operates on the theory that no one understands what an employee is doing quite as well as the employee himself or herself (Mr. Inside or Ms. Inside). AND that left only to his or her own devices, each employee has some blind spots, which only feedback from others (Mr. or Ms. Outside) can correct.

People are as blind to knowing their work has pleased others as they are to their own defects. Consequently, any feedback *must* include praise. Feedback that only offers criticism is *a priori* a defective system.

The mechanism by which an employee keeps his or her own record of achievements is thoroughly described in *Where Do I Go From Here With My Life?* by John C. Crystal and Richard N. Bolles, (1974, Ten Speed Press, 900 Modoc, Berkeley, CA 94707,

452

$7.95, paper) pages 156, 158. See also: *Career Satisfaction and Success: A Guide to Job Freedom* by Bernard Haldane (1974, Amacom, 135 West 50th Street, New York, NY 10020, $9.95, hardcover), chapter Seven.

SOMETHING'S WRONG WITH *THEM*

If evaluation forces you as an employer to reach this conclusion about a whole team of people in your organization or a whole department, with—let us say—twelve or less employees, you will want to look at the general quality of the team:

- If they are all generally inept, the head of the team or department probably needs to surround him- or herself with ineptness, so that he or she will look better. In which case, You Know What You Must Do.
- If they are all generally competent, but just don't seem to work well with each other, the first thing you should have them look at is their functional skills (re-read pages 140-157, earlier in this book, for a refresher course, if you've forgotten what this means). One way of doing this is as follows:

I once met with a team of seven competent people who were not functioning very well together. I sat them in a circle for the better part of a day, and had them do the following exercise: each one, in turn, was asked to describe what he or she thought were the skills which each one of the others had, and liked to use. The key point was "liked to use." So, Bill described what he thought were the skills which Larry (to his left) most enjoyed using. Then Bill described what he thought were the skills which Nan (next to his left, beyond Larry) most enjoyed using. And so on, until Bill had "guessed" about every other member of the team. Then it was Larry's turn to do the same, beginning with Nan (to his left) and so on, around the circle. It was the job of every other person on the team to jot down whatever guesses were being made about his or her skills, and *who made them.* Thus Nan jotted down, first of all, what Bill said about her; then what Larry said about her; etc. When everyone had finished, we then went around the circle again— beginning with Bill—and this time each person was asked to describe what *really* were the skills that he or she most enjoyed using—and *who,* if anyone, had guessed correctly. When we had finished going around the circle the second time, it was discovered that *no one* had guessed anyone correctly, *except the receptionist who had guessed everyone!* That told the team something about how much they had really gotten to know each other as persons (they had been working together for three years). Secondly, it was discovered that some people had been doing things they hated, while right there among their own team was someone who would *love* to be able to do that particular activity or task—but was afraid to say so, previously, for fear of stepping on the toes of the one who was doing it. Thirdly, the team voluntarily exchanged responsibilities among themselves, so that each one was doing what he or she most wanted to do. Result: better teamwork and productivity.

Thus the general rule is: if the team is competent, see if an inventory, discussion, and rearrangement of their functional skill responsibilities will facilitate better teamwork.

If it does not, then you need to look at their self-management skills (again, see pages 140-157), and the issue of each team member's preferred people environment (page 126). It may be that one or more members of the team do not get along with people, Period (they should be reassigned to working individually with Data or Things); or it may be that they don't get along with *this particular kind* of people.

SOMETHING'S WRONG WITH *HIM* (or *HER)*

If you reach this conclusion about a particular individual, it is *crucial* to figure out What's Wrong. Here are the possibilities:

It's a bad job, and no one should be expected to do it. According to the National Occupational Health Survey, 21 million Americans or one out of every four workers are exposed to some hazardous chemical substance that may cause disease or death *(San Francisco Chronicle,* October 3, 1977). Many jobs expose the worker to something equally deadly: a sort of hazardous Emotional Radiation, due to pressure, stress, impossible limits, no support, etc.—all of which inevitably takes its toll *on his or her spirit, body and mind.* Remedy: job restructuring, job division, etc.

The job's fine, but there's a mismatch between this job and that worker. Every job, as you will recall, requires:
- certain functional skills,
- certain work-content skills,
- certain self-management skills.

An employee may have one or two of the above requirements but if he or she lacks the third, whatever that is, there will be a mismatch. Remedy: improve your hiring procedures, especially the information gathering about the job that precedes all interviewing (see the last section in this Appendix). Transfer the employee to a more appropriate job match.

There was, originally, a partially correct match between this job and that worker, but the worker is underemployed (or, as we say in "employerese", overqualified). Either this employee was *always* gifted with more skills than this job gives gainful employment to, or s/he has become more skilled on the job. In any event, an employee who is larger than the job he or she holds, may well become a bored employee who lets balls drop—even as the super-bright student in high school may be so bored in class, that he or she gets poor grades. Remedy: offer free group career counseling classes, preferably on company time, so that the employee may identify how to restructure his or her present job (that is *often* quite possible) to use his or her strongest skills, or what kind of other jobs he or she ought to be aiming at—within this organization, or outside.

One organization I know identifies its underemployed (and motivated) employees by advertising vacancies "in-house" and waiting to see who applies. (It turns out to be an average of five employees for each vacancy.) It then taps the four people who fail to get the job for some group career counseling, on the grounds that "you obviously want to move higher, and we want to help you." The organization figures that even if the employee uses the career counseling to move on out of the organization, that employee becomes a tremendous booster ("You should see the program that X Corporation has for its employees!") — and more than justifies the cost involved.

There was, originally, a correct match between this job and that worker, but the worker has 'burned out'. Burn out, as defined by the pioneer researchers in the subject, Christina Maslach and

Ayala Pines of the University of California, Berkeley, is a kind of disengagement or detachment on the part of a professional from any emotional feelings for the people he or she is serving—in response to stress and overload. (See the article, "Burned Out" by Christina Maslach, in *Human Behavior* Magazine, September 1976—at your local library.) You can tell a person is "burned out" if the job requires him or her to deal with people, and he or she displays some or all of the following symptoms:

Avoiding people more than he or she used to.

Developing negative attitudes toward the people he or she is serving, as revealed by:

• language that makes other people seem like an object or "just a number";

• a negative, cynical or contemptuous attitude toward the people he or she is serving;

• describing the people's problems in detached, totally intellectual, non-emotional, scientific or technological jargon;

• remaining physically as distant as possible from the people he or she is serving.

'Going by the Book' in dealing with people, rather than taking into account the special factors in a particular situation.

Increased escaping from dealing with the people he or she is to serve, through:

• increased conversation with fellow staff;

• shorter work hours;

• sickness, psychosomatic ailments (neck, back), physical rundown-ness, use of crutches (alcohol, drugs);

• quitting.

(These symptoms of burn-out have been discovered in *some* members of all of the following groups: students, mothers, child care workers, physicians, lawyers, clergy, social workers, nurses, psychiatrists, police officers, scientists, etc.) Further interviewing of employees you suspect are burned out will reveal some or all of the following symptoms:

A feeling that nothing they do makes any difference.

A feeling of being all dried up, and having nothing to
give to others.

A feeling of being trapped, and not able to take it any more.

A feeling that things will never get any better.

Remedy for Burn-Out: giving variety in the job-tasks that any one employee must do (time-sharing); reducing the amount of direct, close, involved contact with people; giving employer-sanctioned 'time-outs'; creating support systems, special staff meetings or workshops where the employee can discuss his or her feelings with colleagues; sensitizing employees to the problem, naming it, publicizing its symptoms, identifying how to get help when it appears; setting up helpful models for employees—"detached concern"—as the organization's goal; watching when burn-out typically appears (usually one and a quarter to two years after the employee begins the job); encouraging a program of physical exercise for all employees.

And now, on to the last reason why something may be wrong with an individual employee:

The employee is simply unable to handle this job, because the Job is larger than the employee (as it were). You may just have to fire the employee, but it would help greatly if *first* you identified which kind of skills the employee lacks (the odds are great indeed that he or she lacks the self-management skills necessary—but you just never know until you study the matter, compassionately). Remedy: if you must let him or her go, do them the service of treating them as you would like to be treated, were your roles reversed. Tell him or her what area they are lacking in, and the kinds of courses, apprenticeships, or whatever, where they might overcome this handicap (see pages 155-157).

HEADING EVALUATION OFF AT THE PASS

Oftentimes the problems that evaluation programs uncover turn out to be problems with the organization and its procedures, rather than problems with the individual employee in question. One of the most crucial of these problems with the organization lies in the hiring procedures. A mismatch, or partial mismatch, between job and employee at the time of hiring, will inevitably surface as "an evaluation problem" later. (Or an "employee turnover" problem. Studies of job matching have revealed a turnover rate as low as 0% for well-matched employees vs. a 62% turnover rate at the same company for poorly-matched employees. *The Cleff Job-Matching System,* reported in *Datamation,* February 1, 1971, 1301 South Grove

Avenue, Barrington, IL 60010: "Job/Man Matching in the '70s" by Samuel H. Cleff and Robert M. Hecht.)

Better matching between job and employee requires two steps. First of all, better gathering of information about the job in question. The assumption that "oh, everyone knows what that job involves" can be fatal. Some kind of interviewing of a) the previous incumbent; b) his or her peers; c) his or her subordinates; and d) his or her supervisors is crucial, in order to find out: what does it take to do this job? Some places have devised forms, in order to cut down the time required to gather this information. Here are some excerpts from one such data gathering form, invented some years ago by a man named Bill Stanton, for a county project in California called "SHARED Recruitment"; it is a form for clerical jobs:

JOB ANALYSIS

Instructions: In Column I, mark those jobs which are frequently performed in the position being rated, Place a *1* by the job most frequently performed, a *2* by the job next most frequently performed, a *3* by the job next in the amount of time consumed, and so forth.
Mark only those jobs that use a significant amount of time and make no marks by those that are not done often.

In Column II, check those jobs, if any, (to a maximum of two) that applicants must be particularly well qualified in order to do a good job.

JOBS:	Column 1 *Most Frequent*	Column 2 *Most Important (just 2)*
1 Filing or sorting things very often.		
2 Doing tasks like assembling and folding papers, stuffing envelopes, delivering, copying information most of the day.		
3 Doing mostly telephone answering or receptionist work.		
4 Doing mostly clerical tasks like searching records, filling out forms, maintaining files, preparing form letters.		
5 Typing lots of forms, reports, cards, drafts and memos.		
6 Typing lots of legal documents, contracts, or financial reports where absolute accuracy is very important		
7 Typing final copies from handwritten material where correct spelling, grammar, punctuation and neatness are extremely importan~		
8 Doing mostl~ s~ ~~		

In Column I, mark those job conditions, if any, which are particularly prevalent in the position being rated. Place a *1* by that condition that is most typical, a *2* by the second most typical, a *3* by the third most typical; and so forth.

Mark only those job conditions that are particularly prevalent and make no marks by those conditions that occur less often.

In Column II, mark those conditions, if any, (to a maximum of two) which are particularly critical to good performance.

JOB CONDITIONS:

	Column 1 Typical	Column 2 Critical (no more than 2)
1 Where there are always lots of short deadlines to meet.		
2 Where there is a lot of detailed work and accuracy is critical (like coding information or proofreading).		
3 Where you would be doing the same thing all day (like filing cards or stuffing envelopes).		
4 Where shifts in workload very often demand changes in daily priorities		
5 Where		

In Column I, mark those abilities in which applicants must be competent in order to do a reasonably acceptable job. Mark a *1* by those abilities that are absolutely necessary and a *2* by those that are important, but not as critical. For any ability not really important, leave the column blank.

In Column II, mark those abilities, if any, which would make a superior worker, superior. Put a *1* by the ability most important to a superior worker, a *2* by the ability next most important and a *3* by the ability next in line; and so forth. For any ability not really important in determining a superior work, leave the column blank.

ABILITY:

	Column 1 Must Have	Column 2 Superior Worker
1 Filing alphabetically and numerically.		
2 Organizing and maintaining file systems.		
3 Reading and interpreting complex written instructions.		
4 Memorizing and following directions.		
5 Remembering numerous details having		

I said previously that better matching between job and employee requires two steps. The first is better gathering of information about the job, before starting to interview potential employees, in something like the manner just illustrated. The second is better interviewing of the potential employees, to see if they have the skills or abilities under those conditions *which your information gathering identified.* SHARED Recruitment, not surprisingly, had an employee interview form which was almost identical to the job information gathering form. Excerpts from it follow:

EMPLOYEE INTERVIEW

Review the jobs listed below, and:
- In COLUMN I, mark those that YOU CAN NOW DO AND ARE WILLING TO ACCEPT.
- In COLUMN II, mark those jobs YOU WOULD ACCEPT IF TRAINING WERE GIVEN.
- In COLUMN III, mark the JOBS YOU LIKE MOST, but mark no more than three.
- In COLUMN IV, mark those jobs, if any, in which you have experience equal to at least six months of full-time employment.

(Note: You can make more than one mark on each line.)

JOBS:	COLUMN I Can Do and will Accept	COLUMN II Would Accept as Trainee	COLUMN III Jobs most Liked, No More than three	COLUMN IV More than 6 months Exper.
1 Filing or sorting things very often.				
2 Doing tasks like assembling and folding papers, stuffing envelopes, delivering things, and copying information most of the day.				
3 Doing mostly telephone answering or receptionist work.				
4 Doing mostly clerical tasks like searching records, filling out forms, maintaining files and preparing form letters.				
5 Typing lots of forms, reports, cards, drafts and memos.				
6 Typing lots of legal documents, contracts, or financial reports where absolute accuracy is very important.				
7 Typing final copies from handwritten material where correct spelling, grammar, punctuation and neatness are extremely i...				
8 Doing mostly secretarial work like				

Review the job conditions listed below, and:
- In COLUMN I, mark those you are WILLING TO ACCEPT.
- In COLUMN II, mark the CONDITIONS YOU LIKE MOST, but mark no more than four.
- In COLUMN III, mark those, if any, you have OFTEN EXPERIENCED in prior jobs.

JOB CONDITIONS:	COLUMN I Willing to Accept	COLUMN II Most Liked, no more than four	COLUMN III Had Prior Experience
1 Where there are always lots of short deadlines to meet.			
2 Where there is a lot of detailed work and accuracy is critical (like coding information or proofreading).			
3 Where you would be doing the same thing all day (like filing cards or stuffing envelopes).			
4 Where shifts in workload very often demand changes in daily priorities.			
5 Where your work schedule is very frequently interrupted.			
6 Where you would very often have to teach others.			
7 Where everyone has to help each other a lot.			
8 Where you would have full charge of a clerical function like payroll, personnel, or budget.			
9 Where you would very often be explaining things to customers.			
10 Where you would very frequently be the only person in the office.			
11 Where you would very often answer customer complaints.			
12 Where you would mostly be assisting other clerks to do their jobs.			
13 Where you would often have to carry or lift heavy boxes or supplies.			

(Note: You can make more than one mark on each line.)

THE CONCLUSION OF THE MATTER

Evaluation is merely a 'systematic way' of trying to get at the issue with which every worker must ultimately be concerned: the issue of his or her effectiveness. The secret of that effectiveness begins with a correct match between job and worker, where the skills the job requires are the skills that the worker not only has, but most enjoys using. Therefore the heart of any evaluation program, in an organization, must be the improvement of hiring procedures.

461

Index

Update

To: **THE THREE BOXES OF LIFE**
P.O. Box 379
Walnut Creek, California 94596

The information in the '81 edition needs to be changed regarding

On
page

_____

_____

_____

_____

_____

_____

_____

_____

_____

_____

_____

Name _____

Address _____

_____

OTHER WORKS BY RICHARD N. BOLLES

What Color Is Your Parachute?

Based upon the latest research, this new, completely revised and updated edition is designed to give the most practical step-by-step help imaginable to the career-changer or job-hunter, whether he or she is sixteen or sixty-five. Questions asked throughout the cross-country research upon which this book is based, were: What methods of job-hunting and career-changing work best? What new methods have been developed by the best minds in this field? Is it possible to change jobs without going back for lengthy retraining?
6 × 9 inches, 368 pages, $7.95 paper, $14.95 cloth

The Quick Job-Hunting Map
ADVANCED VERSION

is a practical 32-page booklet of exercises designed to give job-hunters detailed help in analyzing their skills, finding the right career field, and knowing how to find job openings and get hired. The Map is becoming an invaluable tool for career-counselors and agencies as well as for individuals seeking jobs or changing careers.
8½ × 11 inches, 32 pages, $1.25 paper

The Quick Job-Hunting Map
BEGINNING VERSION

Based on the author's original *Quick Job-Hunting Map*, this version for beginners offers special help to new job seekers. For students about to graduate, for house-wives going to work for the first time or returning to work, or for anyone else entering the world of work and facing obstacles in the job hunt, this book gives real and concrete guidance through the maze of the job market.
8½ × 11 inches, 32 pages, $1.25 paper

Tea Leaves — A New Look At Resumes

This booklet is a new look at effective preparation and use of resumes, the routinely submitted yet only occasionally influential tool of the job seeker. Bolles shows how to create a personal profile that will survive the brutal elimination process, reach the hands of the hiring influence, and get you an interview.
6 × 9 inches, 24 pages, $.50 paper

Where Do I Go From Here With My Life?
by John C. Crystal and Richard Nelson Bolles

Here is *the workbook* for the self-motivated individual, student, professional, or anyone who has an interest in a systematic approach to job-hunting and career mobility, bringing together two of the leading people in the field.
9 × 7 inches, 272 pages, illustrated, $9.95 paper

1⊜ Ten Speed Press

P.O. Box 7123, Berkeley, California 94707
When ordering please include $.75 additional for each book for shipping & handling.